Adobe Acrobat

Fourth Edition

Classroom in a Book®

The official training workbook from Adobe

Brie Gyncild & Lisa Fridsma

Adobe Acrobat Classroom in a Book, Fourth Edition

Adobe Press is an imprint of Pearson Education, Inc. For the latest on Adobe Press books, go to adobepress. com. To report errors, please send a note to errata@peachpit.com. For information regarding permissions, request forms, and the appropriate contacts within the Pearson Education Global Rights & Permissions department, please visit www.pearson.com/permissions.

Adobe Inc., 345 Park Avenue, San Jose, California 95110-2704, USA.

ISBN-13: 978-0-13-798363-6

ISBN-10: 0-13-798363-8

1 2023

WHERE ARE THE LESSON FILES?

Purchase of this Classroom in a Book in any format gives you access to the lesson files you'll need to complete the exercises in the book.

1 Go to adobepress.com/AcrobatCIB2023.

2 Sign in or create a new account.

3 Click Submit.

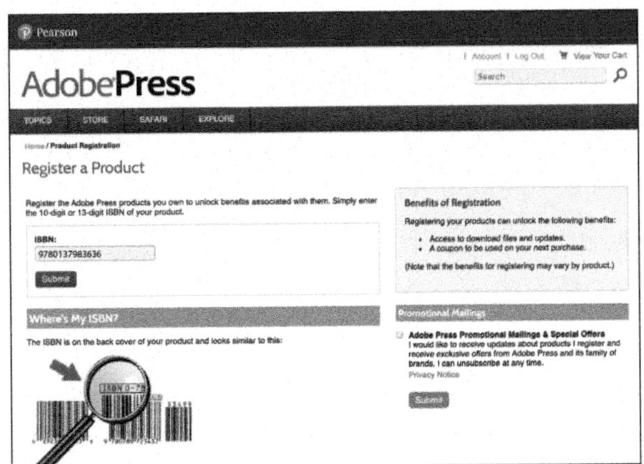

● **Note:** If you encounter problems registering your product or accessing the lesson files or web edition, go to adobepress.com/support for assistance.

4 Answer the questions as proof of purchase.

5 The lesson files can be accessed through the Registered Products tab on your Account page.

6 Click the Access Bonus Content link below the title of your product to proceed to the download page. Click the lesson file links to download them to your computer.

● **Note:** If you purchased a digital product directly from adobepress.com or peachpit.com, your product will already be registered. However, you still need to follow the registration steps and answer the proof of purchase question before the Access Bonus Content link will appear under the product on your Registered Products tab.

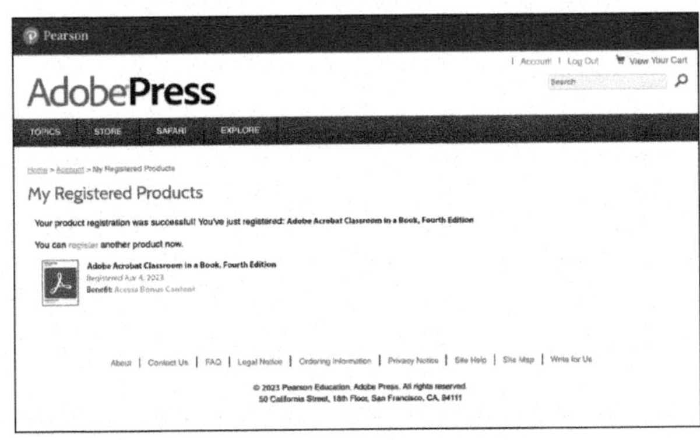

CONTENTS

WHERE ARE THE LESSON FILES? iii

GETTING STARTED 1

About Classroom in a Book 1
Acrobat Pro and Acrobat Standard 2
Prerequisites 2
Installing Adobe Acrobat 2
Options for purchasing Acrobat 3
Starting Adobe Acrobat 3
Online content 3
Adobe Authorized Training Centers 4
Additional resources 5
New Acrobat Experience 6

1 INTRODUCING ADOBE ACROBAT 8

About PDF 10
About Adobe Acrobat 10
About Acrobat Reader 11
About the Acrobat mobile apps 12
Adding Acrobat Reader installers 12
About Acrobat online services 13
Using PDF on the web 13
About the Home view 14
Opening a PDF file 15
Working with toolbars 17
Tools in the Tools pane 19

Working with tools 20
Navigating PDF documents 22
Viewing PDF presentations in Full Screen mode 29
Viewing PDF files in Read mode 31
Customizing the Acrobat toolbar 32
Setting Acrobat preferences for web browsing 32
Customizing the brightness of the user interface 35
Getting help 36
Review questions and answers 37

2 CREATING ADOBE PDF FILES 38

About creating Adobe PDF files 40
Using the Create PDF tool 40
Creating files from the clipboard 43
Dragging and dropping files 44
Saving PDF files to cloud accounts 44
Converting different types of files 45
Inserting a blank page 50
Using PDFMaker 51
Using the Print command to create Adobe PDF files 51
Reducing file size 54
Adobe PDF presets 54
Optimizing PDF files (Acrobat Pro only) 55
Scanning a paper document 56
Making scanned text editable and searchable (Acrobat Pro only) 58
Scan using mobile devices 58
Converting web pages to Adobe PDF 60
Converting web pages in a web browser 64
Review questions and answers 65

3 READING AND WORKING WITH PDF FILES 66

About the onscreen display 68
Reading PDF documents 68
Searching PDF documents 74
Printing PDF documents 76
Printing booklets 80
Filling out PDF forms 81
About flexibility, accessibility, and structure 82
Checking for accessibility (Acrobat Pro only) 84
Making files flexible and accessible (Acrobat Pro only) 87
About tags 90
Using Acrobat accessibility features (Standard and Pro) 91
Sharing PDF files 95
Review questions and answers 97

4 ENHANCING PDF DOCUMENTS 98

Examining the work file 100
Moving pages with page thumbnails 102
Manipulating pages 104
Renumbering pages 106
Applying Bates numbering (Acrobat Pro only) 108
Managing links 109
Working with bookmarks 113
Naming bookmarks automatically 116
Setting document properties and metadata 117
Setting up presentations 118
Review questions and answers 119

5 EDITING CONTENT IN PDF FILES 120

Editing text 122
Redacting text (Acrobat Pro only) 128
Working with images in a PDF file 129
Copying text and images from a PDF file 132
Exporting PDF content to a PowerPoint presentation 134

Saving PDF files as Word documents 137
Extracting PDF tables as Excel spreadsheets 139
Review questions and answers 141

6 USING ACROBAT ON MOBILE DEVICES 142
About the Acrobat mobile apps 144
Getting Started 145
Using the Acrobat Reader app............................145
Using Acrobat in a web browser..........................151
Using the Fill & Sign app 154
Using the Adobe Scan app 156
Review questions and answers 159

7 USING ACROBAT WITH MICROSOFT OFFICE FILES 160
Getting started 162
About Acrobat PDFMaker 162
Converting Microsoft Word files to Adobe PDF (Windows)...163
Creating Adobe PDF files from Word mail-merge templates 168
Converting Word documents to PDF (macOS).............169
Converting Excel documents (Windows)..................170
Converting Excel spreadsheets (macOS) 174
Using the Spreadsheet Split view........................175
Converting PowerPoint presentations (Windows) 176
Converting PowerPoint presentations (macOS) 178
Review questions and answers 179

8 COMBINING FILES 180
About combining files 182
Selecting files to combine................................182
Arranging pages...188
Merging the files...191
Creating a PDF Portfolio (Acrobat Pro) 193
Review questions and answers 195

9 ADDING SIGNATURES AND SECURITY 196
Getting started 198
Viewing documents in Protected Mode (Windows only) 198
About security in Acrobat 199
Viewing security settings 200
Adding security to PDF files 201
About digital signatures 206
Sending a document for others to sign 207
Doing more with e-signatures 213
Using digital IDs 219
Review questions and answers 221

10 USING ACROBAT IN A REVIEW CYCLE 222
About the review process 224
Getting started 224
Adding comments to a PDF document 225
Commenting in Acrobat Reader 227
Working with comments 232
Initiating a shared review 236
Summarizing comments 236
Sending PDF files as email attachments 237
Using a network folder for a shared review 239
Comparing versions of documents (Acrobat Pro only) 240
Review questions and answers 243

11 WORKING WITH FORMS IN ACROBAT 244
Getting started 246
Converting PDF files to interactive PDF forms 246
Types of form fields 248
Adding form fields 249
Specifying an answer format 251
Using image buttons 256
Distributing forms 259

Tracking forms . . . 261
Collecting form data . . . 262
Options for distributing forms . . . 262
Working with form data . . . 264
Calculating and validating numeric fields . . . 265
Review questions and answers . . . 269

12 USING ACTIONS (ACROBAT PRO) 270

About actions . . . 272
Using predefined actions . . . 272
Creating an action . . . 277
Sharing actions . . . 287
Avoiding the Full Screen mode warning . . . 288
Review questions and answers . . . 289

13 USING ACROBAT IN PROFESSIONAL PRINTING 290

Creating PDF files for print and prepress . . . 292
Guidelines for creating print-ready PDF files . . . 293
Preflighting files (Acrobat Pro) . . . 295
Working with transparency (Acrobat Pro) . . . 298
Custom preflight profiles . . . 298
PDF standards . . . 299
What is rasterization? . . . 301
About flattening options in the Flattener Preview dialog box . . . 303
Setting up color management . . . 304
Previewing your print job (Acrobat Pro) . . . 305
Advanced printing controls . . . 308
Review questions and answers . . . 311

INDEX 312

GETTING STARTED

Adobe® Acrobat® is an essential tool in today's electronic workflow. You can use Acrobat Standard or Acrobat Pro to convert virtually any document to Adobe Portable Document Format (PDF), preserving the exact look and content of the original, complete with fonts and graphics. You can edit text and images in PDF documents, initiate reviews, distribute and share documents, create interactive forms, and more.

About Classroom in a Book

Adobe Acrobat Classroom in a Book®, Fourth Edition is part of the official training series for Adobe graphics and publishing software, developed with the support of Adobe product experts. The lessons are designed to let you learn at your own pace. If you're new to Adobe Acrobat, you'll learn the fundamental concepts and features you'll need to master the program. If you've been using Acrobat for a while, you'll find that Classroom in a Book teaches many advanced features, including tips and techniques for using the newest features.

Although each lesson provides step-by-step instructions for working with specific projects, there's room for exploration and experimentation. You can follow the book from start to finish, or complete only the lessons that match your interests and needs. Each lesson concludes with a review section summarizing what you've covered.

Acrobat Pro and Acrobat Standard

This book covers features included in Acrobat Pro and Acrobat Standard. We've noted where a tool or feature described in this book is available only in Acrobat Pro. Features available only in Acrobat Pro include:

- Preflighting documents and other print production tasks
- Creating PDF Portfolios
- Checking PDF documents for accessibility
- Applying Bates numbering and redaction
- Comparing versions of a document
- Using and creating actions
- Converting scanned documents into editable, searchable PDF files

Prerequisites

Before beginning to use *Adobe Acrobat Classroom in a Book, Fourth Edition*, you should have a working knowledge of your computer and its operating system. Make sure you know how to use the mouse, standard menus and commands, and also how to open, save, and close files. If you need to review these techniques, see the printed or online documentation included with your system.

Installing Adobe Acrobat

Before beginning to use *Adobe Acrobat Classroom in a Book, Fourth Edition*, make sure that your system is set up correctly and that you've installed the required software and hardware. You must purchase Adobe Acrobat software separately. For system requirements, see the Adobe website at www.adobe.com/products/acrobat/main.html.

You must install the application onto your hard drive. Follow the onscreen installation instructions.

Some lessons require other Acrobat apps, including the Adobe Acrobat Reader app, Adobe Fill & Sign, and Adobe Scan. You can download and install them all now, or install them when you need them.

Options for purchasing Acrobat DC

Both Acrobat Standard and Acrobat Pro are available by single-app subscription plans or through an Adobe Creative Cloud subscription plan. Which option you choose depends on your individual and organizational needs. However, either an Acrobat or Creative Cloud subscription include access to Adobe Document Cloud services and Adobe's cloud storage. Where Document Cloud services are required for a feature, such as Adobe Sign, we've noted it in the lessons.

You can learn more and compare your options for purchasing Acrobat at https://www.adobe.com/acrobat/pricing.html.

Starting Adobe Acrobat

You start Acrobat just as you would any other software application.

- **Windows:** Choose Start > Programs or All Programs > Adobe Acrobat.
- **macOS:** Open the Adobe Acrobat folder, and double-click the application icon.

Online content

Your purchase of this Classroom in a Book includes online materials provided by way of your Account page on adobepress.com.

Lesson files

To work through the projects in this book, you will need to download the lesson files from peachpit.com. You can download the files for individual lessons or it may be possible to download them all in a single file.

Accessing the lesson files and Web Edition

If you purchased an eBook from peachpit.com or adobepress.com, your Web Edition will automatically appear under the Digital Purchases tab on your Account page. Click the Launch link to access the product. Continue reading to learn how to register your product to get access to the lesson files.

If you purchased an eBook from a different vendor or you bought a print book, you must register your purchase on adobepress.com in order to access the online content:

1 Go to adobepress.com/register.

2 Sign in or create a new account.

3 Enter the ISBN: 9780137983636

4 Answer the questions as proof of purchase.

The Web Edition will appear under the Digital Purchases tab on your Account page.

5 Click the Launch link to access the product.

Note: As you complete each lesson, you will preserve the start files. In case you overwrite them, you can restore the original files by downloading the corresponding lesson files from your Account page at adobepress.com.

Purchase of this Classroom in a Book in any form gives you access to the lesson files you'll need to complete the exercises in this book. All lesson files are copyrighted; you may use them only to complete the exercises in this book.

You can access the lesson files through the Registered Products tab on your Account page. Click the Access Bonus Content link below the title of your product to proceed to the download page. Click the lesson file links to download them to your computer, and then unzip them.

The files are compressed into zip archives to speed download time and to protect the contents from damage during transfer. You must uncompress (or "unzip") the files to restore them to their original size and format before you use them with the book. On a modern operating system, simply double-click a zip archive to open it.

When you begin each lesson, you will navigate to the folder with that lesson number, where you will find all of the project files you need to complete the lesson.

Adobe Authorized Training Centers

Adobe Authorized Training Centers offer instructor-led courses and training on Adobe products. A directory of AATCs is available at https://learning.adobe.com/partner-finder.html.

Additional resources

Adobe Acrobat Classroom in a Book, Fourth Edition is not meant to replace documentation provided with the program or to be a comprehensive reference for every feature. Only the commands and options used in the lessons are explained in this book. For comprehensive information about program features and tutorials, refer to these resources:

- **Adobe Acrobat Learn and Support:** helpx.adobe.com/acrobat.html has comprehensive content you can search or browse, provided by Adobe. This includes hands-on tutorials, a link to Help, answers to common questions, troubleshooting information, and more.
- **Acrobat User Guide:** helpx.adobe.com/acrobat/topics.html is a reference for application features, commands, and tools (press F1 or choose Help > Online Support). You can also download Help as a PDF document optimized for printing at helpx.adobe.com/pdf/acrobat_reference.pdf.
- **Acrobat Forums:** forums.adobe.com/community/acrobat lets you tap into peer-to-peer discussions and questions and answers on Acrobat and other Adobe products.
- **Adobe Creative Cloud Learn:** https://helpx.adobe.com/support/creative-cloud.html provides inspiration, key techniques, cross-product workflows, and updates on new features.
- **Resources for educators:** edex.adobe.com offers a treasure trove of information for instructors who teach classes on Adobe software. Find solutions for education at all levels, including free curricula that use an integrated approach to teaching Adobe software and can be used to prepare for the Adobe Certified Associate exams.

Also check out these useful links:

- **Adobe Exchange:** exchange.adobe.com is a central resource for finding tools, services, extensions, code samples, and more to supplement and extend your Adobe products.
- **Adobe Acrobat product home page:** www.adobe.com/products/acrobat has more information about the product.

New Acrobat Experience

Some Acrobat users with 64-bit operating systems have access to the new Acrobat experience, an enhanced user interface that provides easy access to many Acrobat features. If the new experience is enabled on your system, your screen may not match ours. Most of the steps we provide will work, though you'll have additional ways to access the same tools.

To disable the new experience so that your screen matches ours:

- In Windows, click the hamburger icon (≡) in the upper left corner, and choose Disable New Acrobat.
- In macOS, choose View > Disable New Acrobat.

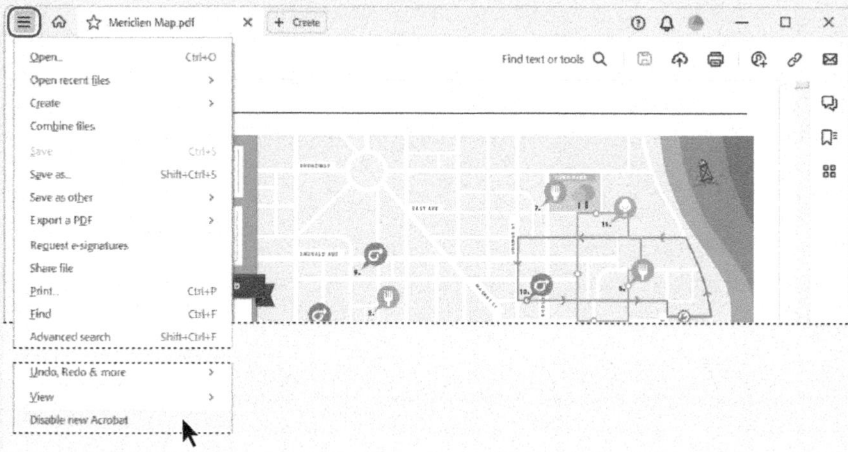

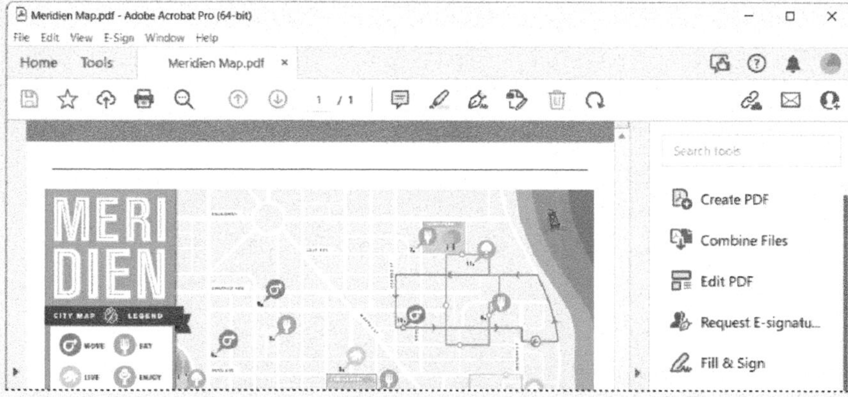

To enable the new experience again, choose View > Enable New Acrobat, and click Restart.

The new user interface includes the following:

- A hamburger menu in Windows that replaces the regular File menu.
- A unified global bar for ease of access and improved document visibility.
- A mega verb bar in the global bar to give access to the Edit, Convert, and Sign PDF tools without switching screens or leaving your document.
- A quick tools pane to add annotations, select text or objects, fill in a PDF form, and customize the tools pane.
- A navigation pane to bookmark, view or navigate pages, and access various viewing options.

A. *Hamburger icon* **B.** *Mega verb bar* **C.** *Quick Tools pane* **D.** *Global bar* **C.** *Navigation pane*

With the new experience enabled, all tools are organized in one section with the new quick tools pane for frequently used tools. When you use any Acrobat tool, the user interface is customized to show the tool's specific options in the left pane. The tools and related options are displayed progressively—as you choose a tool or action in the pane.

1 INTRODUCING ADOBE ACROBAT

Lesson overview

In this lesson, you'll do the following:

- Get acquainted with the Portable Document Format (PDF), Acrobat, and Acrobat Reader.
- Use the Home view to access your files and tools.
- Select tools in the toolbars.
- Use tools in the Tools pane.
- Customize toolbars.
- Navigate a PDF document using the toolbars, menu commands, page thumbnails, and bookmarks.
- Change the view of a document in the document pane.
- View a PDF document in Read mode.
- Learn to use Adobe Acrobat Help.

This lesson will take approximately an hour to complete. Download the project files for this lesson, following the instructions in the Getting Started section under "Accessing the lesson files and Web Edition," if you haven't already done so. As you work on this lesson, you'll preserve the start files. If you need to restore the start files, download them from your Account page.

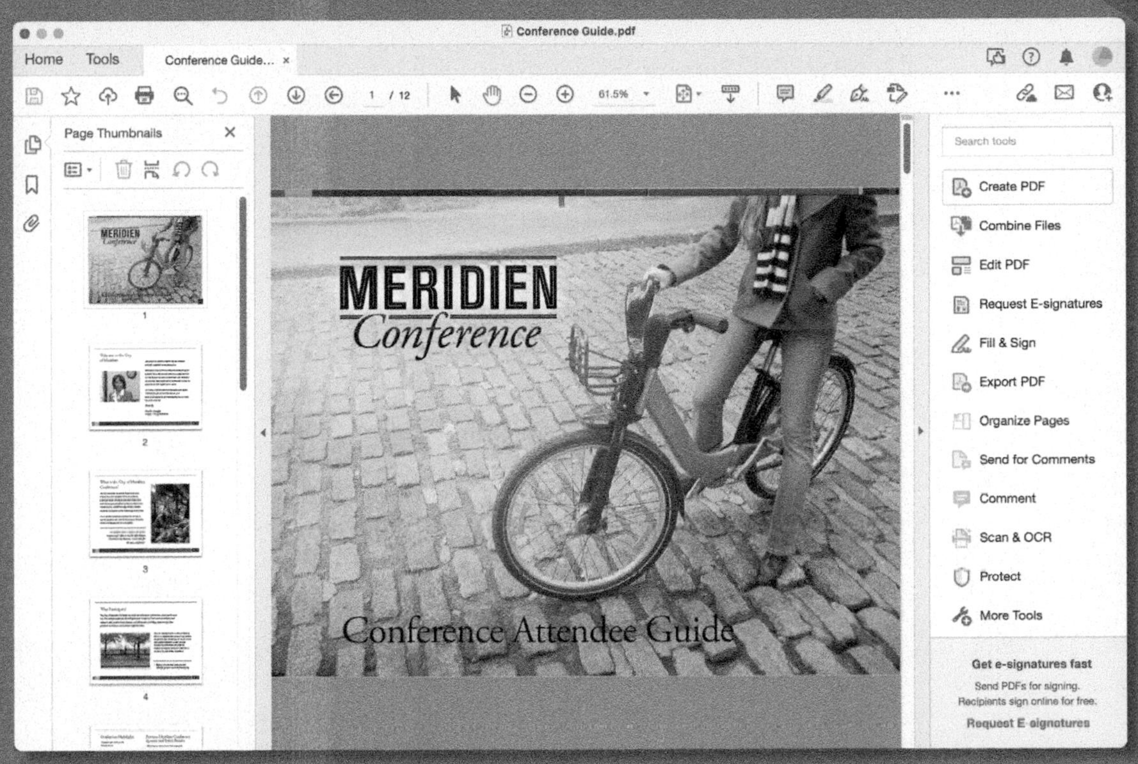

The Acrobat workspace puts the tools you need at your fingertips without cluttering up the screen. You can customize the toolbars for quicker access to tools you use frequently.

About PDF

Portable Document Format (PDF) is a file format that preserves all of the fonts, formatting, colors, and graphics of any source document, regardless of the application and platform used to create the original document. PDF files are compact and secure. Anyone using the free Acrobat Reader can view, navigate, comment on, and print a PDF file. Acrobat Reader users can also complete and return PDF forms and electronically sign PDF documents.

- PDF preserves the exact layout, fonts, and text formatting of electronic documents, regardless of the computer system or platform used to view these documents.
- You can read PDF documents using Acrobat Reader, Acrobat Standard, Acrobat Pro, Acrobat on the web, or Adobe mobile apps.
- PDF documents can contain multiple languages, such as Japanese and English, on the same page.
- PDF documents print predictably, with proper margins and page breaks.
- You can secure PDF files to prevent unauthorized changes or printing or to limit access to confidential documents.
- You can change the view magnification of a PDF page in Acrobat or Acrobat Reader, which is especially useful for zooming in on graphics or diagrams containing intricate details.
- You can share your PDF files using network and web servers, email, discs, other removable media, and Adobe's cloud storage.

About Adobe Acrobat

Adobe Acrobat lets you create, manage, edit, assemble, and search PDF documents. Additionally, you can create forms, initiate review processes, apply legal features, and prepare PDF documents for professional printing.

Almost any document—a text file, a file created in a page-layout or graphics application, a scanned document, a web page, or a digital photo—can be converted to Adobe PDF using Acrobat software or third-party authoring applications. Your workflow and document type determine the best way to create a PDF file.

About Acrobat Reader

Acrobat Reader, available free online, is the global standard for viewing PDF files. It is the only PDF viewer that can open and interact with all PDF documents. Acrobat Reader makes it possible to view, search, digitally sign, verify, print, and collaborate on PDF files without having Acrobat installed.

To install Acrobat Reader, visit get.adobe.com/reader.

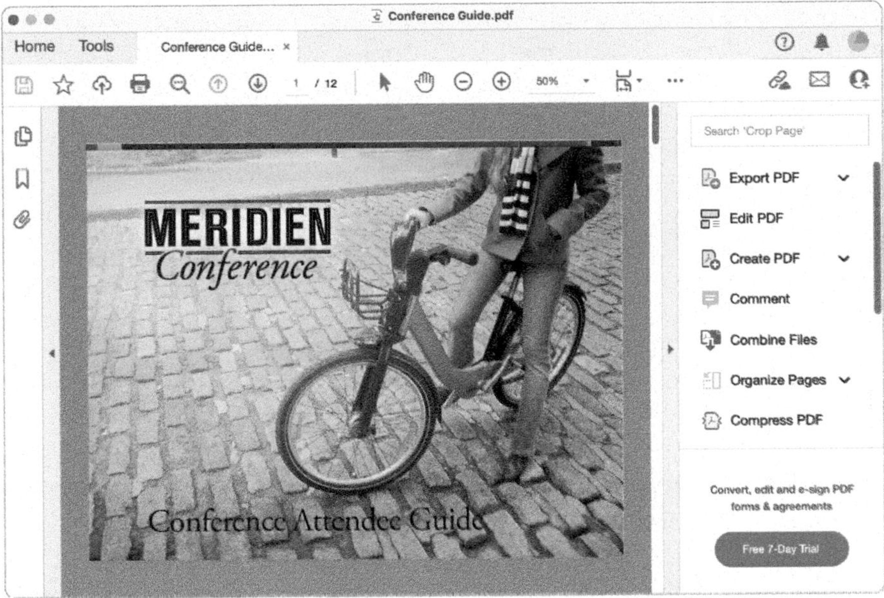

Acrobat Reader can natively display rich media content, including video and audio files. You can also view PDF Portfolios in Acrobat Reader.

In Windows, Acrobat Reader opens PDF files in Protected Mode (known as "sandboxing" to IT professionals). In Protected Mode, Reader confines any processes to the application itself, so that potentially malicious PDF files do not have access to your computer and its system files. To verify that Acrobat Reader is in Protected Mode, choose File > Properties, select the Advanced tab, and view the Protected Mode status.

Note: Adobe strongly recommends that you use Acrobat Reader for Windows in Protected Mode. However, if you need to disable it, choose Edit > Preferences. Then, select General from the list of categories, and deselect Enable Protected Mode At Startup in the Application Startup panel. Restart Acrobat Reader for the change to take effect.

Acrobat for Windows also opens PDF files in Protected Mode by default.

Adding Acrobat Reader installers

Acrobat Reader is available free of charge, making it easier for users to view your PDF documents. You can point users to the Acrobat Reader installers on the Adobe website at get.adobe.com/Reader. You can distribute Acrobat Reader on a local network. If you're distributing documents on a flash drive or other portable storage device , you can include a copy of the Acrobat Reader installers.

If you're providing the Acrobat Reader installers, you should include a ReadMe text file that describes how to install Acrobat Reader and provides any last-minute information.

You may make and distribute unlimited copies of Acrobat Reader, including copies for commercial distribution. For complete information on distributing and giving your users access to Acrobat Reader and the Acrobat Reader mobile app, visit the Adobe website at www.adobe.com/acrobat/pdf-reader/volume-distribution.html.

About the Acrobat mobile apps

The Adobe Acrobat Reader mobile app lets you work with PDF files on tablets and phones, using many of the features available in the desktop version of Acrobat. Adobe Scan, Adobe Sign, and Adobe Fill & Sign apps provide convenient access to specific features on mobile devices. Most lessons in this book focus on the features in the desktop version of Acrobat, but you can learn more about the mobile apps in Lesson 6, "Using Acrobat on Mobile Devices."

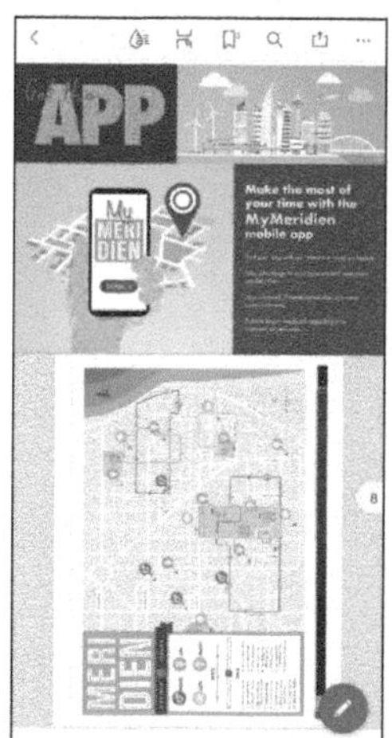

About Acrobat online services

A subscription to Acrobat or Creative Cloud provides free online storage for PDF files so that you can access them from any device, wherever you are. When you use Acrobat in a browser, you also have access to most of the functionality of the desktop version of Acrobat. To access your files and Acrobat features online, go to https://acrobat.adobe.com, and sign in if prompted.

Learn more about working with Acrobat online in Lesson 6, "Using Acrobat on Mobile Devices."

Using PDF on the web

The web makes it possible to deliver electronic documents to a wide and varied audience. Because web browsers can be configured to run other applications inside the browser window, you can post PDF files as part of a website. Visitors to your site can download PDF files or view them inside the browser window using Acrobat Reader.

When including a PDF file as part of your web page, consider directing users to the Adobe website so that the first time they encounter a PDF file, they can download Acrobat Reader, free of charge, if necessary.

PDF files can be viewed one page at a time and printed from the web. With page-at-a-time downloading, the web server sends only the requested page, decreasing downloading time. In addition, you can easily print selected pages or all pages from the document. PDF is a suitable format for publishing long electronic documents on the web, and PDF documents print predictably, with proper margins and page breaks.

You can also download and convert web pages to PDF, making it easy to save, distribute, and print them. (For more information, see Lesson 2, "Creating Adobe PDF Files.")

About the Home view

The Acrobat Home view provides links to tutorials and common tasks, such as exporting a PDF file to Microsoft Word format. By default, the Home view lists files you've recently opened, but you can choose to see files you've scanned, or navigate to PDF files on your local hard drive, Adobe cloud storage, or your account on a cloud service such as Dropbox or Google Drive.

When you select a file in the recent files list, the Home view displays tools for quick access. Selecting a tool opens the selected document with the selected tool active.

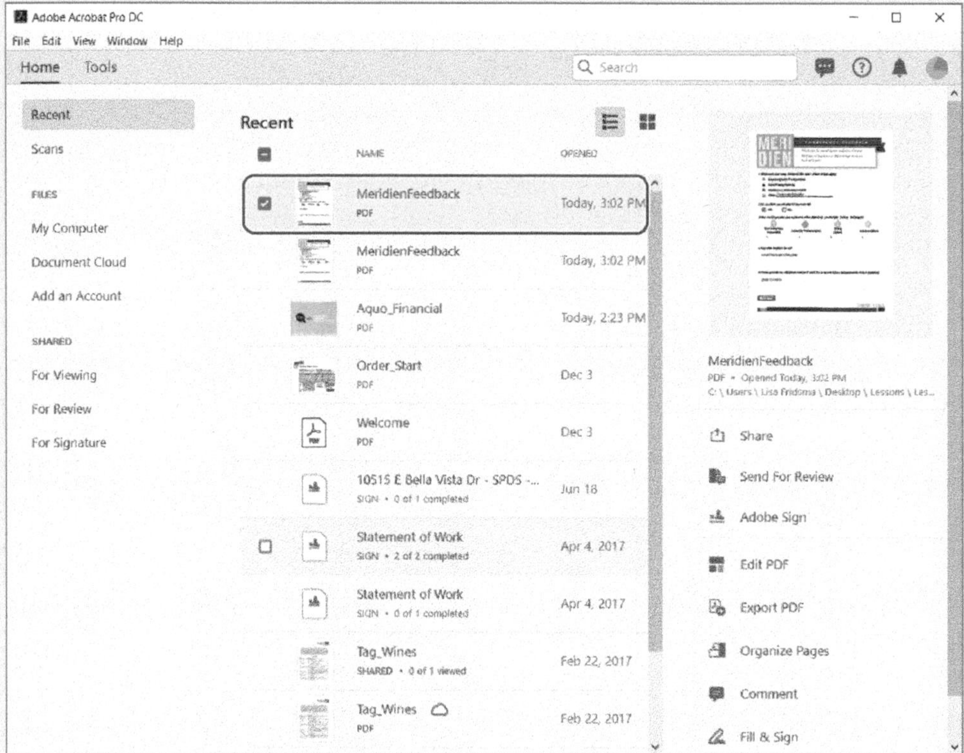

To access tutorials, click the Acrobat Tutorials icon (the question mark) at the top of the Home view.

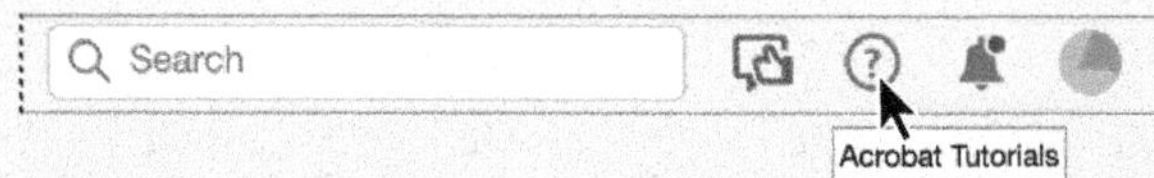

Opening a PDF file

The default Acrobat work area is streamlined to ensure easy access to the tools you'll use most often as you work with PDF files.

1 Start Acrobat.

The Home view lists recently used files.

You want to open a file you haven't opened before, so it isn't included in the list of recent files.

2 Click Your Computer in the Other File Storage area on the left.

3 Click Browse, navigate to the Lesson01/Assets folder on your hard drive, and select the Conference Guide.pdf file.

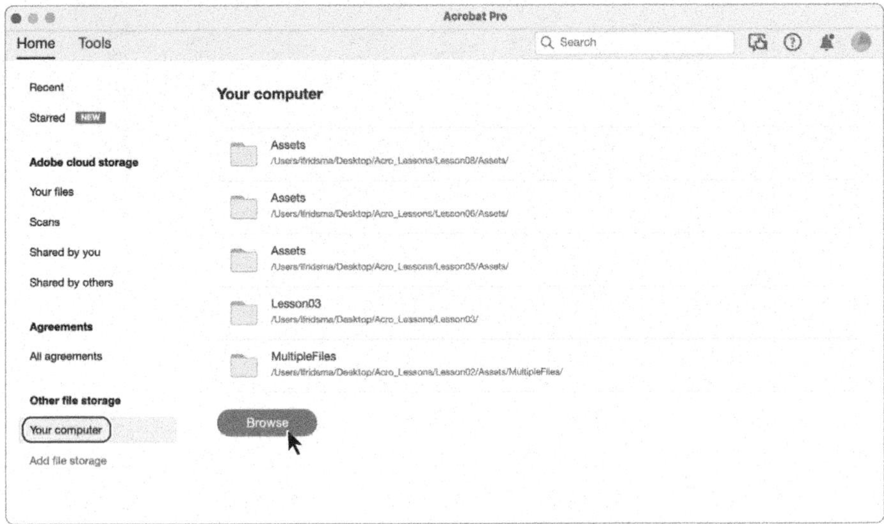

4 Click Open.

The menu bar and a toolbar are visible at the top of the work area. In Acrobat, each open document has its own tab, with its own work area and toolbars. You can access common commands in the menu bar.

▶ **Tip:** If you close the menu bar by choosing View > Show/Hide > Menu Bar, you won't be able to access any menu commands to reopen it. To reopen the menu bar, press F9 (Windows) or Command+Shift+M (macOS) on your keyboard.

Acrobat can open in two different ways—as a standalone application or in a web browser. The associated work areas differ in small but important ways. This book assumes that you are using Acrobat as a standalone application.

5 Move your pointer down to the lower left corner of the document window to reveal the size of this page. (The document window is the part of the workspace that displays an open document.) The page size display disappears when you move the pointer away from the area.

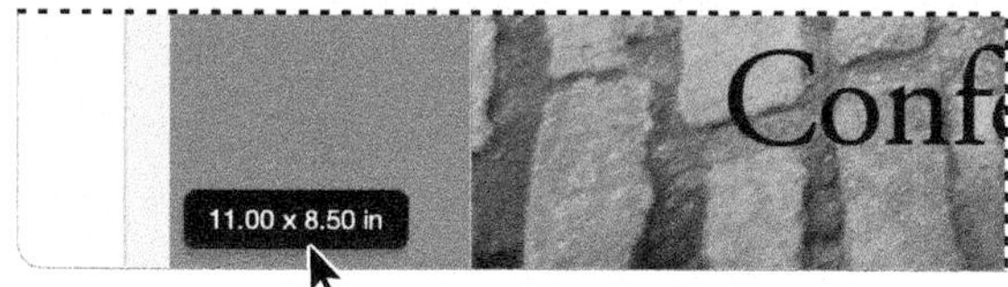

Working with toolbars

The main Acrobat toolbar contains commonly used tools and commands for working with PDF files. You can show additional tools in the toolbar, add tools to the Quick Tools portion of the toolbar, and show recently used tools. The toolbar is designed to be simple and streamlined, giving you the control to add only the tools you use frequently.

Using the toolbar

By default, the top level of the toolbar includes the Home button, the Tools button, and tabs for each open document. In Document view, the lower level of the toolbar is specific to each document; by default, it includes buttons for saving, uploading, or printing a PDF file; the Find Text tool; a few navigation tools; page control tools; and some commenting tools. To use a tool, click it.

To see the name or description of a tool in the toolbar, hover the pointer over the tool.

Using page controls

The page control tools—the Selection (![]) and Hand (![]) tools, page magnification, and page view options—help you navigate the page.

1 Click the Zoom In button (⊕) in the toolbar three times.

Tip: You can undock the page controls from the main toolbar: Click the Move Page Controls Out Of Toolbar button. The separate toolbar appears when you hover the mouse over the bottom of the screen. To redock the page controls, click the Move Page Controls Into Toolbar button.

Acrobat enlarges the view. Now only part of the document appears in the application window.

The default tool in Acrobat is the Selection tool (▶). The Hand tool lets you pan around the document.

2 Click the Hand tool (✋) in the toolbar.

3 With the Hand tool selected, drag the document across the application window to see a different portion of the image.

4 Click the Zoom Out button (⊖) once to see more of the page.

The Zoom tools do not change the actual size of a document. They change only its magnification on your screen.

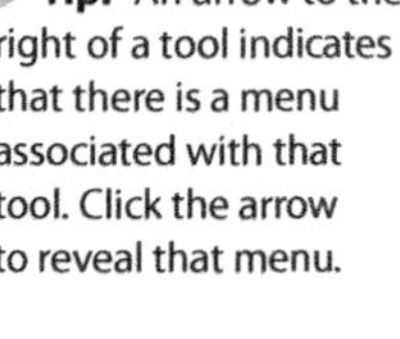

▶ **Tip:** An arrow to the right of a tool indicates that there is a menu associated with that tool. Click the arrow to reveal that menu.

5 Click the arrow on the right side of the magnification text box, and choose Fit Visible from the pop-up menu to display the entire page.

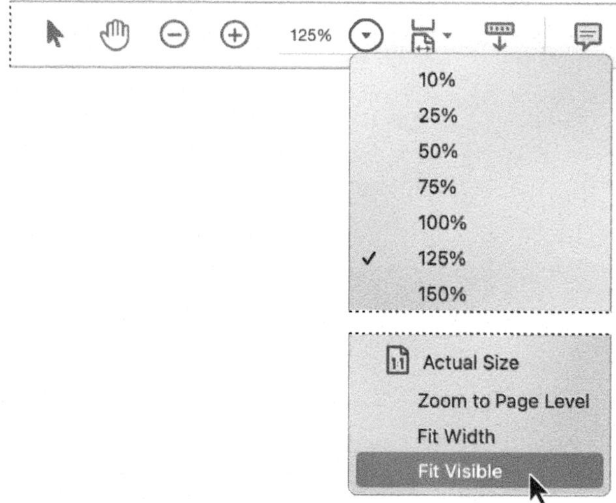

Tools in the Tools pane

By default, the Tools pane displays the most commonly used tools. To add or remove a tool from the pane, click Tools in the main toolbar to open the Tools Center view. Then choose Add Shortcut or Remove Shortcut from the menu beneath a tool. Acrobat uses the current Tools pane configuration in all PDF documents you open until you change the configuration again. (Some of the tools are available only in Acrobat Pro.)

To see the tool names, click the left arrow next to the Tools pane. To show only the icons for each tool, click the right arrow next to the Tools pane.

Commonly used tools include:

- **Create PDF:** Create a PDF file from almost any file or scanned image.
- **Combine Files:** Create a PDF file from multiple PDF files or other documents.
- **Edit PDF:** Edit text, images, links, and other content, and crop pages.
- **Request E-signatures:** Get documents signed electronically and track results.
- **Fill & Sign:** Complete and sign forms electronically.
- **Export PDF:** Export PDF files as Microsoft Office documents, images, HTML web pages, and other formats.
- **Organize Pages:** Rotate, delete, insert, replace, split, extract, and otherwise manipulate pages.
- **Send For Comments:** Invite people to review a shared document and track responses.
- **Comment:** Add, search, read, reply to, import, and export comments.
- **Scan & OCR:** Make text editable, and otherwise improve the quality of scanned documents.
- **Protect:** Apply security features such as file encryption.

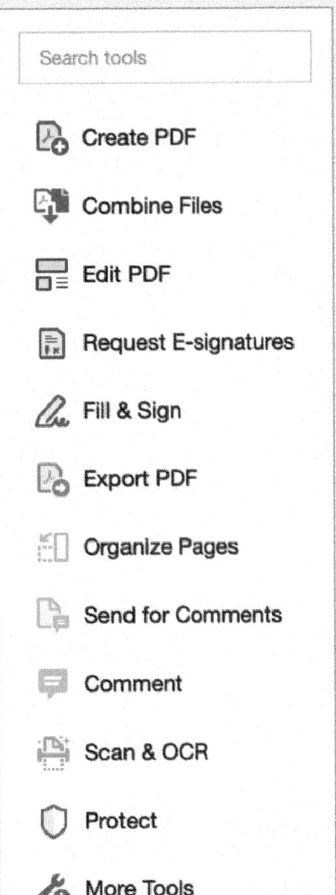

Working with tools

The commands and options you need in order to perform different tasks are grouped in the Tools pane on the right side of the application window. Additional tools are available in the Tools Center; you can access them directly from the Tools Center or add them to the Tools pane. When you select a tool, the user interface changes to provide the options related to that tool.

Selecting tools in the Tools pane

To become familiar with using tools, you'll rotate a page and edit some text.

1 Click Organize Pages in the Tools pane on the right side of the screen.

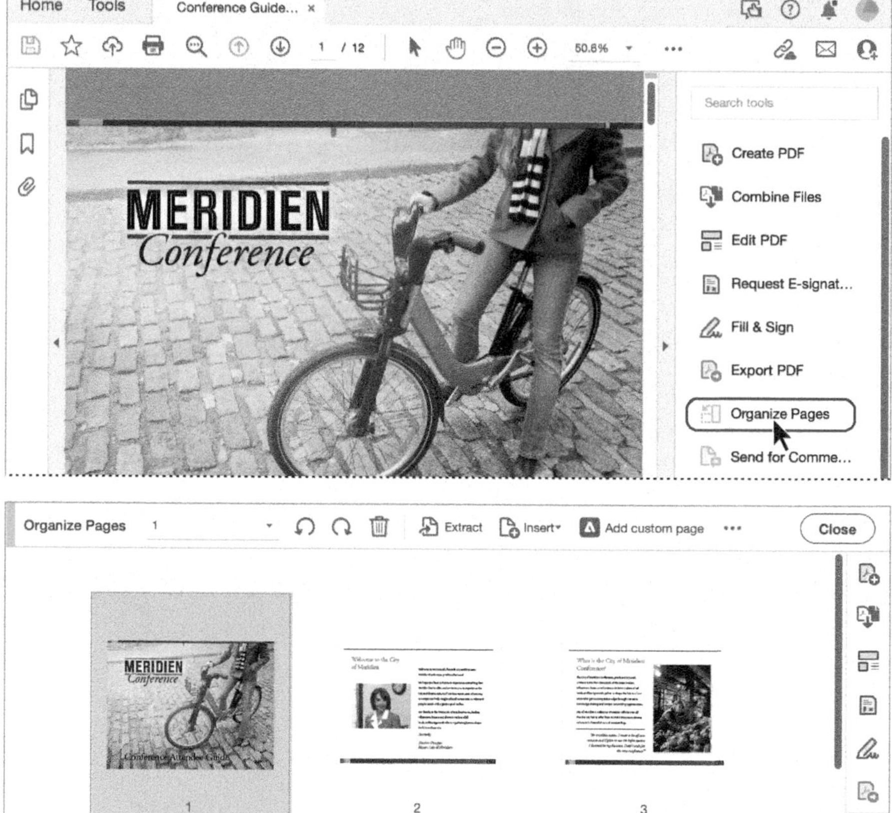

Acrobat displays thumbnail previews of each of the pages in the document, with page numbers shown beneath them. The Organize Pages toolbar appears below the main Acrobat toolbar.

2 Click the page 9 thumbnail. Four icons appear near the selected thumbnail: two rotation icons, a trash icon, and an insertion icon.

The map of Meridien on page 9 is oriented incorrectly. You'll correct it.

3 Click the clockwise rotation icon (↻).

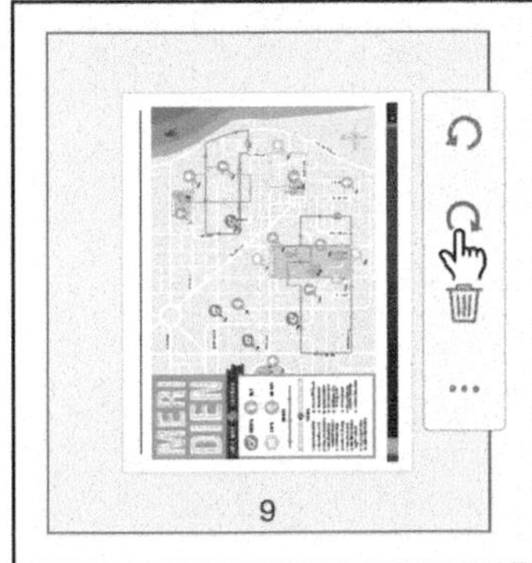

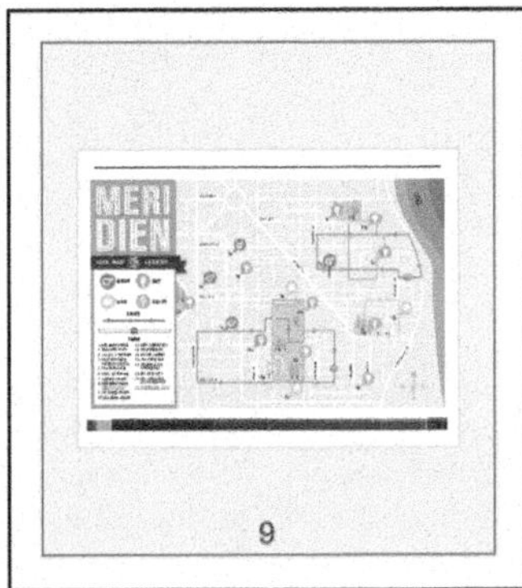

The page rotates to the correct orientation, and no other pages are affected.

4 Click the Close button at the end of the Organize Pages toolbar to return to the main document view.

5 Click Edit PDF in the Tools pane.

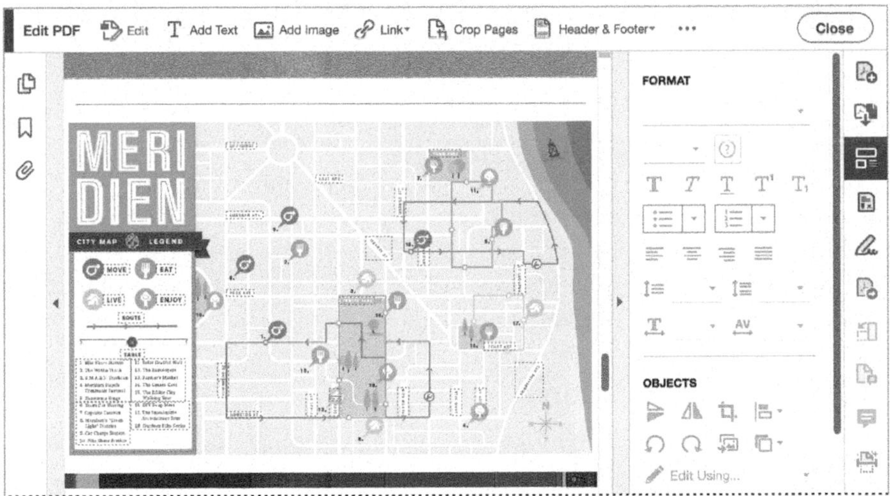

The Edit PDF toolbar appears below the main Acrobat toolbar. On the right side of the application window, a pane displays options related to editing text and images. The document window displays the current page. By default, Edit is selected in the Edit PDF toolbar.

When you select a tool, the user interface changes to show you the options and content you need to effectively use that tool. How it changes varies from tool to tool.

6 In the main toolbar, type **12** in the page number box, and then press Enter or Return to go to that page.

Because Edit is selected in the Edit PDF toolbar, editable content is outlined on the page. A box appears around the text. The pointer changes to an I-beam when you move it over the text.

7 Select the word *and* in the second sentence of the Wireless Internet Access topic.

8 Type **but** to replace the word *and.*

Note: If the original font is not available, Acrobat substitutes a default font and displays a tooltip informing you that the font has been substituted.

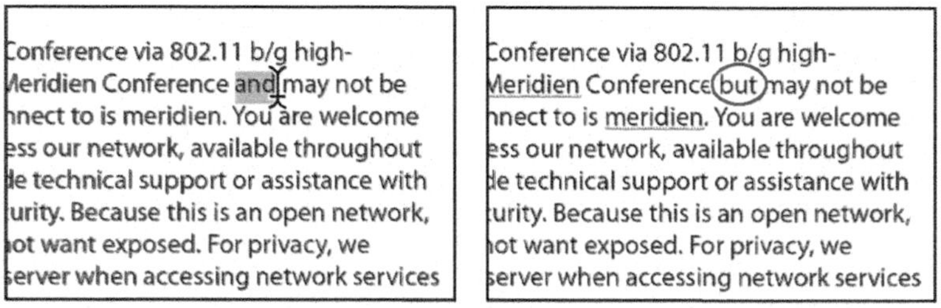

9 Click Close in the Edit PDF toolbar to close the Edit PDF tool.

10 Choose File > Save As.

11 Navigate to the Lesson01/Finished_Projects folder, name the file **Conference Guide_final.pdf**, and click Save. Leave the file open.

Navigating PDF documents

You can zoom in and out, move to different pages, show multiple pages at a time, view multiple documents, and even split a document to view different areas of the same document simultaneously. Many navigation tools are available in more than one place; you can use the method that best suits your workflow.

Changing magnification

Earlier in this lesson, you used the Zoom In and Zoom Out tools, as well as the preset magnification menu, all in the toolbar. You can also change the magnification using commands in the View menu.

1 Choose File > Open, navigate to the Meridien Rev.pdf file in the Lesson01/Assets folder, and click Open.

2 Choose View > Zoom > Fit Height.

The entire PDF document is displayed, fitting the height of the application window.

3 Choose View > Zoom > Zoom To.

4 In the Zoom To dialog box, type **125** for Magnification, and then click OK.

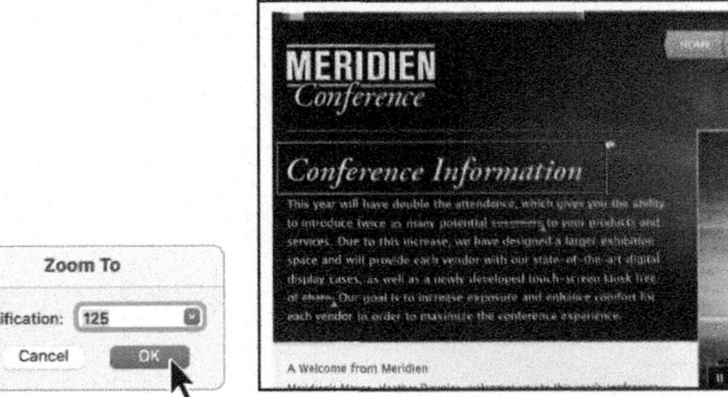

Accessing specific pages

You've used the page number text box in the Acrobat toolbar to go to a specific page. You can also use commands in the View menu or use the Page Thumbnails panel in the navigation pane to quickly move to a different page in the document.

1 Click the Conference Guide_final.pdf tab to display the file you worked with earlier. If the Conference Guide_final.pdf file isn't open, open it.

2 Choose View > Page Navigation > Go To Page.

3 In the Go To Page dialog box, type **6**, and click OK.

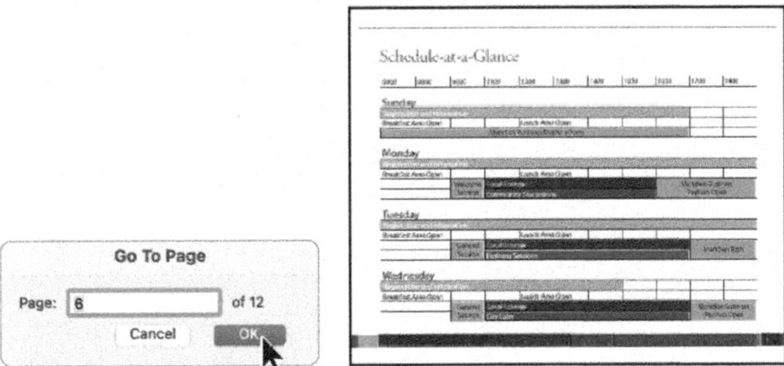

Acrobat displays page 6 of the document.

4 Choose View > Page Navigation > Previous Page.

Acrobat displays page 5 of the document. The Previous Page and Next Page commands serve the same purpose as the Previous Page and Next Page buttons in the Acrobat toolbar.

5 If the navigation pane isn't visible, click the arrow on the left side of the application window to open it.

6 In the navigation pane, click the Page Thumbnails button (![]).

Acrobat displays thumbnails of all the pages in the document. Acrobat automatically creates thumbnails for the pages of a PDF document when you open it.

7 Click the thumbnail for page 3.

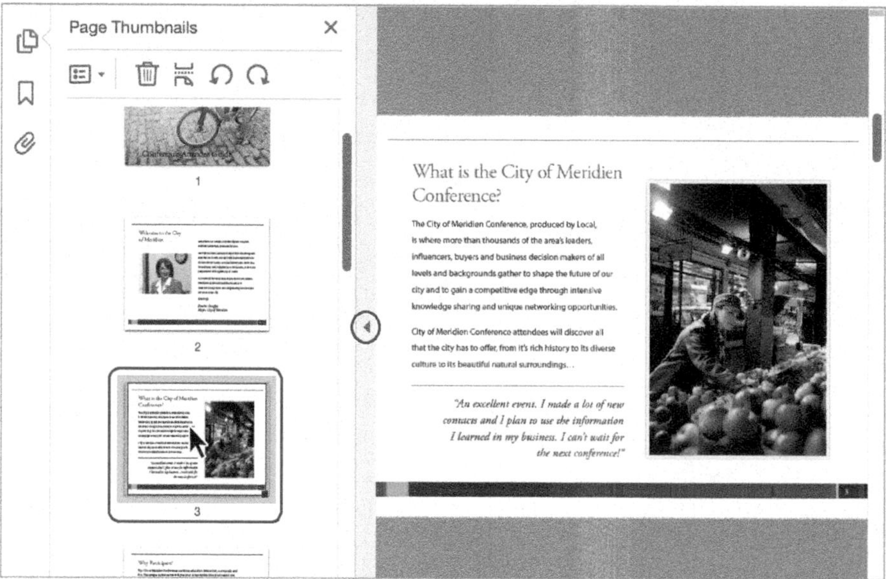

Acrobat displays page 3 of the document.

8 Zoom in to 200%. Notice that the thumbnail highlights the area of the page that is visible at this magnification.

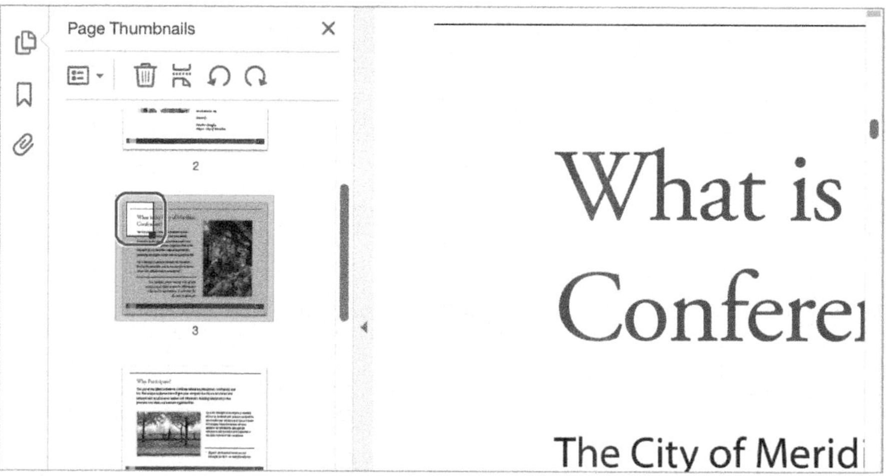

9 Select the Hand tool (☝) in the toolbar.

10 Drag in the document window to see a different area of the page. Notice that the highlighted area in the thumbnail moves accordingly.

Using bookmarks to navigate documents

You can create bookmarks to help viewers navigate PDF documents. Bookmarks act as an electronic table of contents page, providing links directly to the content they describe.

1 Click the Bookmarks button (🔖) directly below the Page Thumbnails button in the navigation pane.

Acrobat displays the bookmarks that have been created for this PDF document.

2 Click the Get the App bookmark.

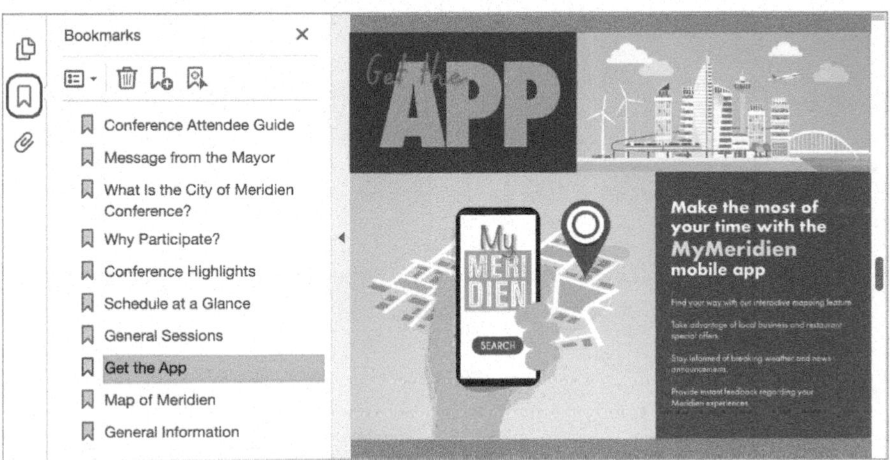

Acrobat displays page 8, which contains information about the city's app.

3 Click the General Sessions bookmark.

Acrobat displays page 7, where the descriptions of the conference sessions begin. You do not need to create a bookmark for each page.

4 Click the General Information bookmark.

Acrobat displays page 10, where the general information begins. You'll create another bookmark to help conference attendees locate information about accessing first aid quickly.

▶ **Tip:** You can create bookmarks for a PDF document in Acrobat, or you can generate them automatically when you create the PDF file using PDFMaker or when you export a PDF file from InDesign.

5 Click the Next Page button (⊕) in the Acrobat toolbar to go to page 11.

6 Select the Selection tool (⮝) in the toolbar, and then select the "First aid information" heading on the page.

7 Click the New Bookmark button (⊞) at the top of the Bookmarks panel.

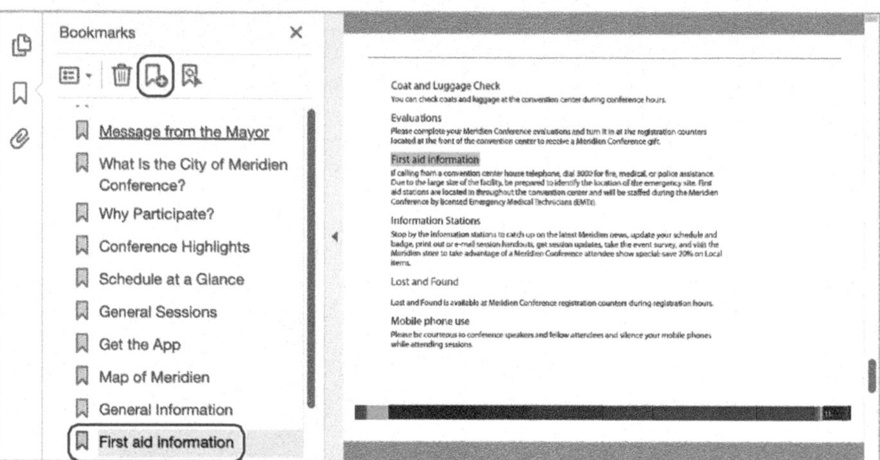

Acrobat adds a new bookmark with the text you selected beneath the General Information bookmark.

8 Drag the new bookmark over the General Information bookmark (directly over the words "General Information"), and then release the mouse button.

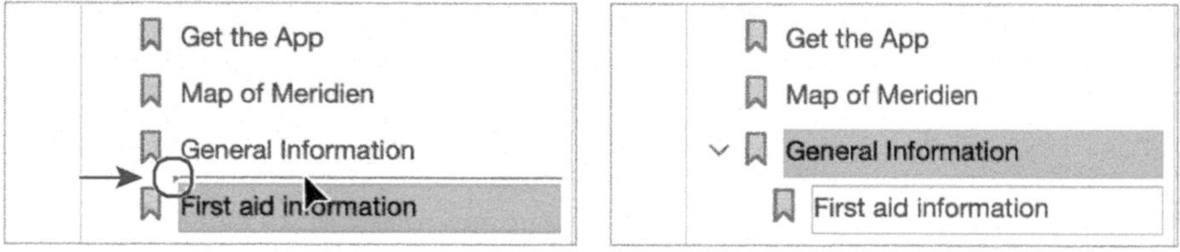

Acrobat indents the new bookmark, nesting it under the General Information bookmark.

9 Close the Bookmarks pane.

Viewing multiple documents

You can work with more than one PDF file at a time, displaying the documents vertically or horizontally. You've opened two PDF documents; you'll view them next to each other.

1 Choose Window > Tile > Vertically.

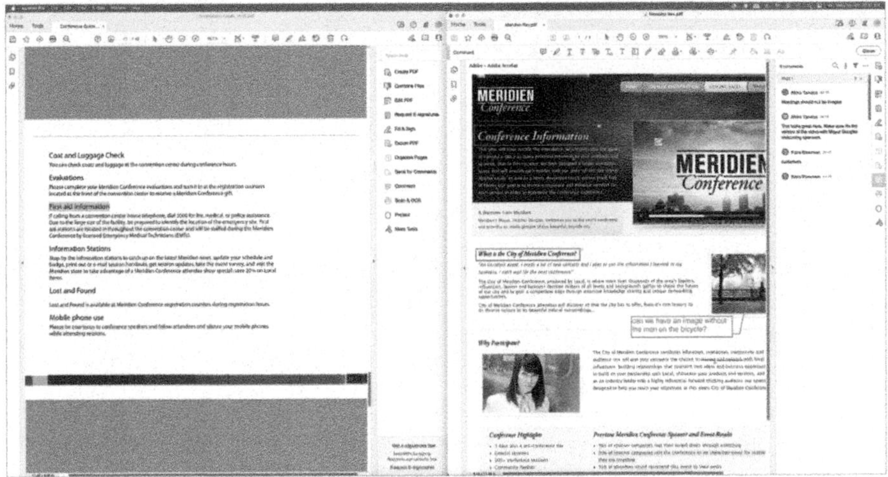

Acrobat displays all the open PDF files side by side. Notice that each document has its own application window, complete with toolbars and panes.

2 Choose Window > Tile > Horizontally.

Acrobat displays the PDF documents in their own application windows once again, but this time they're displayed horizontally.

3 Choose Window > Cascade.

Acrobat displays the active document in front of the others, but you can see the title bar for each of the other open documents.

4 Adjust the windows so you can see the toolbar for each document. Then drag the tab from one of the documents next to the tab for the other; you'll see a blue line. Drop the tab there to return to the standard tabbed document view.

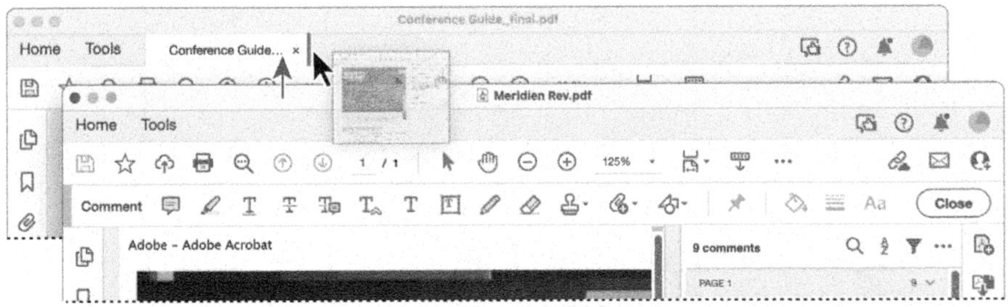

Splitting the view of a document

Sometimes you need to work with different portions of a single document simultaneously, whether it's to ensure you've used consistent wording or to examine differences in images. You can split a document into two views, with the ability to navigate each individually.

1 Click the Conference Guide_final.pdf tab to make it active. Then go to page 9, and choose View > Zoom > Zoom To Page Level.

2 Choose Window > Split.

Acrobat displays the same document twice, each with its own scroll bar. Notice that both copies of the document share the same toolbars and panes.

3 Click anywhere in the top version of the document. It's now the active view.

4 Click the Previous Page button (⊕) to go to the previous page in the top view. Only the top view changes.

5 Click anywhere in the bottom view to make it active.

6 Zoom in to 150%. Only the bottom view changes.

7 Choose Window > Remove Split.

Acrobat restores the document to a single view, displaying whichever view was active when you chose the Remove Split command.

8 Close all open documents without saving changes.

Viewing PDF presentations in Full Screen mode

You can set up a PDF file to be viewed in Full Screen mode, or choose to view any document that way. In Full Screen mode, the menu bar and toolbars are hidden.

1 Choose File > Open, and double-click the Aquo_Financial.pdf file, located in the Lesson01/Assets folder.

2 Click Yes in the Full Screen message box to open this document in Full Screen mode.

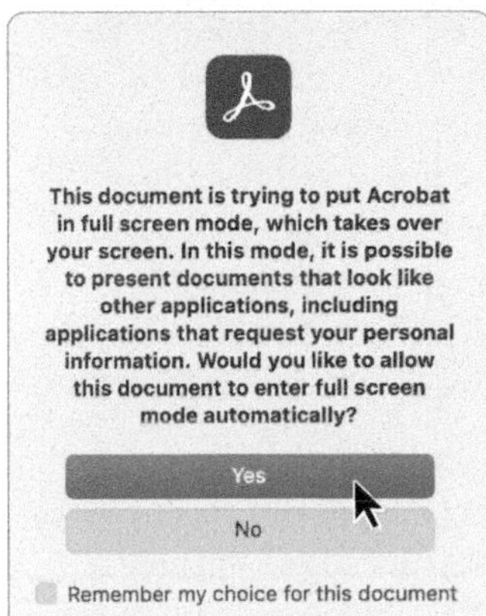

Notice that in Full Screen mode the document occupies all available space on the monitor. All the Acrobat toolbars, menus, and panes have disappeared.

This document is an informational presentation, designed to be viewed exclusively onscreen. The graphics, large type size, and horizontal page layout have been designed for optimal display on a monitor.

You can view any PDF file in Full Screen mode by opening the document in Acrobat and choosing View > Full Screen Mode.

3 Press Enter or Return to page through the presentation. You can also use the arrow keys on your keyboard to move forward and backward.

4 Press the Esc key to exit Full Screen mode.

5 To ensure that navigation controls are always accessible to you, even in Full Screen mode, choose Edit > Preferences (Windows) or Acrobat > Preferences (macOS), and select Full Screen from the list of categories in the Preferences dialog box. Select the Show Navigation Bar option, and click OK to apply your changes.

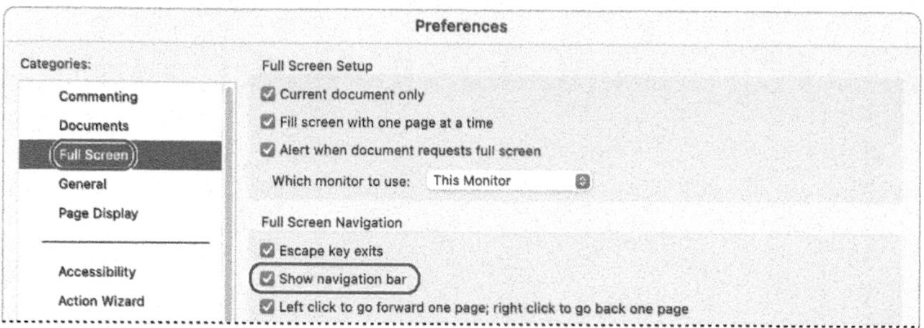

From this point on, whenever you open a document in Acrobat on your computer in Full Screen mode, Acrobat will display Next Page, Previous Page, and Exit Full Screen View buttons at the bottom left of the document window. The buttons appear when you first view the document in Full Screen mode, and then disappear so that they don't obstruct the presentation. To access the buttons, move the pointer over the lower left corner of the screen. Keep in mind that Full Screen viewing preferences are specific to the computer on which you run a PDF presentation, not to the document.

To set a file to open in Full Screen mode, choose File > Properties, click the Initial View tab in the Document Properties dialog box, select Open In Full Screen Mode, and click OK. Then save the document. For more information about document properties and metadata, see Lesson 4, "Enhancing PDF Documents."

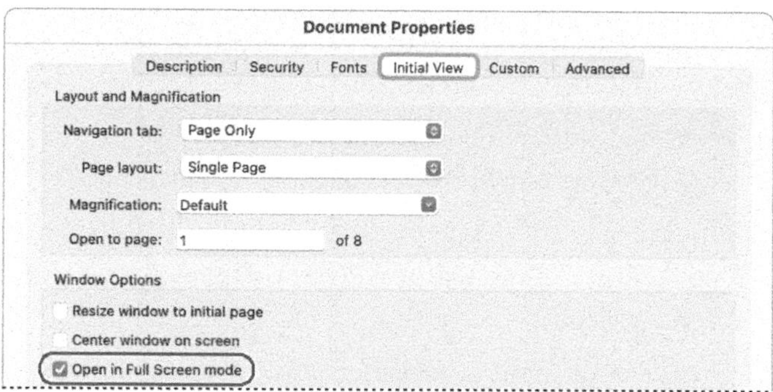

Viewing PDF files in Read mode

You can maximize the screen space available to your PDF document without entering Full Screen mode. Read mode hides all the elements of the work area except the document and the menu bar.

1 Choose View > Read Mode.

2 Move the pointer near the bottom of the window.

A floating toolbar appears briefly when you move the pointer near the bottom of the page. This floating toolbar includes navigational tools that let you zoom in and out, move to different pages, and save or print the file.

3 To restore the work area, click the Show Main Toolbar button (◪) in the floating toolbar, or choose View > Read Mode again.

4 Choose File > Close File, and close the file without saving any changes.

Setting Acrobat preferences for web browsing

You can set the Acrobat Internet preferences to determine how Acrobat loads and displays PDF files from the Internet.

In Acrobat, choose Edit > Preferences (Windows) or Acrobat > Preferences (Mac OS), and select Internet from the categories on the left. By default, several Internet preference options are automatically selected.

- **Display In Read Mode By Default** displays PDF files without toolbars or panes, so that all that appears is a semitransparent floating toolbar when you move your mouse over the lower area of the PDF file. If you deselect this option, PDF files open with toolbars and panes.
- **Allow Fast Web View** downloads PDF documents for viewing on the web one page at a time. If this option is not selected, the entire PDF file downloads before it is displayed.
- **Allow Speculative Downloading In The Background** enables a PDF document to continue downloading from the web, even after the first requested page displays. Downloading in the background stops when any other task, such as paging through the document, is initiated in Acrobat.

For help setting up your browser to enable you to view PDF documents in it, click the link at the top of the Web Browser Options area of the Preferences dialog box to see instructions.

Customizing the Acrobat toolbar

The Acrobat toolbar includes a few commonly used tools by default. You can add tools you use frequently through the Show/Hide commands or by adding them to the Quick Tools section of the toolbar. Changes you make to the toolbar are application-wide, so the toolbar appears the same in any PDF file (until you change the toolbar settings again).

1 Open any document in Acrobat so that you have access to the toolbars.

2 Choose View > Show/Hide > Toolbar Items > Show Page Navigation Tools > Previous View.

Note: If the Previous View button is already in the toolbar, the command in step 2 removes it.

The Previous View button appears in the toolbar, just to the left of the page number.

3 Choose View > Show/Hide > Toolbar Items > Show Edit Tools > Undo.

The Undo button appears in the toolbar, next to the Find button. You may have noticed that the Show/Hide options add commands from the File, Edit, and View menus to the toolbar, positioned in the toolbar according to their menu and sub-menu (such as Page Navigation).

The Quick Tools area of the toolbar contains tools you add through the Tools pane. Almost every tool is available.

4 Choose View > Show/Hide > Toolbar Items > Customize Quick Tools.

The Customize Quick Tools dialog box opens. The tools currently in the Quick Tools toolbar are displayed across the top of the dialog box. Tools you can add are listed below. You'll add the Rotate Left and Rotate Right tools to the toolbar.

5 Click Organize Pages to expand it.

6 Select the Left tool, and then click the Add To Toolbar button to add the tool to the set at the top.

7 Select the Right tool, and then click the Add To Toolbar button.

Note: If the Right tool button is already in the toolbar, you won't be able to add it.

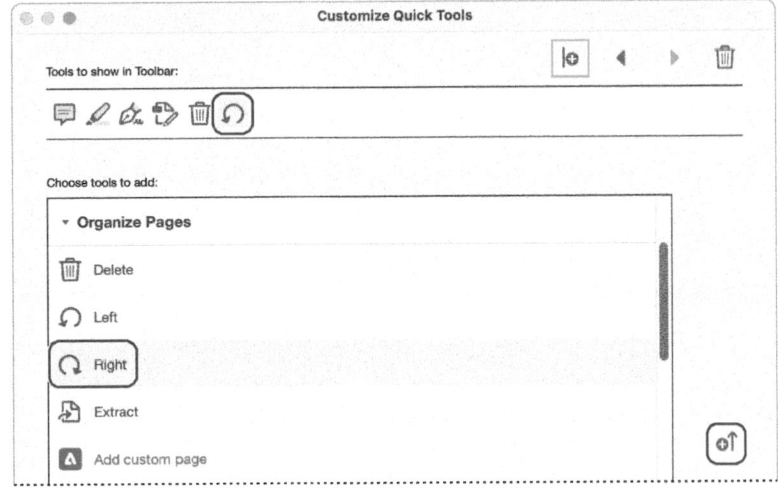

8 Click Organize Pages to collapse the section again, and then scroll up and click Create PDF to expand it.

9 Select PDF From File, and click the Add To Toolbar button.

You've added three buttons to the Quick Tools area of the toolbar. You can rearrange tools, add dividers to organize them visually, and delete tools.

10 With the PDF From File tool still selected, click the left arrow button at the top of the dialog box twice to move it to the left of the rotation tools.

11 Click the Add Divider button at the top of the dialog box to add a divider between the PDF From File tool and the rotation tools.

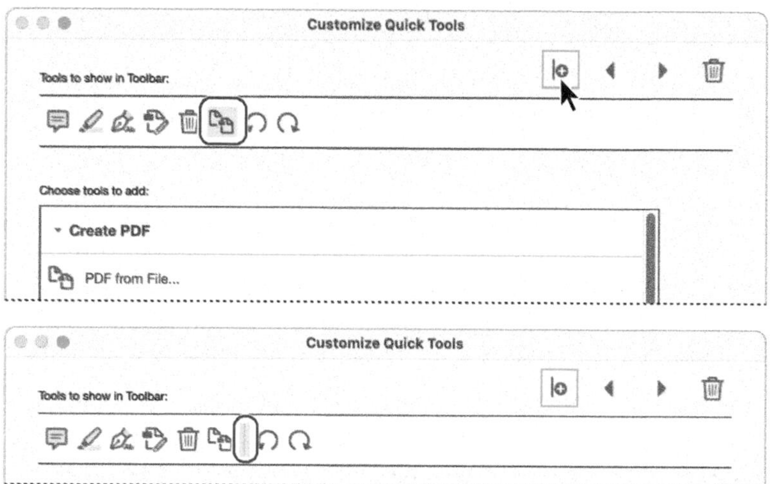

▶ **Tip:** To automatically add the tools you use frequently to the toolbar, choose View > Show/Hide > Toolbar Items > Show Recently Used Tools.

When you click the Add Divider button, Acrobat inserts a divider immediately after the currently selected tool. You can move a divider just as you move a tool, using the right and left arrow buttons at the top of the dialog box.

12 Click Save to save your changes.

The tools and divider you added appear on the right end of the toolbar.

You can customize your toolbar at any time, and you can easily restore the default toolbar settings. You'll do that now.

13 Choose View > Show/Hide > Toolbar Items > Reset Toolbars.

Customizing the brightness of the user interface

By default, Acrobat displays a light gray user interface. It may be easier to see some files accurately with a darker interface. To change the brightness, choose View > Display Theme > Dark Gray.

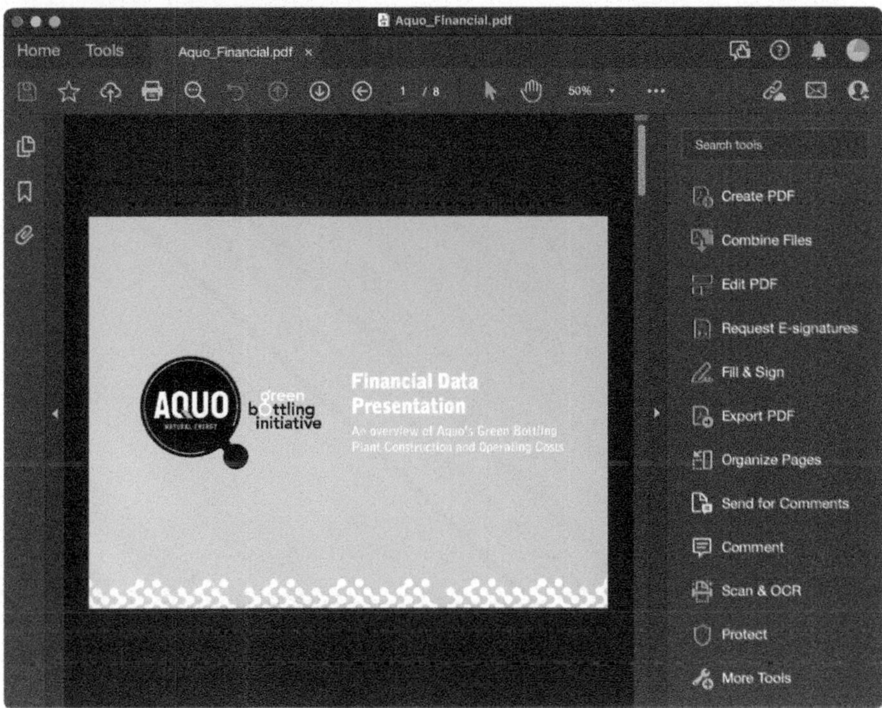

You can set the theme according to your preference. Choose View > Display Theme > Light Gray to return to the default theme, or choose View > Display Theme > System Theme to match the theme of your operating system.

Getting help

The lessons in this book focus on commonly used tools and features in Acrobat. However, you can get complete information on all the Acrobat tools, commands, and features for both Windows and macOS systems from Adobe Acrobat Help online. To access Help, choose Help > Acrobat Help. Acrobat opens your default browser and displays the Acrobat Help page online. In addition to the Help topics, the Acrobat Help page provides links to tutorials to help you learn Acrobat, user forums, and other community resources related to Adobe Acrobat.

Additionally, there are several links to resources for learning about Acrobat in the Getting Started section at the beginning of this book.

Review questions

1 Name two advantages of PDF documents.

2 How do you navigate to a different page in Acrobat?

3 How can you return to your usual work area from Full Screen mode?

Review answers

1 PDF provides several advantages, including the following:

- PDF preserves the exact layout, fonts, and text formatting of electronic documents, regardless of the computer system or platform used to view these documents.
- PDF documents can contain multiple languages, such as Japanese and English, on the same page.
- PDF documents print predictably, with proper margins and page breaks.
- You can secure PDF files to prevent unauthorized changes or printing, or to limit access to confidential documents.
- You can change the view magnification of a PDF page in Acrobat or Acrobat Reader, which is especially useful for zooming in on graphics or diagrams containing intricate details.

2 To navigate to a different page, you can do any of the following:

- Click the Next Page or Previous Page button in the Acrobat toolbar.
- Type a page number in the Acrobat toolbar.
- Choose a command from the View > Page Navigation menu.
- Click a thumbnail in the Page Thumbnails panel in the navigation pane.
- Click a bookmark in the Bookmarks panel in the navigation pane.

3 To exit Full Screen mode and return to your normal work area, press the Esc key on your keyboard.

2 CREATING ADOBE PDF FILES

Lesson overview

In this lesson, you'll do the following:

- Convert a TIFF file to Adobe PDF using the Create PDF tool.
- Convert a file to Adobe PDF using the authoring application's Print command.
- Convert multiple documents into a single PDF file.
- Explore the Adobe PDF settings used to convert files to Adobe PDF.
- Reduce the size of a PDF file.
- Scan a paper document into Acrobat.
- Convert scanned images into searchable text. (Acrobat Pro only)
- Convert web pages to Adobe PDF from Acrobat and directly from a web browser.

This lesson will take approximately 60 minutes to complete. Download the project files for this lesson, following the instructions in the Getting Started section under "Accessing the lesson files and Web Edition," if you haven't already done so. As you work on this lesson, you'll preserve the start files. If you need to restore the start files, download them from your Account page.

You can easily create PDF files from existing files, such as Microsoft Word documents, web pages, scanned documents, and images.

About creating Adobe PDF files

▶ **Tip:** If you have an Acrobat or Creative Cloud subscription, you can convert Microsoft Office and image files to PDF using the Acrobat mobile app. To learn more, see Lesson 6, "Using Acrobat on mobile devices."

You can convert a variety of file formats to Adobe PDF, preserving all the fonts, formatting, graphics, and color of the source file, regardless of the application and platform used to create it. You can create PDF files from images, document files, websites, scanned paper documents, and clipboard content.

If the document you want to convert to PDF is open in its authoring application (for example, a spreadsheet is open in Excel), you can usually convert the file to PDF without opening Acrobat. But if Acrobat is already open, you don't have to open the authoring application to convert a file to PDF.

When you create a PDF file, consider file size and quality (image resolution, for example). When such factors are critical, use a method that allows you to control conversion options. Dragging and dropping files onto the Acrobat icon to create PDF files is fast and easy, but if you want more control over the process, use another method, such as using the Create PDF tool in Acrobat or the Print command in the authoring application. After you specify conversion settings, the settings apply across PDFMaker and Acrobat until you change them.

● **Note:** When you're creating a PDF file from within Acrobat, you must have the application that created the original file installed on your system.

Lesson 7, "Using Acrobat with Microsoft Office Files," describes how to create Adobe PDF files directly from a variety of Microsoft Office applications. Lesson 8, "Combining Files," covers the conversion of multiple file types as you combine files into a single PDF document. In Lesson 13, "Using Acrobat in Professional Printing," you'll learn how to create press-quality PDF files.

If the security settings applied to an Adobe PDF file allow it, you can also reuse the content of the document. You can extract content for use in another authoring application, such as Microsoft Word, or you can reflow the content for use with mobile devices or screen readers. The success with which content can be repurposed or reused depends very much on the structural information contained in the PDF file. The more structural information a PDF document contains, the more opportunities you have for successfully reusing the content, and the more reliably a document can be used with screen readers. (For more information, see Lesson 3, "Reading and Working with PDF Files.")

Using the Create PDF tool

You can use the Create PDF tool in Acrobat to convert a variety of file types, including both image and non-image files, to Adobe PDF. You'll convert a single TIFF image to an Adobe PDF file.

1 Start Acrobat, if it's not already open.

2 Click Tools to open the Tools Center.

3 Click the Create PDF tool in the Create & Edit category.

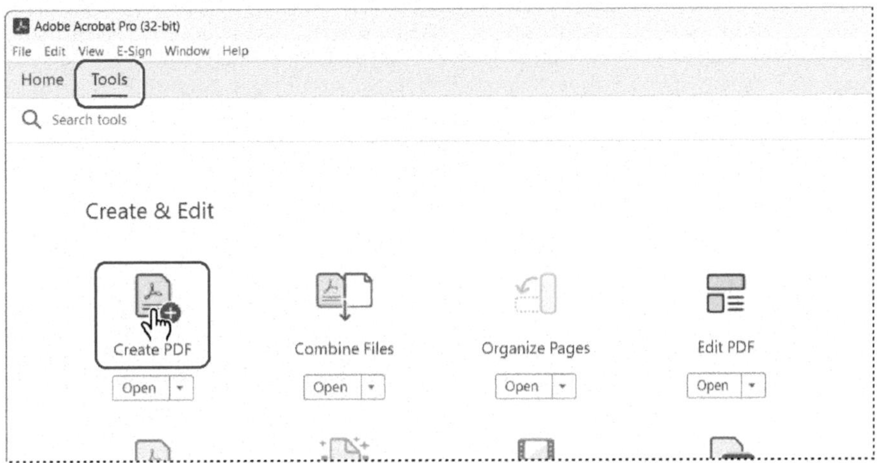

Acrobat displays a list of options for creating a PDF file. Using the Create PDF tool, you can create a PDF document from one or multiple files, a screenshot, a scanned image, a website, clipboard contents, or a blank page. All your options are easily accessible here. Single File is selected by default.

4 With Single File selected, click Select A File.

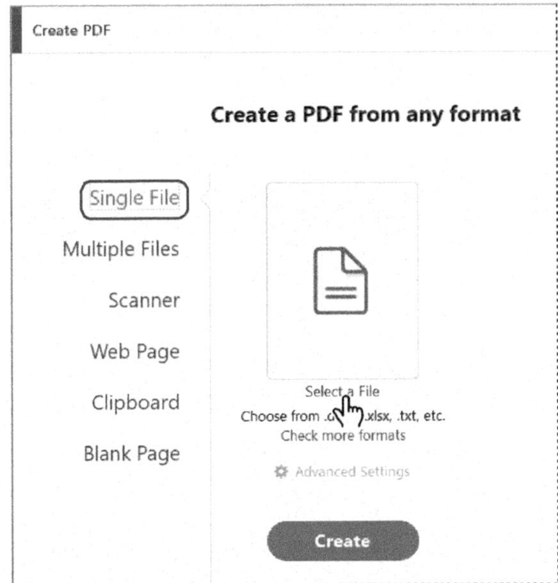

5 In the Open dialog box, navigate to the Lesson02/Assets folder on your hard drive, and select the GC_VendAgree.tif file. Then click Open.

A thumbnail image of the selected file appears, with the filename beneath it.

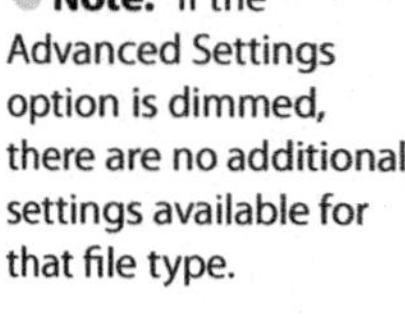
Note: If the Advanced Settings option is dimmed, there are no additional settings available for that file type.

6 Click Advanced Settings.

The settings options vary depending on the file type you've selected. For a TIFF image, the Adobe PDF Settings dialog box includes options for scan optimization, image compression, and color management.

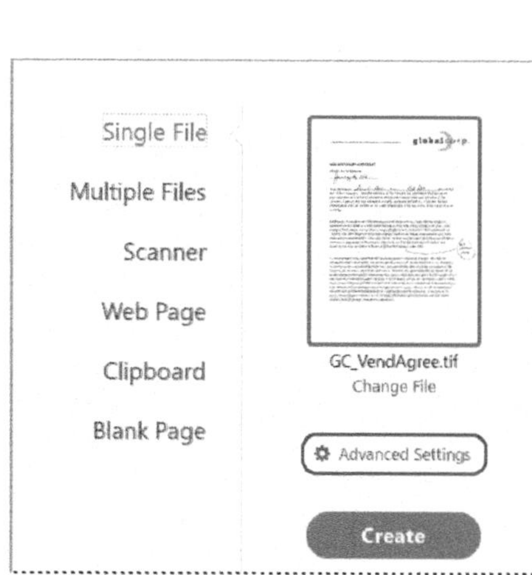

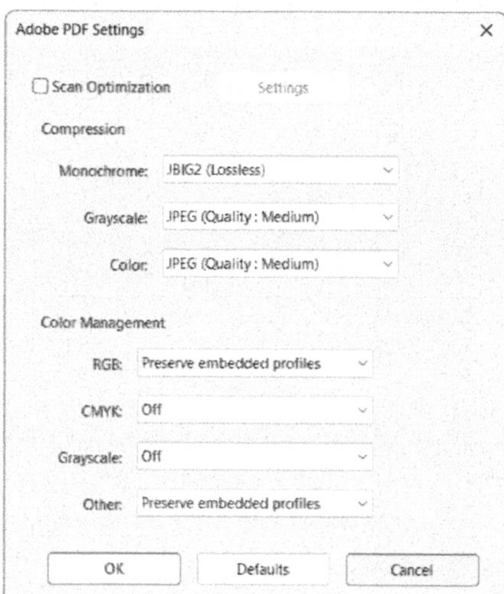

You can also review and edit the settings used to convert your files to PDF in the Convert To PDF panel of the Preferences dialog box.

7 Click Cancel to leave the settings unchanged for this document.

8 Click Create.

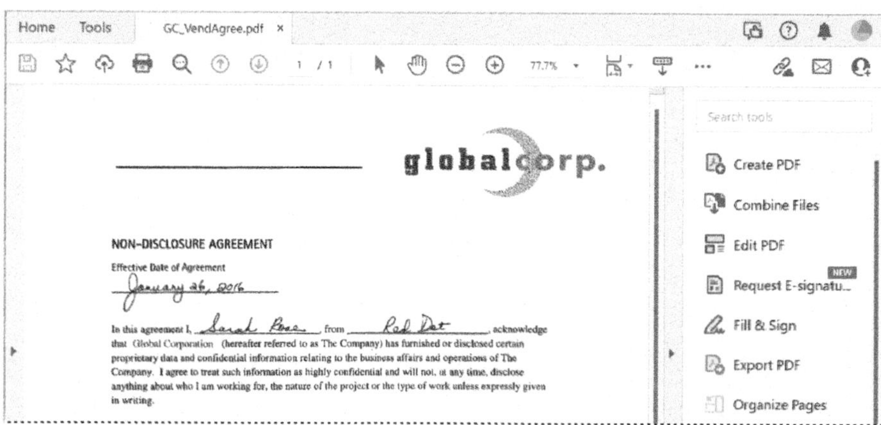

Acrobat converts the TIFF file to Adobe PDF and opens the PDF file automatically.

9 Choose Fit One Full Page from the Fit pop-up menu (icon) on the Page Controls toolbar so that you can see the entire agreement.

Notice that the handwritten note that the signer of the agreement has added is preserved in the Adobe PDF file.

Note: The Fit pop-up menu icon changes to reflect the current view.

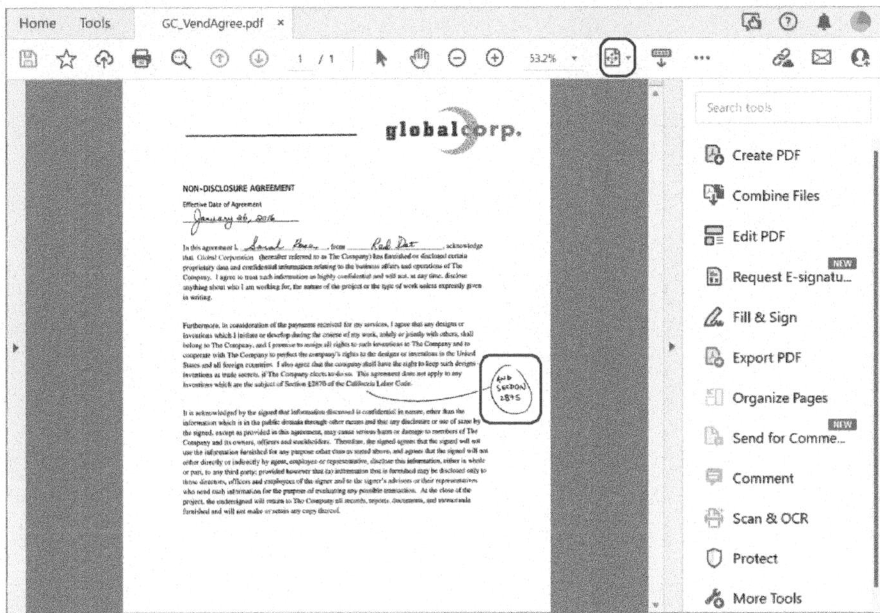

10 Choose File > Save As, name the file **GC_VendAgree.pdf**, and save it in the Lesson02/Finished_Projects folder. Then choose File > Close File to close the PDF file.

Creating files from the clipboard

You can copy content from any type of file, select Clipboard in the Create PDF tool, and then click Create to create a new PDF file. In macOS, you can also select Screenshot in the Create PDF tool to create a PDF file from a screen capture of a window or selection.

You can also easily add text and graphics that you have copied to the clipboard to an existing PDF. Open the PDF file, select the Organize Pages tool, and then choose Insert > From Clipboard.

Saving PDF files to cloud accounts

You can save PDF files directly to your Box, Dropbox, Google Drive, OneDrive, or Sharepoint account. In Acrobat, choose File > Save As, and then click Add File Storage in the pane on the left. Click Add beneath the type of account you want to add, and then sign in and agree to share access with Acrobat. Once you've added an account, it appears among the storage options on the left side of the Save As PDF dialog box. To save the current PDF file directly to your account, choose File > Save As, select the account, name the file, and click Save.

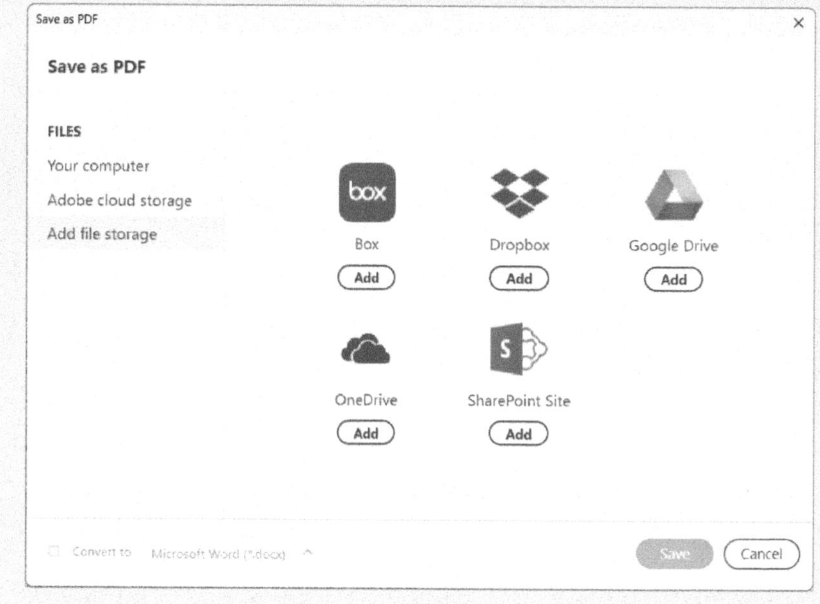

Dragging and dropping files

You can also create Adobe PDF files from many documents simply by dragging the file onto the Acrobat icon or into the document pane in Acrobat (Windows). Acrobat uses the conversion settings you specified the last time you converted a file.

Experiment with dragging the RoadieDog.jpg, Pumpkin.jpg, LoyalFan.jpg, and Tulips.jpg files from the Lesson02/Assets folder into the Acrobat document pane (Windows), onto the Acrobat icon on your desktop, or onto the Acrobat icon in the Dock (macOS). Close any open PDF files when you are finished. You can save the newly created PDF files or close them without saving.

Converting different types of files

You can use the Multiple Files option in the Create PDF tool to easily convert different types of files to Adobe PDF and combine them into one PDF file. If you're using Acrobat Pro, you can also assemble multiple documents into a PDF Portfolio. You'll learn more about combining files and creating PDF Portfolios in Lesson 8, "Combining Files."

Now, you'll convert a file to Adobe PDF and combine it with several other PDF files.

Assembling the files

First, you'll select the files you want to combine, and specify which pages to include. You'll combine a JPEG image file with several PDF files, but you'll include only two pages from one of the PDF documents.

1 In Acrobat, click Tools, and then click the Create PDF tool in the Create & Edit category.

2 Select Multiple Files, and then select Combine Files, and click Next.

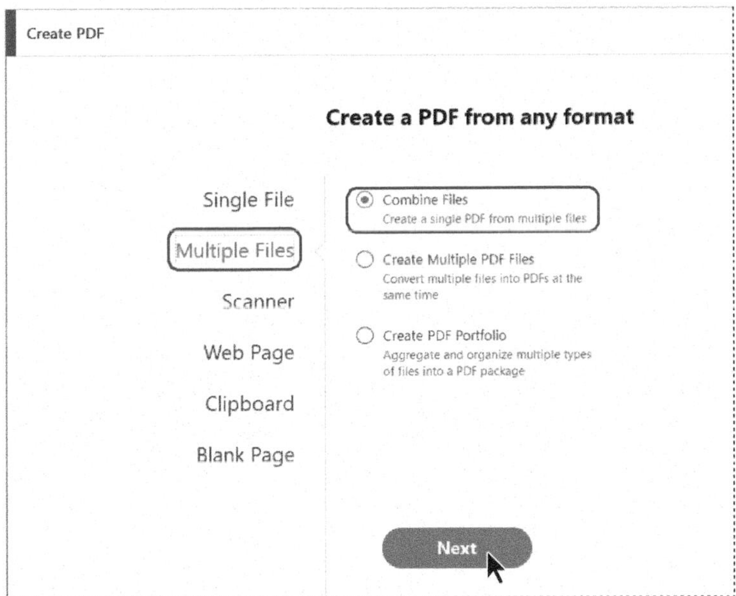

Acrobat opens the Combine Files tool so that you can assemble your documents.

3 Click the Add Files button.

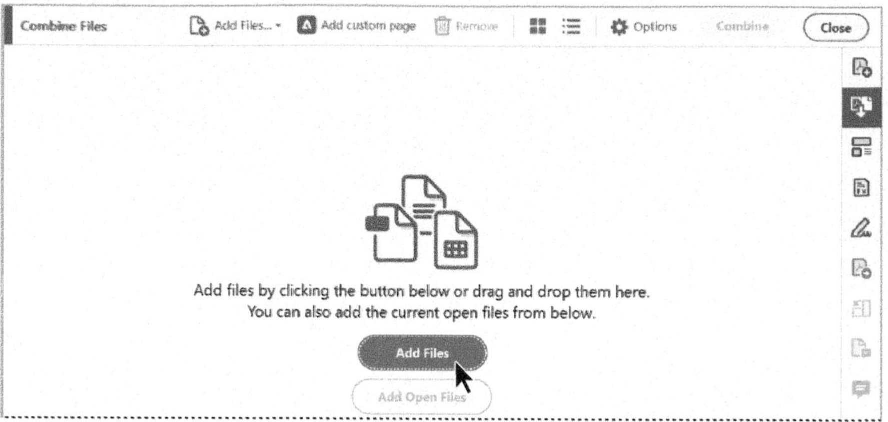

Now you'll select the files that you want to convert and combine. The types of files that you can convert will vary depending on whether you are working in Windows or macOS.

4 In the Add Files dialog box, navigate to the MultipleFiles folder in the Lesson02/Assets folder. Make sure that All Supported Formats is selected in the Show menu. (In macOS, click Options to see the Show menu.)

5 Select the Ad.pdf file. Then Shift-click the Data.pdf file to select the bottle.jpg and Data.pdf files, too.

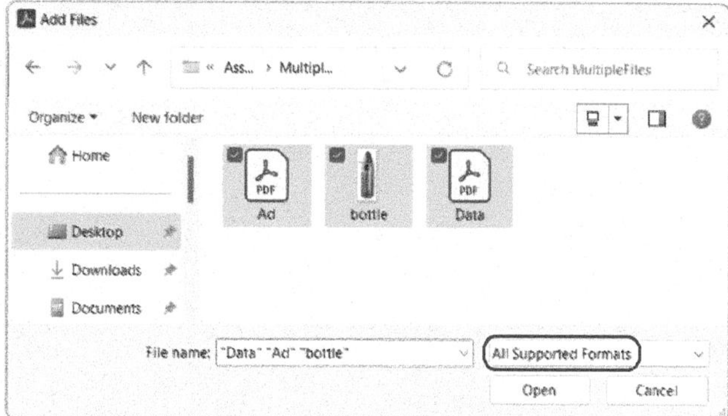

6 Click Open (Windows) or Add Files (macOS).

You can add files in any order, because you can rearrange them in the Combine Files window. You can also use the Remove button to remove any unwanted files.

7 If you see a list of files, click the Switch To Thumbnail View icon in the Combine Files toolbar. Then drag the thumbnail of the bottle.jpg file to the right of the Data.pdf file.

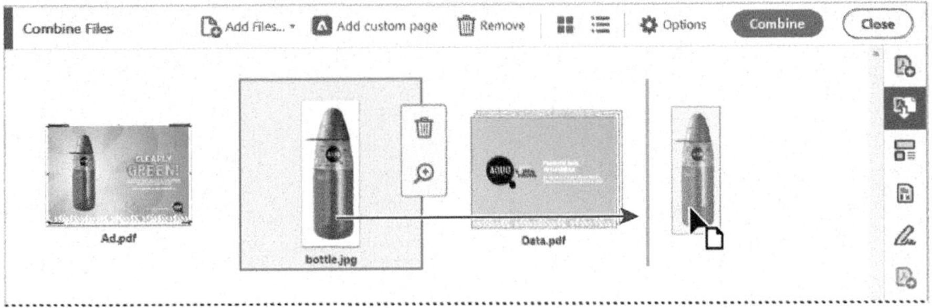

You can convert all pages in a file, or you can select a specific page or range of pages to convert.

8 Hover the mouse over the Data.pdf file, and then click the Expand 8 Pages button (⊖) to see thumbnails of each page in the file.

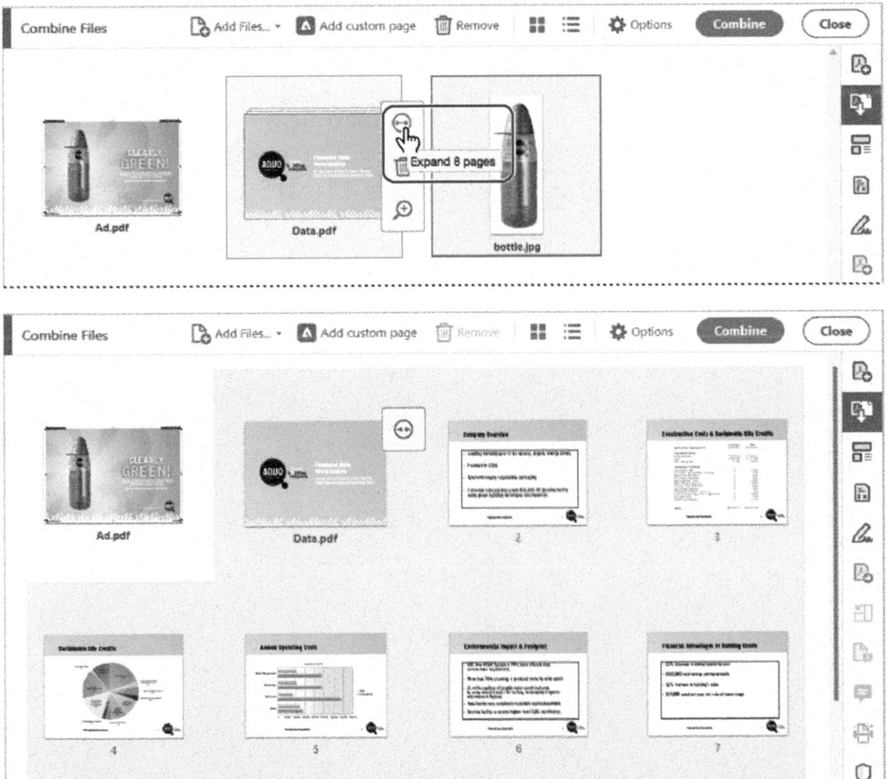

9 Select the first page of the Data.pdf file, and click the Remove button in the Combine Files toolbar.

10 Remove pages 2, 4, 5, 6, and 7 of the Data.pdf file, so that you're left with four thumbnails: Ad.pdf, Data.pdf pages 3 and 8, and bottle.jpg.

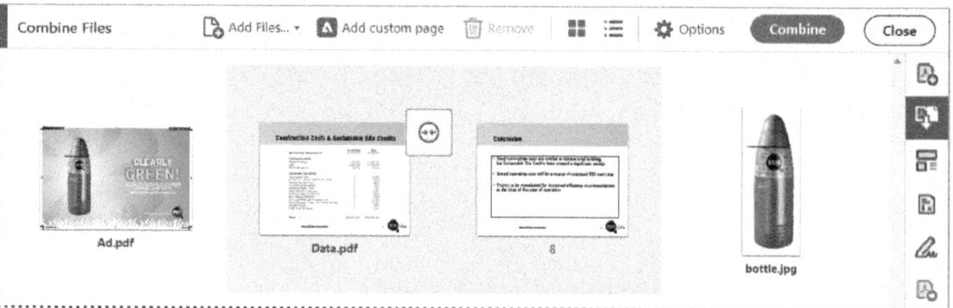

11 Click the Options button (⚙) to specify settings for the PDF file conversion.

12 In the Options dialog box, make sure the middle icon (Default File Size) is selected for File Size and that Save As PDF Portfolio is **not** selected. Then click OK.

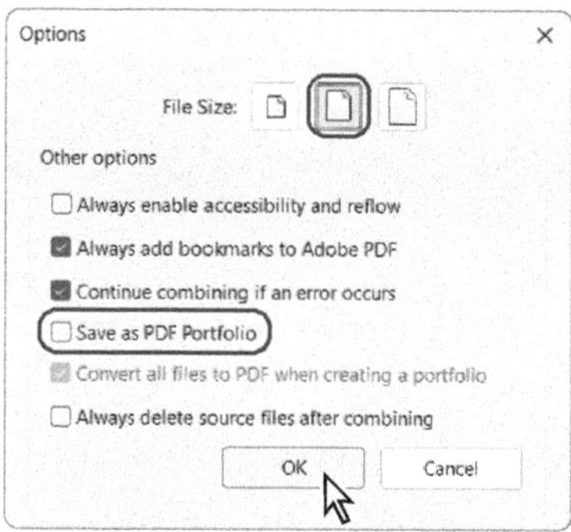

The Default File Size option produces a PDF file suitable for viewing and printing business documents. The Smaller File Size option optimizes files for web distribution. Use the Larger File Size option to prepare documents for high-quality printing.

13 Click Combine.

Acrobat converts any native files into PDF and then consolidates all the selected files into a single file, named Binder1.pdf. The file opens automatically.

14 Use the Next Page (⊕) and Previous Page (⊕) buttons to page through your consolidated documents.

15 Choose File > Save As. Save the file to the Lesson02/Finished_Projects folder, and rename the file **Aquo.pdf**. Click Save.

Without leaving Acrobat, you have converted a JPEG file to Adobe PDF and combined it with other PDF files.

16 Choose File > Close File to close the file.

Inserting a blank page

In Acrobat, you can insert blank pages into a PDF file, which makes it easy to create a transition page or a notes page.

1 In Acrobat, open the Aquo.pdf file you created, and click the Organize Pages tool in the Tools pane.

2 Choose Insert > Blank Page.

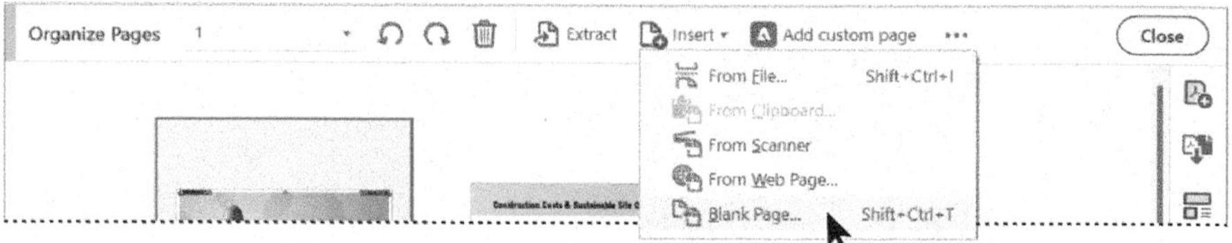

3 In the Insert Pages dialog box, choose After from the Location menu, and select Last in the Page area of the dialog box. Then click OK.

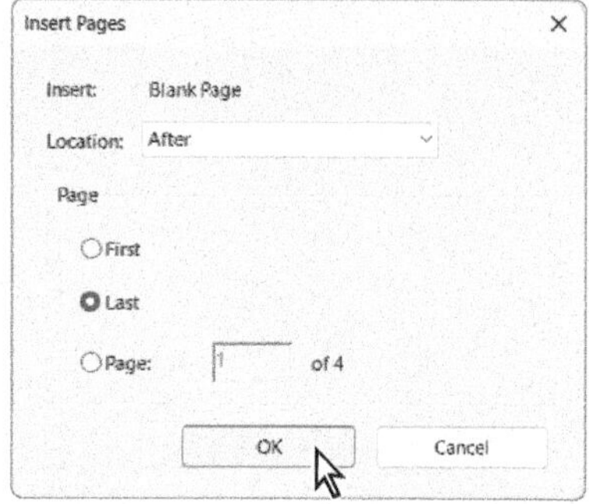

Acrobat adds a blank page, matching the dimensions of the page that preceded it.

4 Click the Edit PDF tool in the Tools pane. The blank page is displayed in the document pane; editing tools are available in the right-hand pane.

5 Click Add Text in the Edit PDF toolbar.

6 Move the pointer over the page; it turns into an I-beam. Click an insertion point at the top of the page.

7 In the Format area of the right-hand pane, change the font (we used Minion Pro Bold).

8 Type **Notes**. Use the Format options to change text attributes, including font size and color.

9 Close the file. You can save your changes if you want to.

Using PDFMaker

When you install Adobe Acrobat, the installer adds Acrobat PDFMaker buttons or menu commands to supported applications, including Microsoft Office applications, supported web browsers, Autodesk AutoCAD, and others. PDFMaker options vary from one application to another, but they always give you the ability to quickly create a PDF file from the source application file. Depending on the application, you can also use PDFMaker to add bookmarks, tag the PDF document to make it more accessible, add security features, or include layers in the PDF file.

For specific information about using PDFMaker in Office, see Lesson 7, "Using Acrobat with Microsoft Office Files." To use PDFMaker in web browsers, see "Converting web pages to Adobe PDF" later in this lesson.

Using the Print command to create Adobe PDF files

As you saw earlier in this lesson, you can easily create Adobe PDF files using the Create PDF tool in Acrobat. However, you can also create an Adobe PDF file from almost any application by using the application's Print command with the Adobe PDF printer (Windows) or the Save As Adobe PDF option (macOS).

Printing to the Adobe PDF printer (Windows)

The Adobe PDF printer isn't a physical printer like one that might sit in your office. Rather, it is a simulated printer that converts your file to Adobe PDF instead of printing it to paper. The printer name is Adobe PDF.

You can use this technique from almost any application, regardless of whether the application has built-in features for creating PDF files. You should be aware, however, that the Adobe PDF printer creates untagged PDF files. (A tagged structure is required for reflowing content to a mobile device and is preferable for producing reliable results with a screen reader.)

The Adobe PDF printer is an easy and convenient way to create a PDF file from almost any document. However, if you're working with Microsoft Office files, the Create Adobe PDF button in the Acrobat ribbon lets you create tagged documents and include bookmarks and hypertext links.

You'll convert a text file to Adobe PDF using the Print command with the Adobe PDF printer. Steps may vary depending on the application and which version of Windows you are using.

1 Open WordPad, a text editor that comes with Windows. In Windows 11, type **WordPad** in the search bar, and then double-click the file. In Windows 10, you can choose the application from your Start menu (it's in the Windows Accessories group).

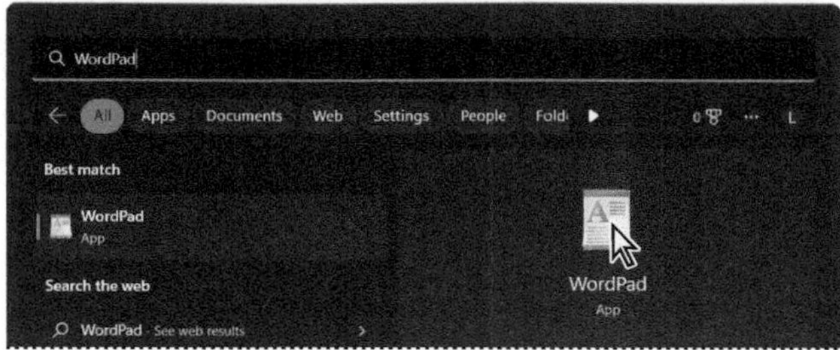

2 In WordPad, click the menu or File tab, and choose Open.

3 Navigate to the Lesson02/Assets folder, and double-click the Memo.txt file.

4 In WordPad, click the menu or File tab, and choose Print.

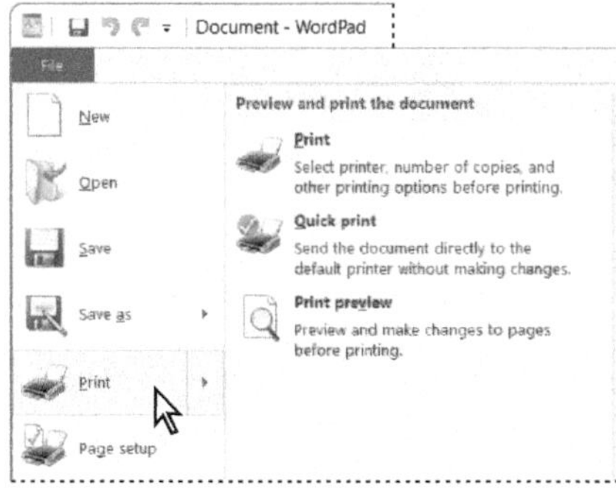

5 Choose Adobe PDF from the list of printers. You may need to scroll to see it.

To change the settings used to convert the text file to Adobe PDF, click Preferences in the Print dialog box or Properties in the Page Setup dialog box. For more information, see the "Adobe PDF Presets" sidebar later in this lesson.

6 Click Print.

7 Save the file using the default name (Memo.pdf) in the Lesson02/Finished_Projects folder, and click Save in the Save PDF File As dialog box.

8 If the PDF file doesn't open automatically, navigate to the Lesson02/Finished_Projects folder, and double-click the Memo.pdf file to open it in Acrobat. When you have reviewed the file, close it, and quit WordPad.

9 Close any open files.

Printing with the Save As Adobe PDF option (macOS)

In macOS, use the Save As Adobe PDF option in the PDF menu in the Print dialog box to print from any application.

1 From your desktop, navigate to the Lesson02/Assets folder, and double-click the Memo.txt file.

The text file opens in a text editor such as TextEdit.

2 Choose File > Print. It doesn't matter which printer is selected.

3 Click the PDF button at the bottom of the dialog box, and choose Save As Adobe PDF.

Note: In some applications, such as Adobe InDesign, click Printer in the Print dialog box to see the PDF menu.

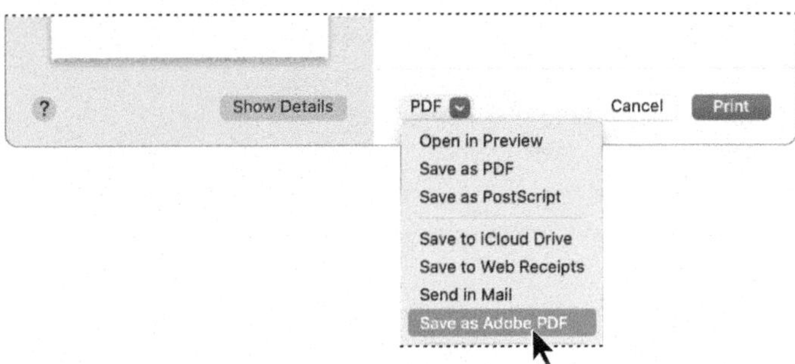

4 In the Save As Adobe PDF dialog box, choose an Adobe PDF Settings file, and choose Adobe Acrobat from the After PDF Creation menu to open the PDF file in Acrobat.

5 Click Continue.

6 In the Save dialog box, accept the default name of Memo.pdf, and save the file to the Lesson02/Finished_Projects folder.

7 Click Save.

The PDF file opens automatically, because you chose Adobe Acrobat from the After PDF Creation menu.

8 Review the file, close it, and quit the text editor application.

You have just converted a simple text document to an Adobe PDF document using the authoring application's Print command.

9 Close any open files.

Adobe PDF presets

A PDF preset is a group of settings that affect the process of creating a PDF file. These settings are designed to balance file size with quality, depending on how the PDF file will be used. Most predefined presets are shared across Adobe Creative Cloud applications, including Adobe InDesign®, Adobe Illustrator®, Adobe Photoshop®, and Acrobat. You can also create and share custom presets to meet your own needs.

For more detailed descriptions of each preset, see Adobe Acrobat Help.

- **High Quality Print** creates PDF files for good-quality printing on desktop printers and proofing devices.
- **Oversized Pages** creates PDF files suitable for viewing and printing engineering drawings larger than 200 by 200 inches.
- **PDF/A-1b** standards are used for the long-term preservation (archival) of electronic documents.
- **PDF/X-1a** standards minimize the number of variables in a PDF document to improve reliability. PDF/X-1a files are commonly used for digital ads that will be reproduced on a press.
- **PDF/X-3** files are similar to PDF/X-1a files, but they support color-managed workflows and allow some RGB images.
- **PDF/X-4** has the same color-management ICC color specifications as PDF/X-3, but includes support for live transparency.
- **Press Quality** creates PDF files for high-quality print production (for example, for digital printing or for separations to an imagesetter or platesetter).
- **Smallest File Size** creates PDF files for displaying on the web or a local network, or for distribution through an email system.
- **Standard** creates PDF files to be printed to desktop printers or digital copiers, published on a disc, or sent to a client as a publishing proof.

Reducing file size

The size of a PDF file can vary dramatically depending on the Adobe PDF settings used to create it. For example, files created using the High Quality Print preset are larger than files created using the Standard or Smallest File Size presets. Regardless of the preset used to create a file, you can often reduce the file size without having to regenerate the PDF file.

You'll reduce the size of the Ad.pdf file.

1 In Acrobat, choose File > Open, navigate to the Lesson02/Assets/MultipleFiles folder, and open the Ad.pdf file.

2 Choose File > Save As Other > Reduced Size PDF.

3 Select Acrobat 10.0 And Later for file compatibility, and click OK.

Be sure to choose a version of Acrobat that your intended audience is likely to have.

4 Name the modified file **Ad_Reduce.pdf**. Click Save to complete the process.

It is always a good idea to save a file using a different name so that you don't overwrite the unmodified file.

Acrobat automatically optimizes your PDF file, a process that may take a minute or two. Any anomalies are displayed in the Conversion Warnings window. If necessary, click OK to close that window.

5 Minimize the Acrobat window. Use Windows Explorer (Windows) or the Finder (macOS) to open the Lesson02/Assets/MultipleFiles folder and view the size of the Ad_Reduce.pdf file. The file size is smaller than that of the Ad.pdf file.

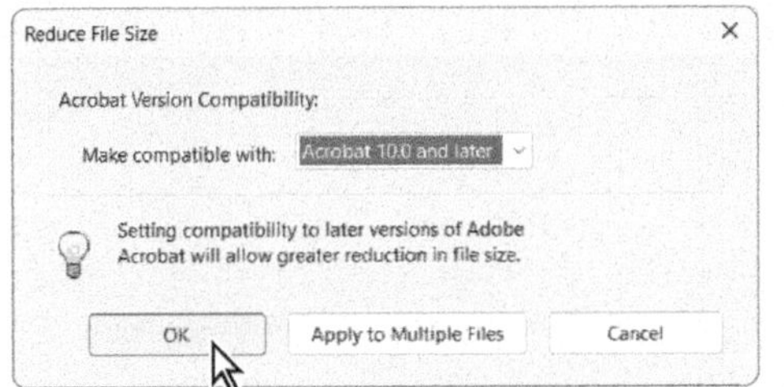

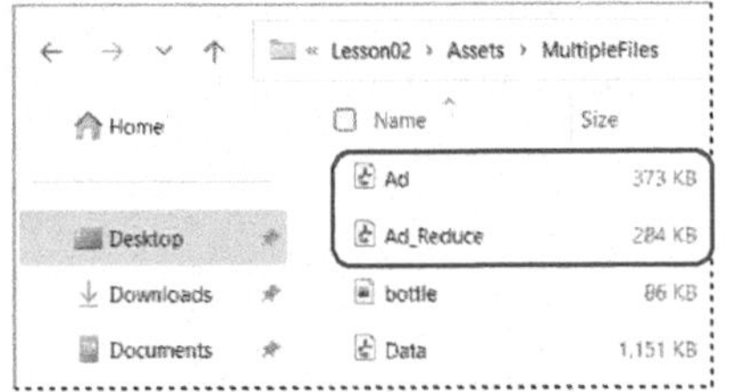

You can repeat steps 1–5 using different compatibility settings to see how they affect file size. Note that some settings might actually increase the file size.

Optimizing PDF files (Acrobat Pro only)

Many factors affect file size and file quality, but when you're working with image-intensive files, compression and resampling are important. In Acrobat Pro, PDF Optimizer gives you greater control over file size and quality.

To access PDF Optimizer, choose File > Save As Other > Optimized PDF.

In the PDF Optimizer dialog box, you can choose from a variety of file compression methods designed to reduce the file space used by color, grayscale, and monochrome images in your document. Which method you choose depends on the kind of images you are compressing. The default Adobe PDF presets use automatic (JPEG) compression for color and grayscale images and CCITT Group 4 compression for monochrome images.

In addition to choosing a compression method, you can resample bitmap images in your file to reduce the file size. A bitmap image consists of digital units called pixels, whose total number determines the file size. When you resample a bitmap image, the information represented by several pixels in the image is combined to make a single larger pixel. This process is also called *downsampling*, because it reduces the number of pixels in the image. (When you downsample or decrease the number of pixels, information is deleted from the image.)

Neither compression nor resampling affects the quality of text or line art.

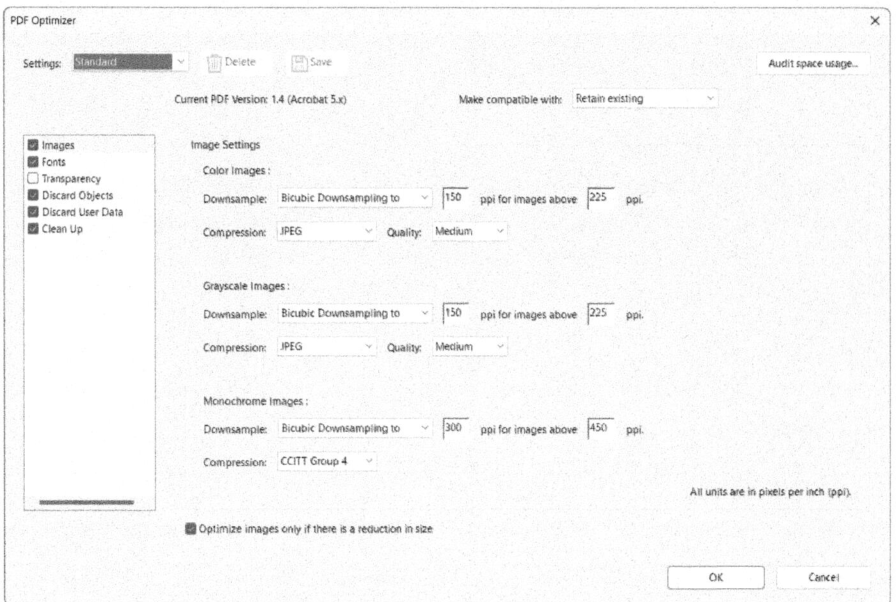

Scanning a paper document

You can scan paper documents to PDF from a broad range of scanners, add metadata while scanning, and optimize your scanned PDF. In Windows, you can choose presets for black and white, grayscale, and color documents, as well as color images. These presets optimize the quality of your scanned documents. You can also define your own conversion settings.

If you do not have a scanner connected to your system, skip this exercise.

1 Insert any one-page document into your scanner, and do one of the following in Acrobat:

- **In Windows:** Open the Create PDF tool, select Scanner, select the scanner you're using, and then select a preset for your document or accept the default. To customize the settings, click the Settings icon next to the preset you choose, and make changes. Click Scan.
- **In macOS:** Open the Create PDF tool, select Scanner, select the scanner you're using, and click Next. Then select options in the Acrobat Scan dialog box, and click Scan.

Note: If Acrobat does not recognize your scanner, refer to your scanner documentation for setup instructions, or contact your scanner manufacturer for troubleshooting help.

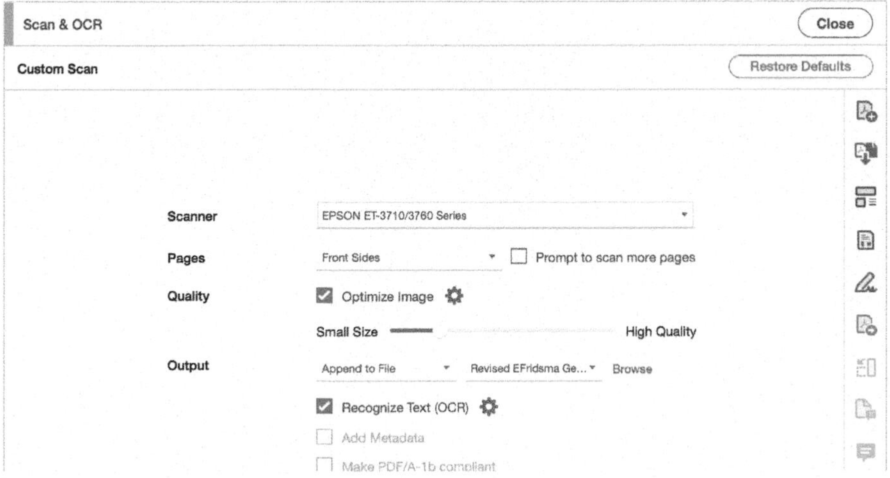

The scan occurs automatically.

2 When prompted, click OK to confirm that the scan is complete.

The PDF file of the scanned document appears in Acrobat.

3 Choose File > Save, and save the scan in the Lesson02 folder as **Scan.pdf**.

4 Choose File > Close to close your document.

Scan using mobile devices

Use your mobile phone or tablet as a scanner. The free Adobe Scan app uses your device's camera to scan a receipt, business card, or other document, automatically detecting borders, removing shadows, and recognizing text. It creates a PDF file of the scan, saved to Adobe cloud storage, so you can access it from anywhere. You'll learn more about Acrobat mobile apps in Lesson 6.

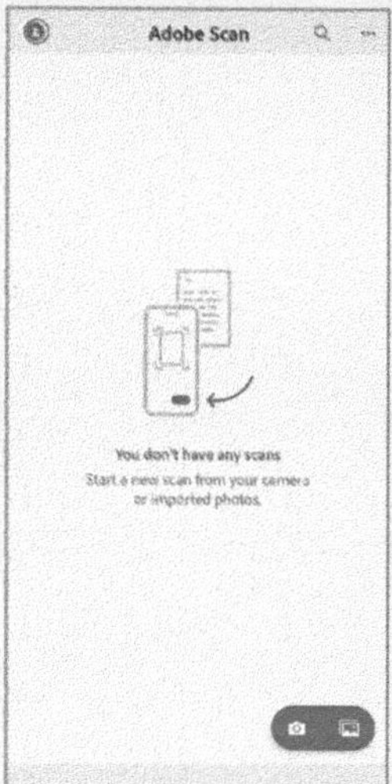

Making scanned text editable and searchable (Acrobat Pro only)

▶ **Tip:** Acrobat Pro can perform OCR automatically when you scan images. Just make sure Recognize Text (OCR) is selected in the scanner preset (Windows) or Acrobat Scan dialog box (macOS) before you scan.

When you convert a file from an application such as Microsoft Word or Adobe InDesign to PDF, the text is fully editable and searchable. However, text in image files, whether scanned documents or files saved in an image format, is not editable and searchable. Using OCR (optical character recognition), Acrobat Pro analyzes the image and replaces portions of it with discrete characters. It also identifies characters it may have analyzed incorrectly.

You'll apply OCR to the PDF document you created from a TIFF image.

1 Choose File > Open, navigate to the Lesson02/Finished_Projects folder, and open the GC_VendAgree.pdf file that you saved earlier.

2 Move the pointer over text in the document. You can select areas in the document, but Acrobat does not specifically select any of the text.

3 In the Tools pane, click Scan & OCR, and then choose Recognize Text > In This File.

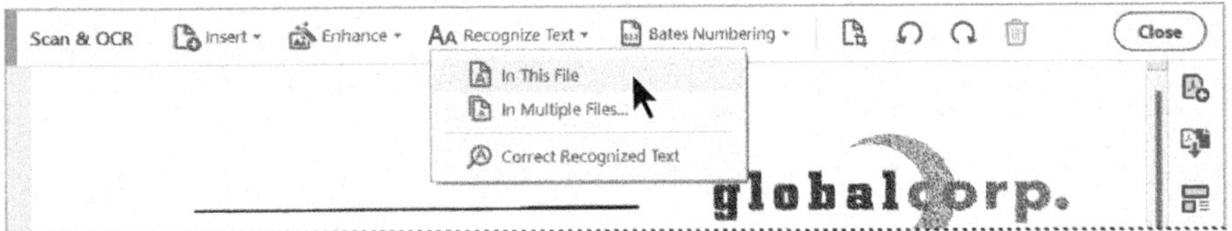

A toolbar with text recognition options appears below the Scan & OCR toolbar.

4 Click Settings to edit the settings for the conversion.

5 In the Recognize Text dialog box, choose Editable Text And Images from the Output menu. Click OK to close the dialog box.

6 Click Recognize Text in the secondary toolbar.

> **Note:** By default, Acrobat converts the document into a searchable image. You can use this setting to convert documents, but the Editable Text And Images option often provides more robust, accurate text conversion.

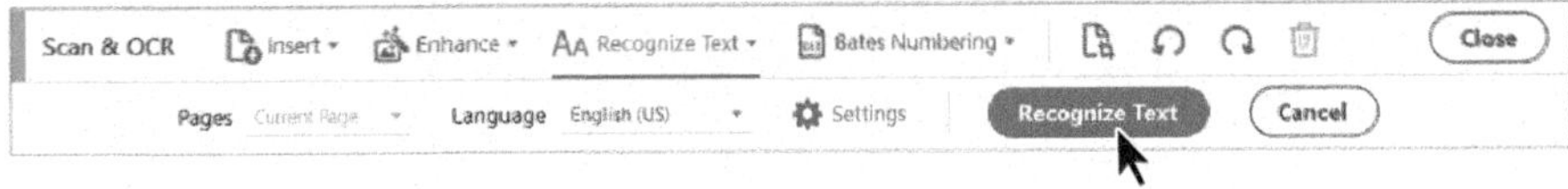

Acrobat converts the document.

7 Select a word on the page. Acrobat has converted the image to editable, searchable text.

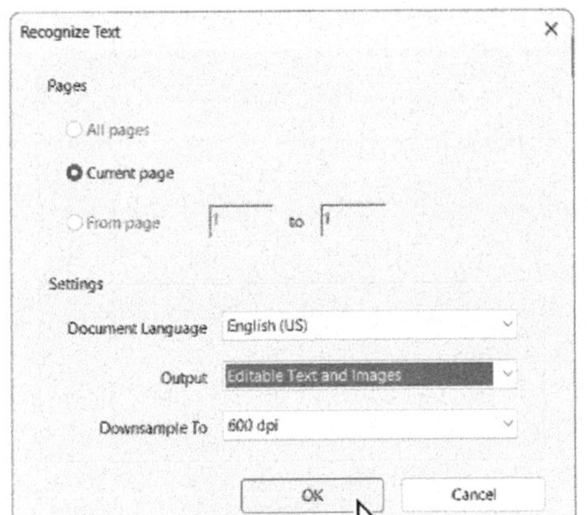

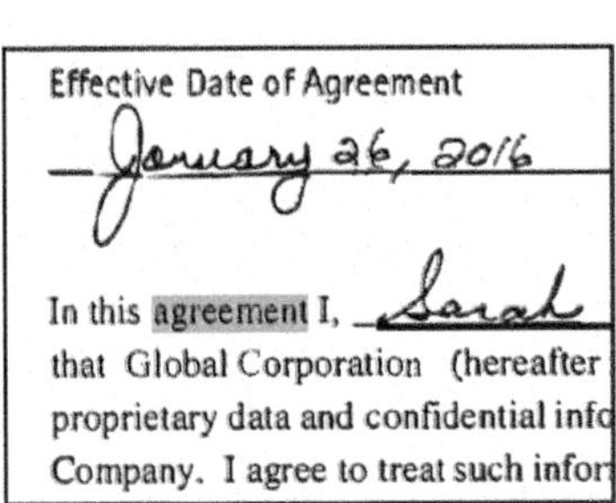

8 Choose Recognize Text > Correct Recognized Text. Acrobat searches the document and identifies any words that may have been converted incorrectly. If it finds any suspect words, you can examine them and correct them as needed. If it doesn't contain any suspects, click OK.

> **Note:** You may also need to use the Edit PDF tool to address issues with spacing.

9 Close the Scan & OCR tool.

10 Choose File > Save As. Navigate to the Lesson02/Finished_Projects folder, and save the file as **GC_VendAgree_OCR.pdf**. Then close the file.

Converting web pages to Adobe PDF

You can convert or "capture" an entire web page or several levels of a multipage website. You can define a page layout, set display options for fonts and other visual elements, and create bookmarks for web pages that you convert to Adobe PDF. The HTML file and all associated files—such as JPEG images, cascading style sheets, text files, image maps, and forms—are included in the conversion process, so the resulting PDF document behaves much like the original web page.

Because converted web pages are in Adobe PDF, you can easily save them, print them, email them to others, or archive them for your own use.

Converting web pages from within Acrobat

Because web pages are updated on a regular basis, when you visit the web pages described in this lesson, the content of the pages may have changed, and you may have to use links other than those described here. However, you should be able to apply the steps in this lesson to virtually any links on any website. If you are working inside a corporate firewall, for example, you might find it easier to complete this exercise using an internal site.

In order to download and convert web pages to Adobe PDF, you must be able to access the web.

Now you'll use the Create PDF tool to convert some web pages.

1 In Acrobat, open the Create PDF tool. (Click Tools to access tools if you're in Home view.)

2 Select Web Page, and then enter the address of the website you'd like to convert. (We used the Adobe Press website at www.adobepress.com.)

3 Select the Capture Multiple Levels option.

You control the number of converted pages by specifying the levels of site hierarchy you wish to convert, starting from your entered URL. For example, the top level consists of the page corresponding to the specified URL, the second level consists of pages linked from the top-level page, and so on. Consider the number and complexity of pages you may encounter when downloading more than one level of a website at a time. A complex site can take a very long time to download. Therefore, we don't recommend selecting Get Entire Site for most websites. Keep in mind that the time it takes to download pages depends on the speed of your Internet connection.

4 Make sure that the Get Levels option is selected, and that 1 is selected for the number of levels.

5 Select Stay On Same Path to convert only pages that are subordinate to the URL you entered.

6 Select Stay On Same Server to download only pages on the same server as the URL you entered.

7 Click Create.

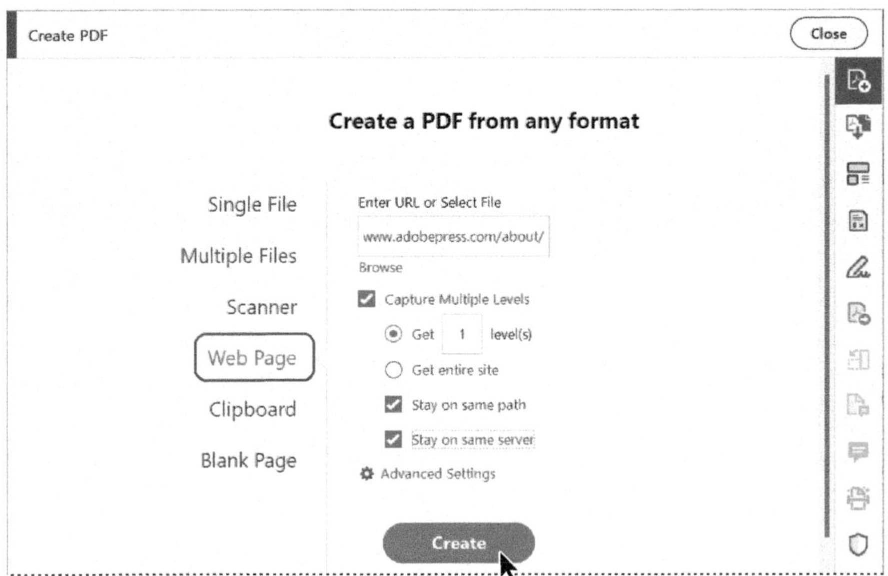

The Download Status dialog box displays the status of the download in progress. When downloading and conversion are complete, the converted website appears in the Acrobat document window, with bookmarks in the Bookmarks panel.

In Windows, if you're downloading more than one level of pages, the Download Status dialog box moves to the background after the first level is downloaded.

If Acrobat cannot download any linked material, it returns an error message. Click OK to clear any error message.

8 Expand the navigation pane, and then click the Bookmarks button to see the bookmarks Acrobat created for the page.

● **Note:** The Adobe Press website changes its content frequently, so your PDF probably won't match ours.

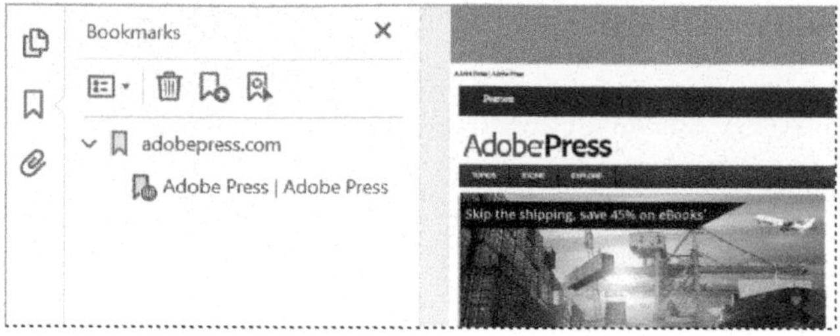

9 Use the Next Page (⊕) and Previous Page (⊕) buttons to move through the pages if more than one page was created.

The converted website is navigable and editable just like any other PDF document. Acrobat formats the pages to reflect your page-layout conversion settings as well as the look of the original website.

10 Choose File > Save As, name the file **Web.pdf**, and save it in the Lesson02/ Finished_Projects folder.

Downloading and converting linked pages

When you click a web link in the Adobe PDF version of the web page that links to an unconverted page, you can download and convert that page to PDF, attaching it to the PDF document you created.

1 Navigate through the converted website until you find a web link to a page that wasn't included in your original conversion. (The pointer changes to a pointing finger when you hover over a link, and a tooltip displays the URL of the link.)

2 Right-click (Windows) or Control-click (macOS) the link, and choose Append To Document from the context menu.

The Download Status dialog box appears again. When the download and conversion are complete, Acrobat displays the linked page, and adds a bookmark for the page to the Bookmarks list.

3 Choose File > Save As, rename the file **Web1.pdf**, and save it in the Lesson02/ Finished_Projects folder.

4 When you're finished looking at your converted web pages, close the PDF file.

Converting web pages in a web browser

In many web browsers, you can create and print an Adobe PDF version of the web page without ever leaving your browser. In supporting browsers, you can use PDFMaker to convert the currently displayed web page to an Adobe PDF file. When you print a converted web page from Acrobat, the page is reformatted to a standard page size, and logical page breaks are added.

Using PDFMaker

To use PDFMaker in a browser:

1 Go to the website you want to save.

2 Click the PDF button ( ) in the toolbar to display the PDF menu.

3 Choose Convert Webpage To PDF.

4 In the Save As dialog box, choose where to save the file, enter a filename, and click Save.

The default filename used by Acrobat is the text used in the HTML tag <TITLE>. Any invalid characters in the web page filename are converted to an underscore when the file is downloaded and saved.

Choose Conversion Settings or Preferences from the PDF menu to create bookmarks, include headers and footers, add tags, and change page layout features such as orientation.

Enabling the extension in a browser

How the Acrobat extension is enabled may differ depending on your browser, its version, and the version of your operating system. Typically, you can follow these steps to enable it if it's not already present:

- In Edge, click the Settings And More menu on the right side of the toolbar, choose Extensions, and then choose Show In Toolbar from the menu next to the Adobe Acrobat extension.
- In Firefox, choose Add-Ons And Themes, and make sure the Adobe Acrobat extension is enabled.
- In Chrome, click the menu button, choose More Tools > Extensions, and make sure the Adobe Acrobat extension is enabled; if you don't see it in the toolbar, click the Extensions icon and pin the Adobe Acrobat extension.

Review questions

1 Name three ways to create a PDF file.

2 How do you print to PDF from an application in Windows?

3 How do you print to PDF from an application in macOS?

4 How can you convert an image file to searchable text in Acrobat Pro?

Review answers

1 You can use the Create PDF tool to create a PDF file from almost any format, from a scanned document, from a web page, or from clipboard data. You can use PDFMaker to create a PDF file from within a supporting application, such as Microsoft Office for Windows. You can use the Print dialog box to create a PDF file from almost any application.

2 To print to PDF from an application in Windows, select the Adobe PDF printer in the Print dialog box, specify your settings, and click Print.

3 To print to PDF from an application in macOS, click the PDF button in the Print dialog box, and then choose Save As Adobe PDF. Specify your settings, and click Save.

4 To convert an image file to searchable text in Acrobat Pro, open the Scan & OCR tool, and then choose Recognize Text > In this File. Then click Recognize Text.

3 READING AND WORKING WITH PDF FILES

Lesson overview

In this lesson, you'll do the following:

- Navigate an Adobe PDF document.
- Change how a PDF document scrolls and displays in the document window.
- Search a PDF document for a word or phrase.
- Fill out a PDF form.
- Print all or a portion of a PDF document.
- Explore the accessibility features that make it easier for users with vision and motor impairments to use Acrobat.
- Add tags and alt text to a PDF document.
- Share a document with others electronically.

This lesson will take approximately 60 minutes to complete. Download the project files for this lesson, following the instructions in the Getting Started section under "Accessing the lesson files and Web Edition," if you haven't already done so. As you work on this lesson, you'll preserve the start files. If you need to restore the start files, download them from your Account page.

Get the most out of the PDF documents you create and read using navigational aids, accessibility features, search tools, and more.

About the onscreen display

▶ **Tip:** To see the printed size of your page, move your pointer into the lower left area of the document pane.

The magnification shown in the toolbar does not refer to the printed size of the page, but rather to how the page is displayed onscreen. At 100% view, each pixel in the page is represented by one screen pixel on your monitor.

How big the page appears onscreen depends on your monitor size and resolution setting. For example, when you increase the resolution of your monitor, you increase the number of screen pixels within the same monitor area. This results in smaller screen pixels and a smaller displayed page, since the number of pixels in the page itself stays constant.

Reading PDF documents

Acrobat provides a variety of ways for you to move through and adjust the onscreen magnification of a PDF document. For example, you can scroll through the document using the scroll bar at the right side of the window, or you can turn pages as in a traditional book using the Next Page and Previous Page buttons in the main toolbar. You can also jump to a specific page.

Browsing the document

You can move to different pages in a document using a variety of navigation methods.

1 In Acrobat, choose File > Open, navigate to the Lesson03/Assets folder, and select the Fall Hiking.pdf file. Click Open.

2 Choose View > Zoom > Actual Size to resize your page.

3 Select the Hand tool (✋) from the toolbar, and then position your pointer over the document. Hold down the mouse button. Notice that the pointer changes to a closed hand when you hold down the mouse button.

4 Drag the closed hand up and down in the window to move the page on the screen. This is similar to moving a piece of paper around on a desktop.

5 Press Enter or Return to display the next part of the page. You can press Enter or Return repeatedly to view the document from start to finish in screen-sized sections.

6 Choose Fit One Full Page (![]) from the Fit pop-up menu (![]) in the toolbar. Click the Previous Page button (![]) in the toolbar as many times as necessary to return to page 1.

7 Click once in an empty portion of the scroll bar. Or, in Windows, you can also position the pointer over the down arrow in the scroll bar and click.

The document scrolls automatically to display all of page 2. In the next few steps, you'll control how Acrobat scrolls and displays PDF pages.

You can also access the Actual Size, Zoom To Page Level, Fit Width, and Fit Visible commands by clicking the arrow to the right of the magnification pop-up menu in the toolbar.

8 Choose Fit To Width Scrolling from the Fit menu in the toolbar, and then use the scroll bar to scroll to page 3 of 4.

The Enable Scrolling option displays pages end to end, like frames in a filmstrip.

9 Choose View > Page Navigation > First Page to go back to the beginning of the document.

10 Choose Fit One Full Page from the Fit menu ( ) in the toolbar to return to the original page layout.

You can use the page number box in the toolbar to move directly to a specific page.

11 Type **3** to replace the current page number, and press Enter or Return.

Acrobat displays page 3.

The scroll bar also lets you navigate to a specific page.

12 Begin dragging the scroll box upward in the scroll bar. As you scroll, a page preview box shows you the current page number. When you see page 2 of 4, release the mouse.

The second page is displayed.

Changing the page view magnification

You can change the magnification of the page view using controls in the toolbar and commands in the View menu.

1 Choose View > Zoom > Actual Size. The magnification changes to 100%.

2 Click the Next Page button (⊕) to move to page 3. Notice that the magnification remains the same.

3 In the toolbar, click the arrow to the right of the magnification text box to display the preset magnification options. Choose 200%.

You can also type in a specific value for the magnification in the text box.

4 Click the arrow to the right of the magnification box, and choose Actual Size to display the page at 100% again.

Next, you'll use the Zoom In button to magnify the view.

5 Select the page number, type **4**, and press Enter or Return to go to page 4.

6 In the toolbar, click the Zoom In button (⊕) once.

7 Click the Zoom In button again to further increase the magnification.

Each click on a Zoom button increases or decreases the magnification by a set amount.

8 Click the arrow to the right of the magnification box, and choose Zoom To Page Level to see the entire page.

Now you'll use the Marquee Zoom tool to magnify the image. The Marquee Zoom tool is hidden by default, so you'll add it to the main toolbar.

9 Choose View > Show/Hide > Toolbar Items > Show Select & Zoom Tools > Marquee Zoom to display the Marquee Zoom tool in the main toolbar.

10 Select the Marquee Zoom tool ( ). Position the pointer near the upper left corner of the image of the colorful walking sticks, and drag to the lower right corner of the walking sticks image.

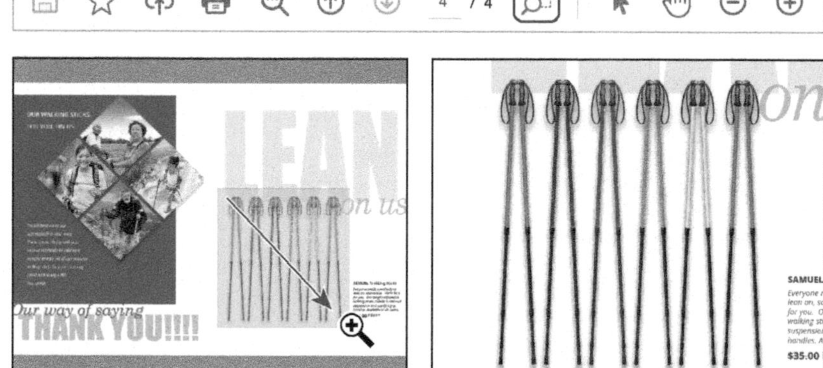

▶ **Tip:** You can show or hide other tools in the main toolbar by choosing View > Show/Hide > Toolbar Items, selecting a category, and then selecting the tool you want to display or hide.

The view zooms in on the area you enclosed.

11 Choose View > Zoom > Zoom To Page Level again.

Using the Dynamic Zoom tool

The Dynamic Zoom tool lets you zoom in or out by dragging the mouse up or down.

1 Choose View > Show/Hide > Toolbar Items > Show Select & Zoom Tools > Dynamic Zoom to add the Dynamic Zoom button to the main toolbar.

2 Select the Dynamic Zoom tool ( ).

3 Click in the document pane. Drag upward or to the left to zoom in, and drag down or to the right to zoom out.

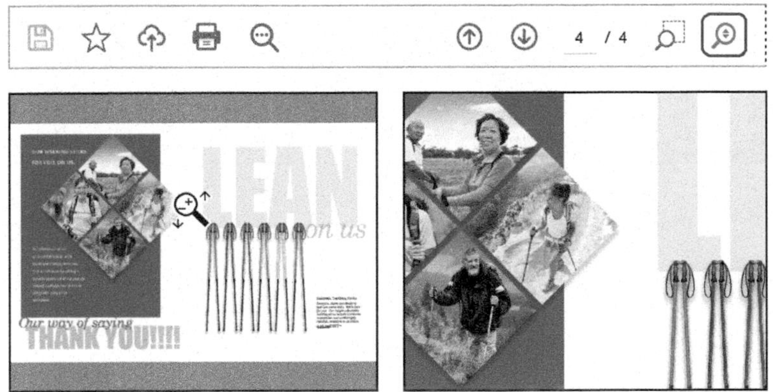

4 When you're finished, select the Hand tool ( ) to deselect the Dynamic Zoom tool, and then choose Zoom To Page Level from the magnification box menu in the toolbar to see the entire page again.

Following links

One benefit of working with electronic documents is that you can convert traditional cross-references into links, which let users jump directly to the referenced section or file. For example, you can make each item in a table of contents a link that jumps to its corresponding area in the document. You can also use links to add interactivity to traditional book elements such as glossaries and indexes.

First, you'll add some navigational tools to the main toolbar.

1 Choose View > Show/Hide > Toolbar Items > Show Page Navigation Tools > Show All Page Navigation Tools.

Now you'll use an existing link to move to a specific area in the document.

2 Click the First Page button (⊜) in the main toolbar to return to the first page.

3 Move the pointer over the special offer medallion. The Hand tool changes to a pointing finger, indicating the presence of a link. Click to follow the link.

This link sends you to page 4.

4 Click the Previous View button (⊝) to return to your previous view of page 1.

You can click the Previous View button at any time to retrace your viewing path through a document. The Next View button reverses the action of your last Previous View.

5 To restore the default toolbar configuration, choose View > Show/Hide > Toolbar Items > Reset Toolbars.

Searching PDF documents

You can quickly search for a word or phrase in a PDF document. For example, if you wanted to find occurrences of the word *boot* in this document, you can use either the Find feature or the Search feature to locate that information. The Find feature locates a word or phrase in the active document. The Search feature locates a word or phrase in one document, across a selection of documents, or in a PDF Portfolio. Both features search text, layers, form fields, and digital signatures.

First, you'll use the Find command to find specific text in the open document.

1 Choose Edit > Find. In the text box in the toolbar that appears in the upper right corner of the application window, type **performance**.

To see the options available with the Find feature, click the settings icon (⚙) on the right side of the text box. You can refine your search, looking for whole words only or specifying uppercase or lowercase letters, and you can also include bookmarks and comments in the search. A check mark next to an option indicates that it is enabled (on).

2 Click Next to start the Find operation.

The first occurrence of *performance* is highlighted on page 2 of the document.

3 Click the Next button in the Find panel to find the next occurrence of the word. Acrobat reports that it found no more matches. Click OK to close the dialog box, and then close the Find panel.

Next, you'll perform a more sophisticated search of the document using the Search feature. In this exercise, you'll search only one document, but you can use the Search feature to search all documents in a folder as well as all documents in a PDF Portfolio. You can even search non-PDF files in a PDF Portfolio.

4 Choose Edit > Advanced Search.

5 To search only the open document, select In The Current Document.

In this search, you'll find references to trekking.

6 In the Search text box, enter **trek**.

7 Click the Show More Options link at the bottom of the Search pane.

8 From the Return Results Containing pop-up menu, choose Match Any Of The Words. This ensures that the search will return all results for "trek," including words that contain additional letters, such as "trekking."

9 Click Search.

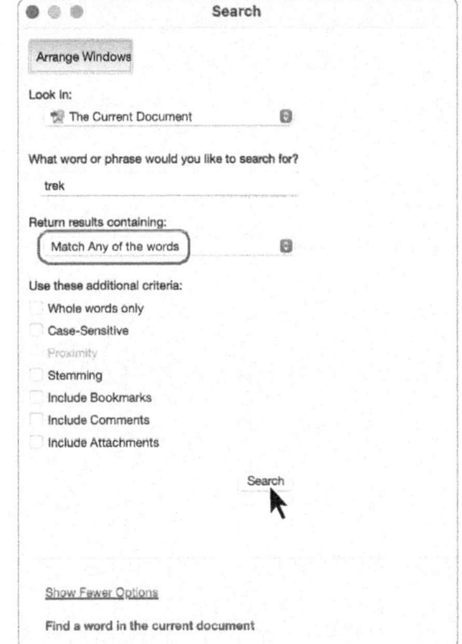

▶ **Tip:** You can also save your search results in Acrobat: Click the Save icon next to the New Search button in the Search pane, and then choose either Save Results To PDF or Save Results To CSV.

The search results are displayed in the Search pane.

10 Click any search result to go to the page that contains that information.

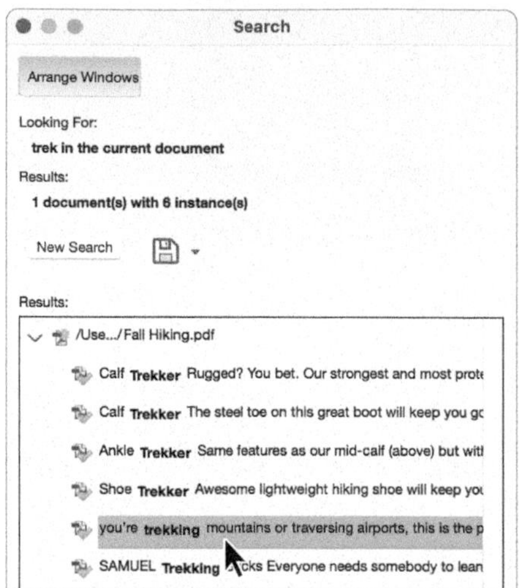

You can check any of the other search results in the Search pane by clicking them.

11 When you're finished, close the Search pane.

In addition to text in the document, the Search feature searches object data and image metadata. When you search multiple PDF documents, Acrobat also looks at the document properties and XMP metadata. If any of your PDF documents have attachments, you can also include those attachments in the search. If you include a PDF index in your search, Acrobat searches indexed structure tags. To search an encrypted document, you must first open the document.

Printing PDF documents

Many of the options in the Acrobat Print dialog box are similar to those you'd find in the Print dialog boxes of other popular applications. For example, you can select a printer and set up parameters such as paper size and orientation. However, Acrobat also gives you the flexibility to print only the current view (that is, what is displayed on the screen at that moment), a selection, a specific page, selected pages, or a range of pages within the PDF file.

You'll instruct Acrobat to print pages you select in the Page Thumbnails panel, a particular view, and discontiguous pages.

1 In the Fall Hiking.pdf document, click the triangle on the left side of the window to open the navigation pane. Then click the Page Thumbnails button in the navigation pane.

2 Click three thumbnails to select the pages you want to print. You can Ctrl-click (Windows) or Command-click (macOS) page thumbnails to select contiguous or discontiguous pages.

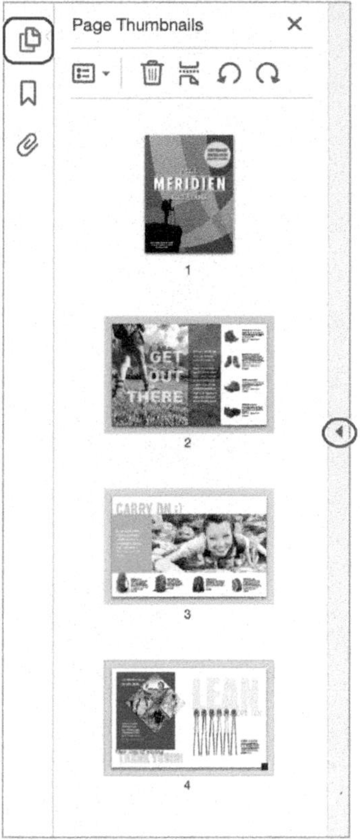

3 Choose File > Print. Select the name of the printer you want to print to. Because you selected pages in the Page Thumbnails panel, the Selected Pages option is selected automatically in the Print dialog box.

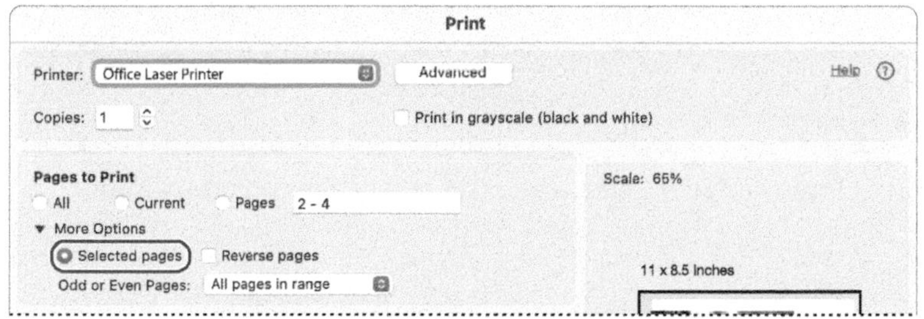

Tip: You can also access the Print dialog box by choosing Print Pages from the context menu.

4 Click OK or Print to print your selected pages. Click Cancel if you don't want to print.

If you need help troubleshooting a printing issue, click the Help link in the upper right corner of the Print dialog box to go to the Adobe website for the latest printing tips and information.

5 After the pages print (or the Print dialog box closes, if you opted not to print), click an empty area of the Page Thumbnails panel to deselect all thumbnails.

6 Close the Page Thumbnails panel.

7 Scroll to page 3 of the document.

8 Zoom in to 200%, and then use the Hand tool (✋) to shift the page so that you see the Jahn Ruck Pack.

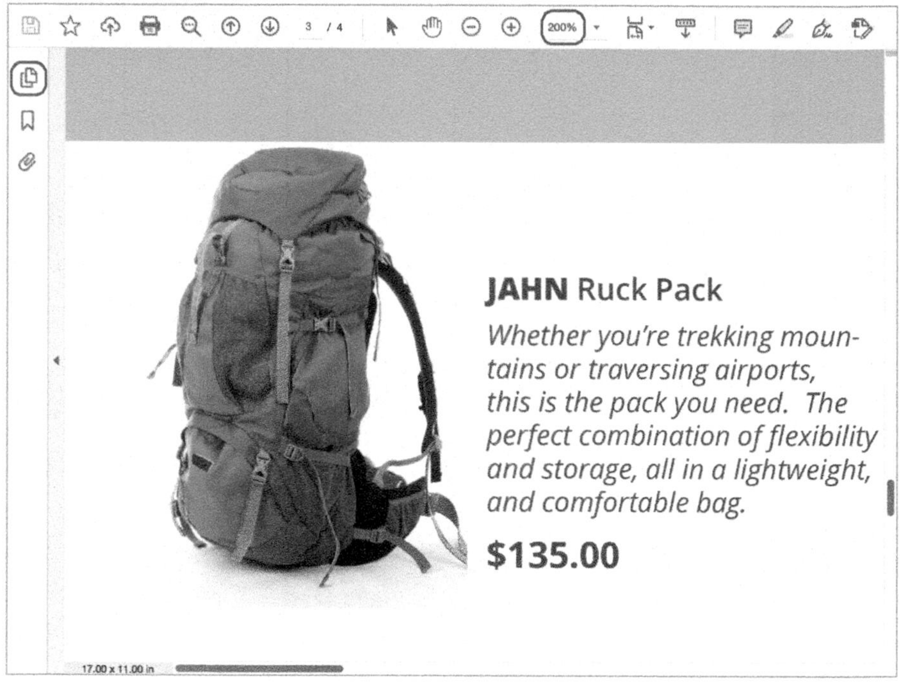

9 Choose File > Print, and select the name of the printer you want to print to.

10 In the Pages To Print area, click More Options. Then select Current View.

The preview changes to represent what is currently visible in the document pane. Click Fit in the Page Sizing & Handling area if it isn't already selected.

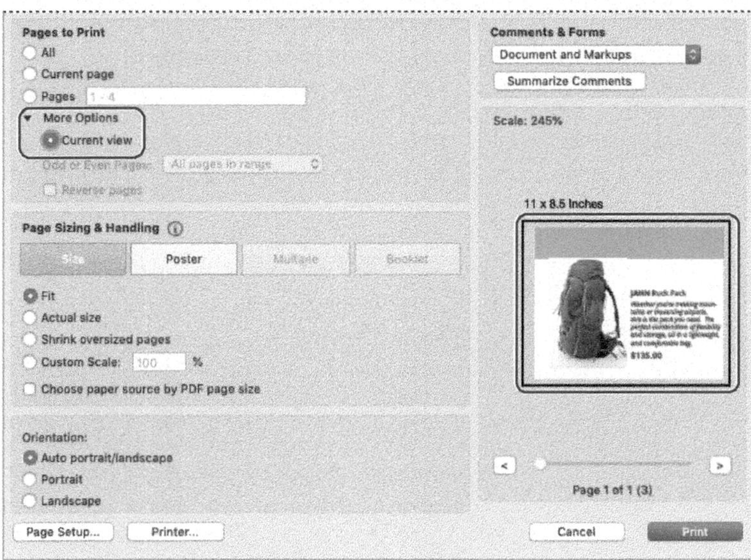

If you print with Current View selected, Acrobat prints only the contents of the document pane. However, you'll select pages to print instead.

11 In the Pages To Print area, select Pages.

12 In the Pages text box, type **1, 3-4**. If you click OK or Print now, Acrobat will print pages 1, 3, and 4. You can enter any set of discontiguous pages or ranges of pages, using commas, in this text box.

13 If you want to print the pages you've selected, click Print or OK. If you don't want to print, click Cancel.

14 Choose File > Close File to close the Fall Hiking.pdf document.

For information on printing comments, see Lesson 10, "Using Acrobat in a Review Cycle."

If your PDF file contains odd-sized pages, you can use the Size options in the Page Sizing & Handling area of the Print dialog box to reduce, enlarge, or divide pages. The Fit option scales each page to fit the printer page size; pages in the PDF file are magnified or reduced as necessary. The Poster options let you tile oversize pages, printing portions of them on several sheets of paper that can be assembled to reproduce the oversize image. You can also specify that the paper source be determined by the document's page size.

Printing booklets

If your printer supports duplex printing, you can print a 2-up, saddle-stitched booklet from Acrobat. Booklets comprise multiple pages that are arranged so that they can be folded to present the correct page order. In a 2-up, saddle-stitched booklet, two side-by-side pages, printed on both sides, are folded once and fastened along the fold. The first and last pages print on the same side of a sheet, the second and next-to-last pages print on other side of that sheet, and so on. When you collate, fold, and staple the double-sided pages, you create a single book with correct pagination.

To print a booklet from Acrobat:

1 Choose File > Print, and select your printer.

2 In the Pages To Print area, specify which pages to print.

3 In the Page Sizing & Handling area of the Print dialog box, click Booklet.

4 Choose additional page-handling options. You can auto-rotate pages, specify the first and last sheet to print, and select the binding edge. The Preview image changes as you specify options. For information about the options, see "Printing booklets" in Adobe Acrobat Help.

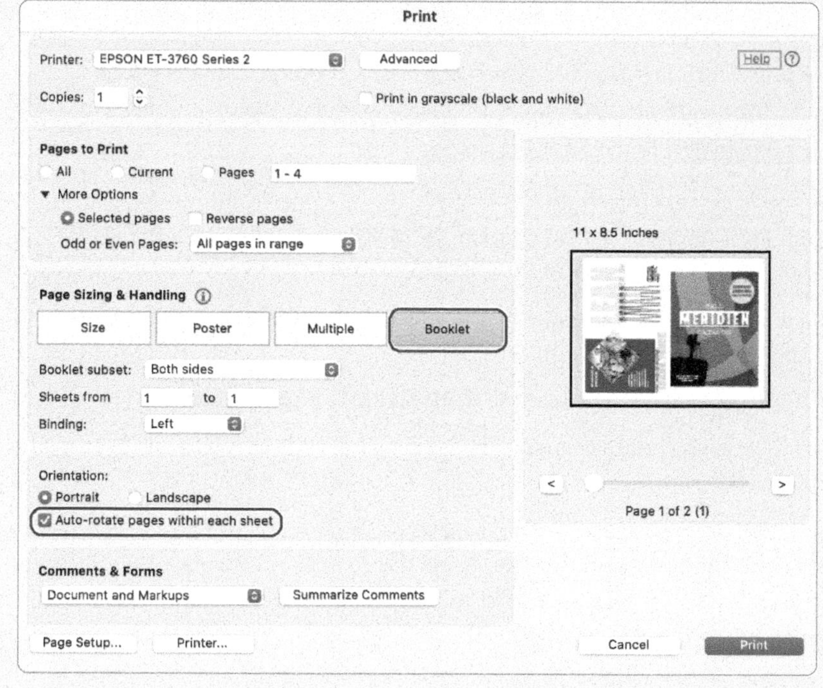

Filling out PDF forms

PDF forms can be interactive or noninteractive. Interactive PDF forms (also called *fillable forms*) have built-in form fields and behave in much the same way as most forms that you encounter on the web or that are sent to you electronically. You enter data using the Selection tool or Hand tool in Acrobat or Acrobat Reader.

Noninteractive PDF forms (flat forms) are pages that have been scanned to create a facsimile of a form. These pages do not contain actual form fields; they contain only the images of form fields. Traditionally, you would print out these forms, fill them out by hand or using a typewriter, and then mail or fax the hard copy. With Acrobat, you can fill out these noninteractive or flat forms online using the Fill & Sign tool or the Add Text tool.

▶ **Tip:** You can fill out PDF forms on a tablet or phone using the Acrobat mobile apps. For more information, see Lesson 6, "Using Acrobat on Mobile Devices."

For information on creating and managing interactive forms, see Lesson 11, "Working with Forms in Acrobat."

You'll fill out fields in an interactive form, and then add information where there is no field using the Add Text tool.

1 Choose File > Open, and navigate to the Lesson03/Assets folder. Select the Contact Update.pdf file, and click Open.

When it opens the document, Acrobat highlights the form fields.

2 Click in the Address field. Enter an address. The text appears in the font and type size chosen by the form creator.

3 Enter an email address and phone number.

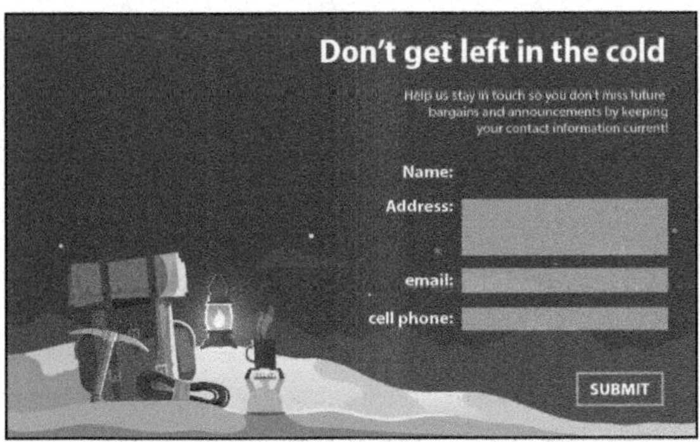

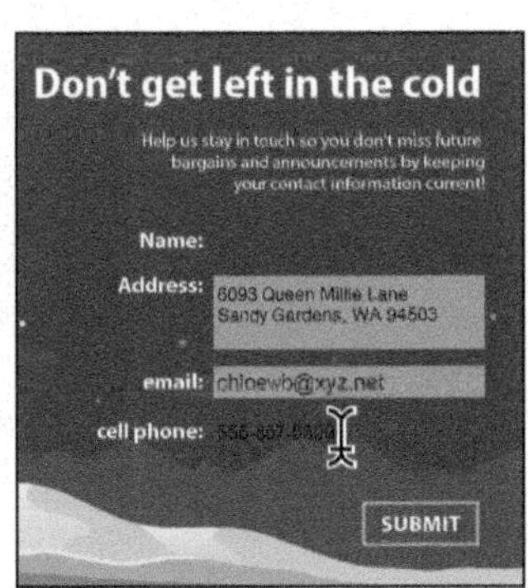

The person who created this form forgot to create an interactive field for the name. You'll add text without requiring a field.

4 In the Tools pane, click the Edit PDF tool to open it. Then click Add Text in the Edit PDF toolbar.

5 Click next to the word *Name*. The pointer is an I-beam.

6 Type your name.

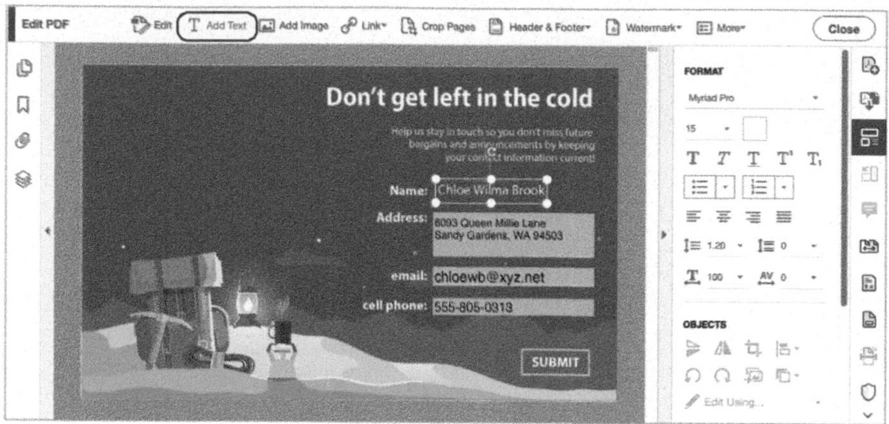

You can use the Add Text tool to add text to any PDF file, unless security settings applied to the document prohibit it. You can customize the text formatting using options in the Format area of the right-hand pane.

7 Close the Edit PDF tool.

8 Choose File > Save As, and save a copy of the form in the Lesson03/Finished_Projects folder, naming the file **Contact Update complete.pdf.**

You can open the saved file if you wish to verify that all your data was saved.

9 Choose File > Close File to close the form.

About flexibility, accessibility, and structure

The accessibility and flexibility of your Adobe PDF files determine how easily people with vision or mobility limitations as well as people using mobile devices can access, reflow, and—if you allow it—reuse the content of your files. You control the accessibility and flexibility of your Adobe PDF files through the amount of structure you build into the source file and the method you use to create the Adobe PDF file.

By making your PDF documents more accessible to users, you can broaden your readership and better meet government standards for accessibility. Accessibility in Acrobat falls into two categories:

- Accessibility features that help authors create accessible documents from new or existing PDF documents. These features include simple methods for checking accessibility and adding tags to PDF documents. With Acrobat Pro, you can also correct accessibility and reading-order problems in PDF files by editing the PDF file structure.
- Accessibility features that help readers who have motion or vision limitations to navigate and view PDF documents more easily. Many of these features can be adjusted by using a wizard, the Accessibility Setup Assistant.

For Adobe PDF files to be flexible and accessible, they must have structure. Adobe PDF files support three levels of structure—tagged, structured, and unstructured. Tagged PDF files have the most structure. Structured PDF files have some structure, but are not as flexible or accessible as tagged PDF files. Unstructured PDF files have no structure. (As you will see later in this lesson, you can add limited structure to unstructured files.) The more structure a file has, the more efficiently and reliably its content can be reused.

Structure is built into a document when, for example, its creator defines headers and columns, adds navigational aids such as bookmarks, and adds alternate text descriptions for graphics. In many cases, documents are automatically given logical structure and tags when they are converted to Adobe PDF.

When you create PDF documents from Microsoft Office files or from files created in Adobe FrameMaker®or InDesign, or when you create Adobe PDF files from websites, the resulting PDF files are tagged automatically.

In Acrobat Pro, if your PDF documents don't reflow well, you can correct most problems using the Accessibility panel or the TouchUp Reading Order tool. However, this is not as easy as creating a well-structured document in the first place. For an in-depth guide to creating accessible PDF documents, visit https://helpx.adobe.com/acrobat/using/create-verify-pdf-accessibility.html.

Checking for accessibility (Acrobat Pro only)

It's always a good idea to check the accessibility of any Adobe PDF document before you distribute it to users. The Accessibility Checker panel tells you if your document has the information necessary to make it accessible. At the same time, it checks for protection settings that would prohibit access.

First, you'll look at the accessibility and flexibility of a tagged PDF file that was created from a Microsoft Word file.

1 Choose File > Open, navigate to the Lesson03/Assets folder, and double-click the Footwear.pdf file.

2 Choose File > Save As, and save the file as **Footwear_Accessible.pdf** in the Lesson03/Finished_Projects folder.

3 In the Tools pane, click the Accessibility tool. If the Accessibility tool isn't listed, click Tools in the main toolbar, and navigate to the Accessibility tool in the Protect & Standardize category. Then, choose Add Shortcut from the pop-up menu beneath the Accessibility tool, and click the Accessibility tool in the Tools pane.

▶ **Tip:** By default, Acrobat displays only some of the tools in the Tools pane. To select which tools appear in the list, click Tools in the main toolbar, and then choose Add Shortcut or Remove Shortcut beneath each tool.

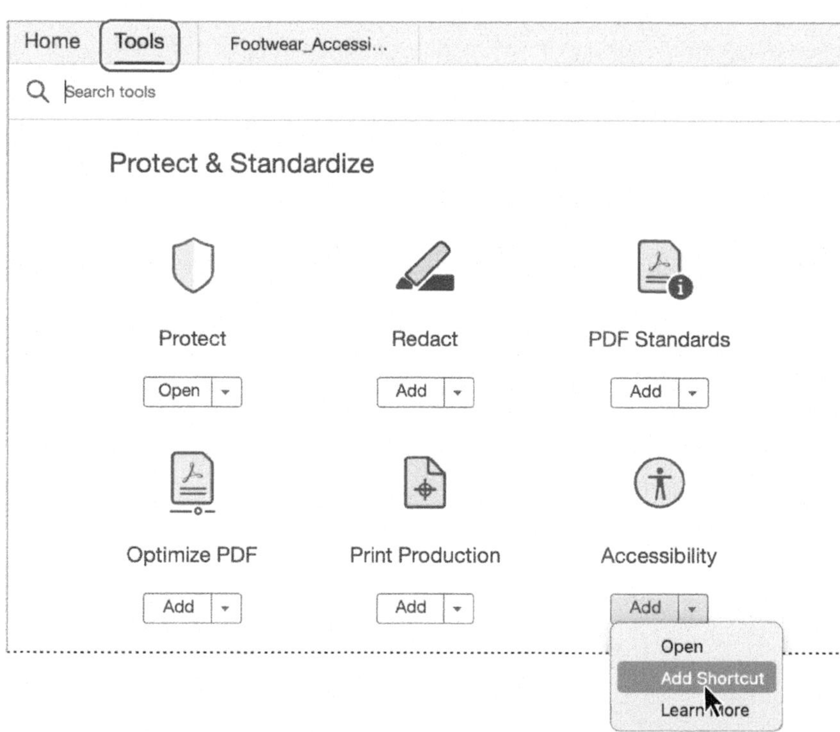

You'll use the Accessibility tool several times in this lesson, so it's handy to have it in the Tools pane. You can remove a tool from the Tools pane at any time by choosing Remove Shortcut from the menu beneath the tool in the Tools Center.

Accessibility options appear in the right-hand pane.

4 Click Accessibility Check in the right-hand pane.

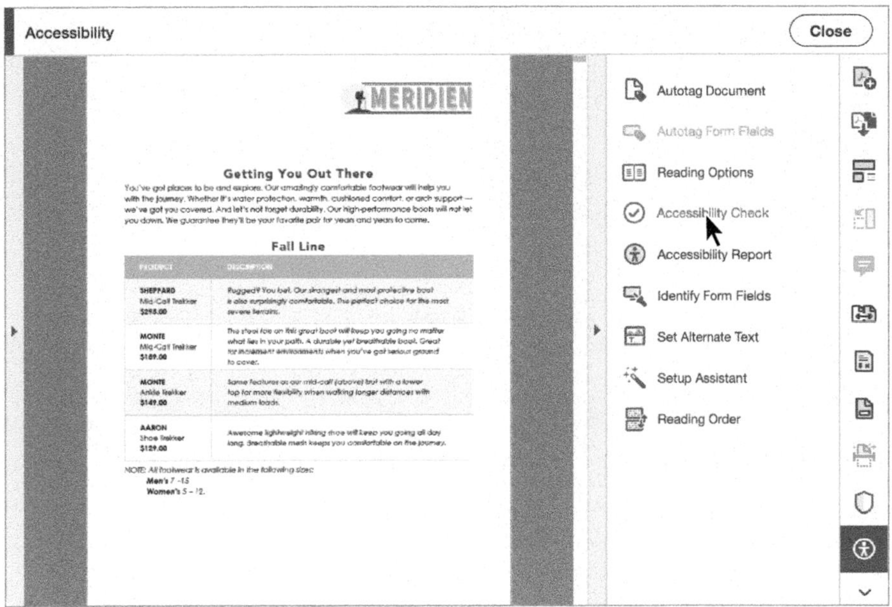

5 Accept the defaults in the Accessibility Checker Options dialog box, and click Start Checking.

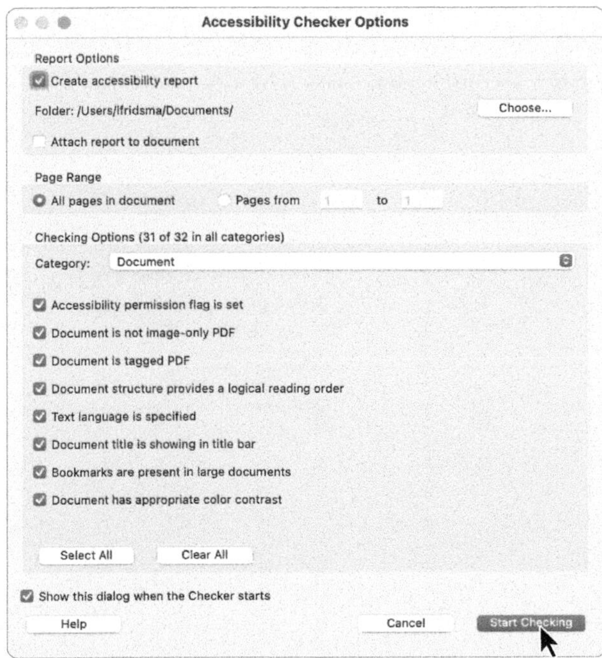

Acrobat quickly checks the document for accessibility issues and displays the interactive Accessibility Checker panel in the navigation pane. There are some issues with this document.

6 Expand the Document category. It lists five issues.

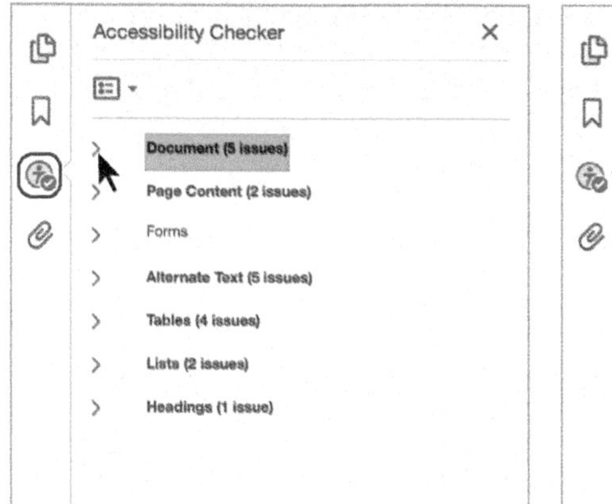

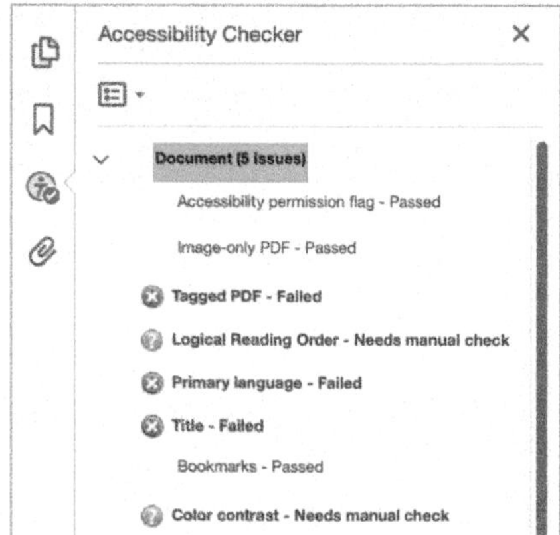

Two of the issues are items that require you to look at the document to determine whether there's a problem (Logical Reading Order and Color Contrast). You'll fix one of the issues now—the title.

In an accessible document, the document title should be included and set to display automatically in the title bar. You can learn what each item in the Accessibility Checker panel refers to by choosing Explain from the options menu at the top of the panel.

7 Right-click or Control-click the Title item, and choose Fix.

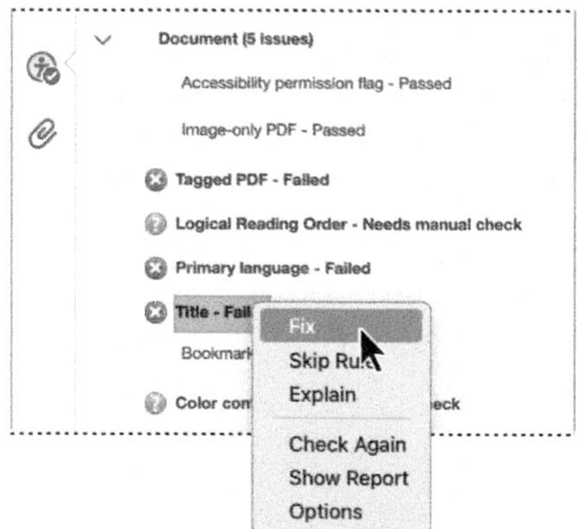

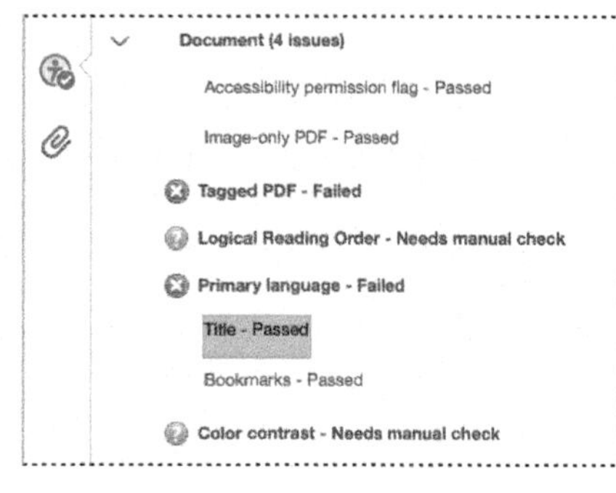

The panel changes to show that the title passed, after Acrobat changed its settings. Had there not been a title already in the document, you'd have been prompted to enter the document title. You can quickly fix most accessibility issues in a document using the interactive Accessibility Checker panel. In the next exercise, you'll use the Make Accessible action to correct the remaining errors.

8 Close the Accessibility Checker panel and the Accessibility tool.

You can add security to your PDF files and still make them accessible. The encryption offered by Acrobat prevents users from copying and pasting text from a PDF file, while still supporting assistive technology.

Making files flexible and accessible (Acrobat Pro only)

Note: You can add tags and alternate text using tools in the Accessibility panel in Acrobat Standard.

Some tagged Adobe PDF documents may not contain all the information necessary to make their contents fully flexible or accessible. For example, your file may not contain alternate text for figures, language properties for portions of the text that use a language other than the default language for the document, or expansion text for abbreviations. (Designating the appropriate language for different text elements ensures that the correct characters are used when you reuse the document for another purpose, that the word can be pronounced correctly when read out loud, and that the document will be spell-checked with the correct dictionary.)

If you're using Acrobat Pro, you can add alternate text and multiple languages using the Tags panel. (If only one language is required, it is easier to choose the language in the Document Properties dialog box.) You can also add alternate text using the TouchUp Reading Order tool.

Using the Make Accessible action

If you're using Acrobat Pro, you can systematically ensure your PDF document is accessible using the Make Accessible action. The action specifies document properties, sets the tab order, adds tags, and adds alternate text to the document.

The Make Accessible action is one of the default actions in the Action Wizard in Acrobat Pro. You'll learn more about using and creating actions in Lesson 12, "Using Actions."

1 Click Tools in the toolbar, and then click the Action Wizard tool in the Customize category.

2 Click Make Accessible in the Actions List pane.

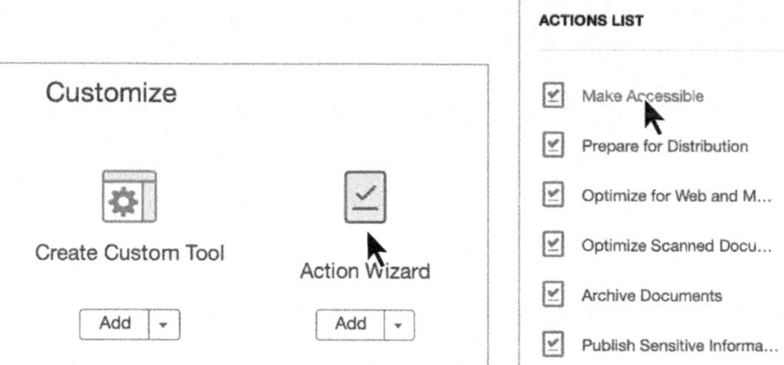

The Actions List pane is replaced by the Make Accessible action pane, which lists the steps included in the action. The action automates steps when possible, and guides you through the steps you need to perform to make your document accessible.

3 Verify that the file in the Files To Be Processed box is Footwear_Accessible.pdf.

4 Click Start.

▶ **Tip:** The Recognition Report is a temporary file and can't be saved. The Accessibility Check feature generates an accessibility report that you can save.

The first section of the Make Accessible action helps you prepare your document settings for flexibility and accessibility.

5 In the Description dialog box, deselect Leave As Is in the Title area, change the title to **Fall Footwear Line**, and click OK.

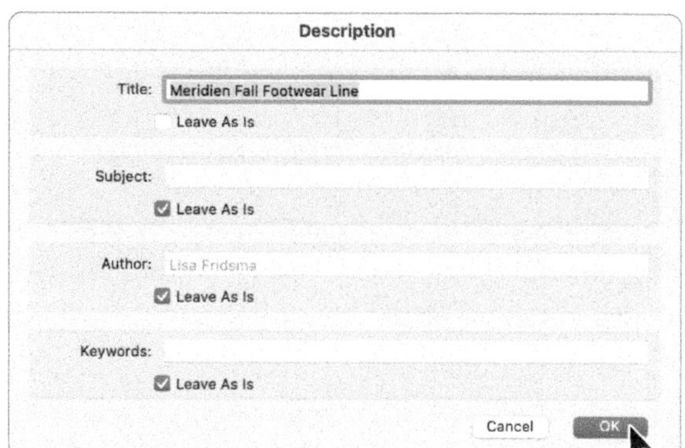

The title in the Description dialog box will appear in the title bar when the document is opened. After you click OK, Acrobat performs the next step automatically, setting the appropriate Open options for the document.

6 Accept the default settings in the Recognize Text - General Settings dialog box, and click OK.

These settings determine how OCR is applied to recognize text for screen readers.

7 When asked whether this document is intended to be a fillable form, click No, Skip This Step.

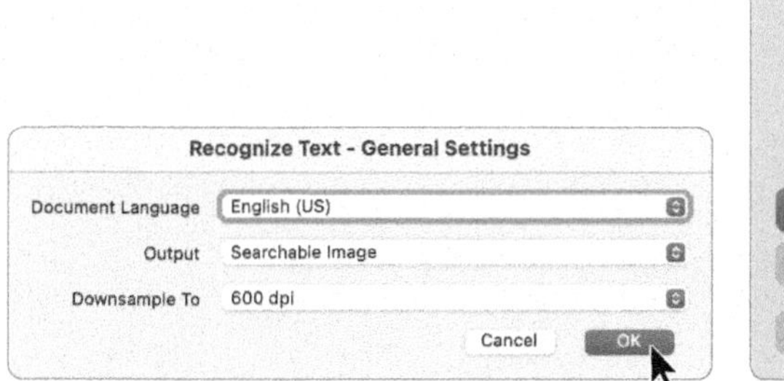

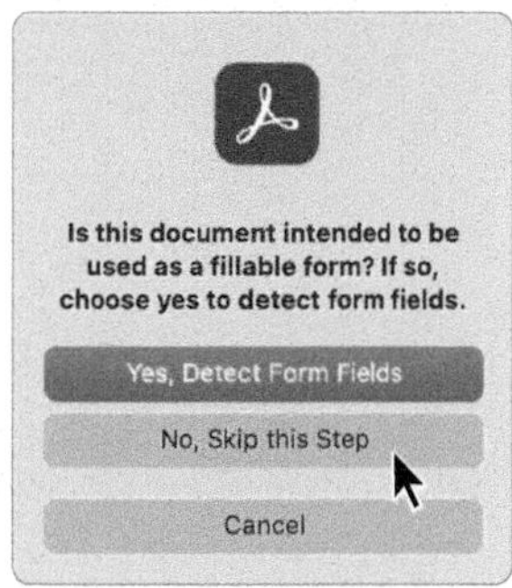

If you had clicked Yes, Acrobat would detect the form fields.

8 Click OK in the Set Reading Language dialog box to accept English as the reading language.

Acrobat automatically performs the next step, adding tags to the document.

9 Click OK when alerted that Acrobat will display any figures with missing alternate text.

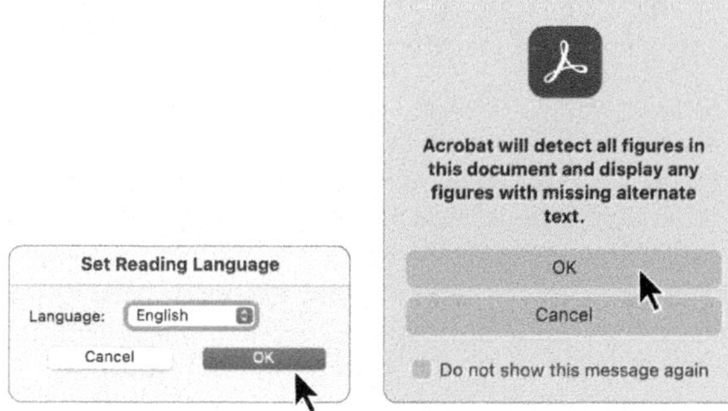

Screen readers use alternate text (often called alt text) to describe non-text elements such as images or figures to a visually impaired person. Acrobat examines your document to ensure that every image has alternate text assigned to it, and prompts you to assign text where it's missing.

10 In the Set Alternate Text dialog box, type **Meridien Logo** as the alt text for the selected image. Then click Save & Close.

11 Click Start Checking in the Accessibility Checker Options dialog box to confirm that the document is now accessible.

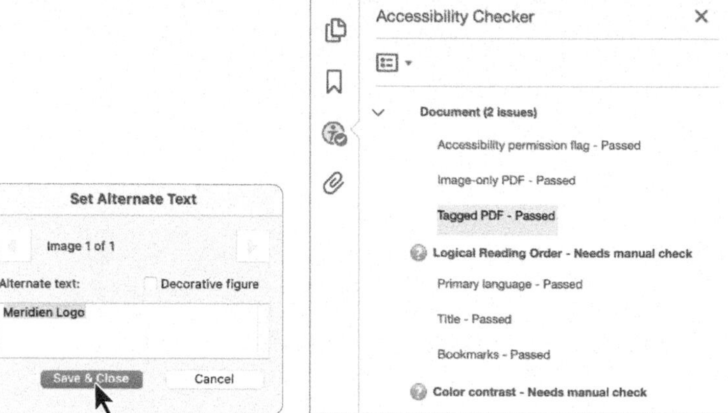

The Accessibility Checker panel now shows only two issues under the Document heading, both items that you would need to confirm manually.

12 Close the Accessibility Checker panel and the Action Wizard tool. Leave the Footwear_Accessible.pdf document open. (Its tab displays "Fall Footwear Line" since you changed the title.)

About tags

When you add tags to a document, Acrobat adds a logical tree structure to the document that determines the order in which page content is reflowed and read by screen readers and the Read Out Loud feature. If you're using Acrobat Pro, you can let Acrobat add tags automatically using the Make Accessible action. In either Acrobat Pro or Acrobat Standard, you can use the Autotag Document option in the Accessibility tool to assign tags, and then review the resulting Recognition Report to see how successful Acrobat was. On more complex pages—pages that contain irregularly shaped columns, bulleted lists, text that spans columns, and so on—Acrobat may mark areas that require some attention. Use the report to navigate to the problem areas of your PDF document by clicking the links for each error. Then, if you're using Acrobat Pro, click Reading Order in the Accessibility tool to correct the problem.

To see how Acrobat has tagged the document, click the Tags button to open the Tags panel in the navigation pane. (If the Tags button isn't displayed, choose View > Show/Hide > Navigation Panes > Tags.) Click the arrow next to Tags to view the tags.

Using Acrobat accessibility features (Standard and Pro)

Many people with vision and motor impairments use computers, and Acrobat provides a number of features that make it easier for them to work with PDF files. Such features include:

- Reflowing text
- Automatic scrolling
- Keyboard shortcuts
- Support for several screen-reader applications, including the text-to-speech engines built into Windows and macOS platforms
- Enhanced onscreen viewing

Reflowing a flexible PDF file

Now you'll take a quick look at how flexible a tagged PDF file is. You'll reflow the PDF file so that you can easily read it at different screen widths.

First, you'll adjust the size of your document window to mimic the smaller screen of a mobile device.

1 Choose View > Zoom > Actual Size to display the document at 100%.

2 Resize the Acrobat window to about 50% of the full-screen display. In Windows, click the Maximize/Restore Down button if the window is currently maximized; if the window isn't maximized, drag a corner of the application window to reduce it. In macOS, resize the document pane by dragging a corner.

Your goal is to resize the Acrobat window so that the ends of the sentences in the document pane are cut off.

3 Choose View > Zoom > Reflow.

The content of the document is reflowed to accommodate the smaller document screen, and you can now read an entire line of text without using the horizontal scroll bar.

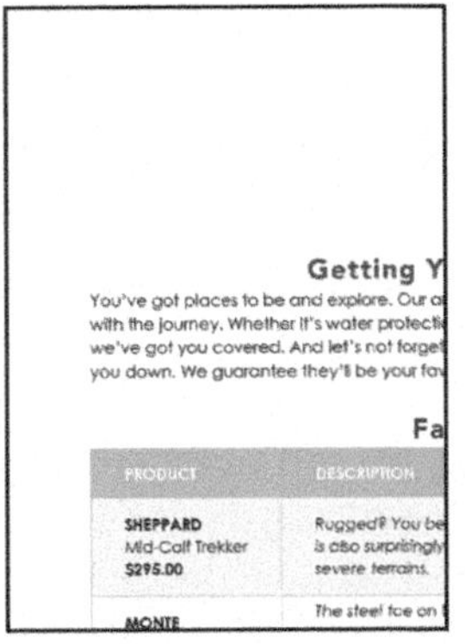

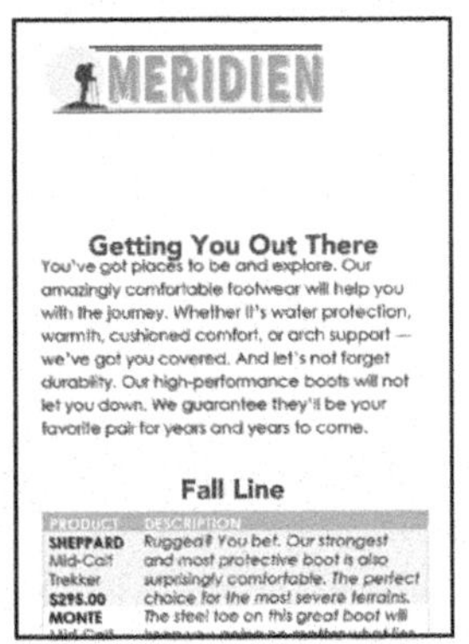

When you reflow text, artifacts such as page numbers and page headers often drop out because they are no longer relevant to the page display. Text is reflowed one page at a time. You cannot save the document in the reflowed state.

Now you'll examine how the display changes when you change the magnification.

4 Choose 400% from the magnification menu in the toolbar.

5 Scroll down the page to see how the text reflows. Again, because the text is reflowed, you don't have to use the horizontal scroll bar to move back and forth across the page to read the enlarged text. The text is automatically contained within the document pane.

6 When you've finished viewing the reflowed text, restore the Acrobat document window to its usual size. Leave the document open.

You can save the contents of a tagged document in a different file format for reuse in another application. For example, if you save this file as accessible text, you'll see that even the contents of the table are saved in an easy-to-use format.

With Acrobat, you can even make some unstructured documents more readily accessible to all types of users. You can add tags to a PDF document using the Add Tags To Document command in any version of Acrobat. However, to correct tagging and order errors, you must be using Acrobat Pro.

Using the Accessibility Setup Assistant

Both Acrobat and Acrobat Reader include an Accessibility Setup Assistant. In Windows, the Accessibility Setup Assistant launches automatically the first time the software detects a screen reader, screen magnifier, or other assistive technology on your system. In macOS, choose Acrobat > Accessibility Setup Assistant or Acrobat Reader > Accessibility > Setup Assistant to open it. (You can also launch the Assistant manually at any time by selecting Setup Assistant in the Accessibility tool in Acrobat.) The Accessibility Setup Assistant walks you through setting the options that control how PDF documents appear onscreen. You can also use it to set the option that sends print output to a Braille printer.

A full explanation of the options you can set in the Accessibility Setup Assistant is available in Adobe Acrobat Help. The options available depend on the type of assistive technology you have on your system. The first panel of the Accessibility Setup Assistant requires you to identify the type of assistive technology you use:

- Select Set Options For Screen Readers if you use a device that reads text out loud or sends output to a Braille printer.
- Select Set Options For Screen Magnifiers if you use a device that makes text appear larger on the screen.
- Select Set All Accessibility Options if you use a combination of assistive devices.
- Click Use Recommended Settings And Skip Setup to use the settings Adobe recommends. (Note that the preferred settings for users with assistive technology installed are not the same as the default Acrobat settings for users who are not using assistive technology.)

In addition to the options you can set using the Accessibility Setup Assistant, you can select a number of options in the Acrobat or Acrobat Reader preferences that control automatic scrolling, reading-out-loud settings, and reading order. You may want to use some of these options even if you don't have assistive technology on your system. For example, you can set your Multimedia preferences to show available descriptions for video and audio attachments.

If you opened the Accessibility Setup Assistant, click Cancel to exit the dialog box without making any changes.

Enabling automatic scrolling

When you're reading a long document, the automatic scrolling feature saves you keystrokes and mouse actions. You can control the speed of scrolling, scroll backward and forward, and exit automatic scrolling with a single keystroke.

Now you'll test the automatic scroll feature.

1 Choose File > Open, and open the Fall Hiking.pdf file. If necessary, resize the Acrobat window to fill your desktop.

2 Choose View > Page Display > Automatically Scroll.

3 You can set the rate of scrolling using the number keys on your keyboard. The higher the number, the faster the rate of scrolling. Try pressing 9 to scroll faster, and then press 1 to scroll slowly. To exit automatic scrolling, press the Esc key.

4 Close the Fall Hiking.pdf file.

About keyboard shortcuts

For some common commands and tools, the keyboard shortcut is displayed next to the command or tool name. A list of keyboard shortcuts is available in Adobe Acrobat Help.

You can also use the keyboard to control Acrobat within a web browser. If the focus is on the web browser, any keyboard shortcuts you use act according to the web browser settings for navigation and selection. Pressing the Tab key shifts the focus from the browser to the Acrobat document and application, so navigation and command keystrokes function normally. Pressing Ctrl+Tab or Command+Tab shifts the focus from the document back to the web browser.

Modifying onscreen elements

You can smooth text, line art, and images to improve onscreen readability, especially with larger text sizes. If you use a laptop or if you have an LCD screen, you can also choose a Smooth Text option to optimize your display quality. Set the options to smooth text in the Page Display preferences.

You can change the color of the background or text displayed on your monitor using the Accessibility Preferences in Acrobat. Color changes affect only the onscreen display, not the printed page or the saved PDF file.

To increase the text size used in bookmark labels, choose Text Size > Large from the options menu of the Bookmarks panel.

You may want to experiment with screen-display options and other accessibility controls to find a combination that best suits your needs.

Setting screen reader and reading-out-loud preferences

After you have installed your screen reader or similar application and set it up to work with Acrobat, you can set the screen reader preferences in Acrobat. You set these preferences in the same panel in which you set the Read Out Loud feature preferences that control the volume, pitch, and speed of the speech; the nature of the voice; and the reading order preferences.

Newer systems (both Windows and macOS) have built-in text-to-speech engines. Although the Read Out Loud feature can read the text of a PDF file out loud, it is not a screen reader. Not all systems support the Read Out Loud feature.

In this exercise, you'll look at the preferences that affect how Adobe PDF documents are read out loud. Unless you have text-to-speech software on your system, you do not need to set these preferences.

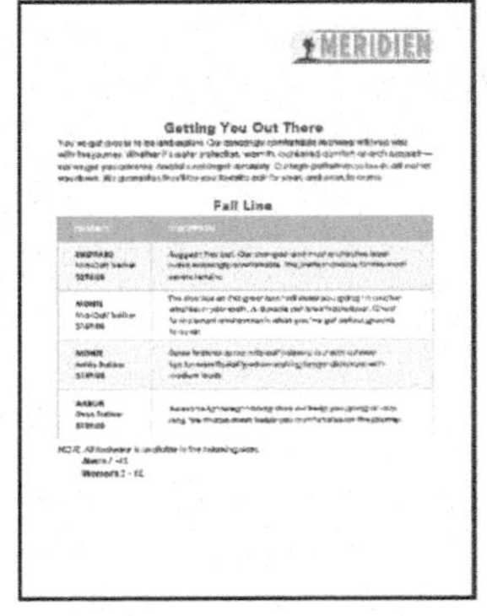

1 Click the Fall Footwear Line tab to make the document active. (If you closed it earlier, open it again.)

2 If your system has text-to-speech software, choose View > Read Out Loud > Activate Read Out Loud.

3 After you have activated the Read Out Loud feature, choose View > Read Out Loud > Read This Page Only. Acrobat reads the page that is currently displayed.

4 To stop the reading, press Ctrl+Shift+E (Windows) or Command+Shift+E (macOS).

You can experiment with the reading options.

5 Choose Edit > Preferences (Windows) or Acrobat > Preferences (macOS), and select Reading from the list on the left. Experiment, if you like.

You can control the volume, pitch, speed, and voice used.

If your system has limited memory, you may wish to reduce the number of pages Acrobat reads before data is delivered page by page. The default value is 50 pages.

6 Click OK in the Preferences dialog box to apply any changes that you make. Or click Cancel to exit the Preferences dialog box without making any changes.

7 To test the settings you changed, choose View > Read Out Loud > Read This Page Only.

8 To stop the reading, press Ctrl+Shift+E (Windows) or Command+Shift+E (macOS).

Sharing PDF files

You can share a PDF document with other people in many ways, including posting it on a website, copying it to a flash drive, or sending it as an email attachment. Acrobat makes it easy to distribute a PDF document to others by attaching the document to an email message or sharing a link to the document in Adobe's cloud storage. The sharing tools are on the right side of the toolbar.

1 With the file still open, click the Send File By Email button (✉) in the main toolbar.

Acrobat displays options for sharing the document.

If you select Attach A Link, Acrobat uploads the document to cloud storage and emails a link to the document. If you deselect Attach A link, Acrobat emails the PDF file as an attachment using your email account.

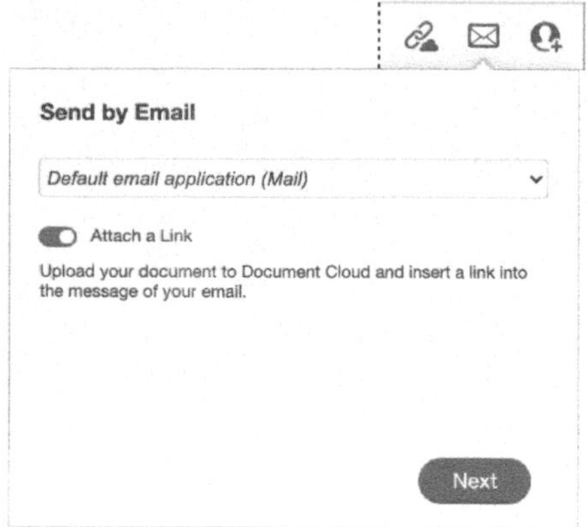

2 Deselect Attach A Link, and then select either Default Email or Webmail. If you select Webmail, choose a webmail service from the pop-up menu, and then add the account information.

Once you've added a webmail account, it appears in the pop-up list so you can select it directly.

3 Click Next.

4 If you're using a webmail account, sign in, and grant access to Acrobat if prompted.

Your email application or webmail program opens with a blank message that has the file attached to it. If you're using Gmail, you may need to click Drafts to see the draft message.

5 Enter email addresses, a subject line, and a brief message.

6 Send the message.

7 Close the document, and close Acrobat.

Review questions

1. Name three methods you can use to navigate to a different page within a document in Acrobat.
2. Name two ways to change the view magnification in a PDF file.
3. How can you determine whether a PDF document is accessible when you're working with Acrobat Pro?
4. How can you print pages that are not next to each other (that is, discontiguous pages) from Acrobat?

Review answers

1. You can move to a different page by clicking the Previous Page or Next Page button in the main toolbar; dragging the scroll box in the scroll bar; entering a page number in the page box in the toolbar; or clicking a bookmark, page thumbnail, or link that jumps to a different page.
2. You can change the view magnification by choosing View > Zoom, and then choosing a view; dragging the Marquee Zoom tool; choosing a preset magnification in the toolbar; or entering a specific percentage in the magnification text box in the toolbar.
3. To determine whether a PDF file is accessible in Acrobat Pro, open the Accessibility tools, and then click Accessibility Check.
4. To print discontiguous pages, either select the page thumbnails, and then choose File > Print, or, in the Print dialog box, select Pages, and then enter the page numbers or ranges you want to print, separated by commas.

4 ENHANCING PDF DOCUMENTS

Lesson overview

In this lesson, you'll do the following:

- Rearrange pages in a PDF document.
- Rotate and delete pages.
- Insert pages into a PDF document.
- Edit links and bookmarks.
- Renumber pages in a PDF document.
- Set document properties and add metadata to a PDF.

This lesson will take approximately 45 minutes to complete. Download the project files for this lesson, following the instructions in the Getting Started section under "Accessing the lesson files and Web Edition," if you haven't already done so. As you work on this lesson, you'll preserve the start files. If you need to restore the start files, download them from your Account page.

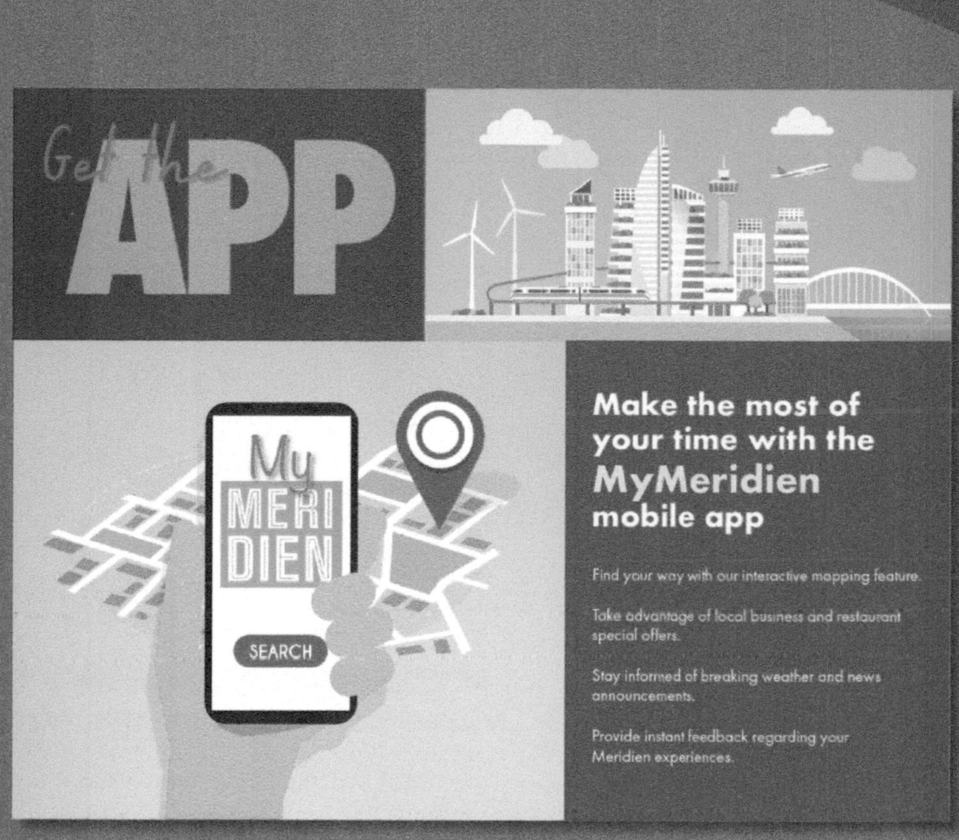

You can rearrange, crop, delete, or insert pages in a PDF document. Or modify a document by editing text or images. You can also add navigational aids such as bookmarks and links.

Examining the work file

You'll work with conference materials for the fictitious Meridien Conference. The conference guide has been designed both for print and for online viewing. Because the guide is in the developmental phase, it contains a number of mistakes. You'll use Acrobat to correct the problems in this PDF document.

1 Start Acrobat.

2 Choose File > Open. Navigate to the Lesson04/Assets folder, select Conference Guide.pdf, and click Open. Then choose File > Save As, click Choose A Different Folder, navigate to the Lesson04/Finished_Projects folder, rename the file **Conference Guide_revised.pdf**, and click Save.

3 Click the small arrow on the left side of the window to open the navigation pane, if it's not already open. Then click the Bookmarks button (🔖) in the navigation pane.

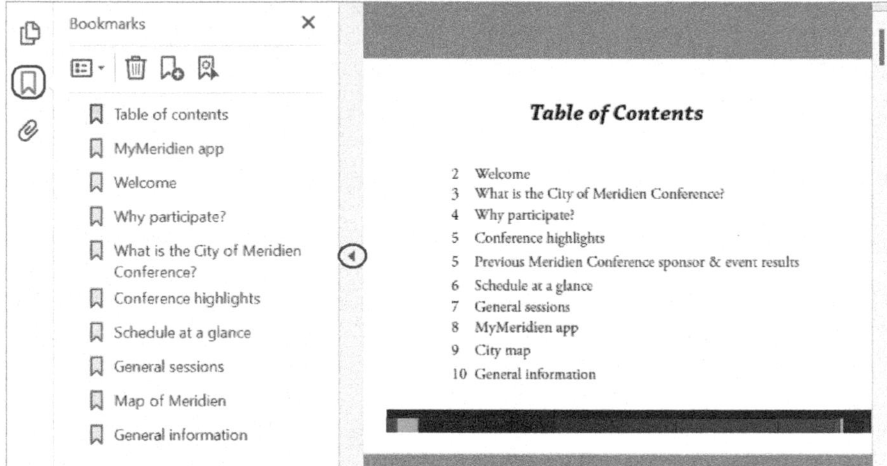

The Bookmarks panel opens, revealing several bookmarks that have already been created. Bookmarks are links to specific points in the document. They can be generated automatically from the table-of-contents entries in documents created by most desktop publishing programs or from formatted headings in applications such as Microsoft Word. You can also create bookmarks in Acrobat. You can specify the appearance of bookmarks and add actions to them.

Notice that the order of bookmarks doesn't correspond with the order in the table of contents. There are a couple of bookmark errors that you'll correct later.

4 Click the Table of contents bookmark to go to the first page of the guide, if you're not there already.

5 In the document pane, move the pointer over the items listed in the table of contents. Notice that the cursor changes to a hand with a pointing finger, indicating that items in the list are links.

6 Click the MyMeridien app entry in the document pane to follow its link. (Be sure to click the entry in the table of contents, not the bookmark in the Bookmarks panel.)

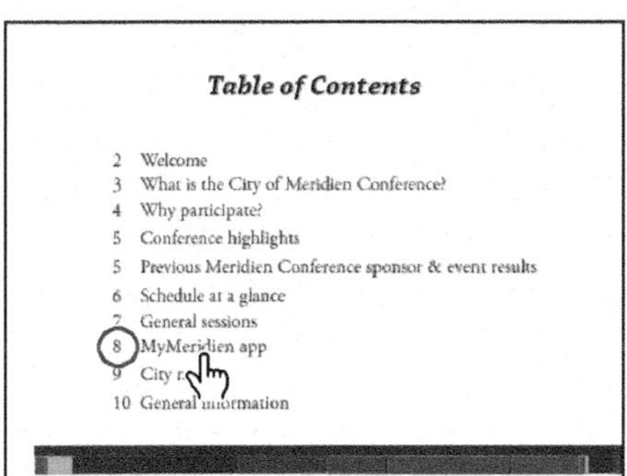

Notice that the page number on the page displayed in the document pane is 2, though the page number in the table of contents showed the page as being page 8. The page is out of order.

7 Choose View > Page Navigation > Previous View to return to the table of contents.

Moving pages with page thumbnails

Page thumbnails offer a convenient way to preview pages. In previous lessons, you used page thumbnails to navigate a document. Now you'll use them to quickly rearrange pages in a document.

1 Click the Page Thumbnails button (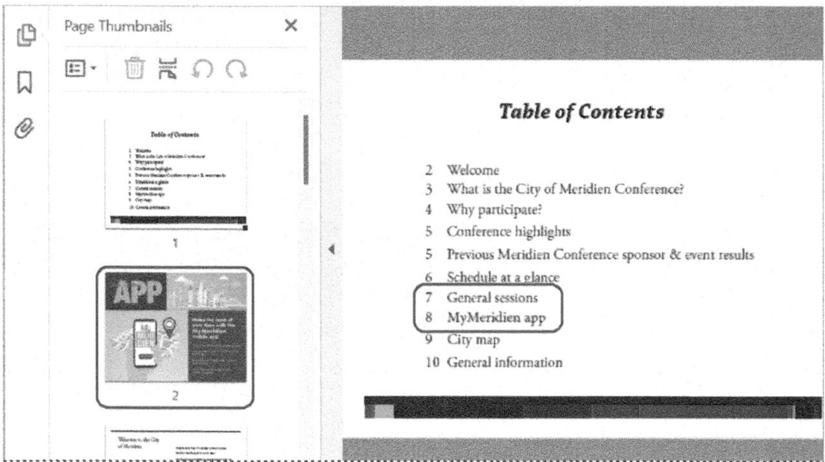) in the navigation pane.

The MyMeridien app page is out of place. According to the table of contents, it should follow the page titled "General sessions."

2 Click the page 2 thumbnail to select it.

3 Drag the selected thumbnail image down until the insertion bar appears between the thumbnails of pages 8 and 9.

4 Release the mouse button to insert the page at its new position. The page numbers change in the Page Thumbnails panel to reflect the new page order.

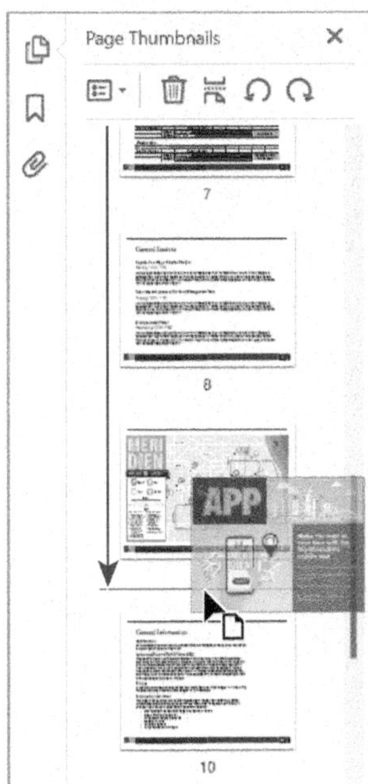

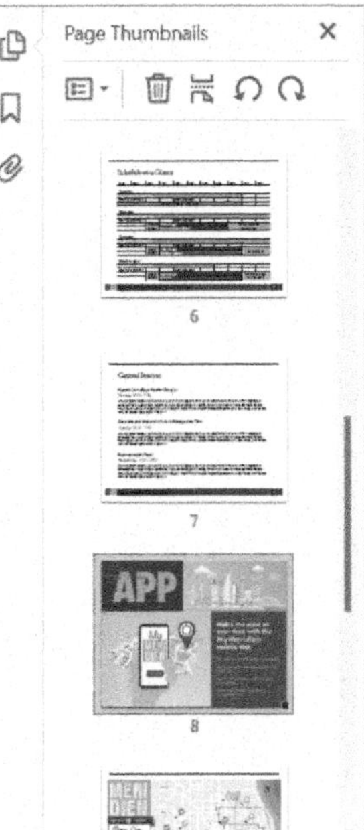

The MyMeridien app page now follows the "General sessions" page and precedes the "City map" page.

5 To check the sequence of pages, choose View > Page Navigation > First Page to go to the first page of the document (if you're not already there), and then use the Next Page button (Ⓥ) to page through the presentation.

6 When you're satisfied that the pages are in the correct order, click the Page Thumbnails button again to close its panel. Then choose File > Save to save your work so far.

Manipulating pages

The first page of the document (page 1 of 13) is the Table of Contents page, and it's rather plain. To make the guide more attractive, you'll add a cover page, which you'll then rotate to match the other pages in the document.

Inserting a page from another file

▶ **Tip:** If you insert a page that is larger than the other pages in a document, you can crop out unnecessary areas of the page. Right-click the page, and choose Crop Pages.

You'll start by inserting the cover page.

1 Click Organize Pages in the Tools pane.

2 Click Insert in the Organize Pages toolbar, and then choose From File.

3 Navigate to the Lesson04/Assets folder, and select Conference Guide Cover.pdf. Click Open or Select.

4 In the Insert Pages dialog box, choose Before from the Location menu, and select First in the Page area. Then click OK. You want to insert this PDF file before any of the pages in your document.

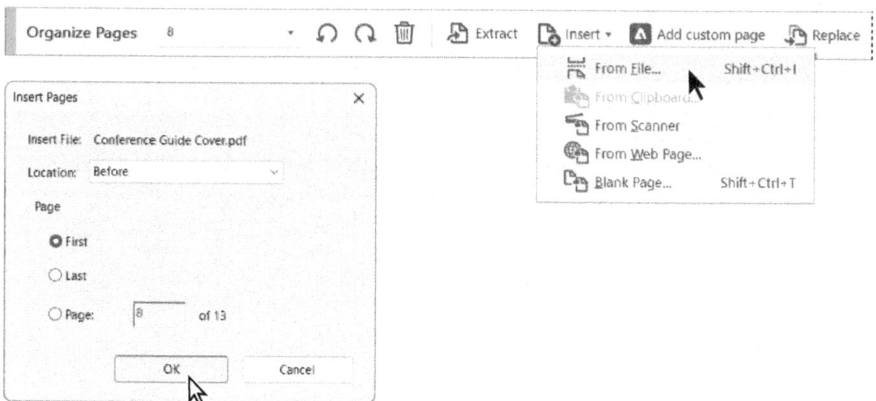

The cover document appears as page 1 in the Conference Guide_revised.pdf document.

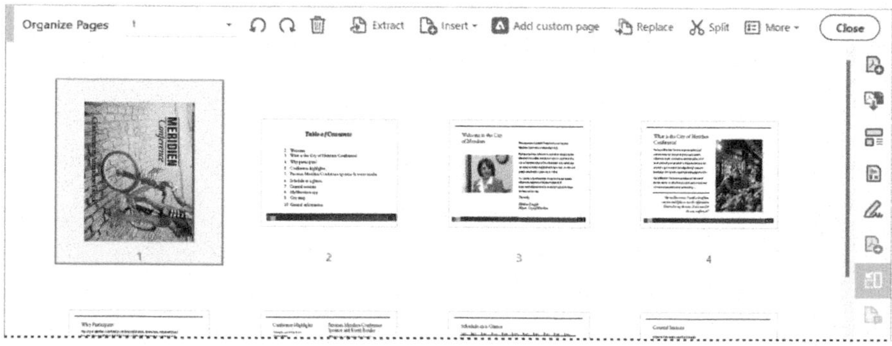

5 Choose File > Save to save your work.

Rotating a page

The cover page is now in the conference document, but it has the wrong orientation. You'll rotate the new page to match the rest of the document.

▶ **Tip:** If you have an Acrobat or Creative Cloud subscription, you can rotate and rearrange pages on a tablet or phone using the Acrobat mobile app. See Lesson 6, "Using Acrobat on Mobile Devices" to learn more.

1 Select the thumbnail for the cover. Two rotation icons, a delete icon, and an icon for more options appear superimposed on the thumbnail.

2 Click the Rotate Counterclockwise icon.

Acrobat rotates the page so that it matches the rest of the document. Only the selected page is rotated.

Deleting a page

The last page in the document doesn't quite fit with the others, and the conference committee has decided to distribute it separately. You'll delete it from the document.

1 Select the thumbnail for the last page in the document (page 14).

2 Click the delete icon.

3 Click OK to confirm that you want to delete the page.

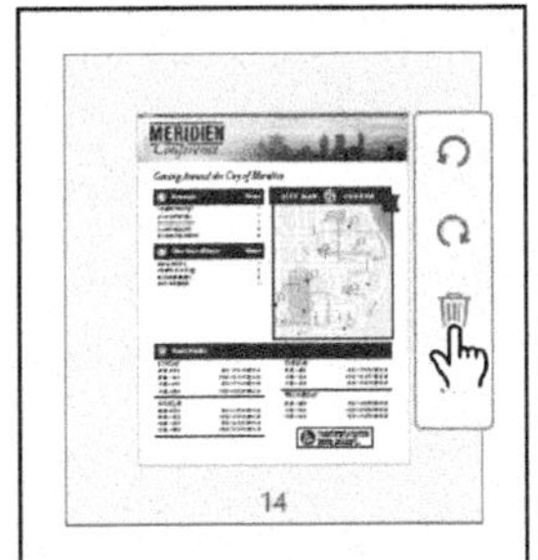

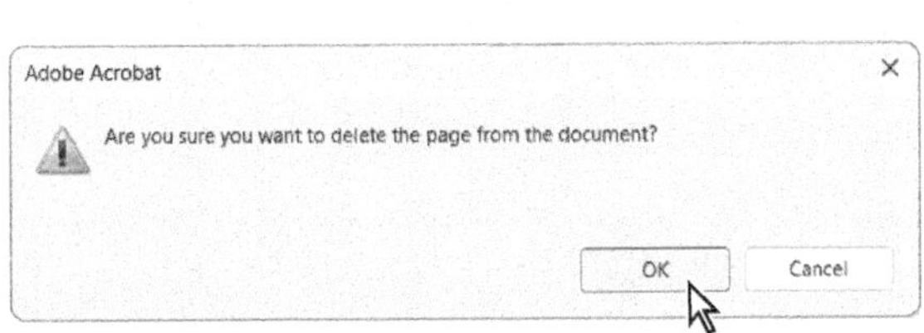

The page is deleted from the Conference Guide_revised.pdf file.

4 Close the Organize Pages toolbar to return to the main document view.

5 Choose File > Save to save your work.

Renumbering pages

You may have noticed that the page numbers on the document pages do not always match the page numbers that appear below the page thumbnails and in the toolbar. Acrobat automatically numbers pages with Arabic numerals, starting with page 1 for the first page in the document, and so on. However, you can change the way Acrobat numbers pages. You'll give the cover page a roman numeral, so that the contents page is page 1.

1 Click the Page Thumbnails button ( ) in the navigation pane to display thumbnails for the document's pages.

2 Click the page 1 thumbnail to go to the cover page.

You'll renumber the first page of the document—the cover page—using lowercase roman numerals.

3 Click the options menu button at the top of the Page Thumbnails panel, and choose Page Labels. The Page Numbering dialog box opens.

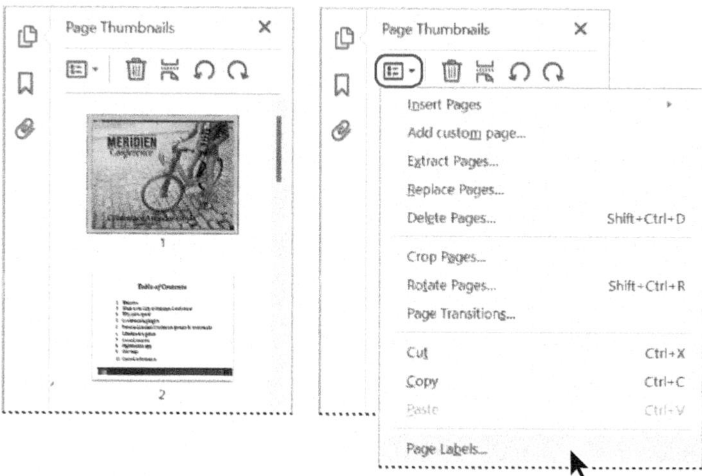

4 For Pages, select From, and make sure **1** to **1** of 13 is specified. For Numbering, select Begin New Section, choose "i, ii, iii" from the Style menu, and enter **1** in the Start text box. Click OK.

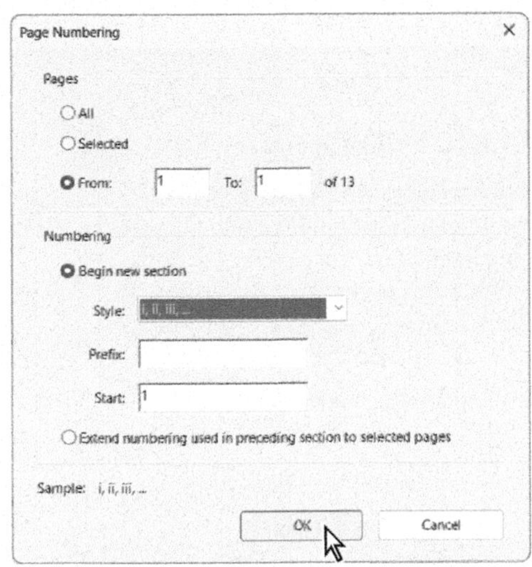

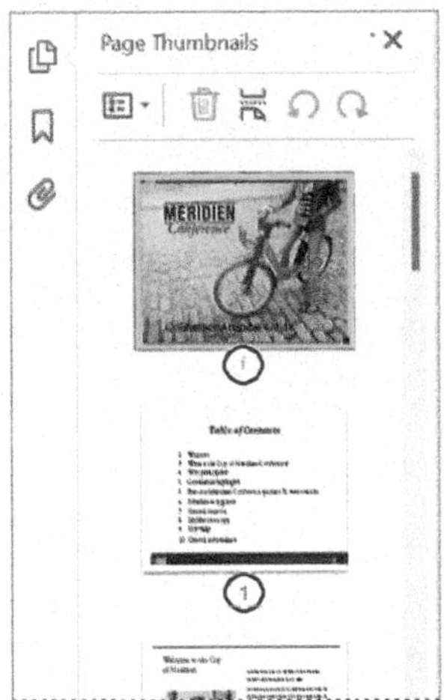

5 Choose View > Page Navigation > Go To Page. Enter **1**, and click OK.

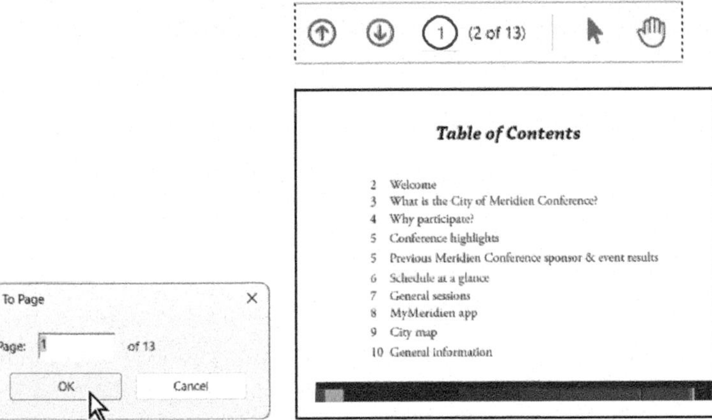

Table of Contents

2 Welcome
3 What is the City of Meridien Conference?
4 Why participate?
5 Conference highlights
5 Previous Meridien Conference sponsor & event results
6 Schedule at a glance
7 General sessions
8 MyMeridien app
9 City map
10 General information

Acrobat displays the Table of Contents page. Because you renumbered the cover page, the number 1 in the page number text box is now assigned to the contents page of the document.

6 Close the Page Thumbnails panel.

7 Choose File > Save to save your changes.

> **Tip:** You can manually add page numbers to the pages of your Adobe PDF document using headers or footers. (Select the Edit PDF tool, and choose Header & Footer > Add.)

Applying Bates numbering (Acrobat Pro only)

Bates numbering is an indexing method used for legal, business, or medical documents in which pages related to a case or project are numbered sequentially with a reference number. Using Acrobat Pro, you can automatically apply Bates numbering as a header or footer to any document or to documents in a PDF Portfolio. (If the PDF Portfolio contains non-PDF files, Acrobat converts the files to PDF and adds Bates numbering.) You can add custom prefixes and suffixes, as well as a date stamp. You can specify that the numbering is always applied outside the text or image area on the document page.

To apply Bates numbering, click Organize Pages in the Tools pane, and then choose More > Bates Numbering > Add.

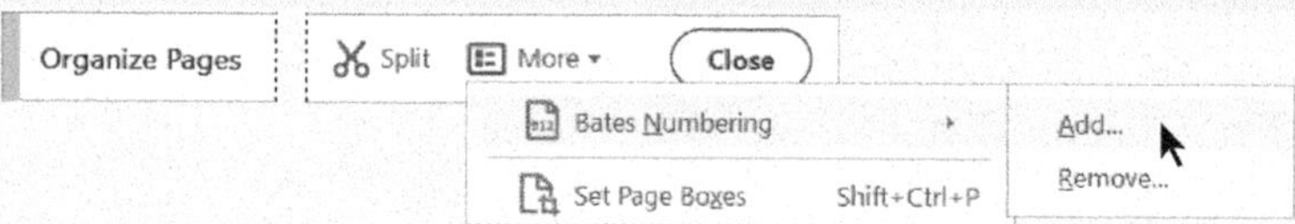

In the Bates Numbering dialog box, add the files you want to number, and arrange them in the appropriate order. Click Output Options to specify the location and naming convention for the numbered files. Click OK to close the Output Options dialog box. Then click OK in the Bates Numbering dialog box to open the Add Header and Footer dialog box, where you can define the style and format of the number—6 to 15 digits, plus prefixes and suffixes.

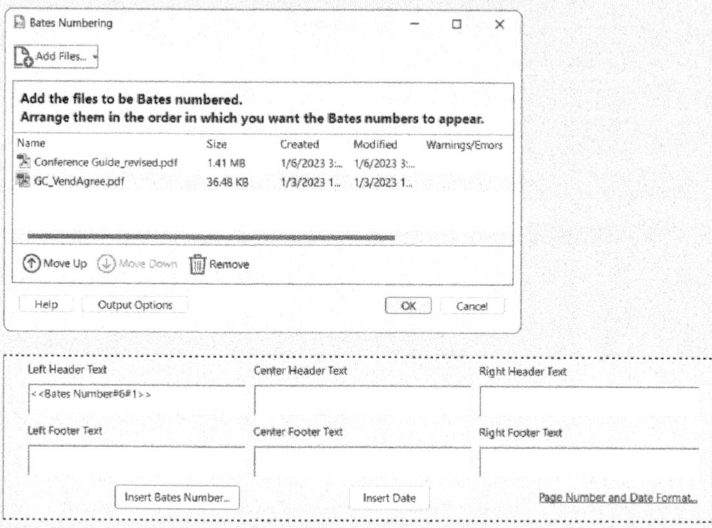

You can't edit Bates page numbering after it's applied, but you can delete it and start over.

For more information on applying Bates numbering and working with other legal features in Acrobat, see Adobe Acrobat Pro Help.

Managing links

Now you'll correct the broken links on the contents page and add a missing link.

▶ **Tip:** To quickly return to your previous view, choose View > Page Navigation > Previous View, or press Alt or Command and the Left Arrow key.

1 Go to page 1, the Table of Contents page, if you're not there already.

2 Click the links for each of the table of contents entries to identify problems.

The link for page 3 and the second link for page 5 go to the wrong pages. There is no link for the last entry. First, you'll correct the links that go to the wrong pages.

3 Click Edit PDF in the Tools pane, and then choose Link > Add/Edit Web Or Document Link. Acrobat outlines the links on the page.

4 Double-click the link for page 3, "What is the City of Meridien Conference?"

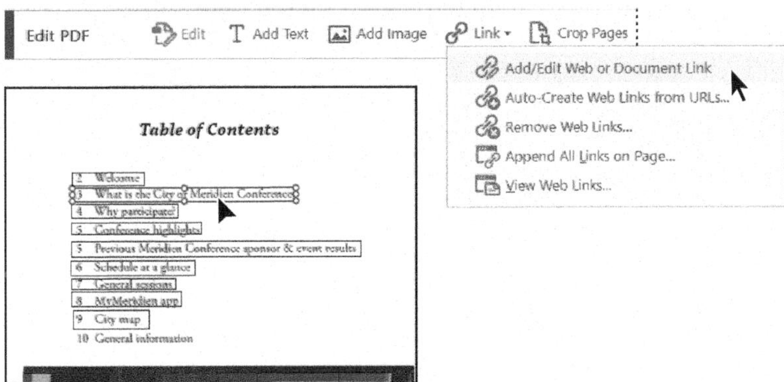

5 In the Link Properties dialog box, click the Actions tab. The action associated with this link is to go to page 3. Click Edit.

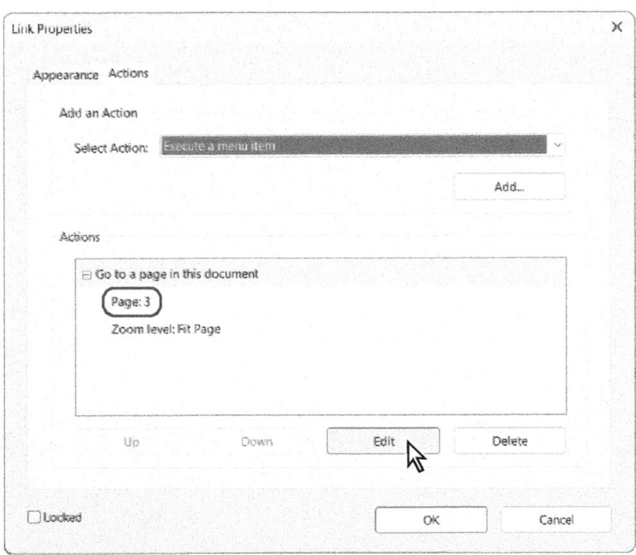

6 In the Go To A Page In This Document dialog box, select Use Page Number, and enter **3** in the Page box. Click OK.

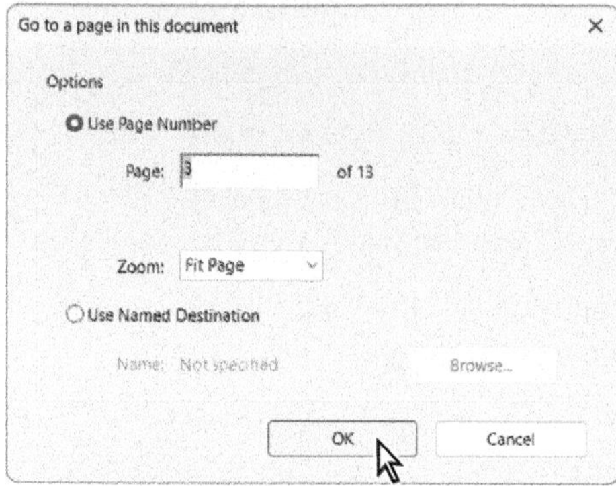

The listed action now goes to page 4. Remember that you renumbered the pages, so page 3 is actually the 4th page in the PDF file.

7 Click OK.

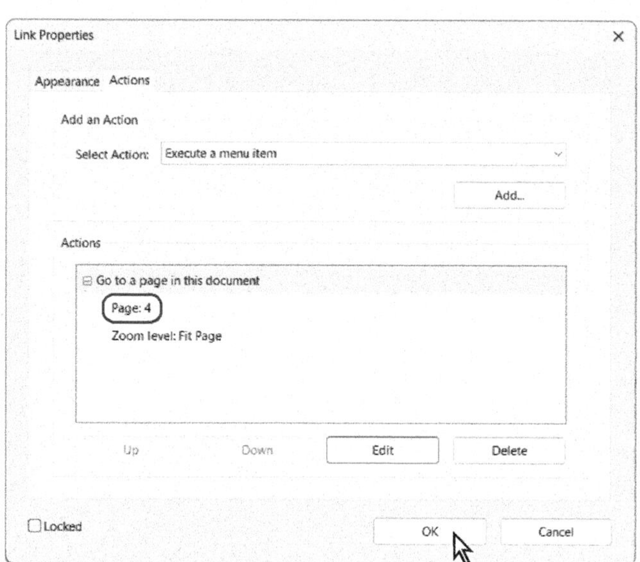

8 In the toolbar, select the Selection tool (![]). Then click the link for page 3. It goes to the appropriate page now. Return to the Table of Contents page.

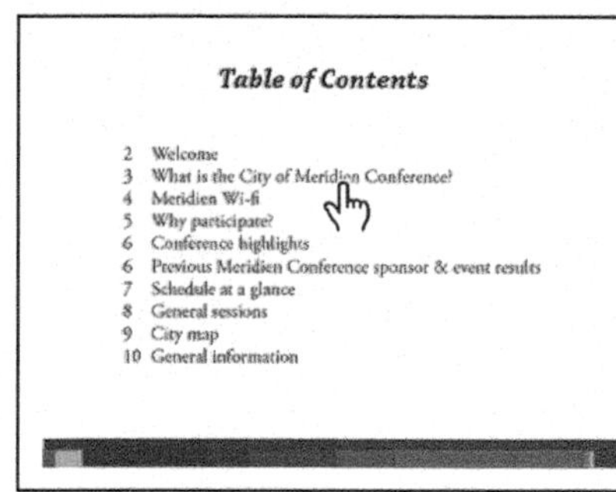

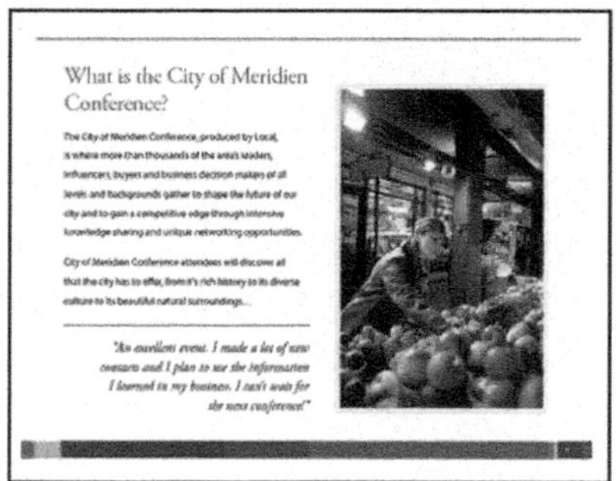

9 Follow steps 3–7 to make the same change for the link to the previous event results, changing the linked page number to page 5.

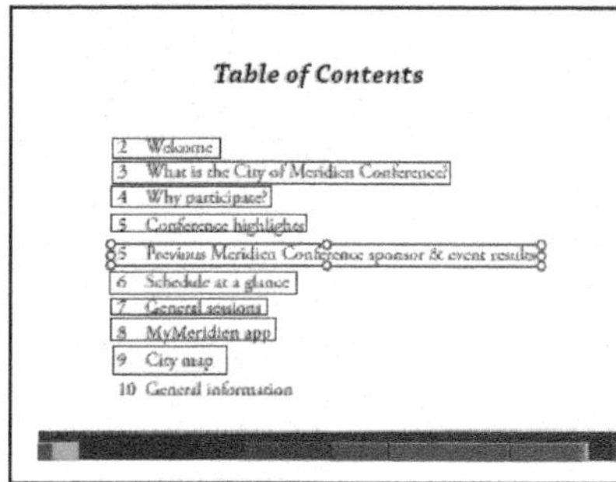

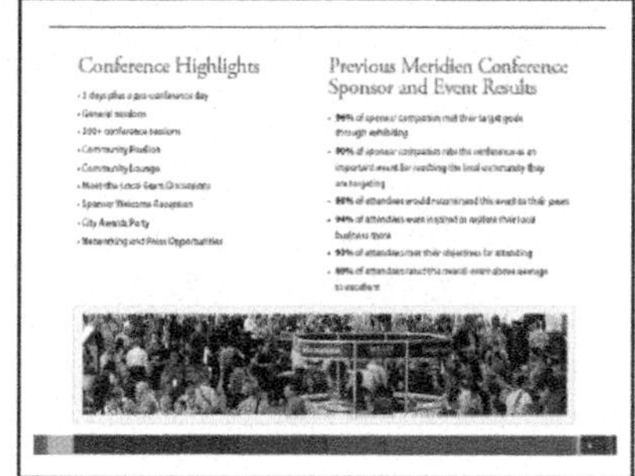

Now you'll create a link for the last entry.

10 Go to page 1 (the Table of Contents page), if you're not there already. If links aren't outlined, choose Link > Add/Edit Web Or Document Link.

11 Drag a link box around the final contents entry, "10 General information."

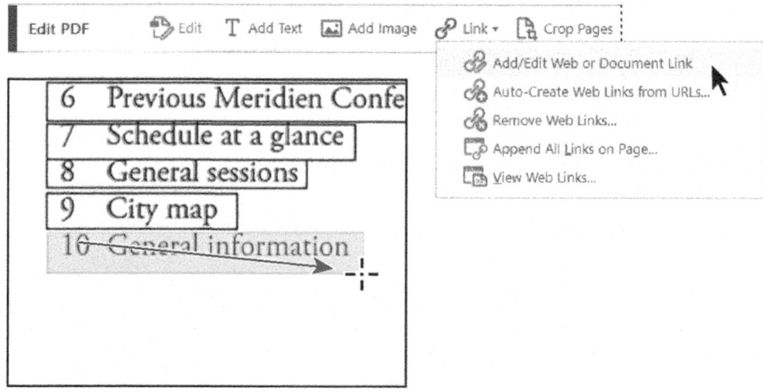

12 In the Create Link dialog box, choose Invisible Rectangle for the Link Type, and select Go To A Page View in the Link Action area. Then click Next.

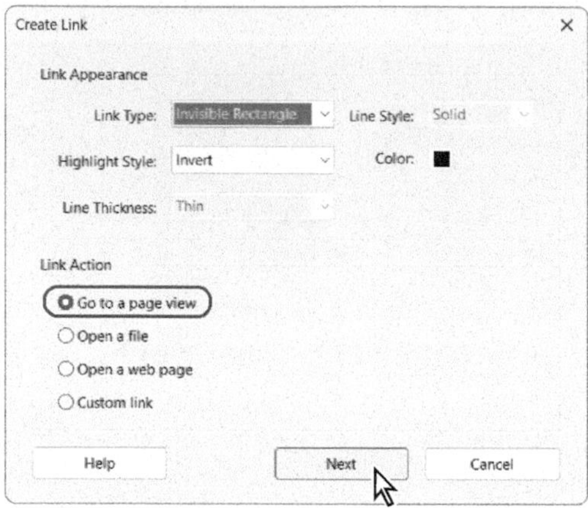

The Create Go To View dialog box appears. Don't click anything until you're on the page that should be linked.

13 Scroll to page 10. When the General Information page is on the screen, click Set Link. Acrobat returns you to the contents page.

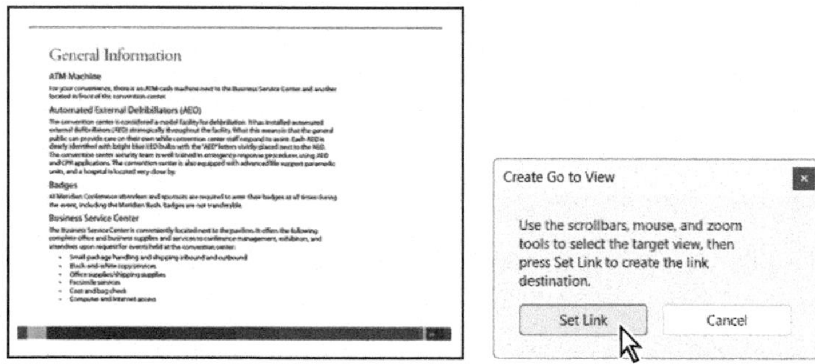

14 Select the Selection tool, and then click the link you just created to test it.

15 Close the Edit PDF panel.

16 Choose File > Save to save your work.

Working with bookmarks

A bookmark is simply a link represented by text in the Bookmarks panel. Many authoring programs automatically create bookmarks that are linked to headings in the text or to figure captions. You can also add your own bookmarks in Acrobat to create a custom outline of a document or to open other documents.

Additionally, you can use electronic bookmarks as you would paper bookmarks—to mark a place in a document that you want to highlight or return to later.

Adding a bookmark

First, you'll add a bookmark for the second topic on page 5, the section titled "Previous Meridien Conference sponsor and event results."

1 Go to page 5 in the document, so that you can see the event results.

2 Open the Bookmarks panel, and then click the Conference highlights bookmark. Your new bookmark will be added directly below the selected bookmark.

3 Click the New Bookmark button ( ) at the top of the Bookmarks panel.

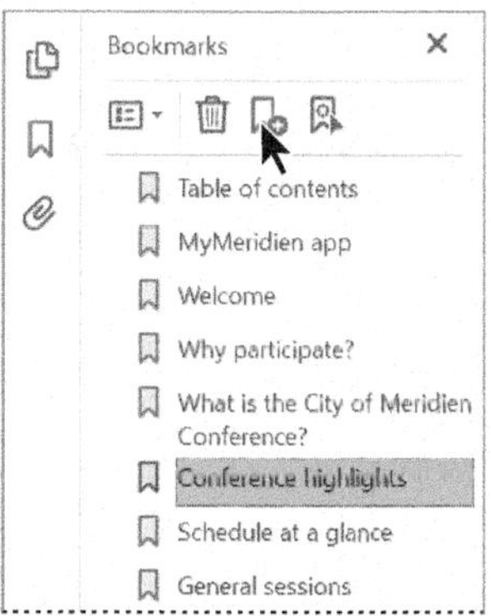

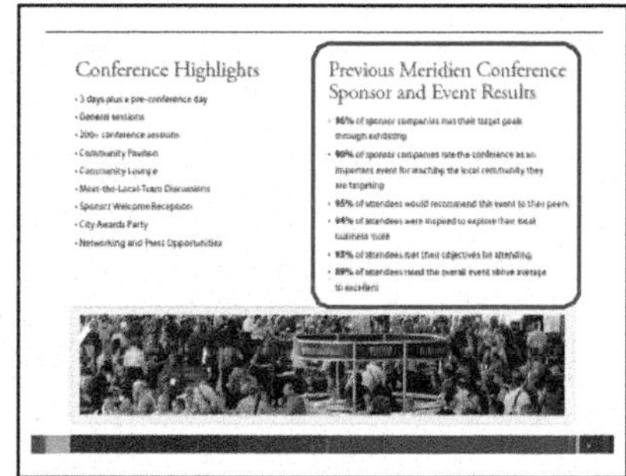

A new, untitled bookmark appears.

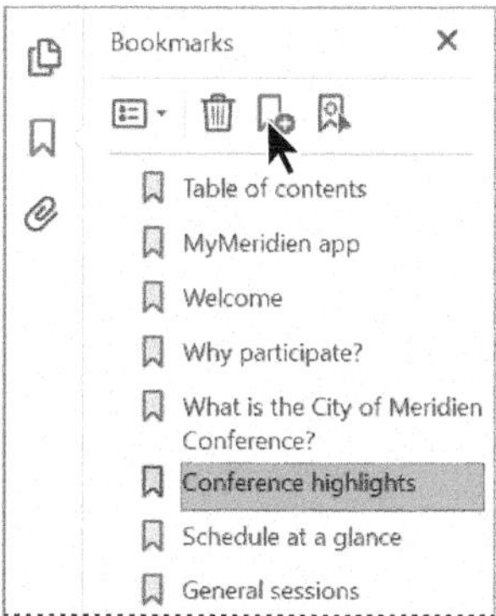

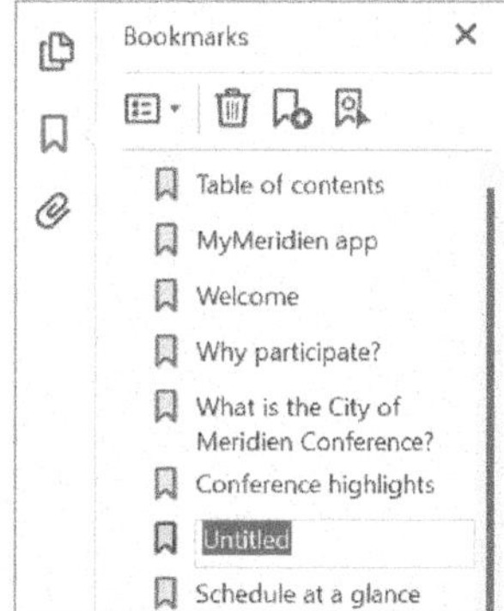

4 In the text box of the new bookmark, type **Previous conference results**. Press Enter or Return to accept the name.

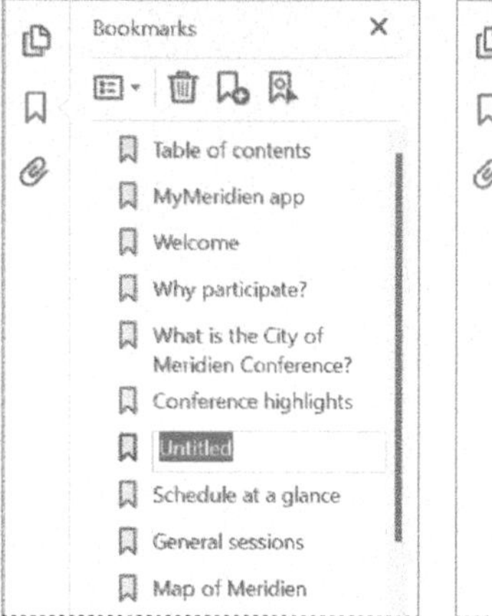

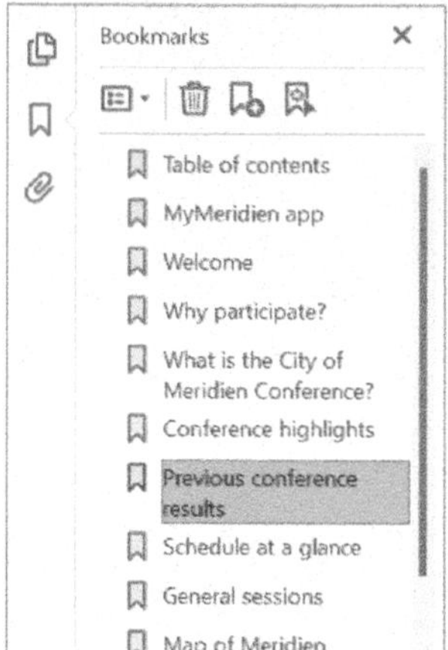

Changing a bookmark destination

A couple of bookmarks link to the wrong pages. You'll change those now.

1 In the Bookmarks panel, click the Why participate? bookmark. The document pane displays the "What is the City of Meridien Conference?" page.

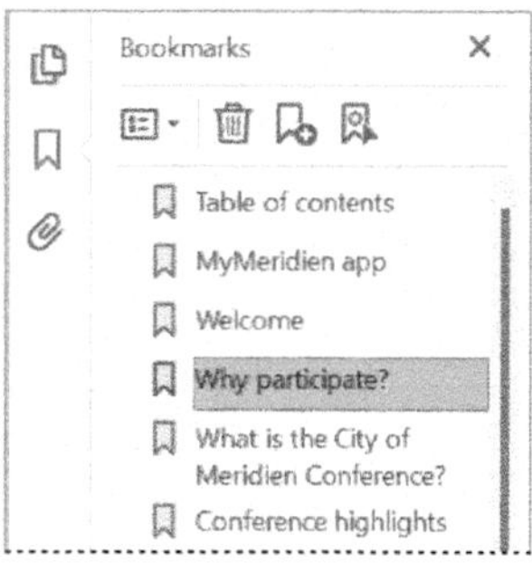

2 Click the Next Page button (⊕) once to go to page 4 (5 of 13) of the document, which is the page you want the bookmark to link to.

3 From the options menu (☰) at the top of the Bookmarks panel, choose Set Bookmark Destination. Click Yes in the confirmation message to update the bookmark destination.

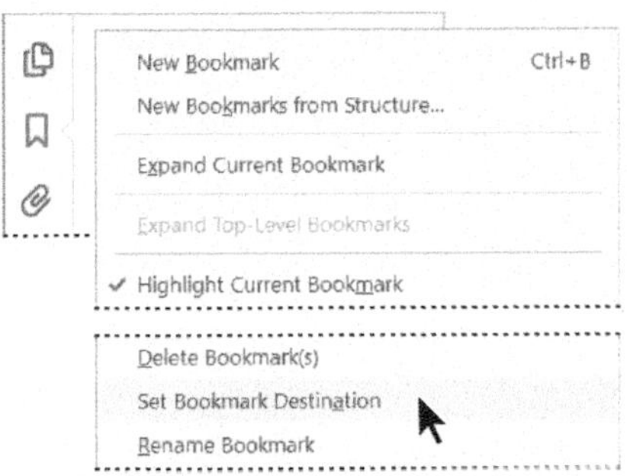

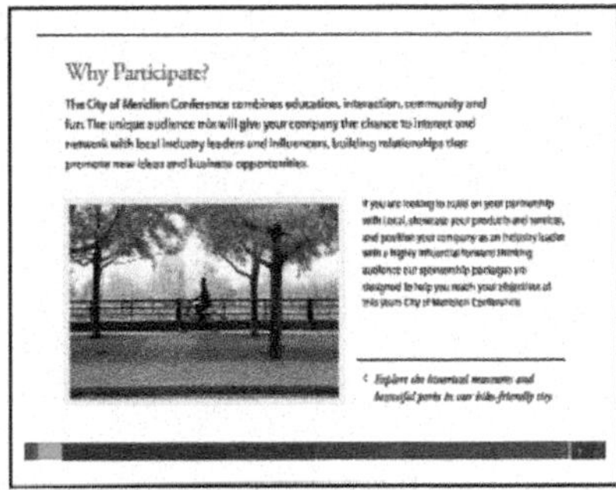

4 Repeat the process to correct the destination of the "What is the City of Meridien Conference?" bookmark, which should be linked to page 3 (4 of 13).

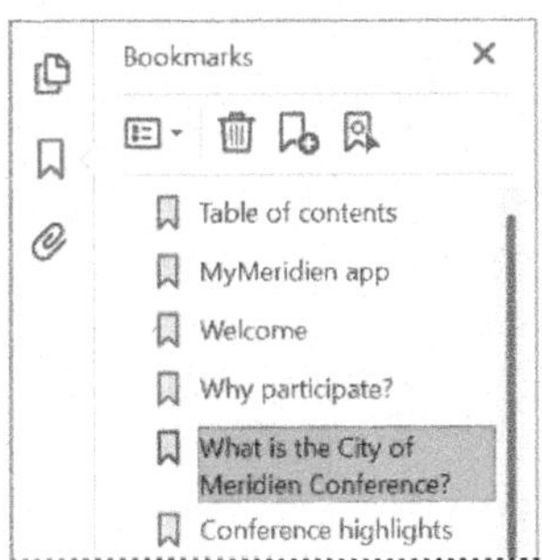

5 Choose File > Save to save the Conference Guide_revised.pdf file.

Moving bookmarks

After creating a bookmark, you can easily drag it to its proper place in the Bookmarks panel. You can move individual bookmarks or groups of bookmarks up and down in the Bookmarks panel, and you can nest bookmarks.

At least one of the bookmarks is out of order in the current document. You'll rearrange them now.

1 In the Bookmarks panel, drag the icon for the MyMeridien app bookmark directly below the icon for the General sessions bookmark.

2 Drag any other bookmarks as needed so that they appear in the same order as the entries in the table of contents.

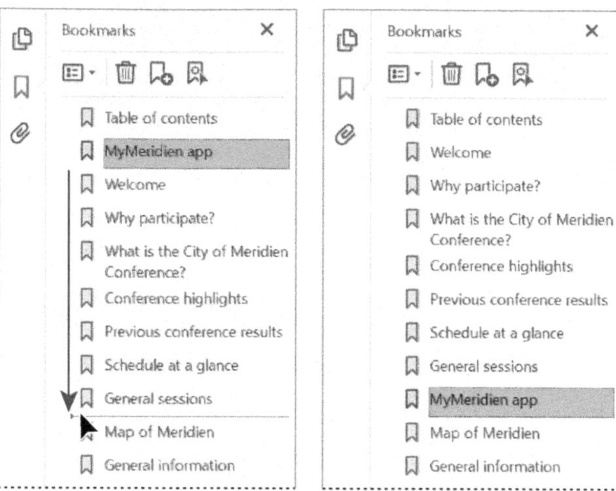

3 Close the Bookmarks panel, and then choose File > Save to save your work.

Naming bookmarks automatically

You can create, name, and automatically link a bookmark by selecting text in the document pane.

1 Navigate to the page you want to link, and set the magnification to the optimal level. The current magnification will be inherited by the bookmark.

2 Drag the I-beam to highlight the text that you want to use as your bookmark.

3 Click the New Bookmark button at the top of the Bookmarks panel. A new bookmark is created in the bookmarks list, and the highlighted text from the document pane is used as the bookmark name. By default, the new bookmark links to the current page view displayed in the document window.

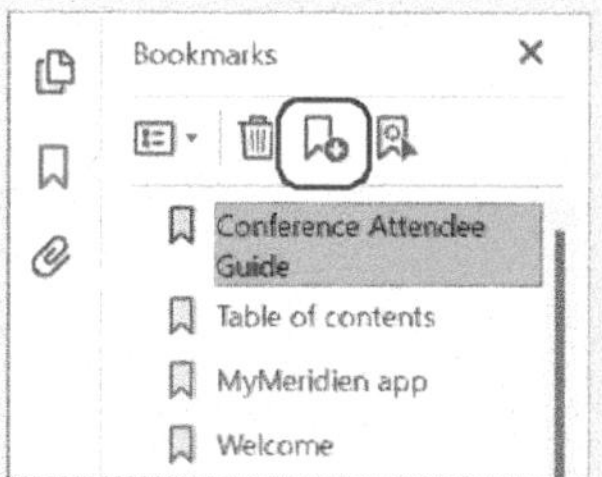

Setting document properties and metadata

You're nearly done with this conference guide. To finish it off, you'll set the initial view, which determines what people see when they first open the file, and add metadata to the document.

1 Choose File > Properties.

2 In the Document Properties dialog box, click the Initial View tab.

3 From the Navigation Tab menu, choose Bookmarks Panel And Page.

When the viewer opens the file, both the page and the bookmarks will be visible.

4 In the Window Options area, choose Document Title from the Show menu.

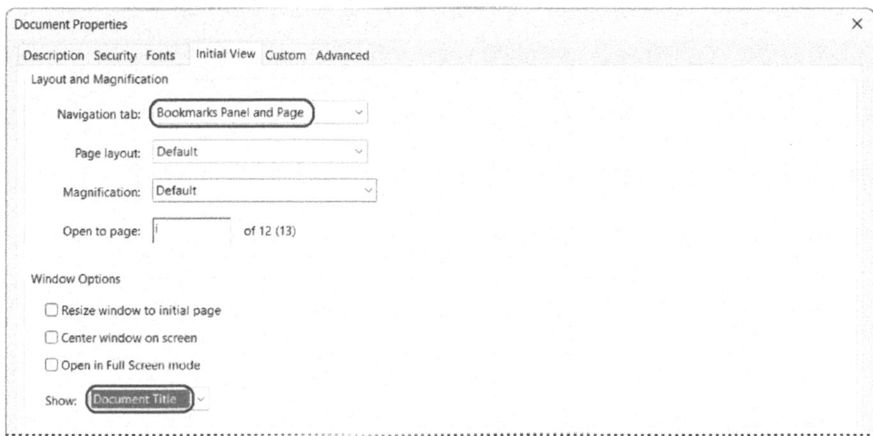

With this option selected, the document title, rather than the filename, will appear in the document's title bar.

5 Select the Description tab.

The document's author has already entered some metadata for the file, including some keywords. Metadata is information about the document itself, and you can use it to search for documents. You'll add some more keywords.

6 In the Keywords field, after the existing keywords, type **; map; vendors**. Keywords must be separated by commas or semicolons.

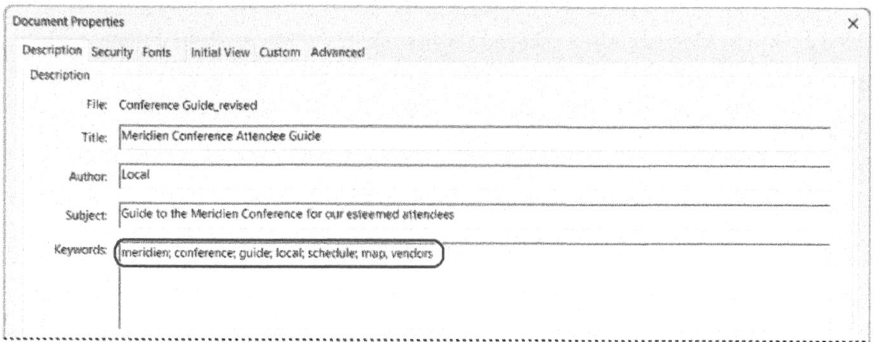

7 Click OK to accept changes in the Document Properties dialog box. Notice that the document title is displayed now, instead of the filename.

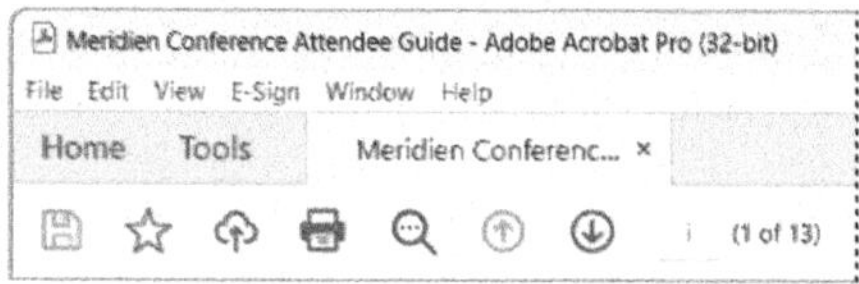

8 Choose File > Save to save your work, and then close all open files and quit Acrobat.

Setting up presentations

Generally, when you make a presentation to a group of people, you want the document to take over the entire screen, hiding distractions such as the menu bar, toolbars, and other window controls.

You can set up any PDF file to display in Full Screen mode in the Initial View tab of the Document Properties dialog box. In the Full Screen tab of the Preferences dialog box, you can set a variety of transition effects to play as you move between pages. You can even set the speed at which pages advance. You can also convert presentations that you've prepared in other programs, such as PowerPoint, to Adobe PDF, preserving many of the authoring program's special effects. For more information, see Adobe Acrobat Help.

Review questions

1 How can you change the order of pages in a PDF document?

2 How do you insert an entire PDF file into another PDF file?

3 How can you correct a link's destination?

4 What is a bookmark?

Review answers

1 You can change the page order by dragging the page thumbnails corresponding to the pages you want to move to their new locations in the Page Thumbnails panel.

2 To insert all the pages from a PDF file before or after any page in another PDF file, select the Organize Pages tool, choose Insert > From File, and then select the file you want to insert. Specify where in the document the pages should be inserted.

3 To correct a link's destination, select the Edit PDF tool, and then choose Link > Add/Edit Web Or Document Link. Next, double-click the incorrect link. Then click the Actions tab in the Link Properties dialog box, click Edit, and type the correct page number in the Page box in the Go To A Page In This Document dialog box. Click OK to close each dialog box.

4 A bookmark is simply a link represented by text in the Bookmarks panel.

5 EDITING CONTENT IN PDF FILES

Lesson overview

In this lesson, you'll do the following:

- Edit text in a PDF document.
- Add text to a PDF file.
- Add and replace images in a PDF file.
- Edit images in a PDF document.
- Copy text and images from a PDF document.
- Export PDF content to a Word, Excel, or PowerPoint document.
- Learn about redacting content.

This lesson will take approximately an hour to complete. Download the project files for this lesson, following the instructions in the Getting Started section under "Accessing the lesson files and Web Edition," if you haven't already done so. As you work on this lesson, you'll preserve the start files. If you need to restore the start files, download them from your Account page.

With Acrobat, you can edit text and other PDF content smoothly and easily. You can also repurpose text, data, and images by copying or exporting content to another application.

Editing text

▶ **Tip:** As you can see, it's easy to make changes to a PDF document. If you want to ensure that your PDF file remains as you intended, apply security settings. For more on security, see Lesson 9, "Adding Signatures and Security."

In Acrobat, you can easily make simple and not-so-simple edits to text in PDF documents, as long as security settings permit it. Whether you're correcting typos, adding punctuation, or restructuring entire paragraphs, Acrobat reflows the text appropriately. You can even use the find-and-replace feature to correct or update multiple instances of a word or phrase in the PDF file. In addition to changes to content, you can edit text attributes such as spacing, point size, and color. If you attempt to change text in a font that is not available on your system, Acrobat prompts you to select a substitute font, and then remembers the substitution later.

Editing a single text block

You'll start by deleting unnecessary text in a document, and then you'll edit a paragraph to make it parallel with other bullet points.

1 Start Acrobat, and choose File > Open. Navigate to the Lesson05/Assets folder, and double-click the Globalcorp_facilities.pdf file.

The Globalcorp_facilities.pdf file is an 18-page document that describes the responsibilities of a department at a fictitious company.

2 Go to page 3 in the document.

The document includes several sections, each with a headline such as "Office Services." Only page 3 includes a subhead ("Things to consider"). You'll delete the text so that it's consistent with the other section pages.

3 Click Edit PDF in the Tools pane.

● **Note:** Acrobat automatically enables Touch Mode when it senses a touch screen on the device you're using.

By default, when you open the Edit PDF tool, Edit is selected in the Edit PDF toolbar, so bounding boxes appear around text blocks and images that are editable. If Acrobat is in Touch Mode, an additional handle appears at the top.

4 Click the "Things to consider" bounding box to select it, and then press the Delete key to remove it. (If you click inside the bounding box, you'll delete individual characters instead of the entire box and its contents.)

5 Go to page 11, which includes bullet points about furniture.

You'll change the second bullet point to start with a verb, making it parallel with all the other bullet points in the document.

6 Select "Purchases of new furniture need prior approval by."

7 Type **Obtain approval from**.

8 Click an insertion point after "Corporate," and type **before purchasing furniture.**

Note: If you're unable to select text in a PDF file, the text may be part of an image. You can convert image text to editable text by using the Recognize Text panel. For more information about text recognition, see Lesson 2, "Creating Adobe PDF files."

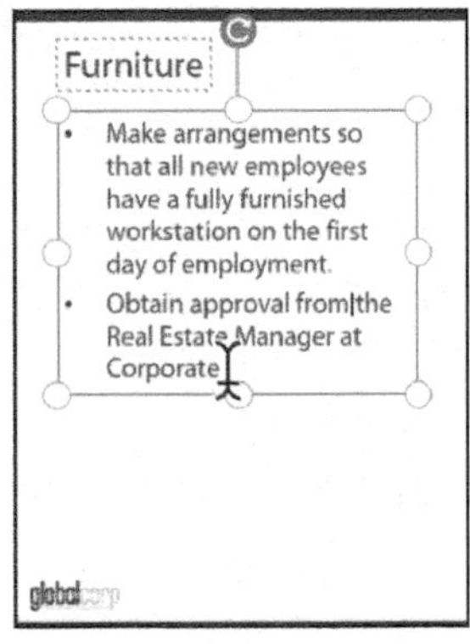

As you delete, replace, or add text, Acrobat reflows the paragraph.

9 Choose File > Save As, and save the file as **Globalcorp_facilities_edited.pdf** in the Lesson05/Finished_Projects folder.

Changing bullet and number list properties

Acrobat recognizes bulleted and numbered lists and provides you with bullet and number options.

1 Click in the text block that includes the bulleted text.

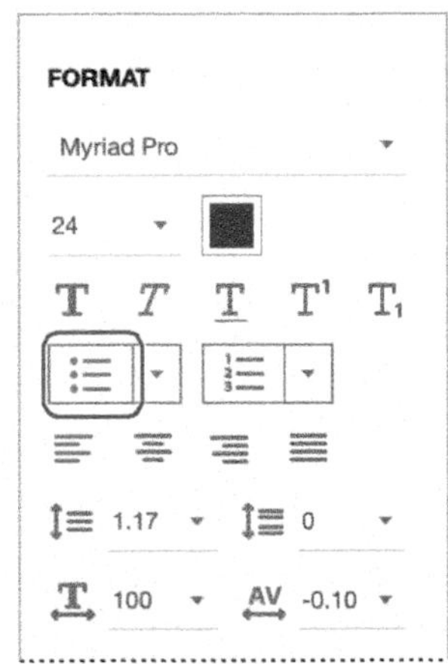

2 Choose the 1.2.3. option from the number list menu in the right-hand pane.

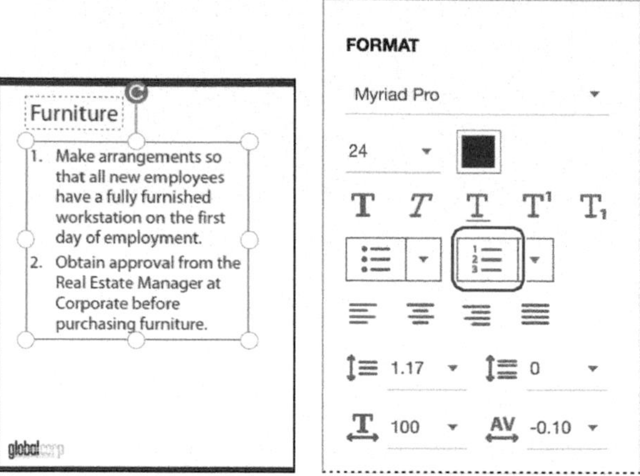

The bulleted list becomes a numbered list, but these items shouldn't be numbered.

3 Select the check mark option from the bullet menu in the right-hand pane.

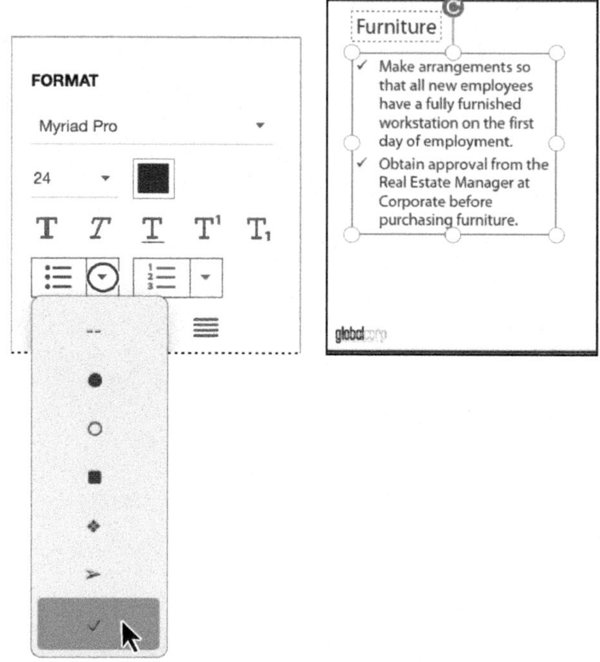

Both bullets become check marks.

Replacing multiple occurrences of text

Acrobat includes a find-and-replace feature similar to one you might use in a word processing or page layout application. You'll use it to replace the word "interface" with the word "communicate" throughout the document.

1 Choose Edit > Find.

2 In the Find panel, type **Interface** in the Find box, and then click Replace With to expand the panel.

> **Tip:** The Find feature is not case-sensitive.

3 Type **Communicate** in the Replace With box.

4 Click Next in the Find panel. Acrobat highlights the next occurrence of the word "interface," on page 10.

5 Click Replace in the Find panel to replace the word.

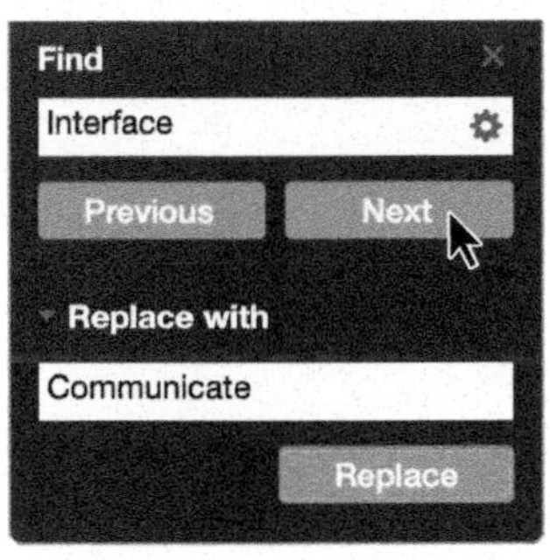

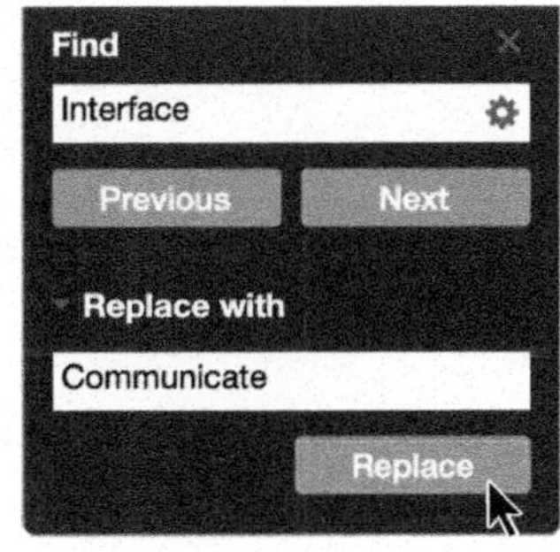

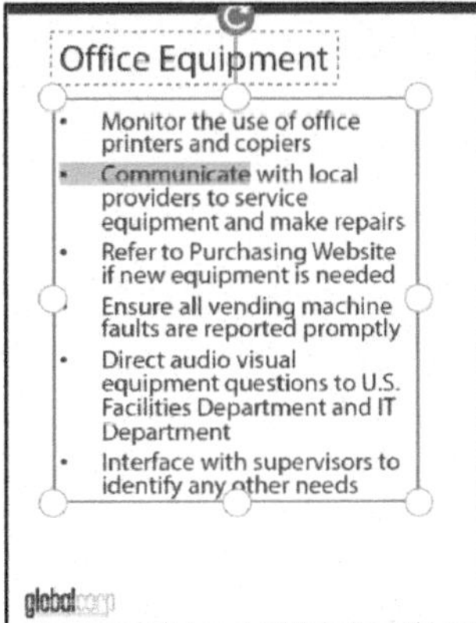

6 Click Next to locate the next occurrence, which is on the same page.

7 Click Replace, and then click Next again. Acrobat finds no instances of the word "interface."

8 Close the Find panel.

Changing text properties

You can change the font, size, type style, alignment, and other attributes of text without leaving Acrobat.

1 Go to page 2, and select the word "Agenda."

2 In the Format area of the right-hand pane, click the color swatch, and select a new color. We used magenta. In macOS, close the Colors panel.

3 With the word "Agenda" still selected, click the Bold icon in the Format area.

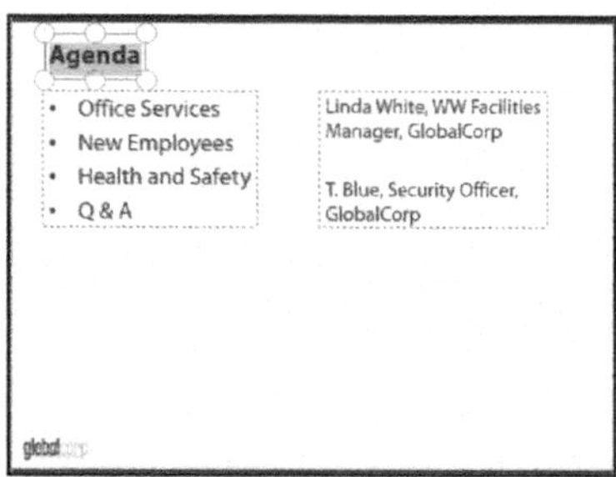

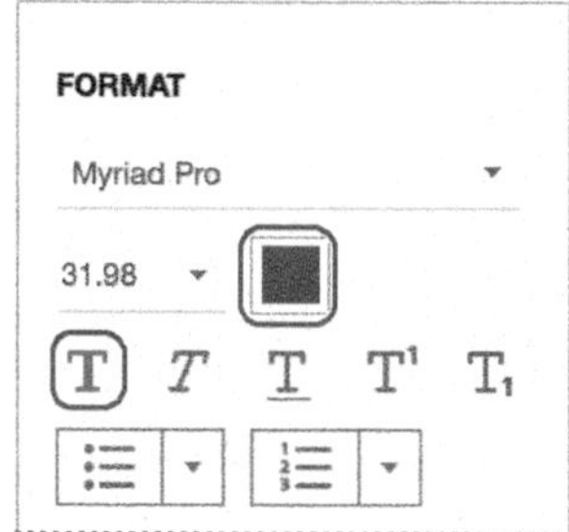

4 Save your changes so far.

Adding text

You can add entirely new text, including new bullet points. You'll add a bullet point to page 11.

1 Go to page 11.

2 Click an insertion point after the period in the second bullet item, and press Enter or Return.

Acrobat creates a new bullet and insertion point indented to match the previous bulleted items.

▶ **Tip:** With the bounding box selected, you can resize items or move them anywhere on the page.

3 Type **Evaluate ergonomic needs and identify solutions.**

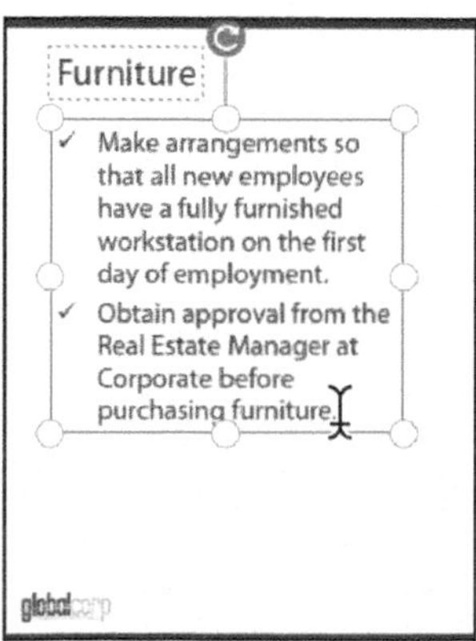

The formatting of the new bullet item matches the previous items.

4 Go to page 18.

You'll add text to this page.

5 Select the bounding box that contains the words "Thank you!," and drag it closer to the top of the blue horizontal stripe.

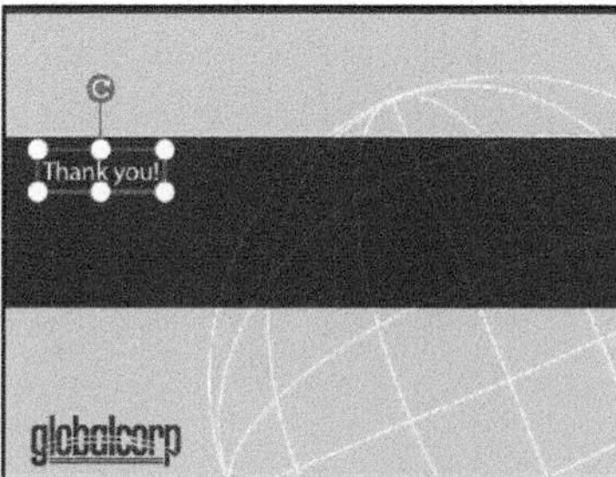

6 Click Add Text in the Edit PDF toolbar.

7 Click a text insertion point directly below the "T" in "Thank you," and type **We look forward to working with you!**

The text appears with the formatting options that are currently selected in the right-hand pane. It matches the existing text on the page.

8 Select the text you just typed, and reduce the font size to 22. If necessary, move the text box to reposition it.

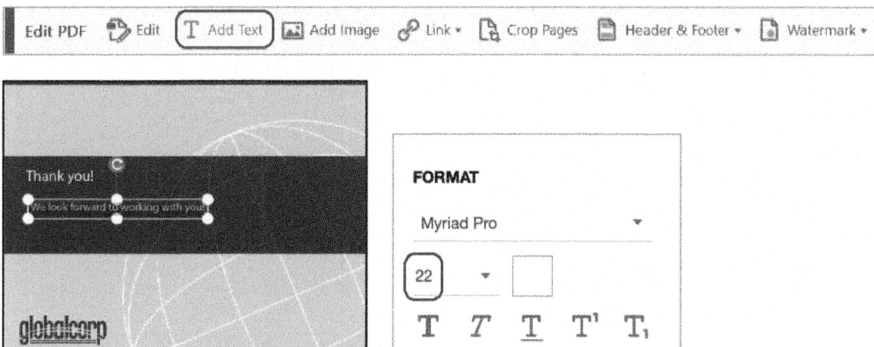

9 Save your work so far.

Redacting text (Acrobat Pro only)

When courts make documents public or companies are required to produce documents that contain potentially confidential or privileged information, such information is often redacted, or hidden. In Acrobat Pro, you can use the Redact tool to automatically search for and permanently remove any privileged information. The Redact tool is in the Protect & Standardize category in the Tools Center.

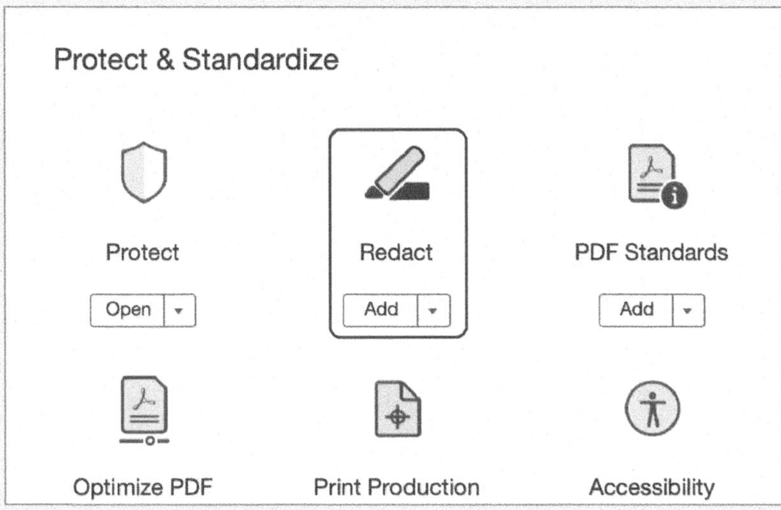

You can search for specific terms, such as names, telephone numbers, or account numbers; you can also search for common patterns. You can redact information using the simple equivalent of a black marker, or add overlay text that identifies the privilege asserted, applicable statutory or code citation, or other basis for the redaction.

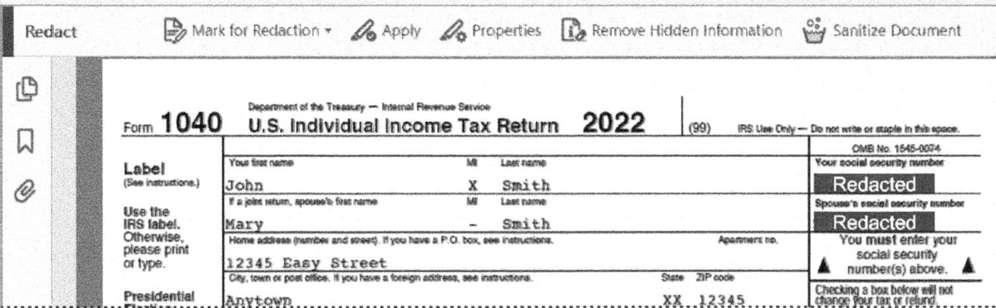

For information about using the Redact tool, see Adobe Acrobat Pro Help.

Working with images in a PDF file

In Acrobat, you can make simple changes to the position or size of an image in a PDF file, add images, or replace images. To make more substantial edits to an image, you can open it in an image-editing application such as Adobe Photoshop, and save it so that Acrobat updates the image in the PDF file.

Replacing images

It's easy to replace an image in a PDF file in Acrobat. You'll replace the image on page 4.

Note: A replacement image may not be the same size as the original image. You may want to adjust the dimensions or aspect ratio of an image before using it in your PDF document.

1 Go to page 4 in the Globalcorp_facilities_edited.pdf file.

2 Select Edit in the Edit PDF toolbar.

3 Right-click (Windows) or Control-click (macOS) the image of the cubicle, and choose Replace Image. Alternatively, you can select the image, and then click the Replace Image icon (![icon]) in the Objects area of the right-hand pane.

4 In the Open dialog box, navigate to the Lesson05/Assets folder, select the New_Reception.jpg file, and click Open.

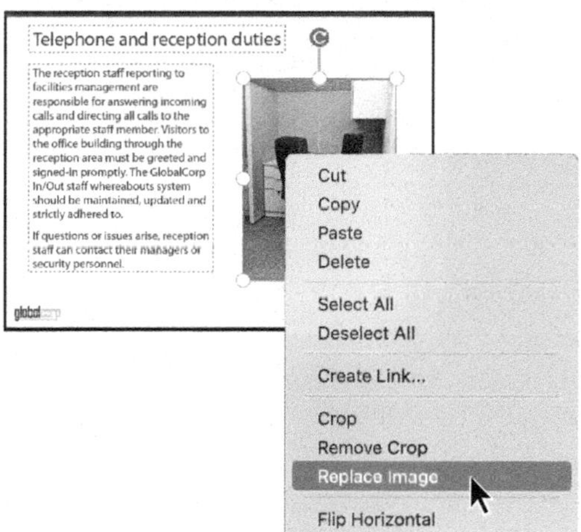

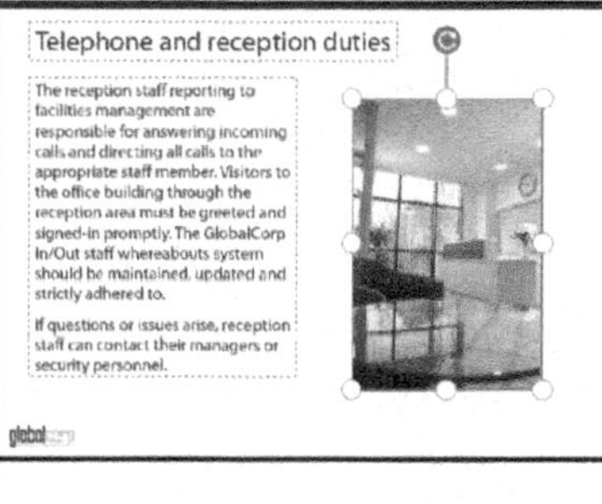

Acrobat replaces the original image with the one you selected.

Adding images

You can also add images to a PDF file. You'll add one to the page that describes mail services.

1 Go to page 5.

2 Select Add Image in the Edit PDF toolbar.

3 In the Open dialog box, navigate to the Lesson05/Assets folder, select the Boxes.jpg file, and click Open.

A thumbnail of the image is attached to the cursor.

4 Click on the right side of the page to place the image. Its upper left corner is aligned with the cursor's position at the time you clicked. You can drag the image to a different position.

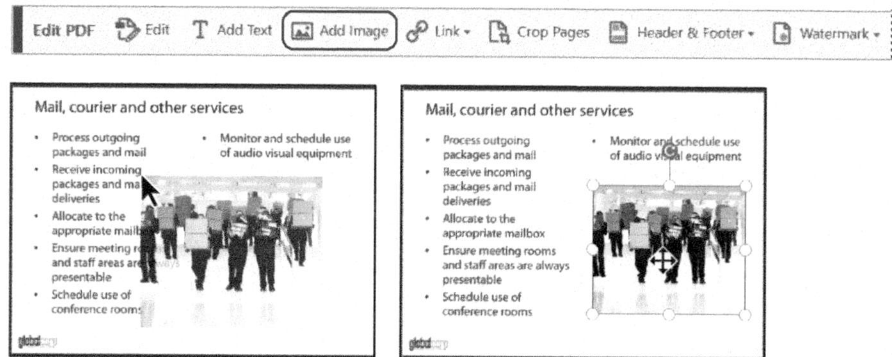

Editing an image in Acrobat

Acrobat is not an image-editing application, but you can make some simple changes to your images without leaving Acrobat. You can rotate, flip, or crop an image in a PDF file.

1 On page 5, select the image of people with boxes.

2 Click the Crop icon (⌗) in the Objects area of the right-hand pane.

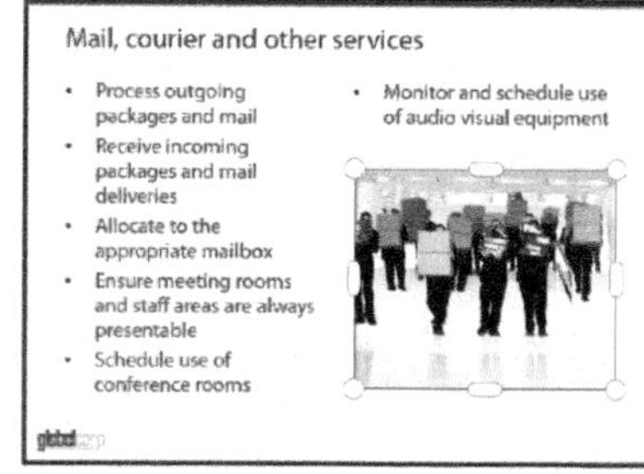

3 Drag the lower right corner up to crop out much of the extra floor and the people to the right of the railing.

4 Drag the upper left corner down to the right, cropping out the people on the far left. The image should clearly focus on the three people in the center now. You can adjust the crop at the top of the image if you want to, or reposition it on either side.

5 Click the Crop icon again to deselect it. If you want to, you can drag the image to reposition it on the page and drag a corner handle to resize it so that it is more aesthetically pleasing.

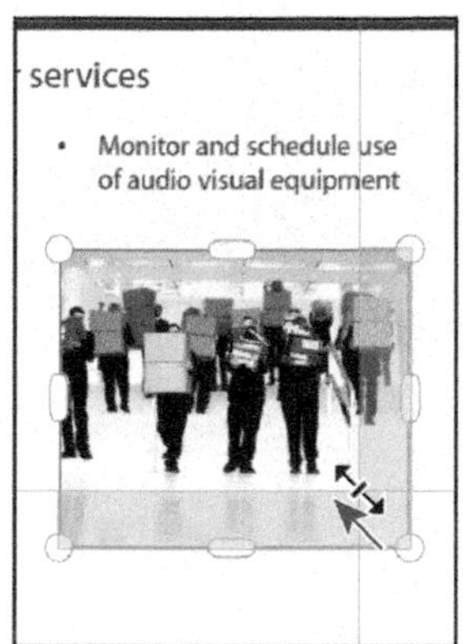

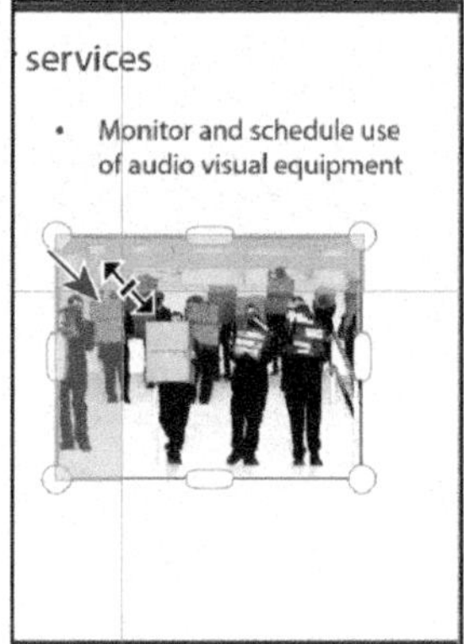

6 Save the PDF file.

Editing an image in another application

If you want to lighten or darken an image, change its resolution, apply filters, or otherwise make substantive edits to it, you can edit it in an image-editing application. In this exercise, you'll make changes to the background image.

1 Select Edit in the Edit PDF toolbar, if it's not already selected.

2 Still on page 5, select the background image for the entire page.

3 Choose an application from the Edit Using menu in the Objects area of the right-hand pane. (Choose Open With to see additional applications.)

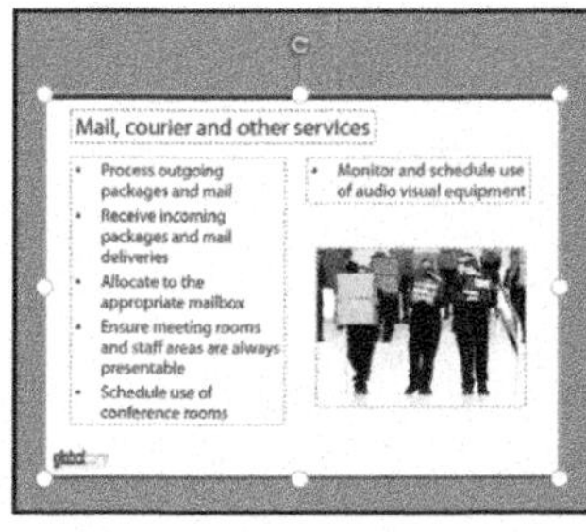

Acrobat lists image-editing applications, such as Adobe Photoshop or Microsoft Paint, that are installed on your system. You may need to browse to find the right application. How extensively you can edit the image depends on the application you open it with.

4 Make changes to the image. For example, you can draw a red box or something equally obvious. Or, you can make a change that fits within the context of the document. Then save or close the image, depending on the application.

5 Return to Acrobat.

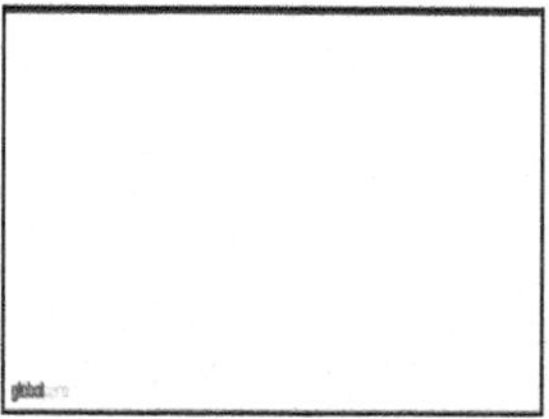

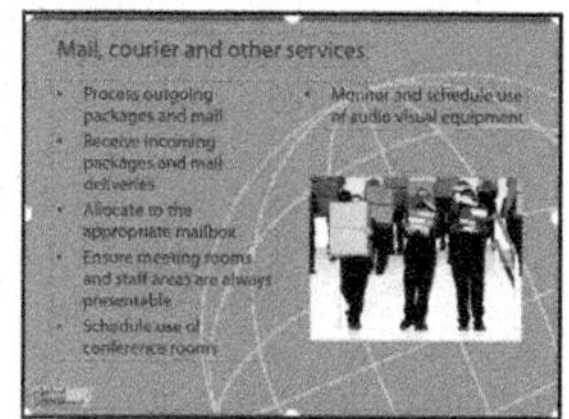

The changes you made appear on the page and will be saved with the PDF file. However, the original image is unchanged.

6 Close the Edit PDF tool and return to Document mode.

Copying text and images from a PDF file

▶ **Tip:** You can change the security settings to prevent people from copying text or images from your PDF file. See Lesson 9, "Adding Signatures and Security."

Even if you no longer have access to the source file for a PDF document, you can reuse the text and images in other applications. For example, you might want to add some of the text or images to a web page. You can copy the text out of the PDF file in rich text format (RTF) or as accessible text so you can import it into a different authoring application for reuse. You can save images from the file in JPEG, TIFF, or PNG format.

If you want to reuse only small amounts of text or one or two images, copy them to the clipboard or to an image format file using the Selection tool. (If the Copy, Cut, and Paste commands are unavailable, the creator of the PDF file may have set restrictions on editing the content of the document.)

You'll copy the text from a page in the facilities document for reuse.

1 Go to page 17.

2 Select the Selection tool (↖) in the toolbar.

3 Move the pointer over the text on the page. Notice that the pointer changes to an I-beam when it is in text-selection mode.

4 Drag the Selection tool across all the text on the page.

5 Right-click or Control-click the text, and choose Copy With Formatting, which preserves the layout.

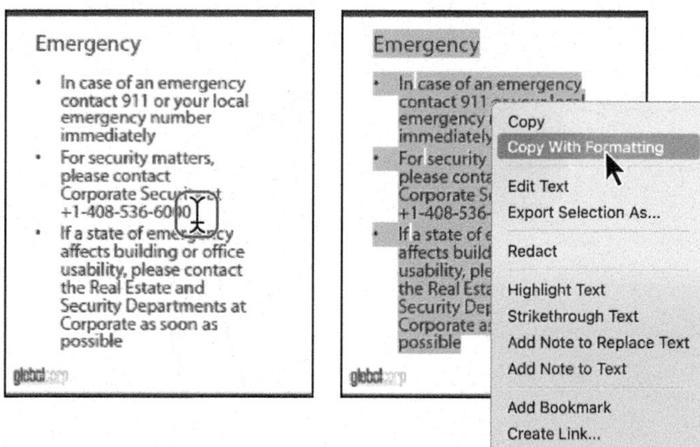

6 Minimize the Acrobat window, open a new or existing document in an authoring application such as a text editor or Microsoft Word, and then choose Edit > Paste.

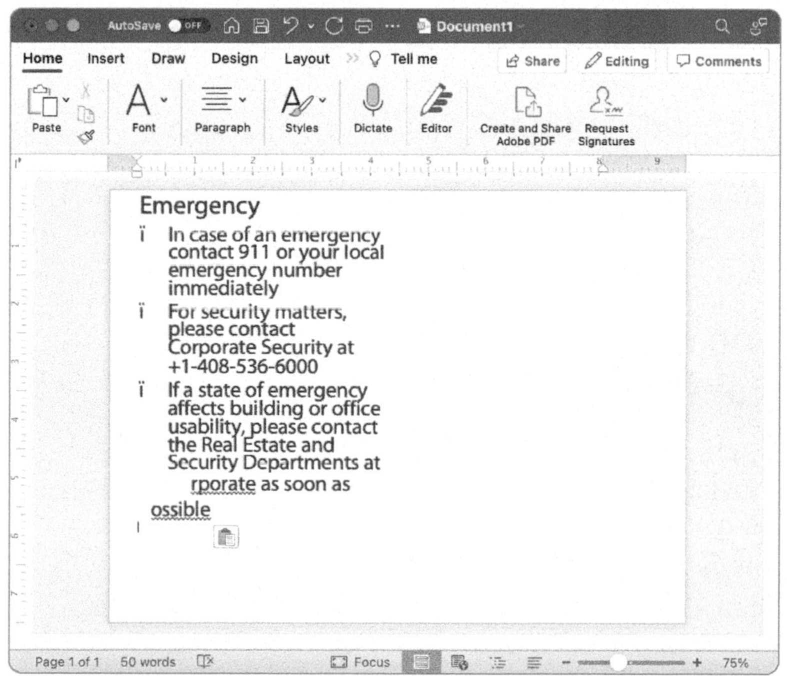

Your text is copied into the document in your authoring application. Acrobat attempts to retain most of the formatting from the PDF file. But as you can see here, in most cases, you'll need to edit and format the text at least a little bit. If a font copied from a PDF document is not available on the system displaying the copied text, Acrobat substitutes the font.

Note: Make sure you closed the Edit PDF tool. If you select text with the Edit option selected, you'll see different options in the context menu.

Tip: You can also copy text and images from all or part of a page using the Snapshot feature. Choose Edit > More > Take A Snapshot, select the area you want to copy, click OK to close the message box, and then paste the image into another application. The resulting image is in bitmap format; any text copied this way is not editable.

You can save individual images for use in another application.

7 Go to page 4 in the document, and select the image.

8 Right-click (Windows) or Control-click (macOS) the image, and choose Save Image As.

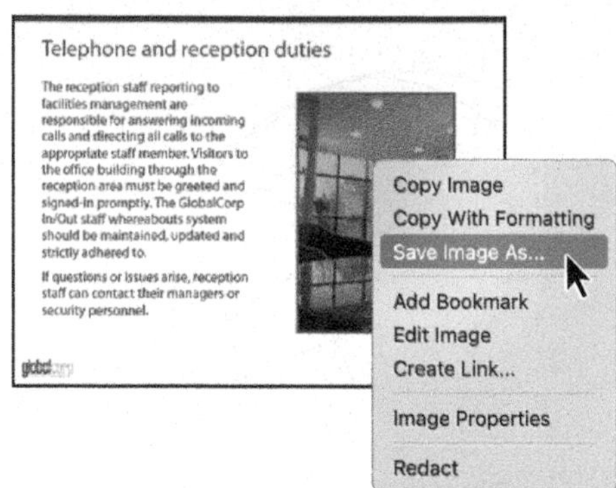

9 In the Save Image As dialog box, name the image **Reception Copy**, and choose JPEG Image Files from the Save As Type (Windows) or Format (macOS) menu. Save the file in the Lesson05/Finished_Projects folder.

10 Close any open documents in other applications, but leave the Globalcorp_facilities_edited.pdf file open in Acrobat.

You've copied text from a PDF document, and you've saved an image for reuse. You can also select both images and text, copy them, and paste them into another application.

Exporting PDF content to a PowerPoint presentation

In Acrobat, you can export a PDF file as a Microsoft PowerPoint presentation. Each page of the PDF document becomes a fully editable slide in PowerPoint, retaining formatting and layout as much as possible.

You can specify whether to include comments and whether to run OCR to recognize text when you save as a PowerPoint presentation. To change the settings, choose Edit > Preferences (Windows) or Acrobat > Preferences (macOS), select Convert From PDF from the list on the left, select PowerPoint Presentation from the Converting From PDF list, and then click Edit Settings.

You'll export the facilities document to a PowerPoint presentation.

1 With the Globalcorp_facilities_edited.pdf file open, open the Tools Center, and click Export PDF.

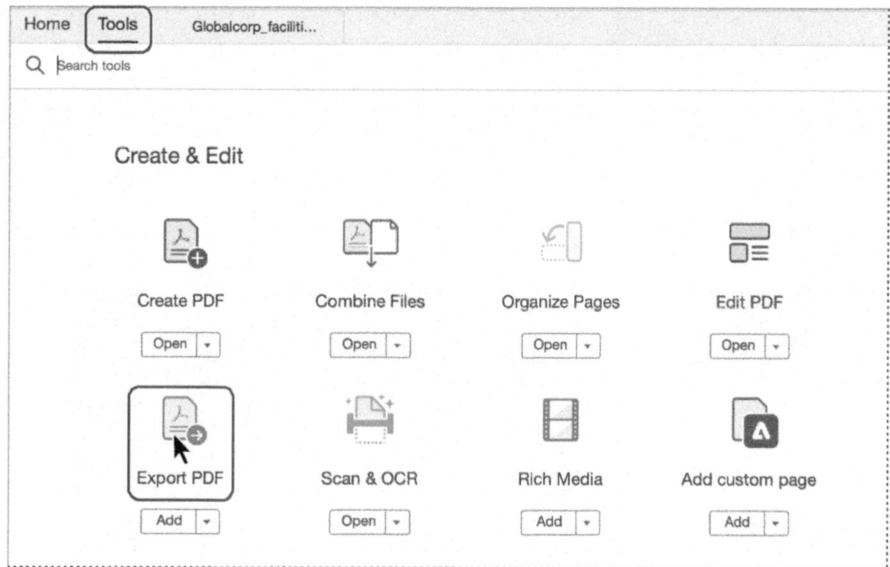

2 Select Microsoft PowerPoint for the format, and then click Export.

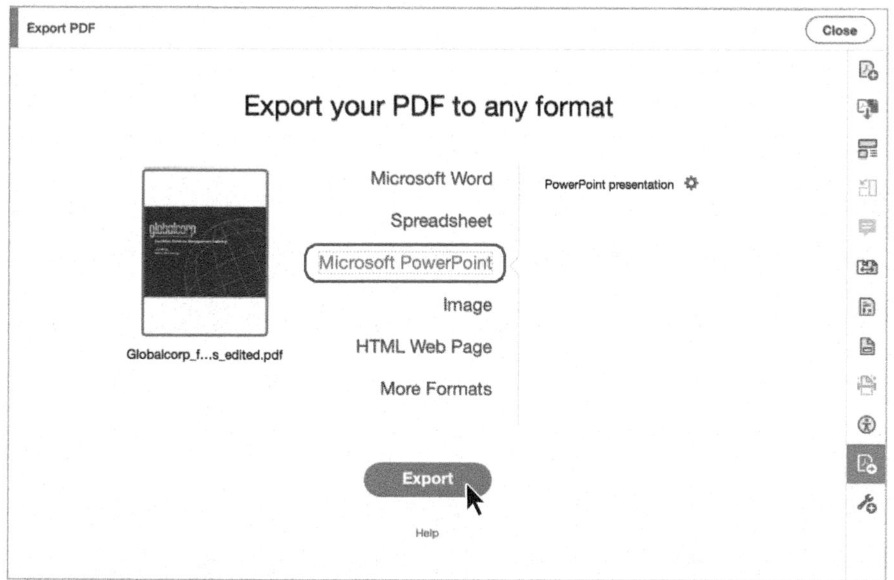

Tip: If you have an Acrobat or Creative Cloud subscription, you can export PDF files to Word, PowerPoint, or Excel on a tablet or phone using the Acrobat mobile app. To learn more, see Lesson 6, "Using Acrobat on Mobile Devices."

3 In the Save As dialog box, select the Lesson05/Finished_Projects folder.

4 Click Save in the Save As dialog box.

5 Preview the presentation in PowerPoint, if it's installed. If you do not have PowerPoint installed, you may be able to preview the presentation using the Preview application or Keynote in macOS.

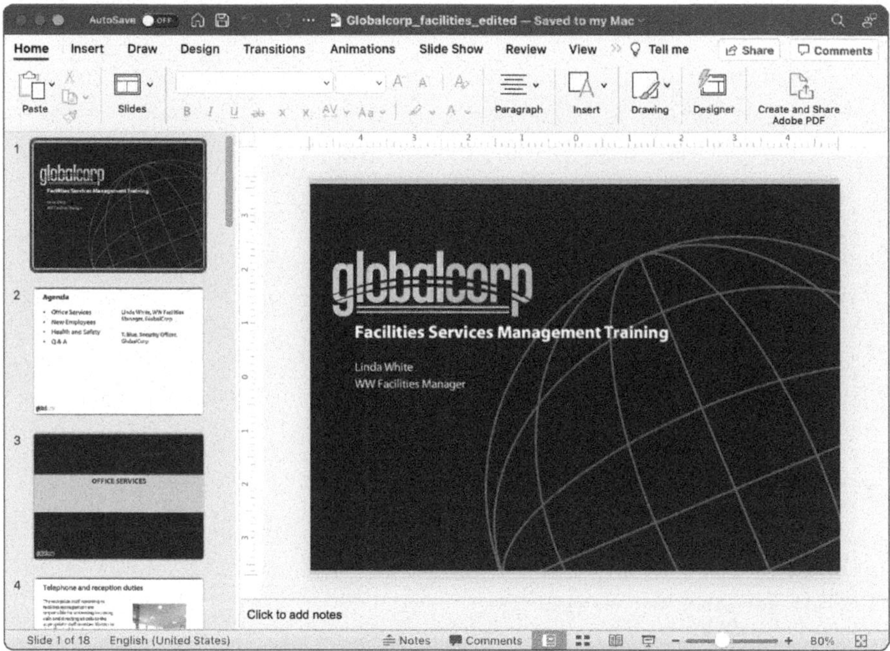

Some text and images may have shifted. When you export a PDF file to a PowerPoint presentation, evaluate each slide carefully, and make any necessary adjustments in PowerPoint.

6 Close the Globalcorp_facilities_edited.pdf file and PowerPoint or any other applications that are open. Leave Acrobat open.

Saving PDF files as Word documents

You can save PDF files as Word documents (either .docx or .doc files), no matter what application the document originated in. You'll save a statement of work for a fictitious company as a Word document.

▶ **Tip:** You can save PDF files as PowerPoint presentations, Word documents, or Excel spreadsheets from Acrobat by choosing an option in the Export PDF tool, choosing File > Export To > [format], or choosing an option from the Save As Type or Format menu in the Save As PDF dialog box.

1 In Acrobat, choose File > Open. Navigate to the Lesson05/Assets folder, and select the Statement_of_Work.pdf file. Click Open.

2 Choose File > Export To > Microsoft Word > Word Document. (If you're using Word 2003 or earlier, choose Word 97-2003 Document, which saves a .doc file.)

3 In the Save As dialog box, change the file destination to the Lesson05/Finished_Projects folder. Then click Settings.

4 In the Save As DOC Settings or Save As DOCX Settings dialog box, select Retain Page Layout. Make sure the other options are all selected. Then click OK.

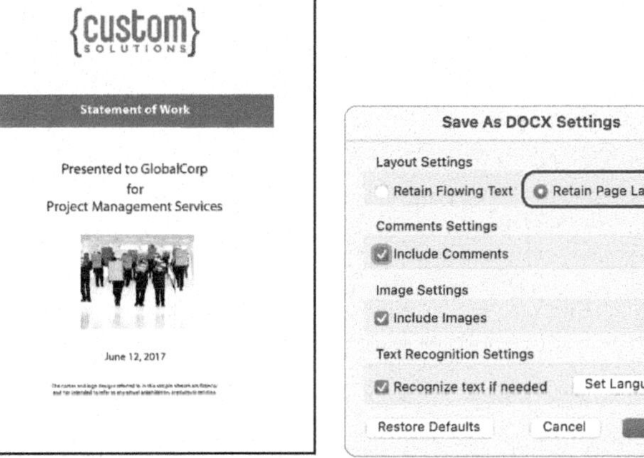

5 Click Save to save the file.

Acrobat displays the status of the conversion process as it works. When you save complex PDF documents, the conversion to Word may take longer. If View Result was selected in the Save As PDF dialog box, the document automatically opens in Word or a similar application.

6 Open the Statement_of_Work.doc or Statement_of_Work.docx file in Word, if it's not already open. You may also be able to open the document in Preview or Pages in macOS, or in another application that can open .doc or .docx files.

7 Scroll through the document to confirm that the text and images have been saved appropriately.

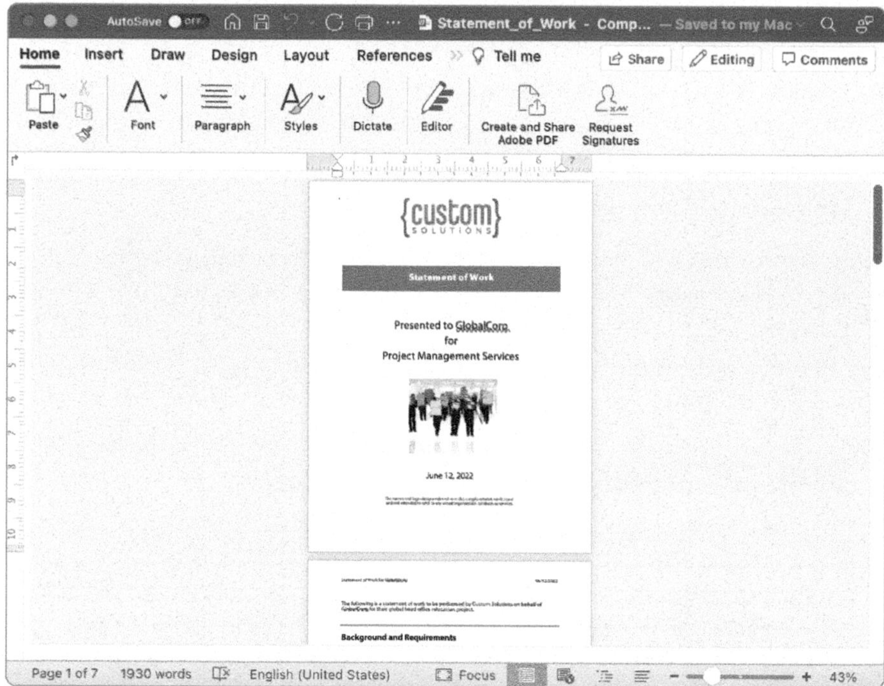

In most cases, Acrobat saves PDF files as Word documents with impressive integrity. However, depending on the way the document was created, you may need to adjust spacing or make minor corrections. Always carefully review a document in Word after you've saved it from Acrobat.

8 Close the PDF file in Acrobat, and then quit Word or any other applications.

Extracting PDF tables as Excel spreadsheets

You can export an entire PDF file or selected tables as Excel worksheets. You'll export a list of restaurants from a PDF document to a new Excel file.

1 In Acrobat, choose File > Open. Navigate to the Lesson05/Assets folder, and select Venues.pdf. Click Open.

The PDF document includes a table of restaurants in the fictitious city of Meridien. You'll export that table to an Excel file.

2 Drag from the upper left corner of the table to the lower right corner, so that the entire table is selected.

3 Right-click or Control-click the selected table, and choose Export Selection As.

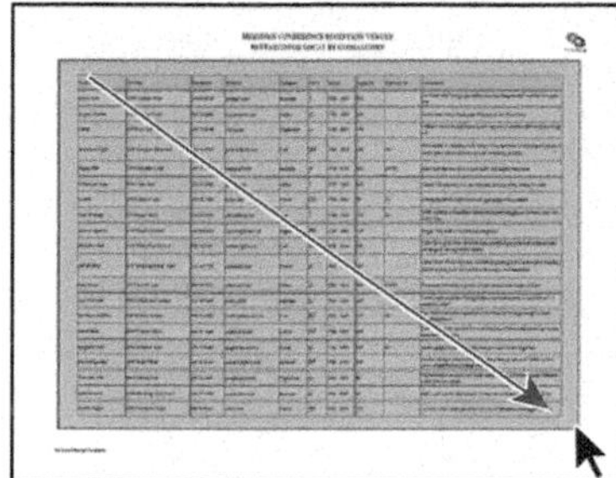

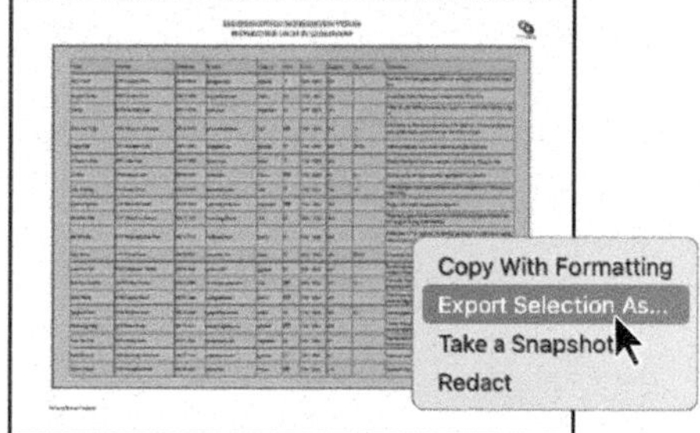

4 In the Export Selection As dialog box, choose Excel Workbook from the Save As Type or Format menu. Name the file **Venues.xlsx**, and save it in the Lesson05/Finished_Projects folder. Then click Save.

Acrobat reports its progress. If View Result was selected in the Export Selection As dialog box, your new spreadsheet opens in Excel or another application automatically.

5 Open the Venues.xlsx file, if it isn't already open. You may also be able to open the file in Preview in macOS or in other applications that can open Excel documents.

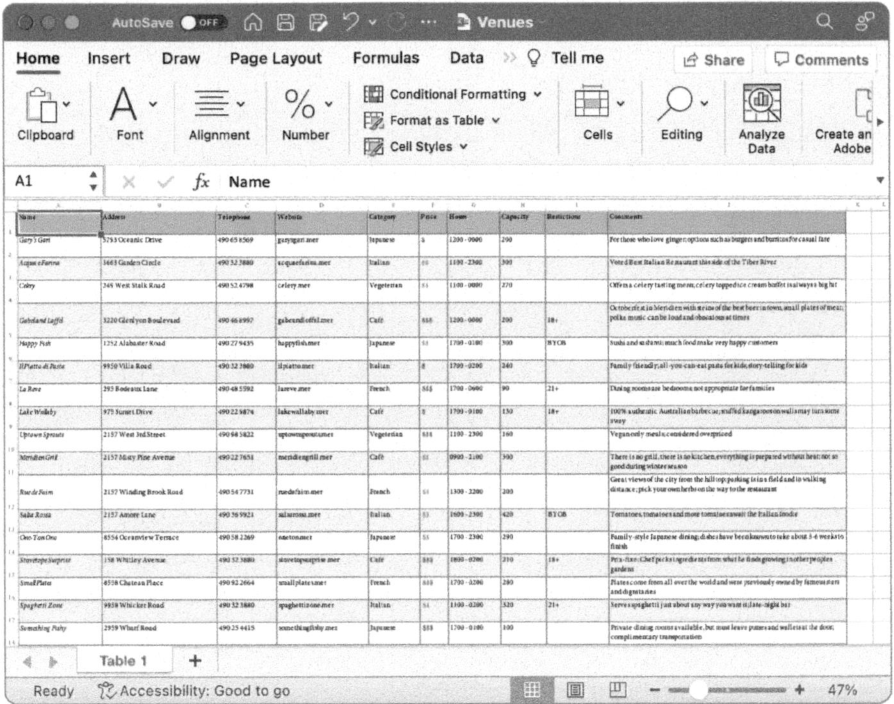

Name	Address	Telephone	Website	Category	Price	Hours	Capacity	Restrictions	Comments
Gary's Gari	5753 Oceanic Drive	490 65 8569	garysgari.met	Japanese	$	1200 - 0000	290		For those who love ginger; options such as burgers and burritos for casual fare
Acqua e Farina	3663 Garden Circle	490 32 3880	acquaefarina.met	Italian	$$	1100 - 2300	300		Voted Best Italian Restaurant this side of the Tiber River
Celery	245 West Stalk Road	490 52 4798	celery.met	Vegetarian	$$	1100 - 0000	270		Offers a celery tasting menu; celery topped ice cream buffet is always a big hit
Gabeland Laffel	3220 Glenlyon Boulevard	490 46 8997	gabeundloffel.met	Café	$$$	1200 - 0000	200	18+	Octoberfest in Meridien with steins of the best beer in town; small plates of meat; polka music can be loud and obnoxious at times
Happy Fish	1252 Alabaster Road	490 27 9435	happyfish.met	Japanese	$$	1700 - 0100	300	BYOB	Sushi and sashimi; much food make very happy customers
Il Piatto di Pasta	9950 Villa Road	490 32 3880	ilpiatto.met	Italian	$	1700 - 0200	240		Family friendly; all-you-can-eat pasta for kids; story-telling for kids
La Reve	295 Bodeaux Lane	490 48 5592	lareve.met	French	$$$	1700 - 0600	90	21+	Dining rooms are bedrooms; not appropriate for families
Lake Wallaby	975 Sunset Drive	490 22 9874	lakewallaby.met	Café	$	1700 - 0100	130	18+	100% authentic Australian barbecue; stuffed kangaroos on walls may turn some away
Uptown Sprouts	2157 West 3rd Street	490 98 5822	uptownsprouts.met	Vegetarian	$$$	1100 - 2300	160		Vegan only meals; considered overpriced
Meridien Grill	2157 Misty Pine Avenue	490 22 7651	meridiengrill.met	Café	$$	0900 - 2100	300		There is no grill, there is no kitchen, everything is prepared without heat; not so good during winter season
Rue de Faim	2157 Winding Brook Road	490 54 7731	ruedefaim.met	French	$$	1300 - 2200	200		Great views of the city from the hilltop; parking is in a field and in walking distance; pick your own herbs on the way to the restaurant
Salsa Rossa	2157 Amore Lane	490 36 9921	salsarossa.met	Italian	$$	1600 - 2300	420	BYOB	Tomatoes, tomatoes and more tomatoes await the Italian foodie
[illegible]	8554 Oceanview Terrace	490 58 2269	[illegible]	Japanese	$$	1700 - 2300	290		Family-style Japanese dining; dishes have been known to take about 3-6 weeks to finish
Stovetop Surprise	158 Whitley Avenue	490 52 3880	stovetopsurprise.met	Café	$$$	1800 - 0200	210	18+	Prix-fixe; Chef picks ingredients from what he finds growing in other peoples gardens
Small Plates	8558 Chateau Place	490 92 2664	smallplates.met	French	$$$	1700 - 0200	280		Plates come from all over the world and were previously owned by famous stars and dignitaries
Spaghetti Zone	9958 Whicker Road	490 32 3880	spaghettizone.met	Italian	$$	1100 - 0200	320	21+	Serves spaghetti just about any way you want it; late-night bar
Something Fishy	2959 Wharf Road	490 25 4415	somethingfishy.met	Japanese	$$$	1700 - 0100	100		Private dining rooms available, but must leave purses and wallets at the door; complimentary transportation

Acrobat appropriately converted the fields in the table.

6 Close any open documents, Acrobat, and other applications.

Review questions

1 How do you edit text in a PDF file?

2 How can you prevent others from editing or reusing content in a PDF file?

3 What kinds of edits can you make to an image in Acrobat?

4 How can you export a PDF file to Microsoft Word, Microsoft Excel, or Microsoft PowerPoint format?

5 How do you copy text from a PDF file?

Review answers

1 To edit text in a PDF file, select Edit PDF in the Tools pane, make sure Edit is selected in the Edit PDF toolbar, and then make your edits. Acrobat reflows the text as you change it.

2 To prevent others from editing or reusing the content of your PDF file, apply security to the document.

3 You can rotate, flip, crop, resize, or replace an image in Acrobat.

4 To export a PDF file to Word, Excel, or PowerPoint format, do one of the following:

- Choose an option from the Export PDF tool.
- Choose File > Export To > [format].
- Choose an option from the Save As Type or Format menu in the Save As PDF dialog box.

5 If you're copying a couple of words or sentences, right-click or Control-click the selected text, and choose Copy With Formatting to retain the formatting when you paste the text.

6 USING ACROBAT ON MOBILE DEVICES

Lesson overview

In this lesson, you'll do the following:

- Learn how to access and download Acrobat apps.
- Comment on PDF files in the Acrobat Reader app.
- Work with PDF files in Adobe's cloud storage.
- Edit PDF files in the Acrobat Reader app.
- Use the Fill & Sign app to complete a form on a mobile device.
- Use the Adobe Scan app to scan a document.

This lesson will take approximately 45 minutes to complete. Download the project files for this lesson, following the instructions in the Getting Started section under "Accessing the lesson files and Web Edition," if you haven't already done so. As you work on this lesson, you'll preserve the start files. If you need to restore the start files, download them from your Account page.

Celebrate the harvest!

People Feeding People produced a bumper crop this year — and not just vegetables. We fed more hungry families, educated more youth about nutrition, trained more gardeners, and hosted more community dinners than ever before.

And it's all because of supporters like you.

Join us to celebrate all that we've accomplished and to look forward to the year ahead.

People Feeding People's
Annual Harvest Celebration
Saturday, October 19
Little Red Schoolhouse
1414 Main Street

Many of the tools you use to work with PDF files in Acrobat on the desktop are also available on the web and in the Acrobat mobile apps, so you can keep working wherever you are.

About the Acrobat mobile apps

The Adobe Acrobat mobile apps let you work on PDF files from anywhere. Many of the features of Acrobat for desktop are available when you access Acrobat on a web browser or use the Adobe Acrobat Reader app, the Adobe Fill & Sign app, or the Adobe Sign app. The Adobe Scan app extends the power of Acrobat so that you can scan a document using the camera on your mobile device.

The user interfaces on the apps are slightly different in iOS and Android.

Adobe Acrobat online - You can use Acrobat online to work with your documents from any computer or device that has Internet access. To access Acrobat in a browser, visit acrobat.adobe.com, and then sign in with your Adobe ID.

Adobe Acrobat Reader app - The free Acrobat Reader app lets you view, organize, export, print, and comment on PDF files on mobile devices. You can also use the app to edit PDF files if you have an Acrobat subscription.

Adobe Fill & Sign app - You can use the Fill & Sign app on a mobile device just as you use the Fill & Sign tool in Acrobat. Open or take a picture of a form, complete it, sign it, and then submit it.

Adobe Acrobat Sign app - This straightforward but powerful app lets you send documents for electronic signature through the Adobe Acrobat Sign service, sign documents yourself, and track documents. You can also set up a form to get a signature in person.

Adobe Scan app - Your mobile phone or tablet becomes your scanner, instantly converting physical documents into PDF files. You can crop or rotate the document in Adobe Scan, or make other changes in Acrobat Reader or Acrobat.

Download any of the apps from the App Store (iOS) or Google Play (Android). The apps are all free; to take full advantage of the features available with your Acrobat or Creative Cloud subscription, sign in using your Adobe ID.

Getting Started

In this lesson, you'll work with PDF documents in apps and in your browser. First, you'll upload the documents to Adobe's cloud storage so they're available to you in the apps.

1 Download and install the Adobe Acrobat Reader, Adobe Fill & Sign, and Adobe Scan apps onto your mobile device(s) if you haven't already. You can access the apps in the App Store (iOS) or Play Store (Android).

2 In Acrobat, choose File > Open, and navigate to the Lesson06/Assets folder.

3 Shift-select Postcard.pdf and Tickets.pdf, and click Open.

4 With Postcard.pdf active, choose File > Save As, and navigate to the Lesson06/Finished_Projects folder. Name the file **Postcard_final.pdf**, and click Save.

5 Click the Save To Adobe's Cloud Storage button in the toolbar.

6 Select the Tickets.pdf tab to make the PDF file active.

7 Choose File > Save As, navigate to the Lesson06/Finished_Projects folder, name the file **Tickets_final.pdf**, and click Save.

8 Click the Save To Adobe's Cloud Storage button in the toolbar.

Both PDF documents are now available on Adobe's cloud storage, so you can open and work with them on any device using a web browser or an Acrobat app. The original versions remain untouched in your Lesson06/Assets folder.

Using the Acrobat Reader app

You'll view the Postcard PDF file, comment on it in the Acrobat Reader app, and make some simple edits to the document as well. Changes you make to the PDF file will be saved to the version stored in Adobe's cloud storage, which is accessible from the other apps, the web, and Acrobat.

You can view, annotate, share, or print PDF files. You can also rotate or delete pages in a document using the Organize Pages tool, combine documents into one PDF document using the Combine Files tool, and convert native documents to PDF using the Create PDF tool, all available in the app on both phones and tablets.

Opening PDF files in the Acrobat Reader app

You can open PDF files that are already stored on your phone or tablet; Adobe's cloud storage; or Dropbox, Google Drive, or other remote accounts. You'll open the Postcard_final PDF file you just saved to the cloud.

1 Open the Acrobat Reader app on a mobile device. You'll have access to a few more features on a tablet, but most are available on a mobile phone.

2 Sign in using your Adobe ID if you're prompted to do so. Click Home if the Home view isn't active.

The Home view opens. It displays your recent files, including files you've recently worked with or saved to cloud storage.

3 Tap Files at the bottom of the screen to see other documents. Then, tap Adobe Cloud Storage.

4 Select Postcard_Final from the list of documents in Adobe cloud storage.

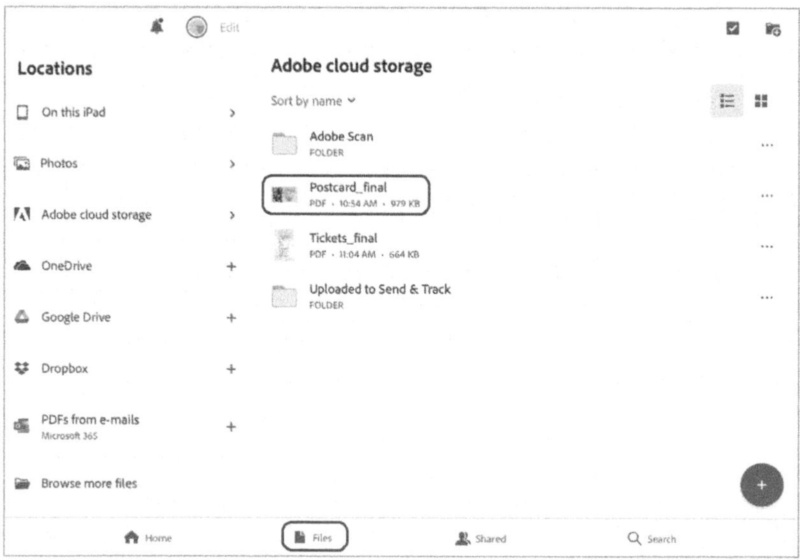

Acrobat Reader displays the postcard.

5 Tap the Liquid View button at the top of the screen if it isn't already enabled.

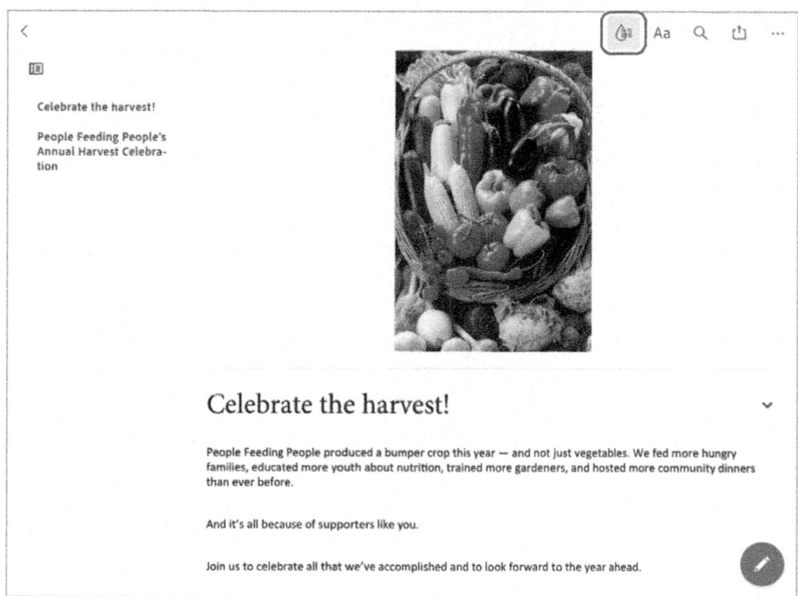

When Liquid View is selected, Acrobat reflows the contents. Liquid view makes it easier to read PDF files on a small screen, but you want to review the PDF document in its intended format, so you won't use Liquid view now.

6 Tap the Liquid View button to disable it. Acrobat Reader displays both pages of the postcard.

7 Tap the View Settings button at the top of the screen, and choose Single Page (iOS) or Page-By-Page (Android).

A single page of the document appears.

8 Turn the device sideways, if it isn't already, so you can see the wide postcard. Tap the PDF file to display it without menus.

9 Swipe to the left to see the back of the postcard (the second page).

10 Tap the PDF file to display the menus again, and then tap the View Settings button, and select Continuous (iOS) or Continuous Pages (Android).

You'll be commenting on the file in the next exercise, and it's easier to highlight or select text in Continuous Pages view.

Commenting on PDF files in Acrobat Reader

You can add notations to any PDF file. You'll add a comment to this draft of the postcard. Changes you make to the document are saved to the version in the cloud immediately.

1 Tap the Edit button in the lower right corner, and choose Comment.

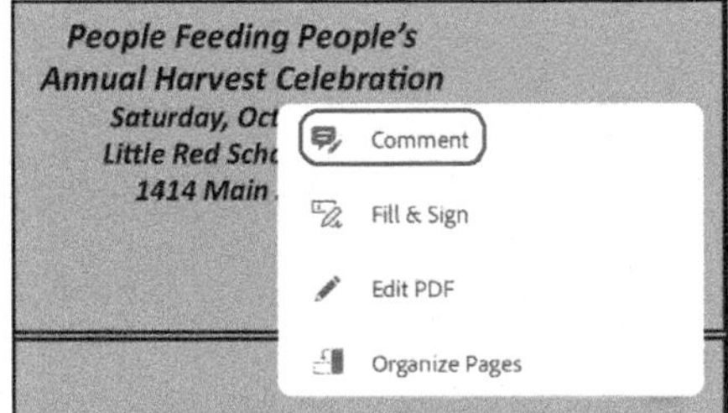

2 Tap the Sticky Note tool, and then click near the end of the text on the second page, and type **Where can they get tix?** Click Post or the right arrow to apply the note.

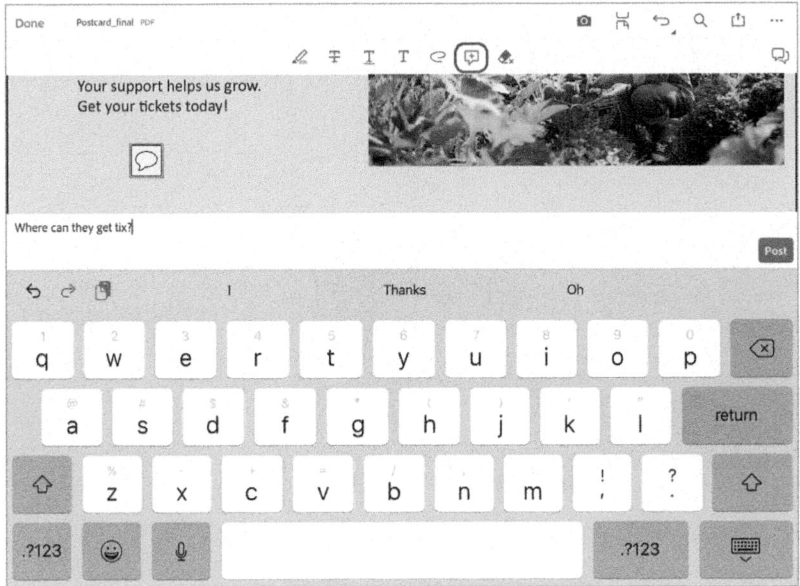

3 If prompted, enter your name to identify your comments, and click Save.

4 Tap the Highlight tool, and then tap, hold, and drag your finger over some text to highlight it.

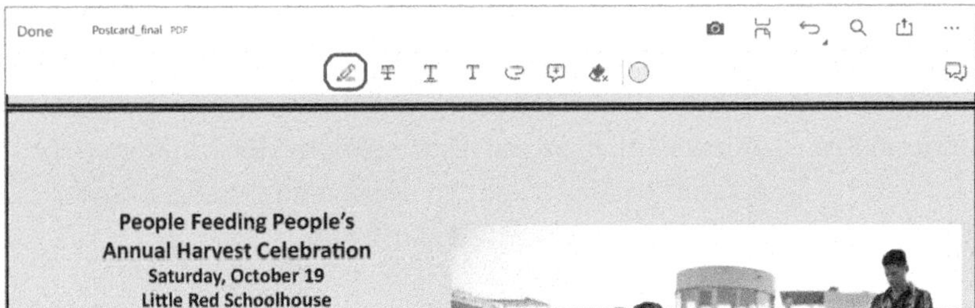

You can add sticky notes, highlight text, strike through or underline text, add text, and draw on the page. To add comments to highlights and other notations, tap the notation, and type a comment.

Depending on your device, tap the Comments button on the right side of the toolbar to see all the comments in the document, or tap a comment to see its contents, and then tap the Comment List button to show all the comments.

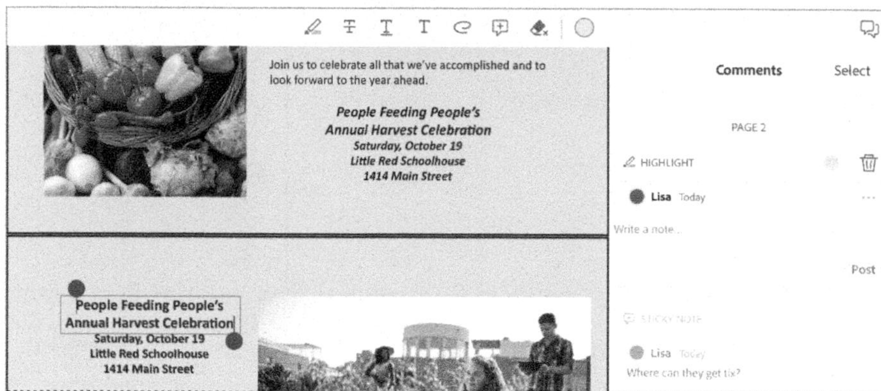

5 Tap the Undo button at the top to undo the highlighting. If the Undo button isn't available, tap the highlight and tap the Delete button.

6 Tap Done (iOS) or the Check mark button (Android) or the Back button in the top left corner to accept your notations and exit commenting mode. Acrobat Reader saves your changes to the document in the cloud.

Editing PDF files in Acrobat Reader

In the Acrobat Reader app, you can make simple text and image edits to PDF files. You'll correct a spelling error and adjust the size and position of an image on the postcard.

1 Tap the Edit button in the lower right corner, and choose Edit PDF.

2 Scroll to see the second page. Click the text block. If you're using a phone, tap Edit Text.

3 Tap an insertion point before the *v* in *Hors d'oervres*, which is spelled wrong. Backspace to delete the letter *r*, and then type **u**. On a phone, click Save or Done when you've made the change.

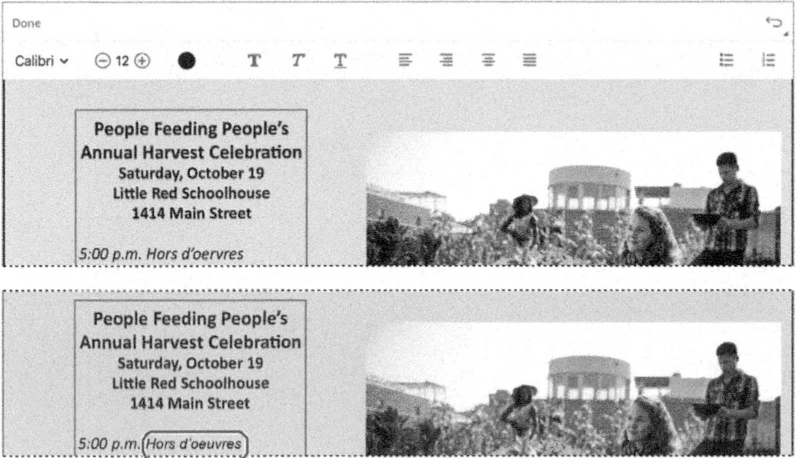

4 Tap and hold your finger down over the photo's bounding box to select and highlight it. Then drag it up slightly on the page. Drag the lower left corner handle down and to the left to make the image larger.

5 When you're satisfied with the changes you've made, tap Done or the Check mark button at the top of the screen to exit editing mode. Acrobat saves the changes to the cloud.

6 Tap the Back button at the top of the screen to return to the Home view.

Using Acrobat in a web browser

Acrobat in a browser includes the same Home view you see in Acrobat on the desktop and in the Acrobat Reader app, but it also provides a Quick Start set of tools to help you do what you want to do quickly.

You can access Acrobat in a browser on a computer or on a device. It provides some features that aren't available in the Acrobat Reader app, such as the ability to send documents for review. You'll use Acrobat on the web to share the Postcard PDF file for review.

1 Open a browser on a computer or a device, and then type **acrobat.adobe.com** into the browser.

2 Sign in with your Adobe ID if you're prompted to do so.

Acrobat displays the Home view.

3 Click the Postcard_final file in the Recent files list to open it.

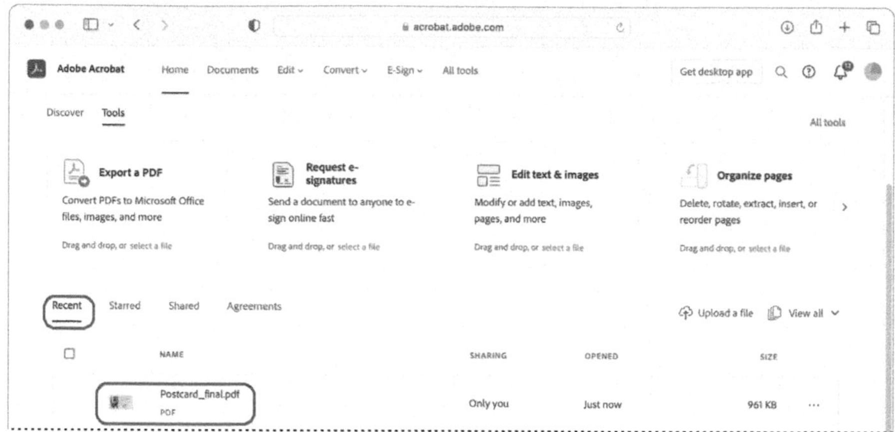

Acrobat displays both pages of the Postcard_final document. The toolbar displays the Edit, Convert, and Request E-signature tools.

4 Click the Discover button (◎) in the toolbar to display the Tools panel on the left side of the screen, if it's not already open.

5 Click the Share tool in the Tools panel. (You may need to scroll down to see it.)

6 In the Share Document dialog box, enter an email address for a reviewer. (You can enter your own email address or a colleague's.) Enter a personalized message if you want to. Make sure Allow Comments is enabled, and click Add Deadline if you want to specify a date by which comments are due. Then click Invite.

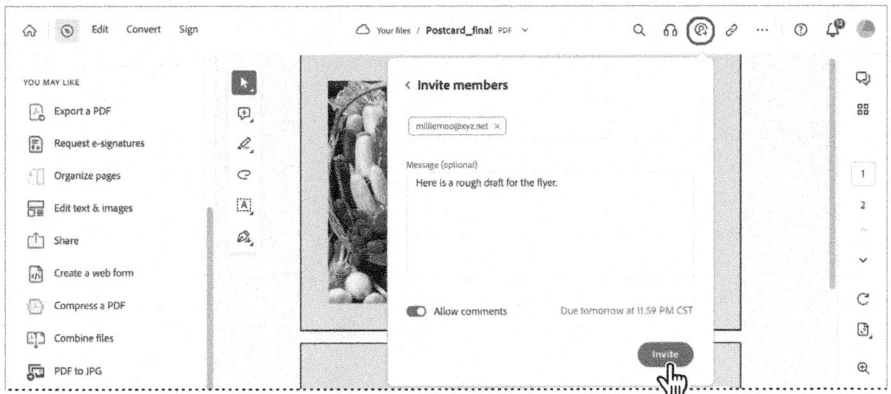

Acrobat sends the PDF document for review and reports its status.

Acrobat displays the PDF file in Review mode, with existing comments listed on the side near their placement on the page.

7 Click the Home button (⌂) to return to Home view. In the document list, the Postcard_final.pdf document has Shared for the Sharing status, and if you set a deadline, it's listed under the file name.

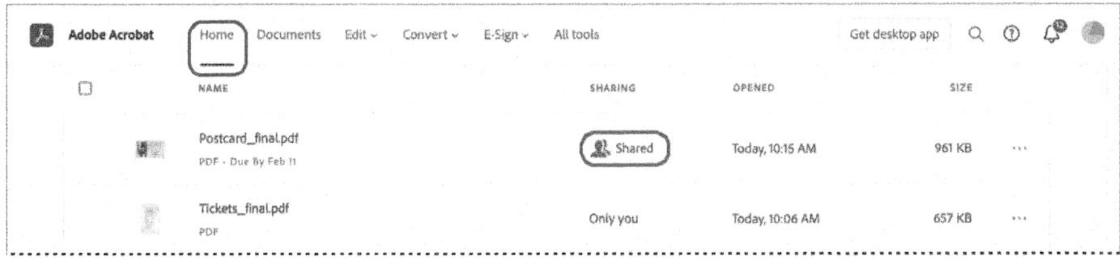

You'll learn more about commenting and shared review processes in Lesson 10, "Using Acrobat in a Review Cycle."

8 In the Home view, select the Tickets_final.pdf file. Then click the Add Your Signature tool in the Quick Tools toolbar.

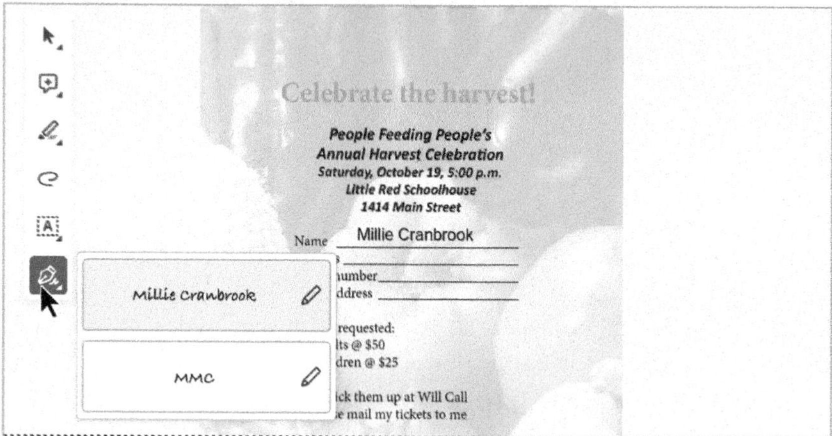

You could sign the document here in the browser, but you'll use the Fill & Sign app so you can set up a profile.

9 Click the Home button to return to the Home view.

Using the Fill & Sign app

The Adobe Fill & Sign app performs the same function as the Fill & Sign tool in Acrobat or the Acrobat Reader app. Because it's available on your mobile device, you can complete forms wherever you are. The Fill & Sign app also lets you create a profile that you can use to quickly complete standard form fields. You'll use the Fill & Sign app to complete the ticket order form for an event. The steps required depend on the device you're using; they may differ slightly from those listed here.

1 Open the Fill & Sign app on your device. Sign in to your Adobe account if you aren't already signed in.

The app displays forms that have been accessed recently in Acrobat on the web or on your device. The app displays only the PDF files it recognizes as forms.

2 Tap the Profile button (👤).

3 Enter a full name, first name, last name, and information for any other fields you'd like to be able to complete quickly.

The profile includes standard identity and contact information. You can add custom fields that you encounter frequently, too.

4 Tap Settings, or, on some devices, tap the menu icon at the top of the screen, and choose Settings.

In the Settings panel, you can choose whether to store your profile online for use on other computers and devices.

5 In iOS, tap Done, and then tap Close or anywhere else on the screen to close the Profile panel. On an Android device, tap the back button to close the Settings panel.

6 Tap the Tickets_final PDF file to open it.

7 Tap at the beginning of the Name field to click an insertion point. Then tap the Profile button, and select Full Name to enter it.

8 Tap next to *Adults* to insert text, and type the number **2**. Tap the small capital A to reduce the text size; tap the large capital A to increase the size of the text.

9 Tap the Will Call box, and tap the check mark to add it to the box, or tap the menu button (. . .) in the floating toolbar, and then tap the check mark.

Note: If the Tickets_final PDF file isn't listed, email it to yourself and open it from your device.

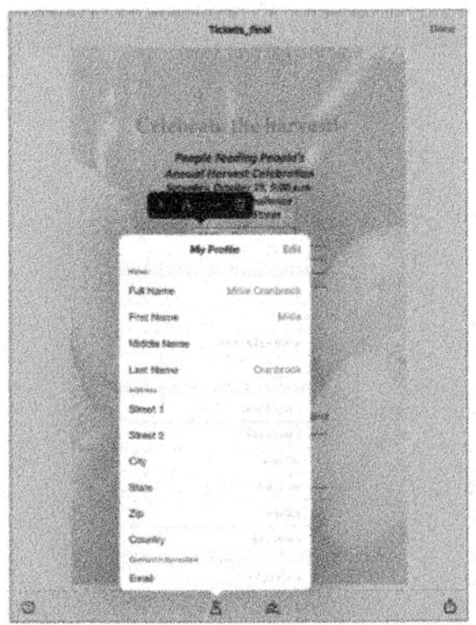

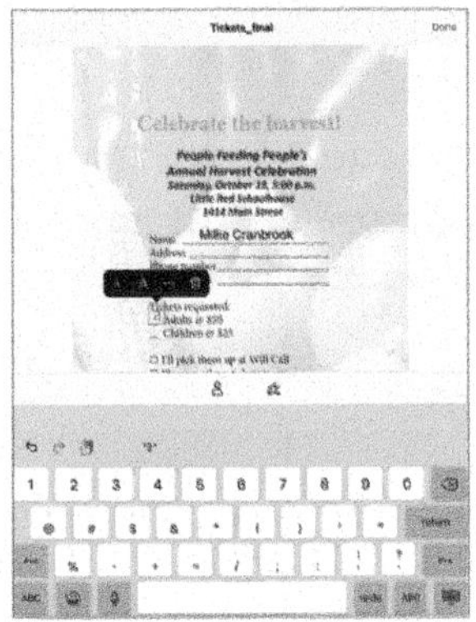

10 Tap the signature field, and then tap the Signature button. Tap Create Signature, sign a name, and then tap Done. (If your signature is already shown, tap it instead.) You may need to reposition your signature.

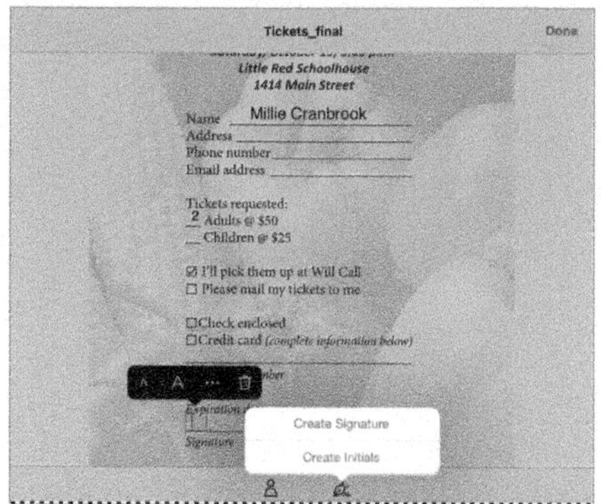

You can save your signature in your profile for use online in other Adobe apps.

11 Tap the Share button, and tap your Mail app icon to email the completed form. You can log in to your email account and send the form to yourself, or tap the back button to return to Adobe Fill & Sign.

12 Tap Done or the back button to return to the Home view of the Adobe Fill & Sign app.

Had you been ordering tickets, you'd have completed the entire form, and you could submit it using email, print it, or save it to Adobe cloud storage and then upload it to a website.

Using the Adobe Scan app

You can use the Adobe Scan app to use the camera on your phone or tablet as a scanner. Once you've scanned a document, you can use Acrobat to recognize text, share the document, convert it into a form, and generally do anything you can do with any other PDF file.

You can open Adobe Scan directly, and you can also access Adobe Scan from within the Acrobat Reader app by tapping Scan in the tools menu. The app's interface is different on different devices; the interface described here may be slightly different from the one you use.

1 Open Adobe Scan on your device.

2 Tap the Profile button in the upper left corner to open the Settings panel.

3 Tap Preferences, and make sure Run Text Recognition is enabled if you want to scan text-based documents into editable PDF documents. If you want to save the original scans to your photos, tap Save Originals To Photos or Save Originals To Gallery.

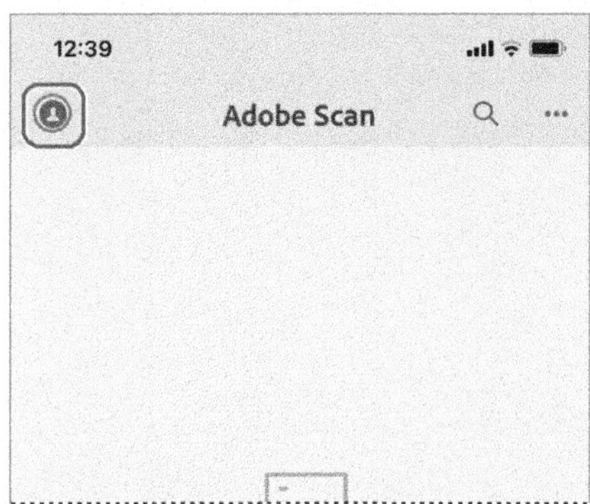

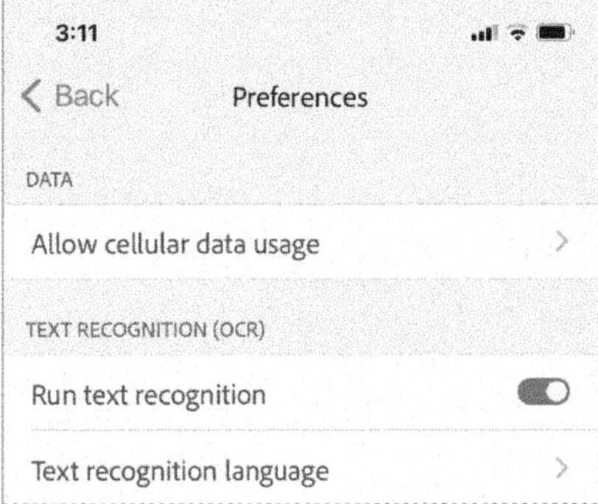

4 Tap Back, if necessary, and then tap Done or close the Settings menu to return to the Home view.

5 Tap the Camera button in the lower right corner to activate your camera. Give permission for the app to use your camera if prompted.

6 Tap the Auto-Capture button, next to the Capture button, to disable it.

When Auto-Capture is enabled, the Adobe Scan app identifies documents and takes the photo automatically. When it's disabled, you must press the Capture button manually.

7 Position your device over a document, and press the Capture button.

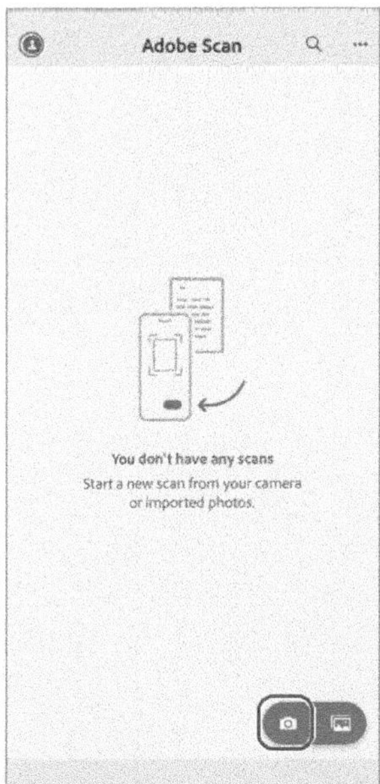

8 Tap the Scans thumbnail in the lower right corner to see the scan. If you see a Quick Actions option, tap Continue.

9 Tap the Crop button in the bottom toolbar to adjust the borders of the image. Tap the check mark or the Crop button when you're done. (Depending on your settings, you may also be able to adjust borders immediately after scanning.)

10 Tap the Rotate button to rotate the scanned image one-quarter turn clockwise, if necessary.

11 Tap the Filters button to change the color and mood of the image.

12 Tap Save PDF when you're satisfied with the scan. The scan is saved to Adobe cloud storage.

Review questions

1. Which commenting tools are available in the Acrobat Reader app?
2. How can you use Acrobat in a web browser?
3. Why would you want to save a profile in the Fill & Sign app?

Review answers

1. The Acrobat Reader app includes the Sticky Note, Highlighter, Strikethrough, Underline, Add Text, and Drawing tools for commenting on PDF documents.
2. You can use Acrobat in a web browser to view and work with your PDF documents from any computer or device. When you make changes to a PDF document in the Acrobat Reader app, those changes are saved to the PDF document in the cloud.
3. A profile can help you complete form fields much faster, as you can select previously designated answers to populate fields.

7 USING ACROBAT WITH MICROSOFT OFFICE FILES

Lesson overview

In this lesson, you'll do the following:

- Convert a Microsoft Word file to Adobe PDF.
- Convert Word headings and styles to PDF bookmarks. (Windows only)
- Convert Word comments to PDF notes. (Windows only)
- Change the Adobe PDF conversion settings. (Windows only)
- Convert a Microsoft Excel file to Adobe PDF.
- Use the Spreadsheet Split view.
- Convert a Microsoft PowerPoint presentation to Adobe PDF.

This lesson will take approximately 45 minutes to complete. Download the project files for this lesson, following the instructions in the Getting Started section under "Accessing the lesson files and Web Edition," if you haven't already done so. As you work on this lesson, you'll preserve the start files. If you need to restore the start files, download them from your Account page.

Statement of Work
for
Local

Meridien Conference
Promotion Program

Presented by

April 22, 2023

Using Acrobat PDFMaker and the Create PDF tool in Acrobat, you can easily convert Microsoft Office documents to PDF. In Windows, PDFMaker settings also let you convert Word headings to bookmarks, include comments, and start email-based reviews.

Getting started

How you convert Microsoft Office documents to PDF depends on your operating system, which application you're using, and its version. When you install Acrobat, it adds Acrobat PDFMaker to Microsoft Office 2013 or later applications in Windows—including Microsoft Word, Microsoft Excel, and Microsoft PowerPoint. In macOS, it adds Acrobat PDFMaker to Microsoft Word 2016 or later and to Microsoft PowerPoint and Excel 2019 or later.

You need to have one or more of the applications listed above installed on your system to complete the exercises. If you do not use these Microsoft Office applications, skip this lesson. Visit the Adobe website (www.adobe.com) to see which versions of Microsoft Office are supported.

Because the process for converting PDF documents is so different depending on the operating system, we've separated the exercises for Windows and macOS. If you are using only one operating system, skip the sections regarding the other operating system.

This lesson assumes you are using Microsoft Office 365, but the steps are similar in other versions.

About Acrobat PDFMaker

Acrobat PDFMaker makes it easy to convert Microsoft Office documents to PDF. When you install Acrobat in Windows, it automatically installs PDFMaker for supported Microsoft Office applications (Microsoft Office 2013 and later) it finds on the system. In macOS, Acrobat installs PDFMaker for Microsoft Word 2016 or later, Microsoft PowerPoint 2019 or later, and Microsoft Excel 2019 or later. PDFMaker options are available on the Acrobat ribbon. In Windows, you can control the settings used in the PDF conversion, automatically email the PDF file, and set up an email review process without ever leaving the Microsoft application; PDFMaker can also attach your Office source file to the PDF file.

PDF files are often substantially smaller than their source files. You can also create PDF/A-compliant files from Office files in Windows.

If you don't see the Acrobat ribbon in your Windows application, choose File > Options, select Add-Ins in the Options dialog box, and select Acrobat PDFMaker Office COM Addin. Then close and restart your Microsoft application.

In Windows, Acrobat installs essentially the same buttons and commands in Word, PowerPoint, and Excel. There are, however, some application-specific differences.

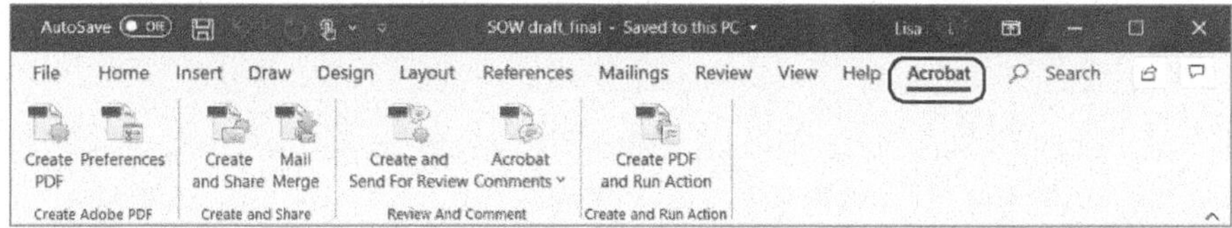

Acrobat PDFMaker on macOS installs just two buttons: Create PDF and Preferences.

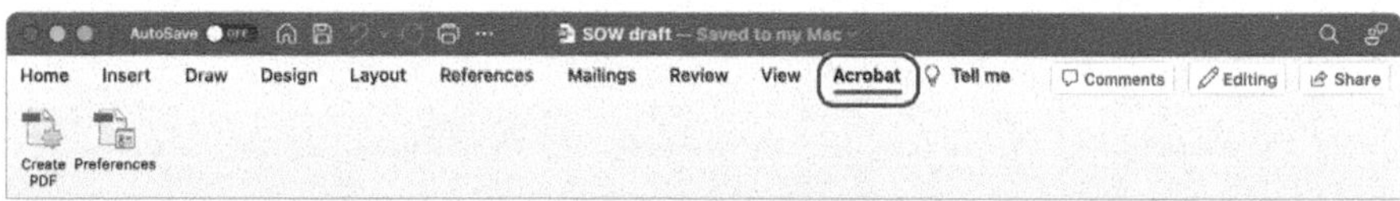

Converting Microsoft Word files to Adobe PDF (Windows)

Word is a popular authoring program that makes it easy to create a variety of types of documents. Word documents often include text styles and hyperlinks and may contain comments added during a review process. When you create an Adobe PDF document from your Word document in Windows, you can convert text using specific Word styles, such as headings, to Acrobat bookmarks, and you can convert comments to Acrobat notes. Hyperlinks in a Word document are preserved when it is converted to PDF. Your Adobe PDF file will look just like your Word file and retain the same functionality, but it will be equally accessible to readers on all platforms, regardless of whether they have the Word application. PDF files created from Word files can also be tagged, improving accessibility and making the content easy to repurpose.

Tip: With an Acrobat or Creative Cloud subscription, you can convert Microsoft Office files to PDF on a tablet or phone using the Acrobat mobile app.

Converting Word headings and styles to PDF bookmarks

If your Word document contains headings and styles that you want to convert to linked bookmarks in Adobe PDF, you must identify these headings and styles in the Acrobat PDFMaker dialog box. (Word Heading 1 through Heading 9 styles are converted automatically.) You'll convert a statement of work document that was formatted using custom styles. You'll need to make sure that the styles used are converted to linked bookmarks when you create the Adobe PDF file.

1 Start Microsoft Word.

2 Depending on your version, click Open or choose File > Open. Then navigate to the Lesson07/Assets folder, and double-click the SOW draft.docx file.

3 If the document opens in Protected View mode, click Enable Editing.

4 Choose File > Save As, rename the file **SOW draft_final.docx**, and save it in the Lesson07/Finished_Projects folder.

First, you'll change the PDF settings to create bookmarks based on the styles used in the document.

5 Click Acrobat in the menu bar to open the Acrobat ribbon, and then click Preferences.

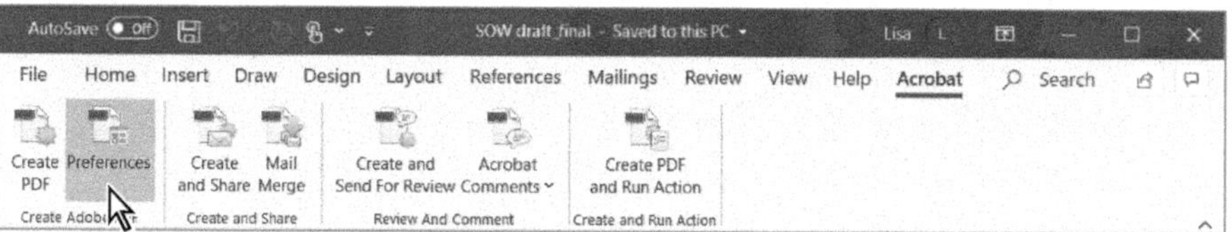

The Acrobat PDFMaker dialog box contains the settings that control PDF conversion. There are different tabs available, depending on the application. In Word, the dialog box includes a Word tab and a Bookmarks tab.

6 Click the Bookmarks tab to select which styles are used to create bookmarks.

By default, all headings are converted to bookmarks. You'll select a few styles to convert instead.

7 Deselect Convert Word Headings To Bookmarks to deselect the headings.

8 Scroll down the list, and select the Bookmark option for each of the following styles: Second Level, Third Level, Top Level, and Title. These are the styles you want to use to create bookmarks.

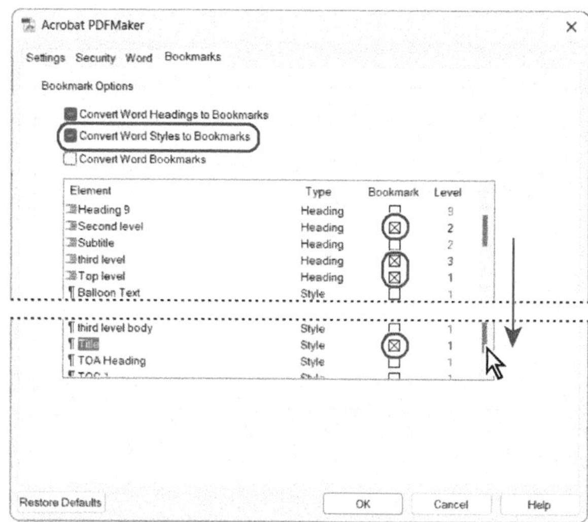

Notice that the level for Title and Top Level is automatically set to 1, Second Level is set to 2, and Third Level is set to 3. These are the hierarchical levels of PDF bookmarks. To change the level setting for a style, click its level number, and then choose a new level from the pop-up menu.

Any settings that you make in the Bookmarks tab apply only to the conversion of Word documents.

Converting Word comments to PDF notes

You needn't lose any comments that have been added to your Word document when you convert the document to Adobe PDF: You can convert them to PDF notes. There are two comments in this document that need to remain available in the PDF.

1 Click the Word tab in the Acrobat PDFMaker dialog box, and make sure Convert Displayed Comments To Notes In Adobe PDF is selected.

The Comments area displays information about the comments that will be included. Make sure that the box in the Include column is selected.

2 To change the color of the note in the Adobe PDF document, click repeatedly on the icon in the Color column to cycle through the available color choices. We chose blue.

3 To have the note automatically open in the PDF document, select the Notes Open option. You can always close the note in the PDF document later if you wish.

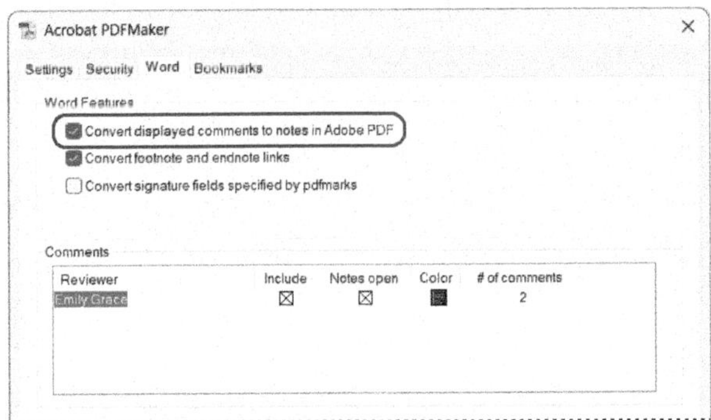

Any settings that you make in the Word tab apply only to the conversion of Word documents.

Specifying the conversion settings

In every Office application for Windows, PDFMaker includes the Settings tab, which is where you can select the conversion settings that determine how the PDF file is created. For most purposes, the predefined settings files (or presets) work well. However, if you need to customize the conversion settings, click Advanced Settings, and then make the changes appropriate for your file.

You'll convert this document using the Standard settings file.

1 Click the Settings tab.

2 From the Conversion Settings menu, choose Standard.

3 Verify that View Adobe PDF Result is selected. When this option is selected, Acrobat automatically displays the Adobe PDF file you create as soon as the conversion is complete.

4 Make sure that Create Bookmarks is selected.

5 Make sure that Enable Accessibility And Reflow With Tagged Adobe PDF is selected. Tagging PDF files makes them more accessible.

For more information on making your PDF files accessible, see Lesson 3, "Reading and Working with PDF Files."

6 Select Attach Source File to attach the Word document to the PDF file. This option can be useful if you want the viewer to have access to the original for editing purposes.

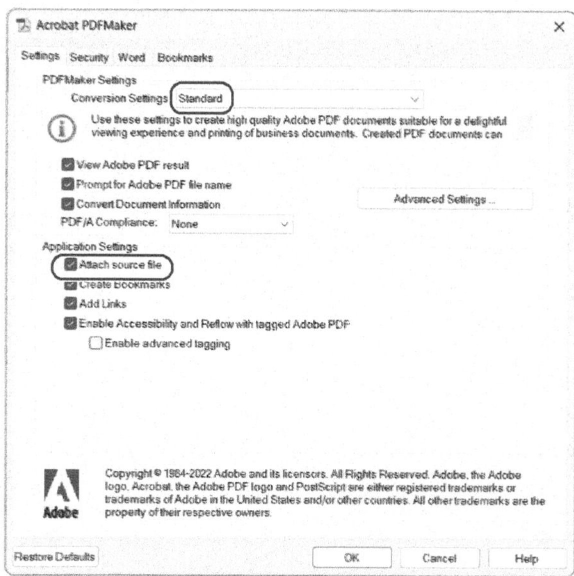

Note: Acrobat PDFMaker will use these conversion settings for converting Word documents until you change them.

7 Click OK to apply your settings, and then choose File > Save.

Converting your Word file

Now that you've defined the settings to be used for the conversion, you're ready to convert your Word file to Adobe PDF.

1 Click the Create PDF button on the Acrobat ribbon.

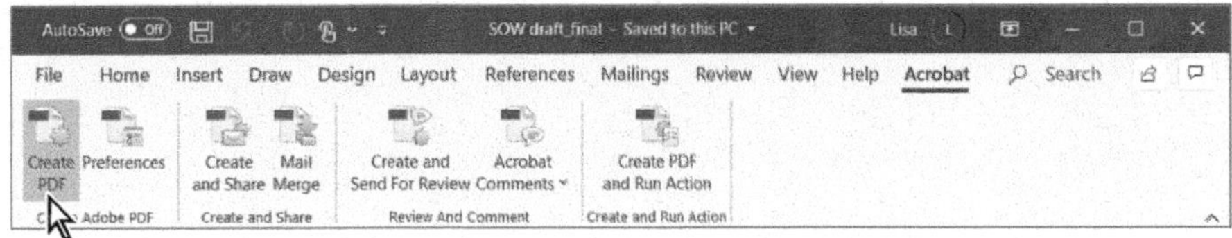

2 In the Save Adobe PDF As dialog box, navigate to the Lesson07/Finished_Projects folder, and name the file **SOW draft.pdf**. Click Save.

PDFMaker converts the Word document to Adobe PDF. The status of the conversion is shown in the Acrobat PDFMaker message box.

Because you selected View Adobe PDF Result, Acrobat automatically displays your converted file. Notice that the Word notes are displayed in the open Acrobat Comments pane.

3 Scroll if necessary to see the first note. After you have read the notes, click Close to exit the Comment tool.

▶ **Tip:** In Acrobat, you can edit headers and footers in PDF files created from Office files.

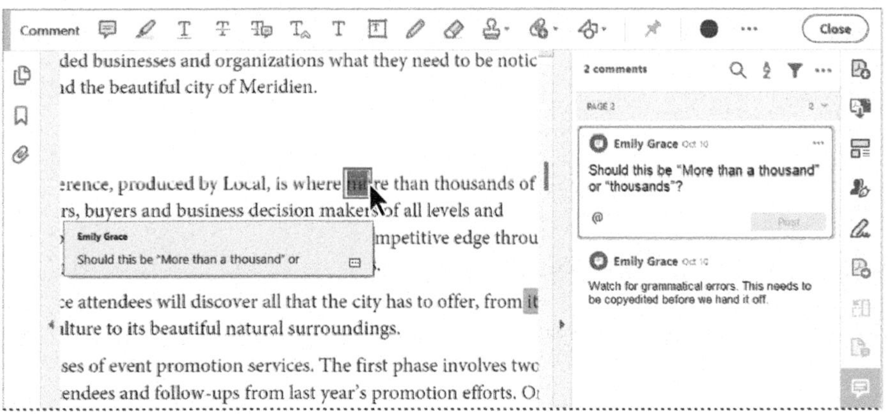

4 Click the Bookmarks button (🔖) in the navigation pane, and view the bookmarks that were created automatically.

In Acrobat, when you select a bookmark in the navigation pane, the link takes you directly to the heading, not the top of the page that contains the heading.

5 Click the Attachments button (📎) in the navigation pane to verify that your original Word file is attached.

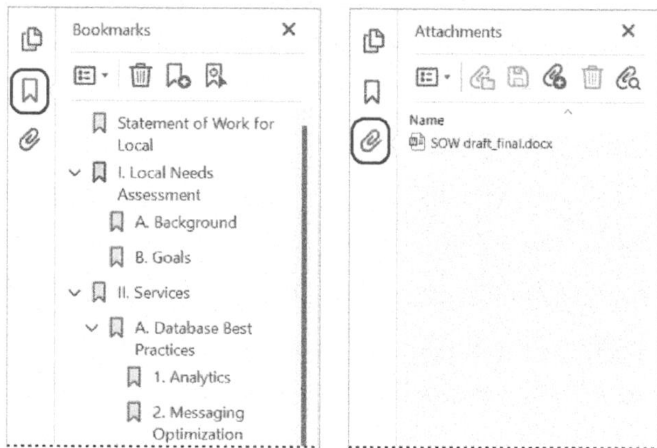

▶ **Tip:** If you simply want to convert your Microsoft Office file to Adobe PDF using the current PDFMaker conversion settings, you can drag the Office file onto the Acrobat icon on your desktop or into an empty document pane in the Acrobat work area.

6 When you have finished reviewing the file, close it.

7 Choose File > Exit to quit Acrobat.

8 Quit Microsoft Word.

Creating Adobe PDF files from Word mail-merge templates

Word mail-merges generate documents such as form letters, which are personalized with the names and addresses of the individuals to whom they will be sent. In Windows, with Acrobat PDFMaker, you can use a Word mail-merge template and its corresponding data file to output mail-merges directly to PDF. You can even set up PDFMaker to attach those PDF files to email messages that are generated as the PDF files are created. Click the Mail Merge button in the Acrobat ribbon to start the process. For more information, see Adobe Acrobat Help.

Converting Word documents to PDF (macOS)

You can quickly convert a Microsoft Word 2016 or later document to PDF in macOS using the Acrobat ribbon in Word. The Create PDF button on the Acrobat ribbon uses the Create Adobe PDF cloud service to convert the file; to use this service, you must be signed in to Acrobat and be connected to the Internet. Acrobat uses the current page settings for the document to make the conversion and automatically creates bookmarks from heading styles.

1 Open Word.

2 Click Open or choose File > Open. Then navigate to the Lesson07/Assets folder, and double-click the SOW draft.docx file. Choose File > Save As, rename the file **SOW draft_final.docx**, and save it in the Lesson07/Finished_Projects folder.

3 Click Acrobat, and then click Preferences on the Acrobat ribbon.

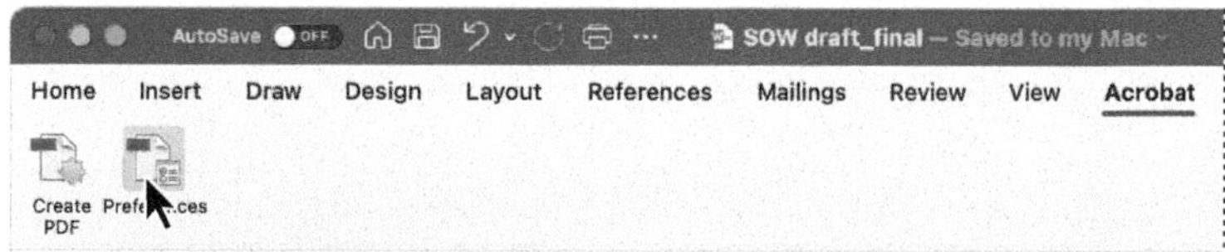

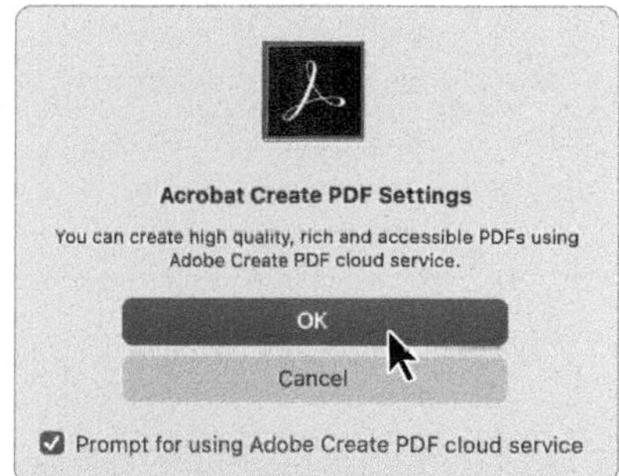

The Acrobat Create PDF Settings dialog box opens. Select Prompt For Using Adobe Create PDF Cloud Service if you want Acrobat to ask you before using the Adobe Create PDF cloud service when you click Create PDF in the Acrobat ribbon.

4 Click OK to close the dialog box.

5 Choose File > Page Setup to see the page settings Acrobat will use. Click OK to accept the settings.

6 If you made any changes, save the document.

7 Click Create PDF on the Acrobat ribbon. If prompted, click Yes to use the Adobe Create PDF cloud service.

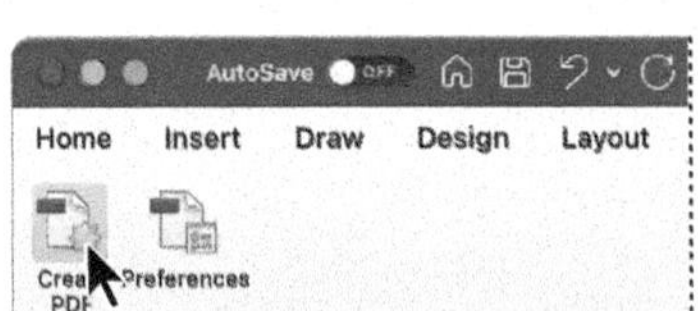

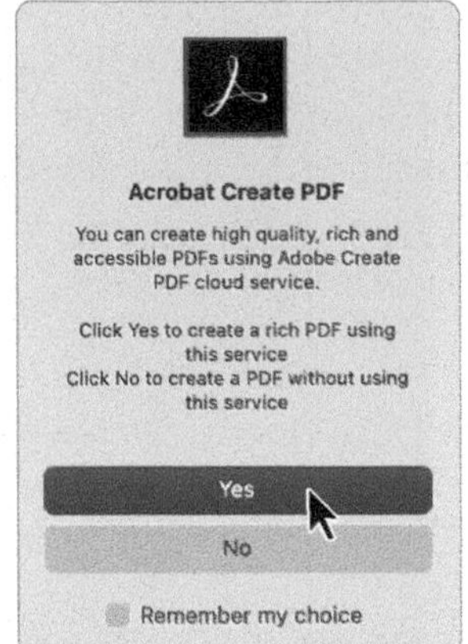

The converted PDF document opens in Acrobat.

8 Close the PDF document, and quit Word.

Converting Excel documents (Windows)

When you convert Excel documents to PDF in Windows, you can easily select and order the worksheets you want to include, retain all links, and create bookmarks. You'll create an Adobe PDF file from an Excel document after customizing the conversion settings.

Converting the entire workbook

You can choose to convert an entire workbook, a selection, or selected sheets to PDF. In this exercise, you'll convert an entire workbook.

1 Start Microsoft Excel.

2 Depending on your version, click Open or choose File > Open. Then, navigate to the Lesson07/Assets folder, and open the Financials.xlsx file.

3 If the file opens in Protected View mode, click Enable Editing.

4 Choose File > Save As, rename the file **Financials_final.xlsx**, and save it in the Lesson07/Finished_Projects folder.

This Excel file includes two worksheets. The first lists construction costs, and the second shows operating costs. You'll need to convert both of these sheets to include them in the PDF. You'll start by changing the PDF conversion settings.

5 Click Acrobat to open the Acrobat ribbon.

6 Click Preferences in the Acrobat ribbon.

7 In the Settings tab of the Acrobat PDFMaker dialog box, choose Smallest File Size from the Conversion Settings menu, because you're going to be emailing the PDF file.

8 Select the Fit Worksheet To A Single Page option.

9 Make sure that the Enable Accessibility And Reflow With Tagged Adobe PDF option is selected. When you create tagged PDF files, you can more easily copy tabular data from PDF files back into spreadsheet applications. Creating tagged PDF files also makes them more accessible.

10 Select the Prompt For Conversion Settings option to open a dialog box at the beginning of the file conversion process, which will allow you to specify which sheets to include and in what order.

PDFMaker will use these conversion settings when converting Excel documents to PDF until you change the settings.

11 Click OK to apply your settings.

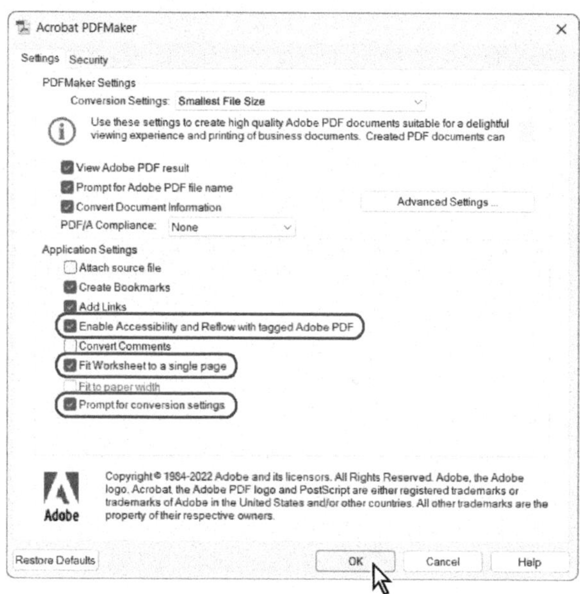

In Acrobat, you can convert an oversized worksheet to a PDF document that is one sheet wide and several sheets long. In the Settings tab of the Acrobat PDFMaker dialog box, the Fit Worksheet To A Single Page option adjusts the size of each worksheet so that all the entries on that worksheet appear on the same page of the PDF file. The Fit To Paper Width option adjusts the width of each worksheet so that all the columns on that worksheet appear on one page in the PDF document.

Creating the PDF file

You'll convert the Excel workbook to a PDF file. PDFMaker uses the settings you specified earlier.

1 Click the Create PDF button on the Acrobat ribbon.

2 In the Acrobat PDFMaker dialog box, select Entire Workbook.

This is the dialog box where you'd select specific material or worksheets, if you wanted to.

3 Click Convert To PDF.

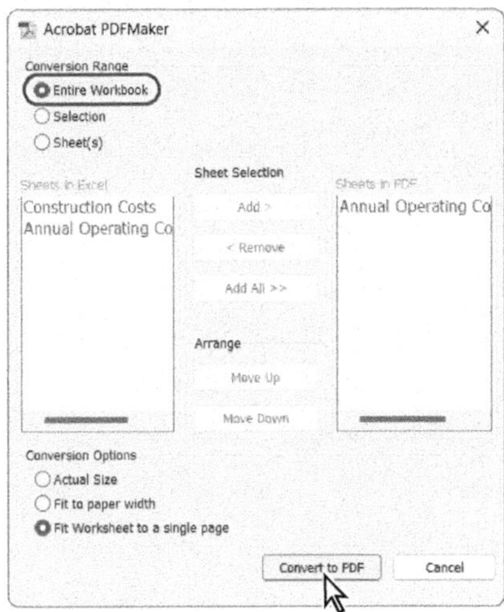

4 In the Save Adobe PDF File As dialog box, click Save to save the file as **Financials_final.pdf** in the Lesson07/Finished_Projects folder.

Acrobat opens the PDF document automatically if View Result was selected in the Save Adobe PDF File As dialog box.

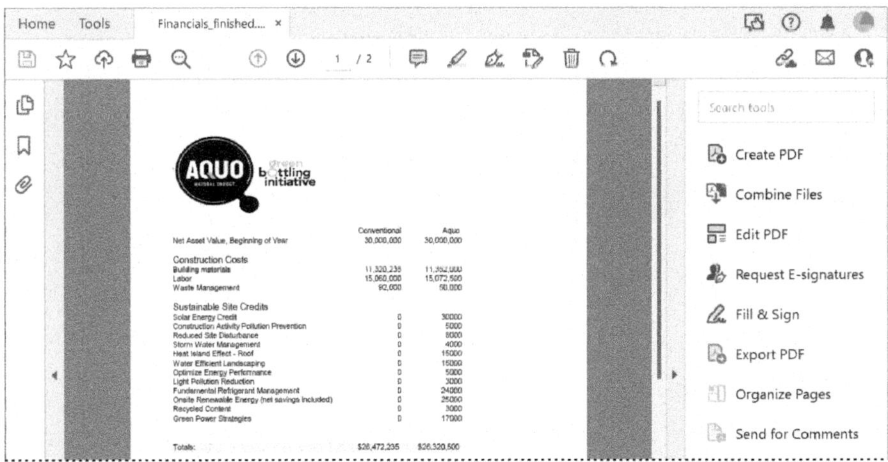

5 Review the Financials_final.pdf file in Acrobat, and then close the PDF file and close Excel.

Converting Excel spreadsheets (macOS)

You can quickly convert a Microsoft Excel 2019 or later document to PDF in macOS using the Acrobat ribbon in Excel. The Create PDF button on the Acrobat ribbon uses the Create Adobe PDF cloud service to convert the file; to use this service, you must be signed in to Acrobat and be connected to the Internet. Acrobat uses the current page setup settings in Excel to convert the document.

1 Open Excel.

2 In Excel, click Open, or choose File > Open. Then, navigate to the Lesson07/Assets folder, and double-click the Financials.xlsx file. Then choose File > Save As, rename the file **Financials_final.xlsx**, and save it in the Lesson07/Finished_Projects folder.

3 Choose File > Page Setup. Select Landscape for Orientation. Then click OK.

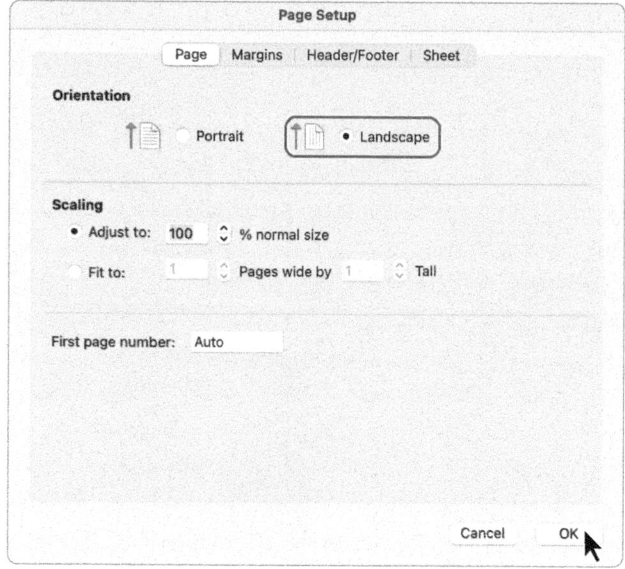

4 Choose File > Save to save the changes you made.

5 Click Acrobat to open the Acrobat ribbon.

6 Click Create PDF on the Acrobat ribbon. If prompted, click Yes to use the Adobe Create PDF cloud service.

Acrobat uploads the file to Adobe's cloud storage and converts it. It then opens the PDF file in Acrobat.

7 Scroll through the document.

8 Close the PDF document, and quit Excel.

Note: If you're using an earlier version of Excel, you may not have an Acrobat ribbon. To convert a spreadsheet to PDF, specify file settings in Excel, and then open Acrobat, and choose File > Create > PDF From File.

Using the Spreadsheet Split view

Whether you've converted an Excel worksheet in Windows or on macOS, when you work with spreadsheets, it is often useful to be able to keep the column or row names in view while scrolling up and down columns or across rows. The Spreadsheet Split command in Acrobat lets you do this.

1 In Acrobat, choose File > Open. Navigate to the Lesson07/Assets folder, and open the GE_Schedule.pdf file.

This schedule is difficult to read onscreen because the type size is small if you have the view set to Fit Page. You'll use the Spreadsheet Split command to look more closely at some of the data. First you'll change the view of the page.

2 Choose Window > Spreadsheet Split to divide the document pane into four quadrants.

You can drag the splitter bars up, down, left, or right to resize the panes.

In Spreadsheet Split view, changing the zoom level changes the magnification in all the quadrants. (In Split view, you can have a different zoom level in each of the two windows.)

3 Drag the vertical splitter bar so that the categories fill the left pane.

4 Drag the horizontal splitter bar so that it is directly below the column headings.

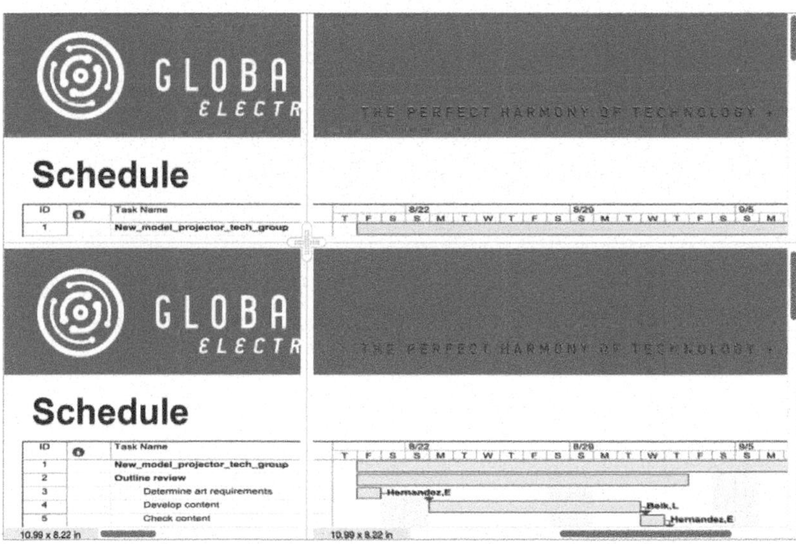

5 Use the vertical scroll bar to scroll down through the categories. Because the column headers remain visible, it is easy to evaluate the schedule for each task.

6 When you are finished exploring the Spreadsheet Split view, close the GE_Schedule.pdf file without saving your work.

Converting PowerPoint presentations (Windows)

You can convert Microsoft PowerPoint presentations to PDF in the same way that you convert Microsoft Word documents. However, there are additional options available to help you preserve the look and feel of the presentation. You'll convert a simple presentation and preserve its slide transitions.

1 Start PowerPoint. Depending on the version of PowerPoint, click Open or choose File > Open. Then navigate to the Lesson07/Assets folder, and open the Projector Setup.pptx file.

2 If the file opens in Protected View mode, click Enable Editing.

A Push transition has been applied to the slides in this file.

3 Click Acrobat to open the Acrobat ribbon.

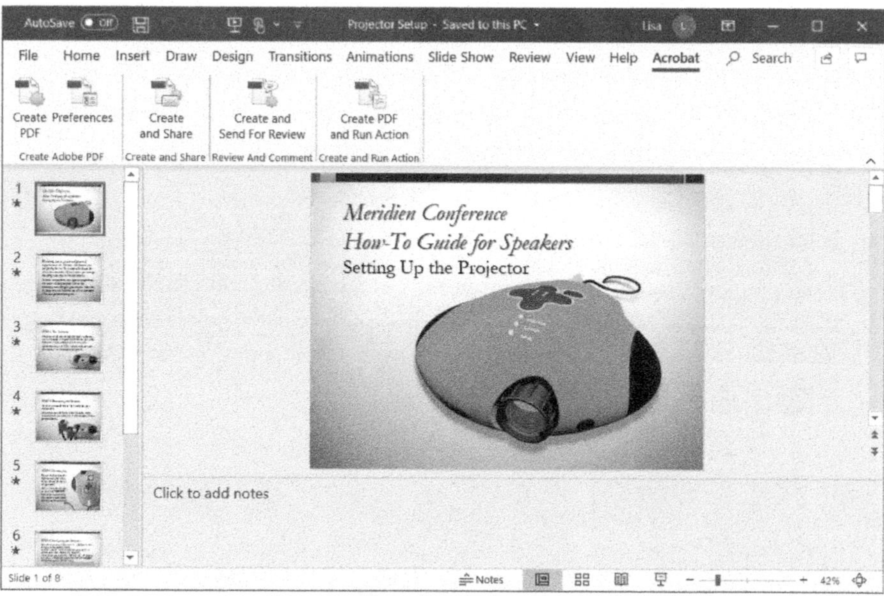

4 Click Preferences in the Acrobat ribbon.

5 Select the Settings tab, and then select Convert Multimedia and Preserve Slide Transitions. Make sure View Adobe PDF Result is selected, too.

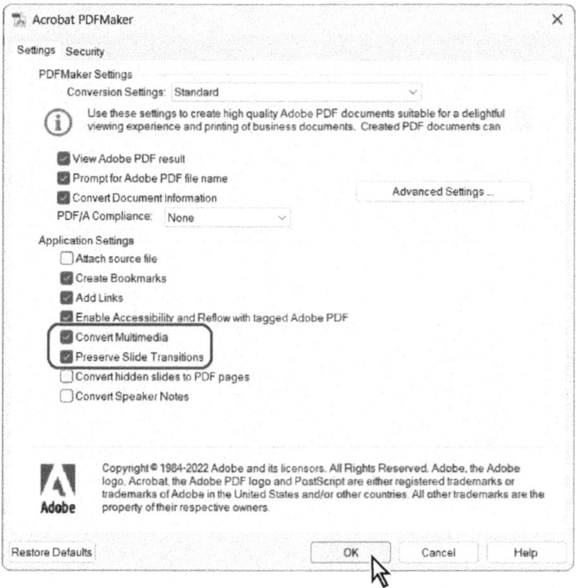

6 Click OK.

You can include speaker's notes and hidden slides, and specify other settings.

7 Click Create PDF in the Acrobat ribbon. Name the file **Projector Setup_final.pdf**, and save it to the Lesson07/Finished_Projects folder. Then click Save in the Save Adobe PDF dialog box. Acrobat opens the PDF file after conversion.

8 In Acrobat, choose View > Full Screen Mode. Then press the arrow keys to move through the presentation. The Push slide transitions remain in the PDF file. Press the Esc key to exit Full Screen mode. Then, close the PDF file and PowerPoint.

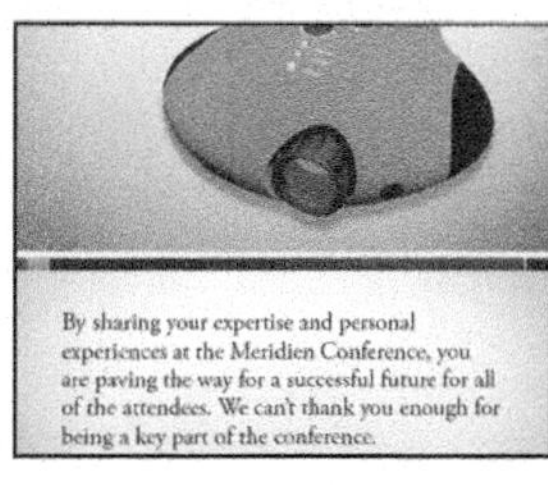

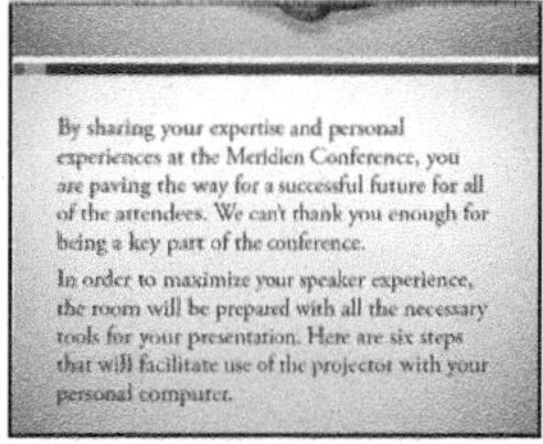

Converting PowerPoint presentations (macOS)

In Acrobat for macOS, you can convert Microsoft PowerPoint 2019 or later presentations to PDF the same way that you convert Word documents. Acrobat uses the current page setup settings in PowerPoint to convert the document. Because Acrobat uses the Create Adobe PDF cloud service to convert the document, you must be connected to the Internet and signed in to Acrobat to use the feature.

1 Open PowerPoint.

2 In PowerPoint, choose File > Open. Then navigate to the Lesson07/Assets folder, and double-click the Projector Setup.pptx file. Choose File > Save As, name the file **Projector Setup_final.pptx**, and save it to the Lesson07/Finished_Projects folder.

3 Choose File > Page Setup, and confirm the settings are appropriate. Click OK to close the dialog box.

4 If you made any changes, choose File > Save to save the changes you made.

5 Click Acrobat to open the Acrobat ribbon.

6 Click Create PDF in the Acrobat ribbon. If prompted, click Yes to use the Adobe Create PDF cloud service.

Acrobat uploads the file to Adobe's cloud storage and converts it. It then opens the PDF file in Acrobat.

7 Scroll through the document.

8 Close the PDF document, and quit PowerPoint.

Review questions

1 In Windows, how can you be sure that Word styles and headings are converted to Acrobat bookmarks when you convert Word documents to Adobe PDF using PDFMaker?

2 How can you scroll through a spreadsheet in Acrobat without losing sight of the column headings?

3 Can you retain slide transitions when you save a PowerPoint presentation to PDF in Windows?

4 How can you quickly convert an Excel 365 document to PDF in macOS?

Review answers

1 If you want Word headings and styles to be converted to bookmarks in Acrobat, select them for conversion in the Acrobat PDFMaker dialog box in Word for Windows. In Microsoft Word, click Preferences in the Acrobat ribbon, and click the Bookmarks tab. Make sure that the required headings and styles are selected.

2 To see column headings while you review the content of a spreadsheet, choose Window > Spreadsheet Split, which divides the document pane into four quadrants. Move the divider bars where you want them, and then scroll through the rows.

3 Yes, you can retain slide transitions when you save a PowerPoint presentation to PDF in Windows. To do so, click Preferences in the Acrobat ribbon, and then make sure Preserve Slide Transitions is selected. PDFMaker uses those settings until you change them.

4 In macOS, you can quickly convert an Excel document to PDF using the Create Adobe PDF cloud service, as long as you're signed in to Acrobat and connected to the Internet. Make sure the file is ready to convert. In Excel, click Acrobat to open the Acrobat ribbon, and then click Create PDF.

8 COMBINING FILES

Lesson overview

In this lesson, you'll do the following:

- Quickly and easily combine files of different types into one PDF document.
- Select individual pages to include in a combined PDF file.
- Customize a combined PDF file.
- Learn how to create a PDF Portfolio (Acrobat Pro only).

This lesson will take approximately 45 minutes to complete. Download the project files for this lesson, following the instructions in the Getting Started section under "Accessing the lesson files and Web Edition," if you haven't already done so. As you work on this lesson, you'll preserve the start files. If you need to restore the start files, download them from your Account page.

You can easily combine multiple files, including files of different file types, into a coherent PDF document. You can even select which pages to include from each document.

About combining files

In Acrobat, you can assemble multiple files into an integrated PDF document. You can combine files of different formats, created in different applications. As long as you have applications installed that support the native documents' formats, they'll automatically be converted to PDF. For example, you could assemble all the documents for a specific project, including text documents, email messages, spreadsheets, CAD drawings, and PowerPoint presentations. When you combine the files, you can select specific pages from each document and then rearrange them. Acrobat converts each to PDF and then assembles them into a single PDF file.

If you have Acrobat Pro, you can choose to combine files in a PDF Portfolio. Files in a PDF Portfolio do not need to be converted to PDF; they can remain in their original format but are assembled into a coherent document. For more information, see the sidebar "Creating a PDF Portfolio" at the end of this lesson.

Selecting files to combine

In this lesson, you'll create a combined PDF file that contains documents for the board meeting of a fictitious beverage company. You'll assemble several PDF files, a logo, a Microsoft Word document, and a Microsoft Excel spreadsheet. You can select which pages of each document to include in the combined PDF file.

Note: Acrobat requires the native application be installed in order to convert a document to PDF. If you do not have Word or Excel installed on your computer, you will not be able to include those files in your combined PDF. You can skip those files and complete the exercise without them.

Adding files

First, you'll select the files you want to include in the combined PDF file.

1 Start Acrobat.

2 Click Tools.

3 In the Tools Center, click the Combine Files tool in the Create & Edit category.

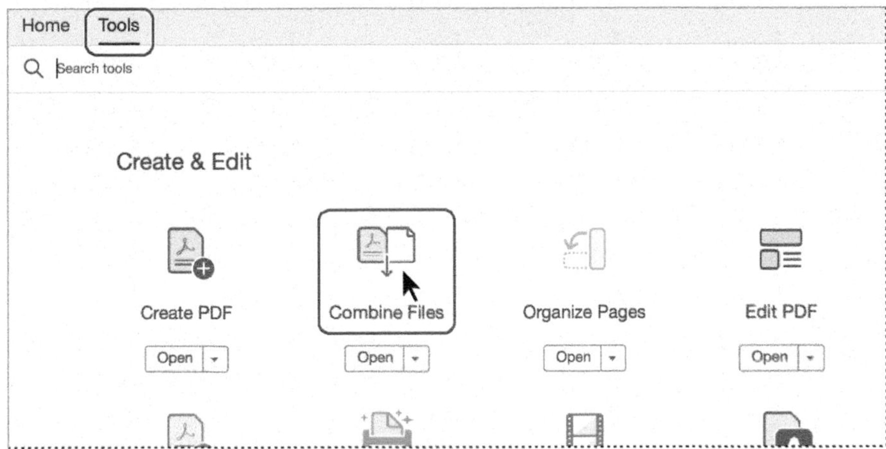

The Combine Files dialog box appears.

4 Click Add Files.

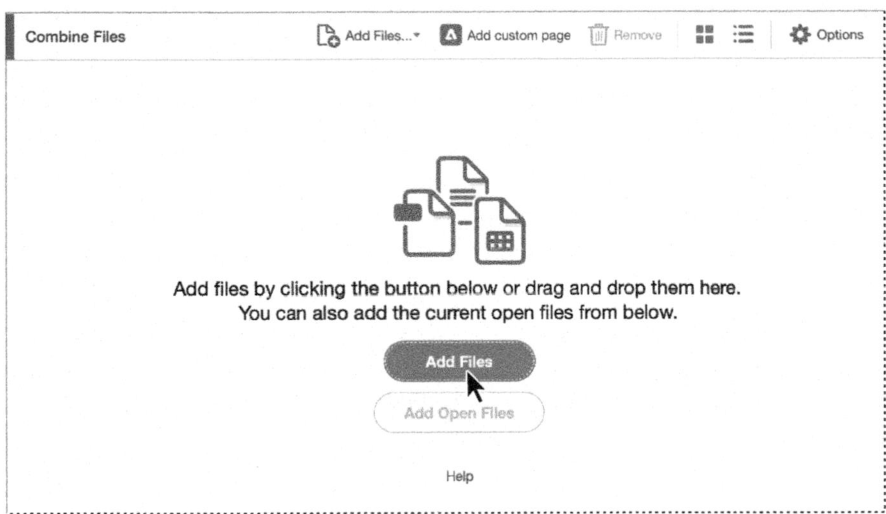

5 Navigate to the Lesson08/Assets folder.

The folder contains a GIF file, an Excel spreadsheet, a Word document, and several PDF files.

6 Select Aquo_Bottle.pdf, and then Shift-click Logo.gif to select all the following files, and click Open (Windows) or Add Files (macOS):

- Aquo_Bottle.pdf
- Aquo_Building.pdf
- Aquo_Costs.pdf
- Aquo_Fin_Ana.xls
- Aquo_Mkt_Summ.doc
- Aquo_Overview.pdf
- Logo.gif

If you do not have the required software installed to convert a document, you won't be able to select it.

Browsing files

Acrobat displays a thumbnail for each selected file in the Combine Files dialog box. You can use those thumbnails to preview a document, select specific pages to include, delete a file, or rearrange the pages in the final file.

Note: In macOS, the source applications (Microsoft Word, Excel, and PowerPoint) may open as you select the files. Acrobat uses the source applications to create the thumbnails it displays in the Combine Files dialog box.

1 Select the Aquo_Bottle.pdf thumbnail.

2 Move the cursor over the thumbnail. Acrobat displays the filename, size, modification date, and the number of pages it contains.

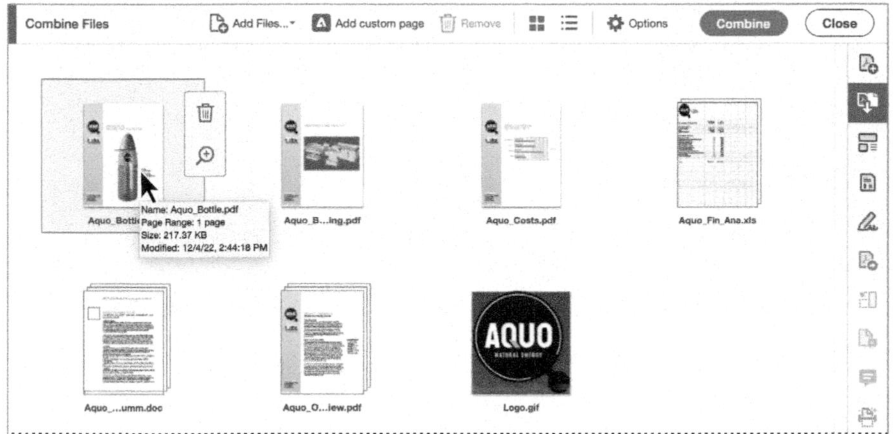

3 Click the magnifying glass on the thumbnail to zoom in to the full page.

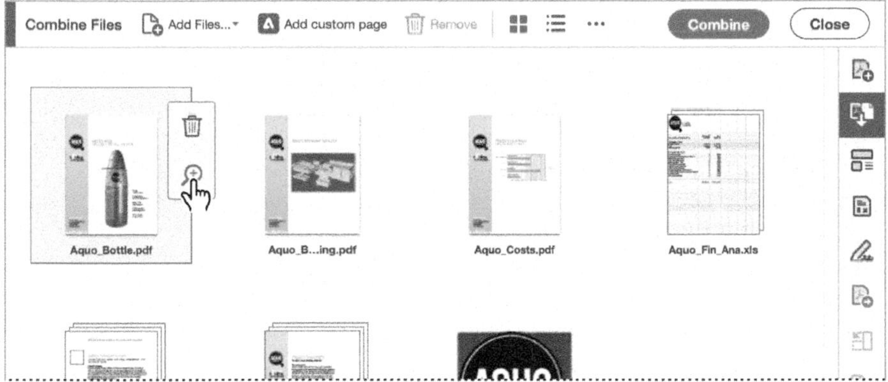

4 Click anywhere in the dialog box outside of the preview page to close the preview box.

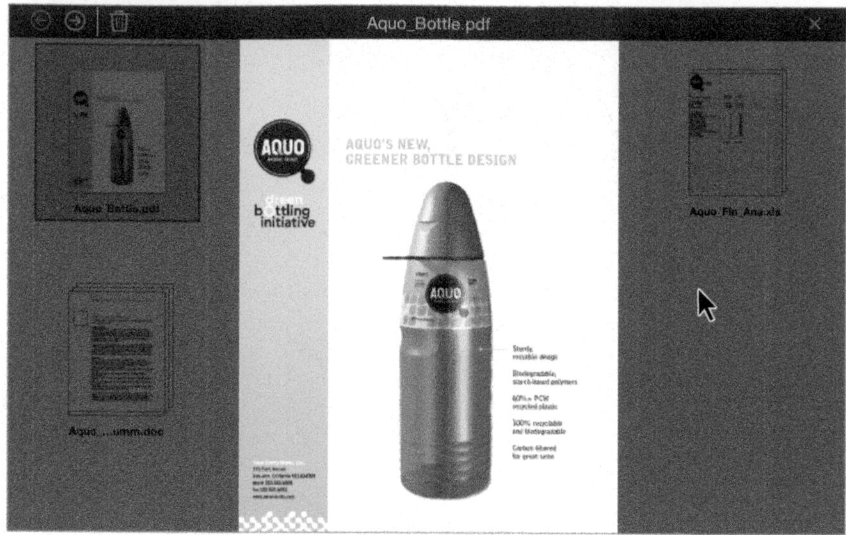

5 Move the cursor over the Aquo_Overview.pdf thumbnail, and click the Expand 3 Pages icon (a double-headed arrow) to see each of the pages in the document.

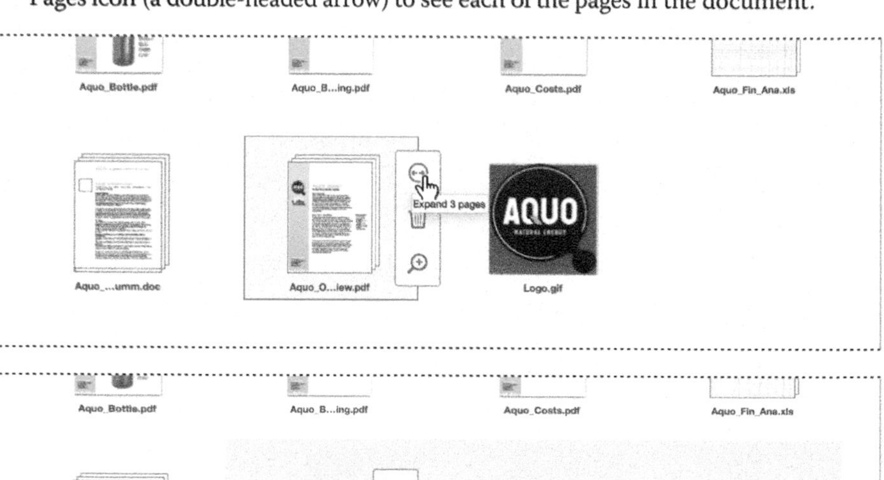

You can preview each page separately, rearrange them, or delete them from the combined PDF file.

6 Select the thumbnail of the third page in the Aquo_Overview.pdf file, and then click the Remove button (🗑) at the top of the dialog box.

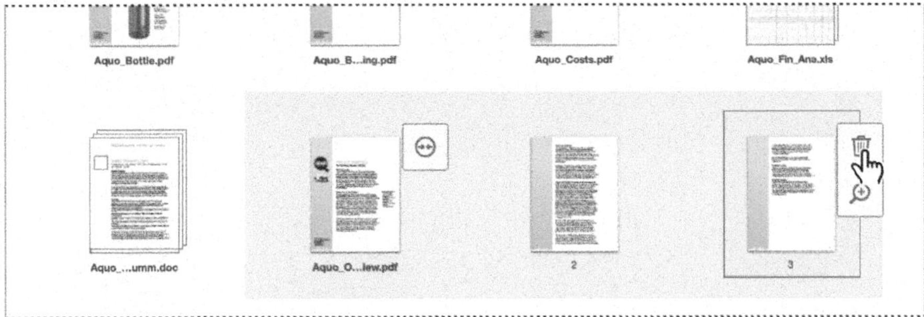

Only two pages remain in the document.

7 Click the Collapse Document button (inward-pointing arrows) over the Aquo_Overview.pdf thumbnail to collapse the document back to a single thumbnail.

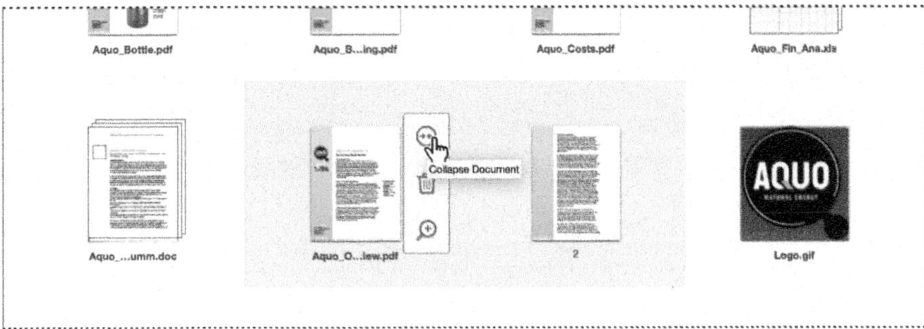

Note: If you weren't able to add the Aquo_Fin_Ana.xls file to the Combine Files dialog box, skip step 8.

8 Move the cursor over the Aquo_Fin_Ana.xls file, and then click the Expand Two Pages icon to view the two worksheets it contains.

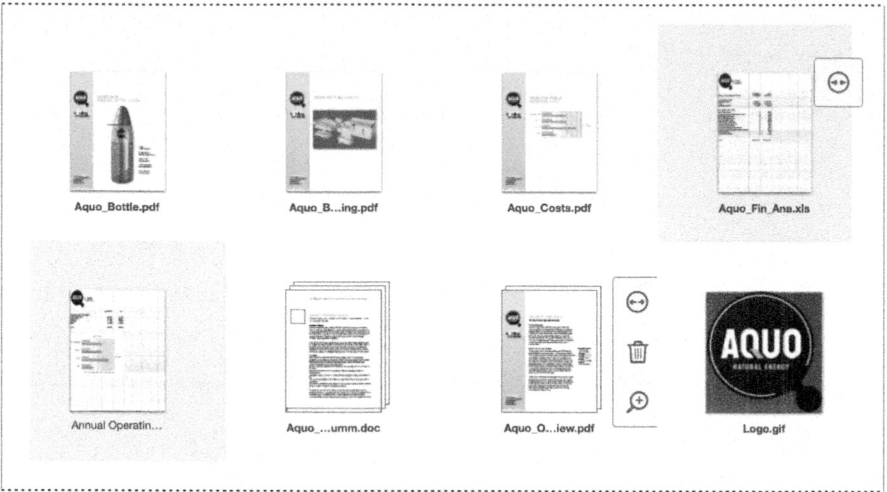

Arranging pages

You can organize the pages in the merged file before you actually create it. Just drag and drop thumbnails in the Combine Files dialog box to place them in the order you want them to appear.

1 Drag the Logo.gif file to the top of the dialog box, so that it's the first file, before Aquo_Bottle.pdf.

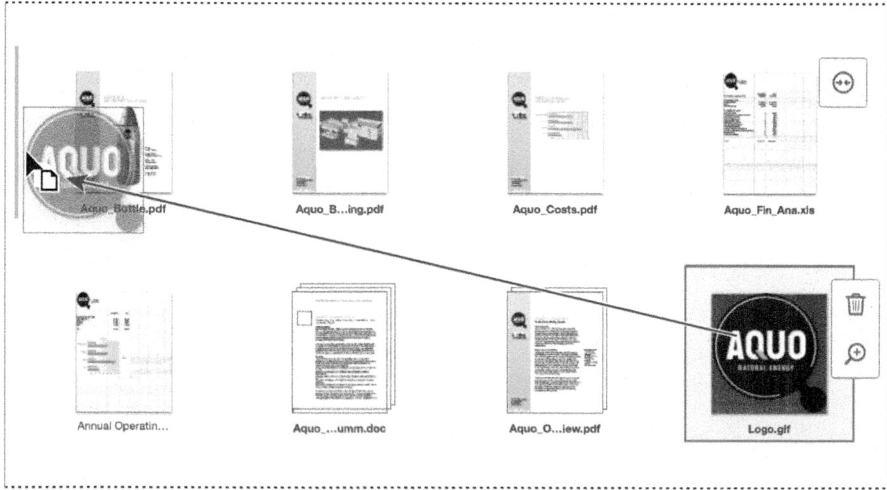

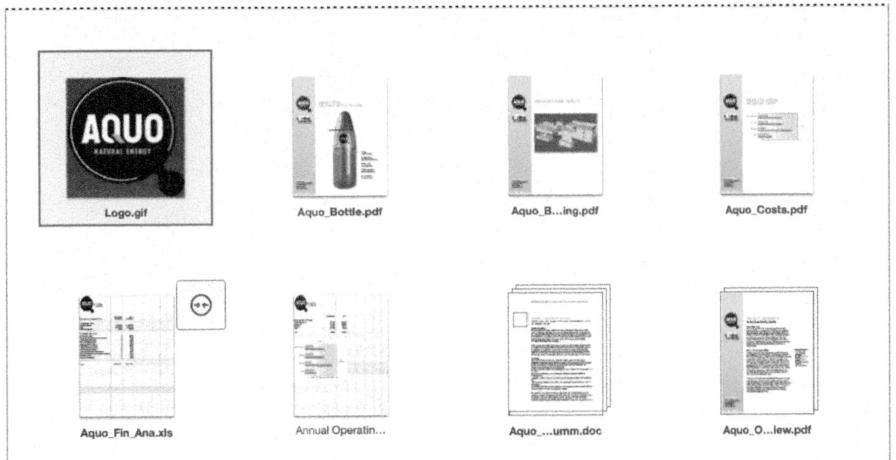

2 Drag the first worksheet in the Aquo_Fin_Ana.xls file so that it appears right after the Aquo_Mkt_Summ.doc file.

Note: If you were unable to add the Aquo_Fin_Ana.xls file, skip step 2. Likewise, ignore any files in step 3 that don't appear in the Combine Files dialog box on your system.

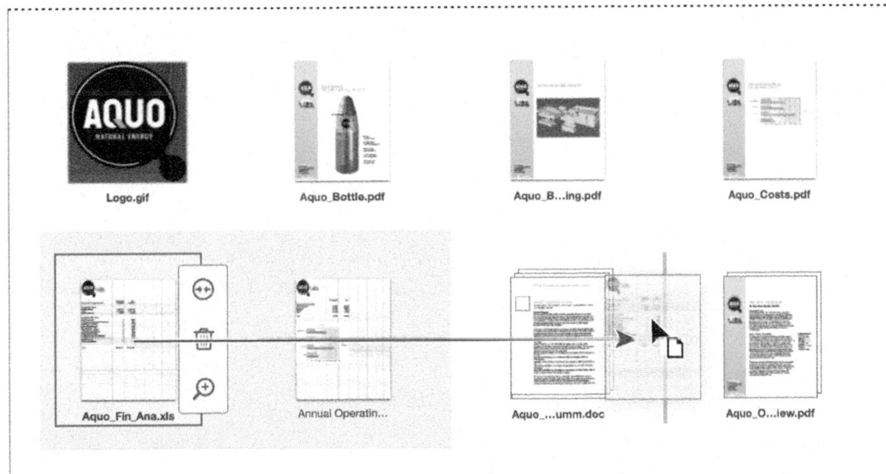

You can arrange documents, or individual pages within those documents.

3 Collapse any expanded documents, and then arrange the remaining documents so that they appear in the following order:

- Logo.gif
- Aquo_Bottle.pdf
- Aquo_Overview.pdf
- Aquo_Building.pdf
- Aquo_Costs.pdf
- Second sheet of Aquo_Fin_Ana.xls
- Aquo_Mkt_Summ.doc
- First sheet of Aquo_Fin_Ana.xls

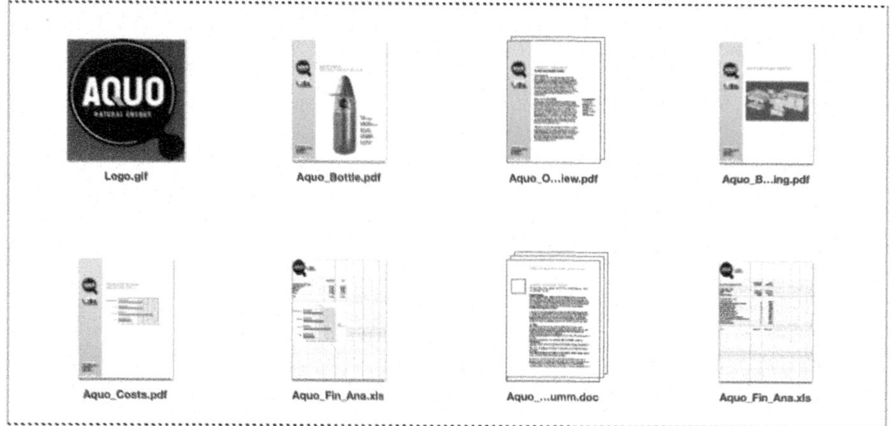

4 Click the Switch To List View button at the top of the dialog box to see the filenames and information instead of thumbnails.

Merging the files

When you've selected the pages you want to include and arranged them in the appropriate order, you're ready to combine the files.

1 Click the Options icon (⚙) at the top of the Combine Files dialog box.

2 In the Options dialog box, make sure the Default File Size option is selected.

The Smaller File Size option uses compression and resolution settings that are appropriate for onscreen display. The Default File Size option creates PDF files for business printing and viewing onscreen. The Larger File Size option uses High Quality Print conversion settings.

3 Make sure Always Add Bookmarks To Adobe PDF is selected.

When this option is selected, Acrobat creates bookmarks for the file as it converts and combines the documents.

4 Make sure Save As PDF Portfolio is **not** selected so that Acrobat combines all the files into a single combined PDF document.

5 Click OK to close the Options dialog box.

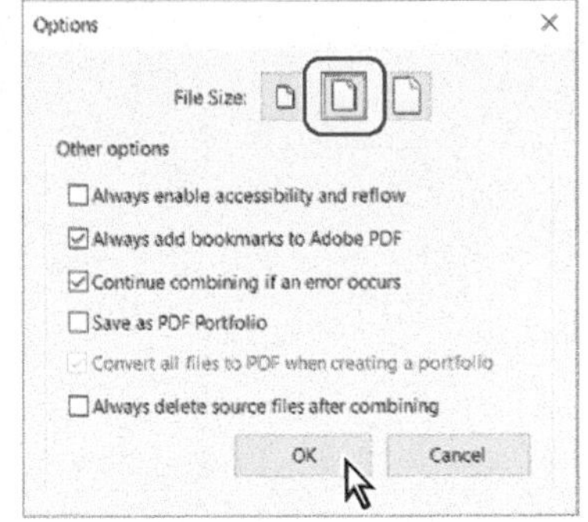

6 Click Combine.

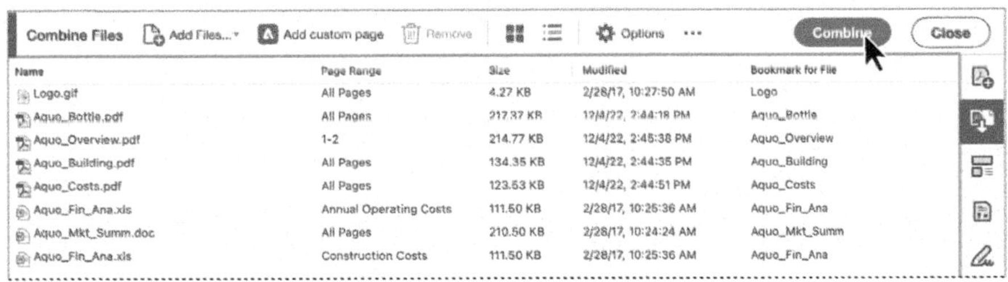

Acrobat reports its progress as it converts individual documents to PDF format and then combines the files. Some source applications may open and close during the conversion process. When Acrobat has finished merging the documents, it opens the resulting file, named Binder1.pdf.

7 Click the Bookmarks button ( ) in the navigation pane to view the bookmarks Acrobat created for the document.

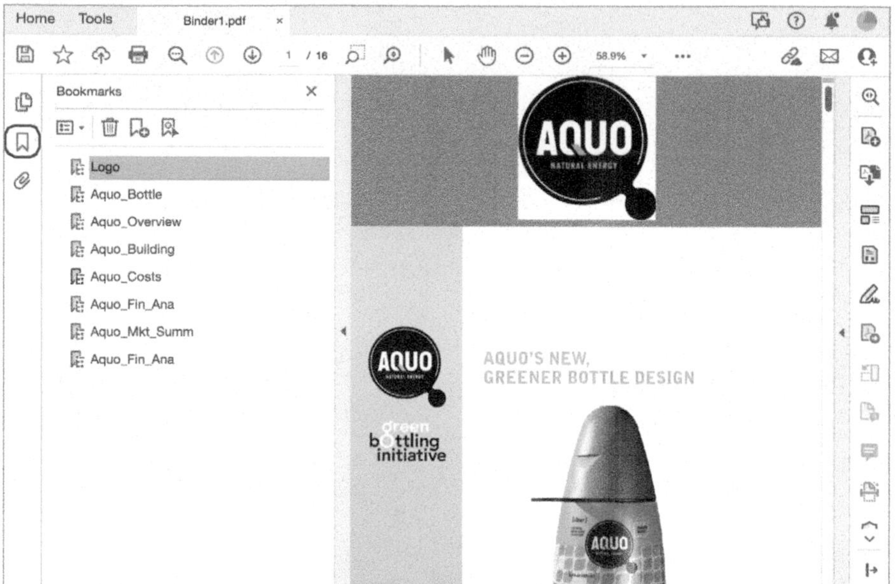

Because you moved a worksheet separately from the rest of the Excel document, that document is included twice in the list of bookmarks. In Windows, Acrobat creates additional bookmarks for individual pages, nested under the bookmark for the document name. Depending on your goals for the document, you might want to edit the bookmarks.

8 Browse through the document. The pages are in the order you specified.

9 Choose File > Save As, and save the document as **Aquo presentation** in the Lesson08/Finished_Projects folder.

10 Close the Aquo presentation.pdf file.

Creating a PDF Portfolio (Acrobat Pro)

In Acrobat Pro, you can assemble files of different formats into a PDF Portfolio. You do not need to convert files to PDF to include them in a PDF Portfolio.

PDF Portfolios offer several advantages over files merged into an ordinary PDF file or native files stored separately:

- You can add and remove component documents easily.
- You can quickly preview component files without having to pause for Open or Save dialog boxes.
- You can edit individual files within the PDF Portfolio without affecting the other files. You can also edit non-PDF files in their native applications from within a PDF Portfolio; any changes you make are saved to the file within the PDF Portfolio.
- You can search the entire PDF Portfolio or individual component documents, including non-PDF component files.
- You can add non-PDF files to an existing PDF Portfolio without converting them to PDF.

To create a merged PDF Portfolio:

1 Choose File > Create > PDF Portfolio.

The Create PDF Portfolio dialog box is similar to the Combine Files dialog box.

2 Click Add Files at the top of the dialog box, and then choose Add Files.

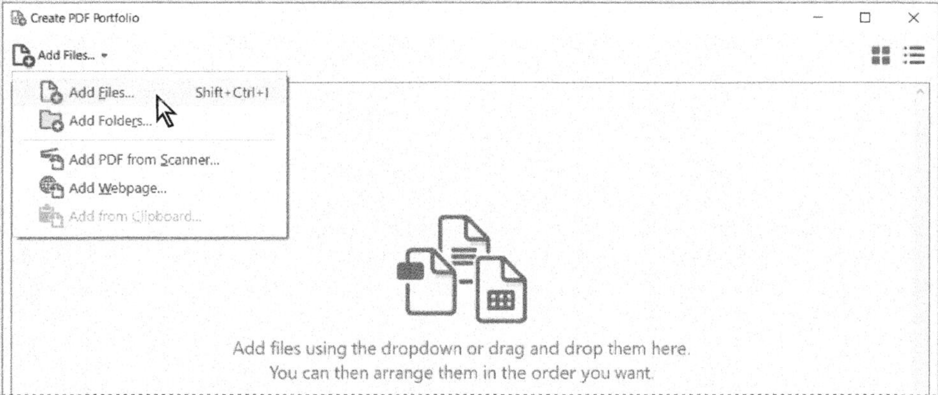

3 Select the files you want to include, and click Open (Windows) or Add Files (macOS).

4 Arrange the files in the order you want them to appear in the PDF Portfolio.

5 Click Create.

Acrobat opens the PDF Portfolio, named Portfolio1.pdf. It lists the Portfolio components in the navigation pane on the left.

continues on next page

Creating a PDF Portfolio (Acrobat Pro) (continued)

To navigate the PDF Portfolio, click a component name on the left, or use the Previous and Next buttons in the document taskbar.

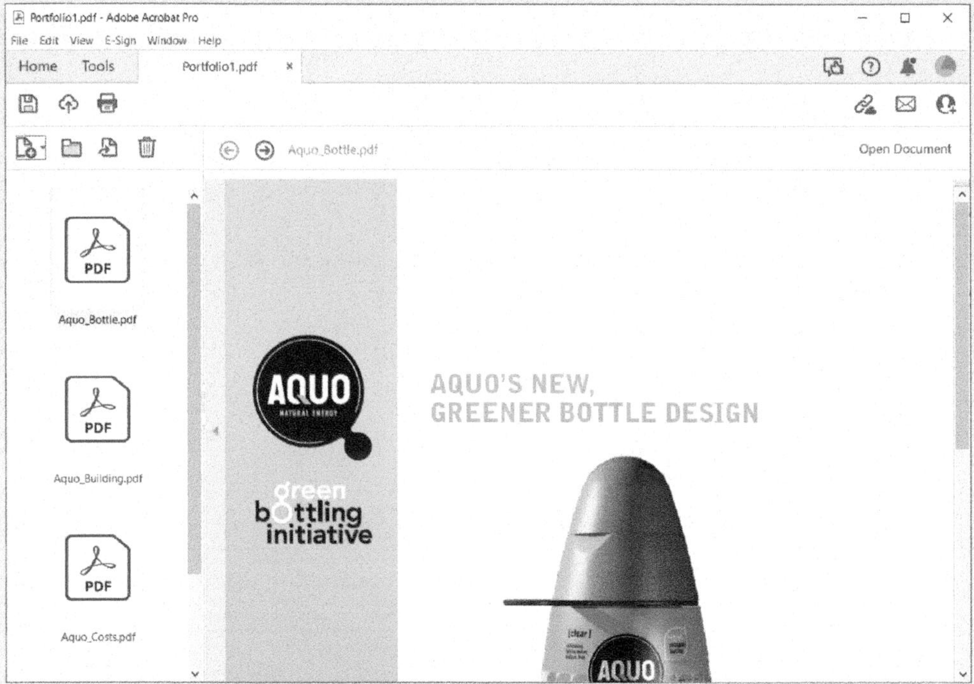

If the selected component is not a PDF document, click Open Document to open the document in its native application, such as Microsoft Word. If the selected document is a PDF file, clicking Open Document opens a separate copy of the PDF document. You can extract individual documents from a PDF Portfolio, whether they're PDF files or native documents. To extract a file, select the document in the PDF Portfolio, and then choose File > Extract File From Portfolio. Name the file, choose a folder for it, and click Save.

6 Choose File > PDF Portfolio.

The Save As PDF dialog box opens.

7 Select a folder for the PDF Portfolio, and then name it, and click Save.

Review questions

1 Can you include documents in non-PDF formats in a combined PDF file?

2 How do you arrange pages in a combined PDF file?

3 Why would you want to preview or browse a file in the Combine Files dialog box?

4 Name one advantage of a PDF Portfolio.

Review answers

1 Yes, you can include documents in any format in a combined PDF file, as long as you have the application that created the document installed. Acrobat converts documents to PDF as it combines the files.

2 To arrange pages in a combined PDF file, drag their thumbnails in the Combine Files dialog box.

3 It's handy to be able to preview or browse files in the Combine Files dialog box so that you can determine whether you want to include each file or all the pages of a file, and in which order.

4 PDF Portfolios provide several advantages:

- You can add and remove component documents easily, including non-PDF files.
- You can preview component files quickly.
- You can edit individual files within the PDF Portfolio independently.
- PDF Portfolios contain all their components, so you can share them easily.
- You can search the entire PDF Portfolio, including non-PDF component files.

9 ADDING SIGNATURES AND SECURITY

Lesson overview

In this lesson, you'll do the following:

- Use Acrobat in Protected Mode (Windows only).
- Apply password protection to a file to restrict who can open it.
- Apply a password to prevent others from printing or changing a PDF file.
- Use Acrobat Sign to send documents for digital signatures.
- Learn how to send forms in bulk and track them.
- Learn how to use Acrobat forms to collect payments.
- Learn about creating and using digital IDs in Acrobat.

This lesson will take approximately 45 minutes to complete. Download the project files for this lesson, following the instructions in the Getting Started section under "Accessing the lesson files and Web Edition," if you haven't already done so. As you work on this lesson, you'll preserve the start files. If you need to restore the start files, download them from your Account page.

Statement of Work

Presented to GlobalCorp
for
Project Management Services

June 12, 2023

The names and logo designs referred to in this sample artwork are fictional and not intended to refer to any actual organization, products or services.

You can keep your PDF documents secure through password protection, certification, and digital signatures.

Getting started

Acrobat provides several tools to help you secure your PDF documents. You can use passwords to prevent unauthorized users from opening, printing, or editing PDF files. With an Acrobat or Creative Cloud subscription, you can use Acrobat Sign to send a document to others for their digital signatures. Alternatively, you can use digital IDs to sign documents and certify PDF documents, and you can use a certificate to encrypt PDF documents so that only an approved list of users can open them. If you want to save security settings for later use, you can create a security policy that stores security settings. In Acrobat Pro, you can also permanently remove sensitive content from your PDF documents using the Redaction feature (see Lesson 5, "Editing Content in PDF Files").

First you'll learn about Protected Mode in Acrobat and Acrobat Reader for Windows, and then you'll work with the security features in Acrobat.

Viewing documents in Protected Mode (Windows only)

Note: Acrobat Reader is not automatically installed with Acrobat. If you want to install it, download the free installer at get.adobe.com/reader. You may not be able to install Acrobat Reader with Acrobat installed.

By default, Acrobat and Acrobat Reader for Windows open PDF files in Protected Mode (known as "sandboxing" to IT professionals). In Protected Mode, all processes are confined to the application itself, so that potentially malicious PDF files do not have access to your computer and its system files.

To complete this exercise, you must use Acrobat for Windows.

1 Open Acrobat in Windows.

2 Choose File > Open, and navigate to the Lesson09/Assets folder.

3 Select Travel Guide.pdf, and click Open.

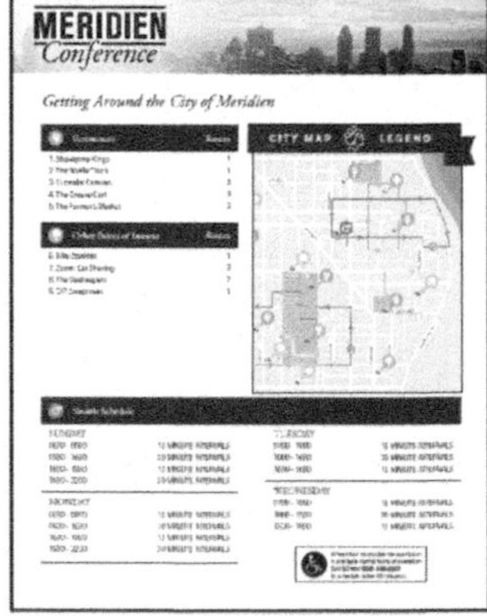

The Travel Guide.pdf file opens. In Protected Mode, you can access all of the menus and tools in Acrobat or Acrobat Reader. However, the PDF file cannot make calls to your system outside the application environment.

4 Choose File > Properties.

5 In the Document Properties dialog box, click the Advanced tab.

6 View the Protected Mode status at the bottom of the dialog box. It's On by default.

You can always confirm that a document is open in Protected Mode by viewing the Document Properties dialog box.

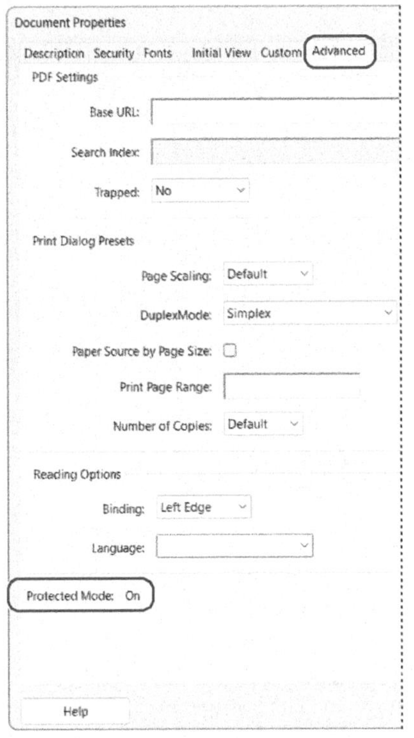

7 Click OK to close the Document Properties dialog box. Then close the Travel Guide.pdf file.

Adobe strongly recommends that you open documents in Protected Mode. However, some third-party plug-ins may not work in Protected Mode. If you need to disable Protected Mode, choose Edit > Preferences, select Security (Enhanced) from the list of categories, and deselect Enable Protected Mode At Startup. You'll need to restart Acrobat or Acrobat Reader for the changes to take effect.

About security in Acrobat

You can secure a PDF document using any of the following security methods:

- Add passwords and set security options to restrict opening, editing, and printing PDF files.
- Encrypt a document so that only a specified set of users has access to it.
- Save the PDF file as a certified document. Certifying a PDF file adds a certifying signature (which may be visible or invisible) that lets the document author restrict changes to the document.
- Apply server-based security policies to PDF files (for example, using Adobe LiveCycle Rights Management). Server-based security policies are especially useful if you want others to have access to PDF files for a limited time.

Note: You can use FIPs mode in Acrobat and Acrobat Reader to restrict data protection to Federal Information Processing Standard (FIPS) 140-2 approved algorithms. In FIPS mode, you cannot apply password-based security policies or create self-signed certificates. For more information, see Acrobat Help.

Viewing security settings

When you open a document that has restricted access or some type of security applied to it, you'll see a Security Settings button (🔒) in the navigation pane to the left of the document window.

1 Start Acrobat. Then choose File > Open, navigate to the Lesson09/Assets folder, and open the Sponsor_secure.pdf file. If the Acrobat Security Settings dialog box appears, click Cancel; if the Trusted Certificates Update dialog box appears, click OK.

2 Notice that "(SECURED)" appears after the filename in the title bar.

3 Open the Comment tool, and notice that the commenting and text markup tools are unavailable.

4 Click the triangle on the left side of the document window to open the navigation pane, if it isn't already open. Click the Security Settings button (🔒) in the navigation pane to view the security settings. Click the Permission Details link to view more detail.

The Document Properties dialog box lists each action and whether it is allowed. As you read down the list, you'll see that commenting is not allowed, which is why the related tools are dimmed. Signing, printing, editing, and other actions are also not allowed in this document.

5 When you have finished reviewing the information, click OK to close the Document Properties dialog box.

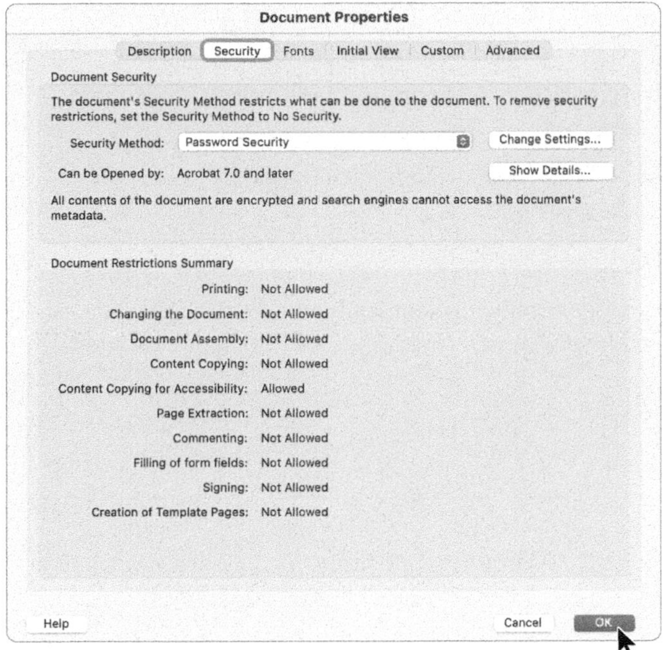

6 Choose File > Close File to close the Sponsor_secure.pdf file.

Adding security to PDF files

You can add security to your Adobe PDF files when you first create them, or you can add it later. You can even add security to files that you receive from someone else, unless the creator of the document has limited who can change security settings.

Now, you'll add password protection to limit who can open your document and who can change the security settings.

Adding passwords

You can add two kinds of passwords to protect your Adobe PDF documents. A Document Open password allows only users who enter the password to open the document. A Permissions password allows only users who enter the password to change the permissions for the document, so that they can print or modify the document or perform other changes you've restricted.

Tip: As long as you have the password, you can open password-protected and encrypted PDF files on tablets and phones using the Acrobat mobile app. To learn more, see Lesson 6, "Using Acrobat on Mobile Devices."

You'll add protection to a logo file so that no one can change its contents and so that unauthorized users can't open and use the file.

1 Choose File > Open, navigate to the Lesson09/Assets folder, and open the Local_Logo.pdf file.

There is no Security Settings button in the navigation pane, because no security has been applied to this document.

2 Choose File > Save As, save the file in the Lesson09/Finished_Projects folder, and name the file **Local_Logo1.pdf**.

3 Click Protect in the Tools pane.

4 In the Protect toolbar, click Advanced Options, and choose 2 Encrypt With Password. Click Yes when Acrobat asks whether you want to change the security on the document.

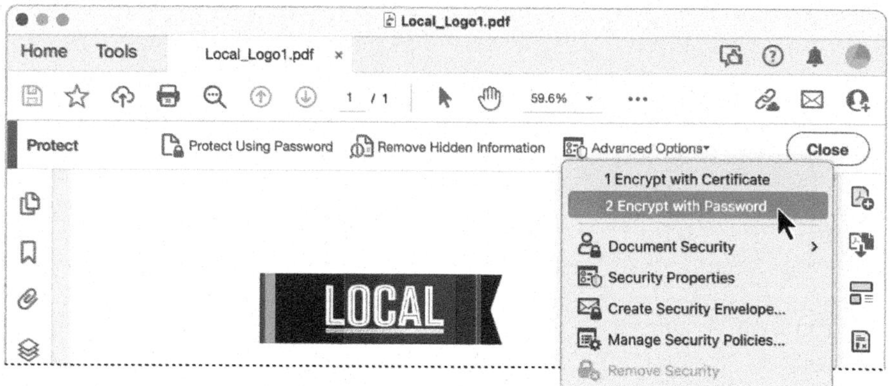

The Password Security – Settings dialog box opens.

Note: If you think that some of your viewers may still be using Acrobat 6.0 or Acrobat 7.0, select a different option. Be aware, however, that this setting may use a lower encryption level.

First, you'll set the compatibility level; if you change the compatibility level after entering passwords, you may have to enter them again.

5 Make sure Acrobat X And Later is selected in the Compatibility menu.

6 Select the Require A Password To Open The Document option, and then type **Logo1234;^bg** for the password.

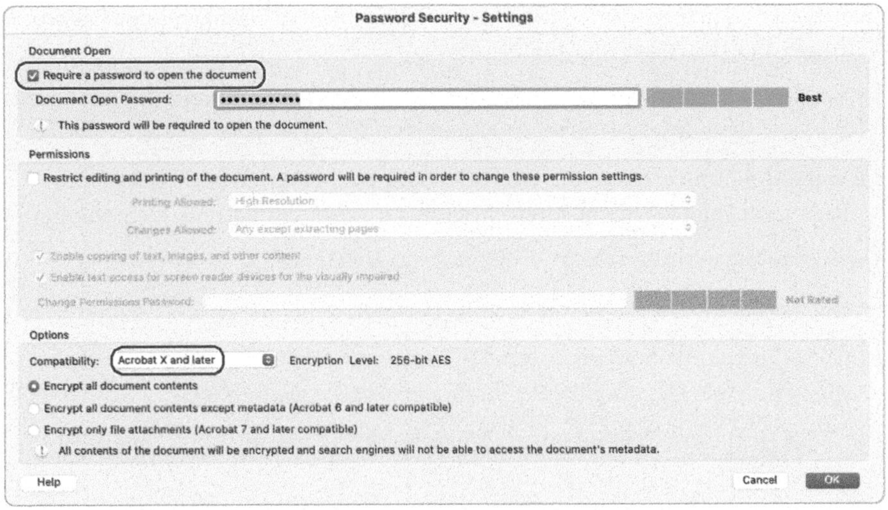

Acrobat rates the password's strength. Stronger passwords include both uppercase and lowercase letters, numbers, punctuation marks, and symbols. Longer passwords also tend to be harder to guess. If it's critical that a document remain confidential, use a strong password. You'll share this password with anyone who you want to allow to open the document. Remember that passwords are case-sensitive.

Now you'll add a second password that controls who is allowed to change printing, editing, and security settings for the file.

7 Under Permissions, select Restrict Editing And Printing Of The Document.

8 From the Printing Allowed menu, choose Low Resolution (150 dpi). You can prohibit printing, allow only low-resolution printing, or allow high-resolution printing.

9 From the Changes Allowed menu, choose Commenting, Filling In Form Fields, And Signing Existing Signature Fields to allow users to comment on the logo. You can prohibit all changes, some changes, or only prohibit viewers from extracting pages.

10 In the Change Permissions Password box, type **Logo5678;^bg**. Your open password and permissions password can't be the same.

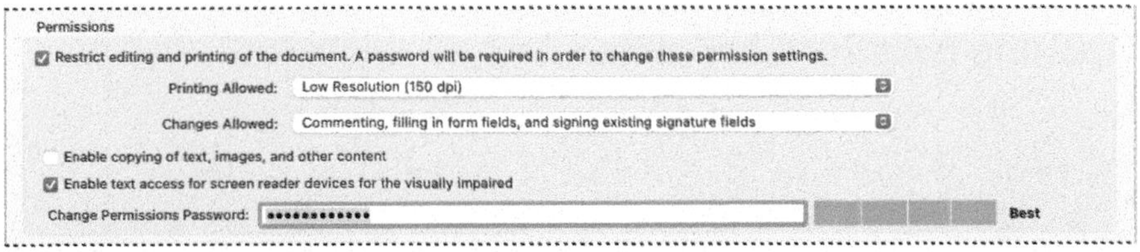

11 Click OK to apply your changes.

Tip: Always record your passwords in a secure location. If you forget your password, you can't recover it from the document. You might also want to store an unprotected copy of the document in a secure location.

12 In the Confirm Document Open Password dialog box, re-enter the Open Password, **Logo1234;^bg**. Then click OK.

13 Read the alert that warns you that some third-party applications may not honor the security settings in the PDF file, and click OK to clear the alert.

14 In the Confirm Permissions Password dialog box, re-enter the Permissions Password, **Logo5678;^bg**. Then click OK, and click OK again to clear the alert.

The security changes don't take effect until you save the file.

15 Choose File > Save to save the security changes.

16 Click the Security Settings button (🔒) in the navigation pane, and then click the Permission Details link. The limitations you set are in effect.

17 Click OK to close the Document Properties dialog box, and then choose File > Close File to close the Local_Logo1.pdf file.

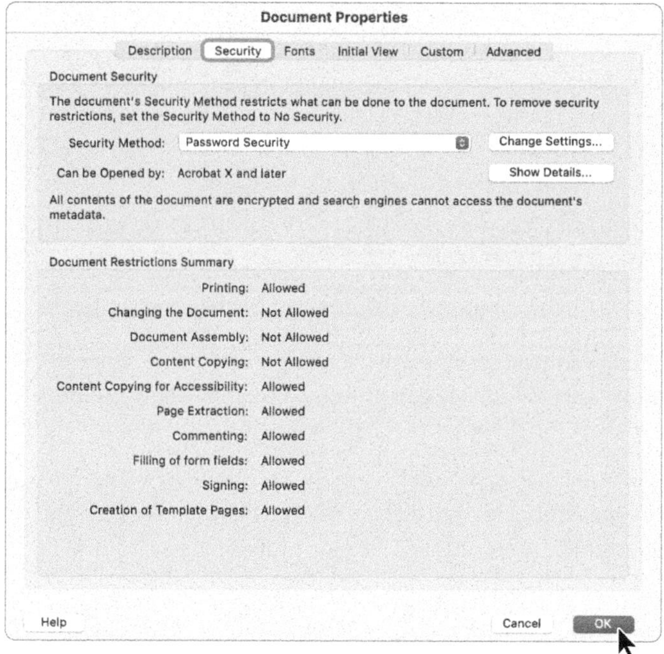

Opening password-protected files

Now you'll check the security that you've added to your file.

1 Choose File > Open, and open the Local_Logo1.pdf file in the Lesson09/ Finished_Projects folder.

Acrobat prompts you to enter the required password to open the file.

2 Enter the password (**Logo1234;^bg**), and click OK.

Notice that "(SECURED)" has been appended to the filename at the top of the application window.

Now you'll test the permissions password.

3 Click the Security Settings button (🔒) in the navigation pane if it's not already open, and click the Permission Details link.

4 In the Document Properties dialog box, choose No Security from the Security Method pop-up menu.

Acrobat prompts you to enter the Permissions password.

5 Enter the password (**Logo5678;^bg**), and click OK; then click OK again to confirm that you want to remove security.

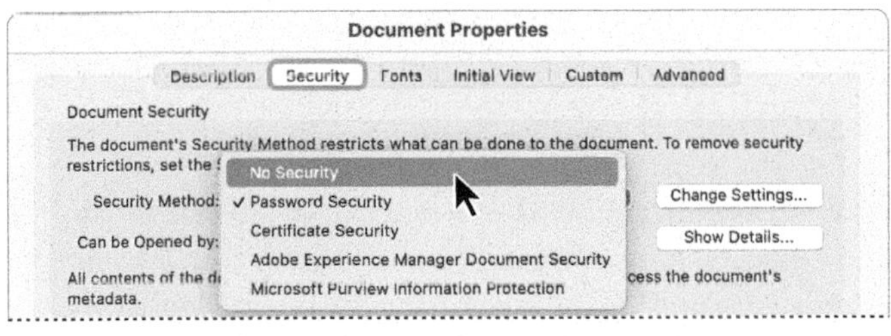

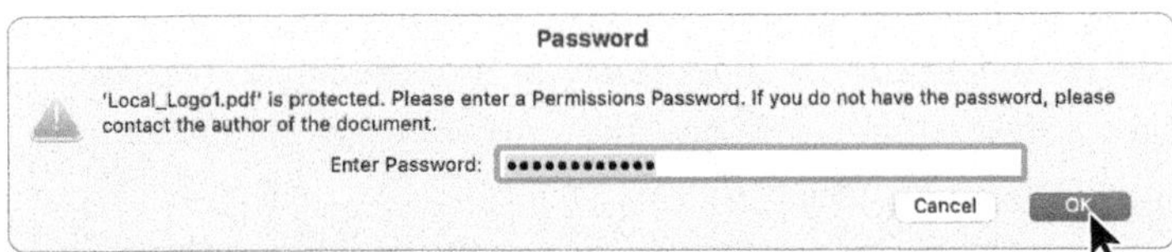

All restrictions are now removed from the file.

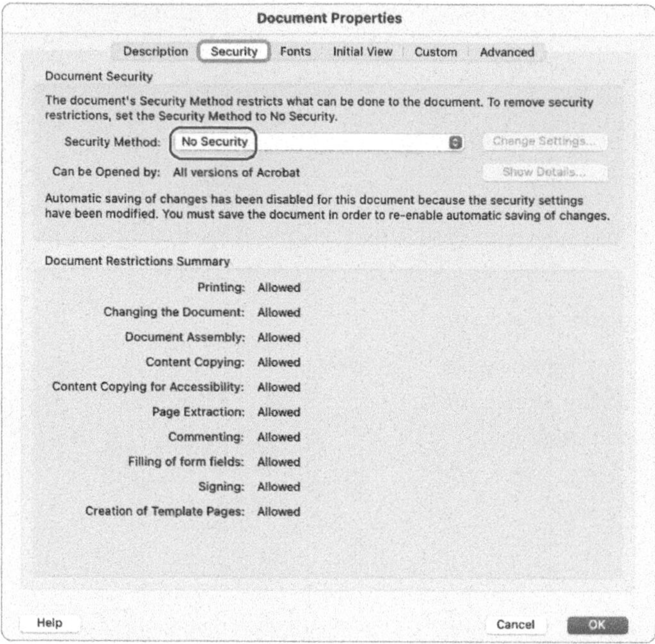

6 Click OK to close the Document Properties dialog box.

7 Choose File > Close File, and close the file without saving the changes. Because you aren't saving your changes, the passwords remain in effect next time you open the file.

About digital signatures

Signing a document electronically offers several advantages, not least of which is that you can return the signed document via the internet rather than having to fax it or send it by courier. Although digitally signing a document doesn't necessarily prevent people from changing the document, it does allow you to track any changes made after the signature is added and revert to the signed version if necessary. (You can prevent users from changing your document by applying appropriate security to the document.)

With an Acrobat or Creative Cloud subscription, you can use Acrobat Sign (formerly Adobe Sign) to sign a document or send it out for signatures. Acrobat Sign makes the process of signing documents electronically fast and simple.

You can also sign a document using certificates. To do so, obtain a digital ID from a third-party provider or create a digital ID (self-signed digital ID) for yourself in Acrobat. The digital ID contains a private key that is used to add the digital signature and a certificate that you share with those who need to validate your signature.

For information about Adobe security partners that offer third-party digital IDs and other security solutions, visit the Adobe website at www.adobe.com. To learn how to create and use your own digital ID, see "Using digital IDs" on page 217.

Sending a document for others to sign

The easiest way to invite someone else to sign a document electronically is to use Acrobat Sign. You'll prepare a document for Acrobat Sign, and then send it out for signatures. If you're working with others, you'll send it to a colleague to sign. However, if you're working alone, you'll need to have an alternate email address to use; you can create free email addresses through services such as Gmail or Yahoo Mail.

Preparing the form

If you send a document without preparing it, Acrobat Sign affixes signature and email fields to the bottom of the document. That may be all you need if, for example, you require only confirmation that someone has read a document. However, most forms require signatures or initials in specific locations, and many require other information as well. You'll prepare a form with standard signature blocks for the client (GlobalCorp) and the vendor (Custom Solutions).

1 In Acrobat, choose File > Open, navigate to the Lesson09/Assets folder, and double-click Statement of Work.pdf.

This document is a contract for services. The signature blocks are on the last page, but they aren't yet set up as form fields. You'll prepare the form before sending it for a signature.

2 Click Tools, and then click the Prepare Form tool to open it.

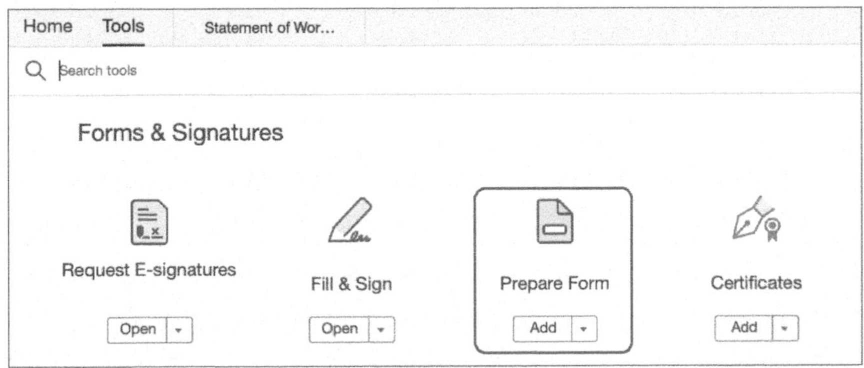

3 Make sure Statement of Work.pdf is the selected document, and select This Document Requires Signatures. Then click Start.

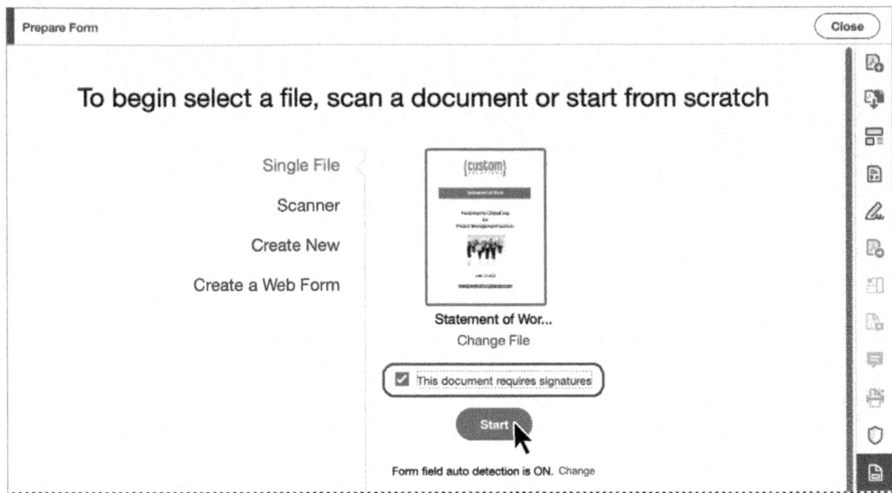

Acrobat opens the Prepare Form tool and analyzes the document for existing and likely form fields.

4 Click OK when Acrobat reports that no form fields were found.

5 Go to page 4 in the document to see the signature lines.

6 Select the Signature Field tool () in the Prepare Form toolbar.

7 Drag a signature form field above the GlobalCorp signature line.

8 Make sure Signer is chosen in the Who Needs To Sign This Field? menu.

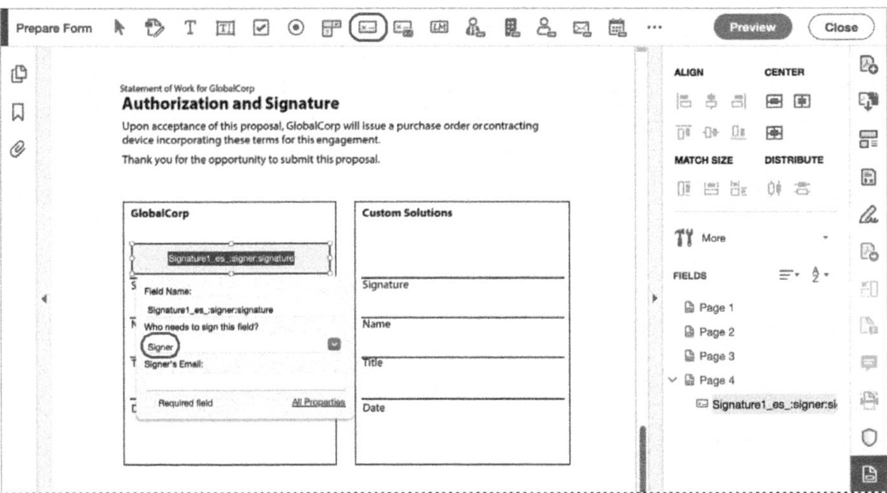

When Sender or one of the Signer options is chosen, the form field becomes an Acrobat Sign field. If Anyone is chosen in the Who Needs To Sign This Field? menu, Acrobat Sign won't recognize the field. You can add the signer's email address, too.

9 Select the Name Field tool (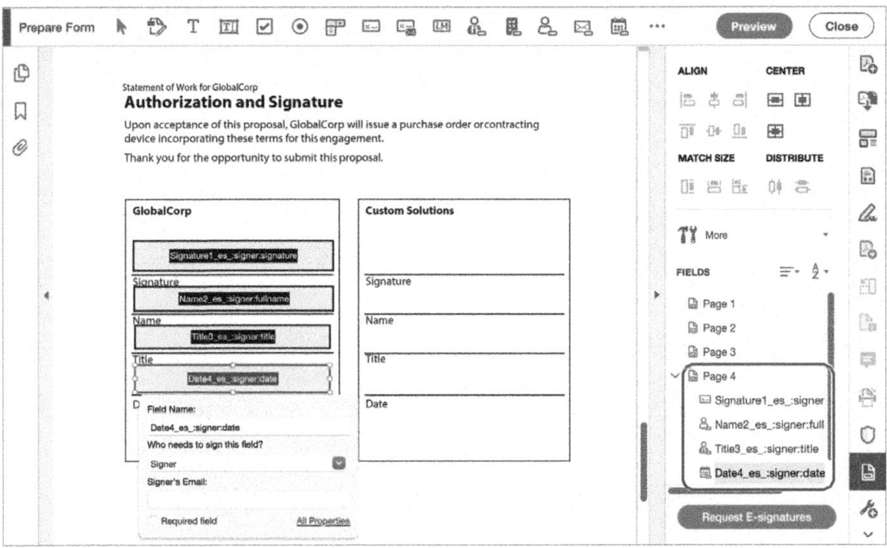) in the Prepare Form toolbar, drag a field above the GlobalCorp Name line, and make sure Signer is chosen in the Who Needs to Sign This Field? menu.

10 Select the Title Field tool () in the Prepare Form toolbar, drag a form field above the GlobalCorp Title line, and make sure Signer is chosen.

When the recipient signs the signature line, Acrobat Sign will automatically populate the Name field with the signer's name. It will also automatically add the current date to the Date field.

11 Select the Date Field tool () in the Prepare Form toolbar, drag a form field above the GlobalCorp Date line, and make sure Signer is chosen.

You've created the fields for the GlobalCorp signer. Now you'll create the fields for the Custom Solutions representative. Because Custom Solutions is sending the document, you'll choose Sender from the Who Needs To Sign This Field? menu.

12 Select the Signature Field tool, and drag a form field above the Custom Solutions signature line.

13 Choose Sender from the Who Needs To Sign This Field? menu. You may need to scroll up to see the option.

14 Use the Name Field, Title Field, and Date Field tools to add the remaining fields, choosing Sender from the Who Needs to Sign This Field? menu each time.

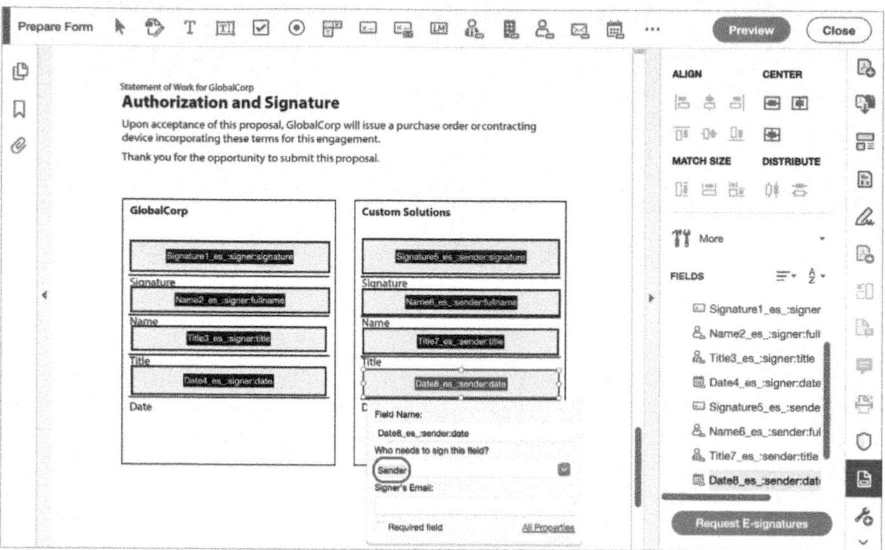

Sending the document

All the form fields are in place and recognizable by Acrobat Sign, so you're ready to send the document. You'll send it to another person to sign for GlobalCorp and to yourself to sign for Custom Solutions. When you enter email addresses in the Acrobat Sign dialog box, Acrobat Sign sends the document to each address in the order they're entered. That is, the document is sent to the first person to sign, and when it's been signed, the document—including the first person's signature—is sent to the second person to sign, and so on.

1 Click Request E-signatures in the right-hand pane.

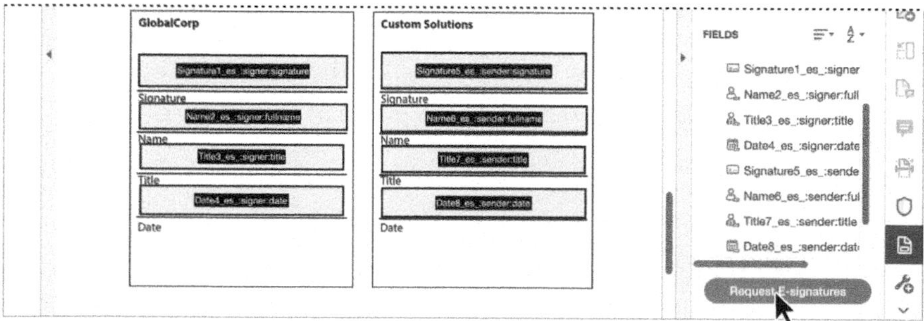

2 Enter the email address of the person who should sign the document first, and press Enter or Return. For this exercise, use a colleague's email address or an alternate address you've created. This person will be prompted to sign the fields that are specified for the Signer.

3 Just after the first signer's email address, add the email address from which you're sending the document. This should be the email address associated with your Adobe ID. You'll be prompted to sign the fields specified for the Sender.

4 Customize the message if you want to, and then click Specify Where To Sign.

Note: Acrobat compares the email address you enter with your address book. If it doesn't find the address you enter, it may prompt you to enter an address again. Click the address you already entered to proceed.

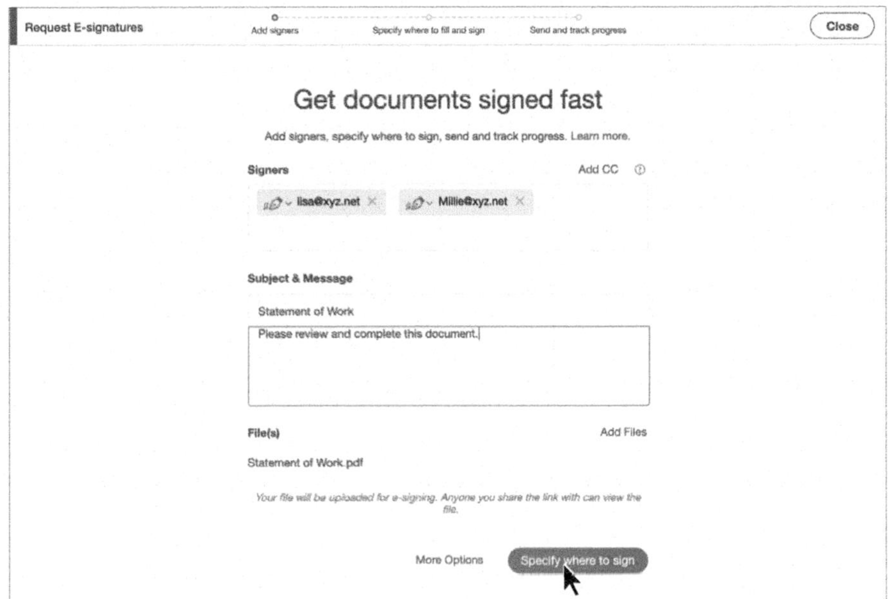

Acrobat uses Acrobat Sign to send the documents for signature. It uploads the document, and then analyzes the form fields.

5 Scroll to page 4 to verify that the form fields are correct.

6 Click Send.

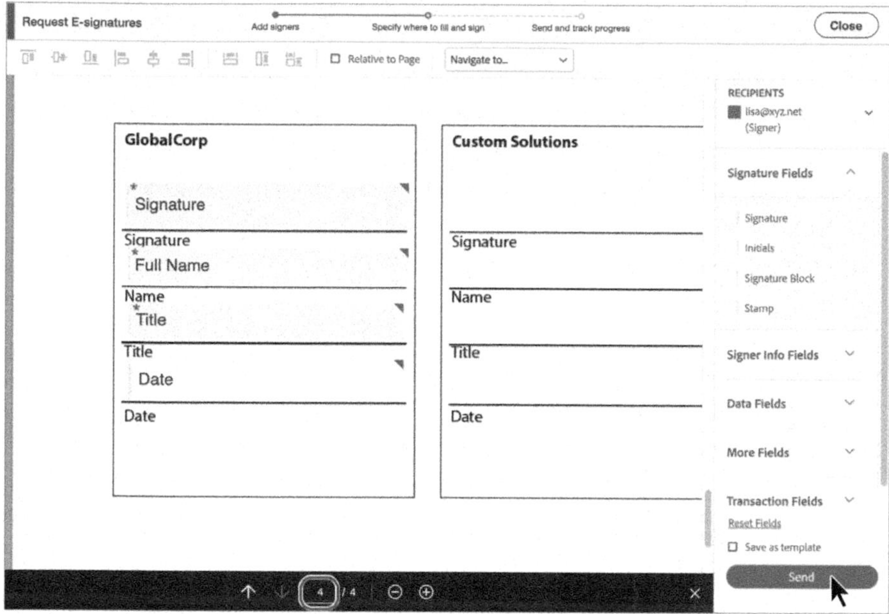

Acrobat Sign reports that your document has been sent for signature, and that when it's been fully signed, all parties will receive final copies. Acrobat Sign also emails you to confirm that the document has been sent for signature.

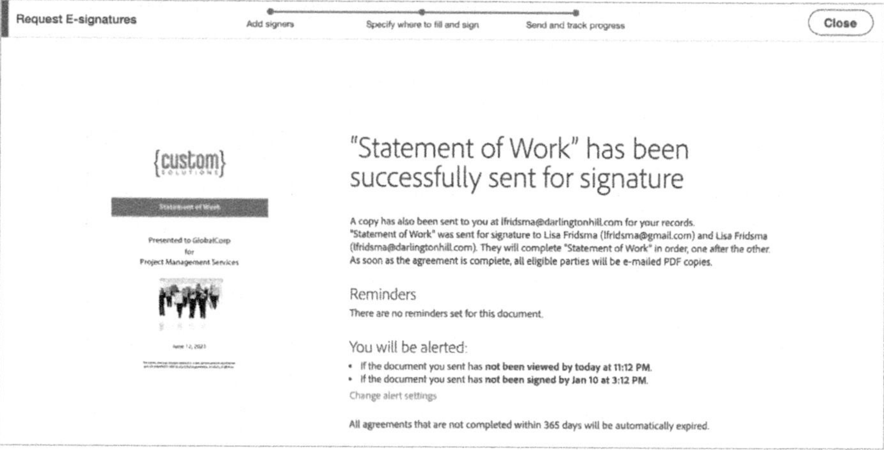

Doing more with e-signatures

There are several ways to sign documents and request signatures. You can use the Fill & Sign tool to sign and complete forms that don't include fields. Using Acrobat on the web, you can send similar documents to multiple people for signatures, or use Acrobat Sign to request payment along with a signed document.

Using the Fill & Sign tool

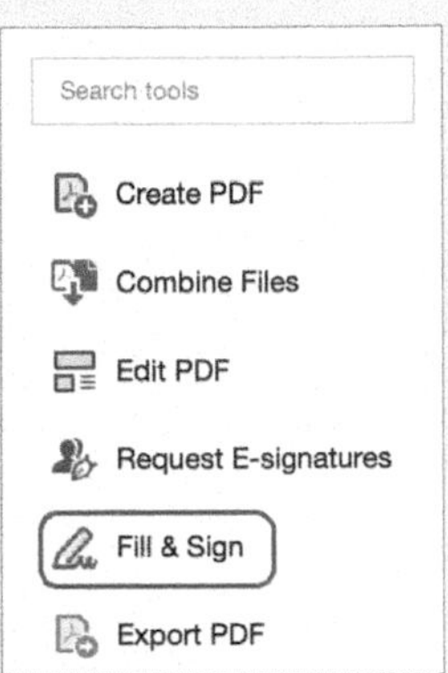

With the Fill & Sign tool, you can fill in a form that doesn't include Acrobat form fields, and you can sign anything anywhere. If you're signing legal documents, you should probably use Acrobat Sign or a digital ID to sign your document. But if you're signing a permission slip or other more casual document, the Fill & Sign tool gives you the flexibility to sign without having to create form fields.

To sign a document using the tool, click Fill & Sign in the Tools pane. Then click Sign Yourself in the Fill & Sign toolbar, and choose Add Signature or Add Initials (or choose your name or initials, if Acrobat already has your name and initials stored). Type your name, if it's not already there. You can change the style, draw your signature, or even import a scanned image of your signature. Click Apply. The cursor becomes your signature; just click it where you want your signature to appear.

To fill in other fields, select the Add Text tool in the Fill & Sign toolbar, position the cursor on the page, and start typing. Click outside the text box to accept what you've typed.

Download the Fill & Sign app to use the tool on mobile devices. You can use your stylus or finger to add your signature on a phone or tablet.

continues on next page

Doing more with e-signatures (continued)

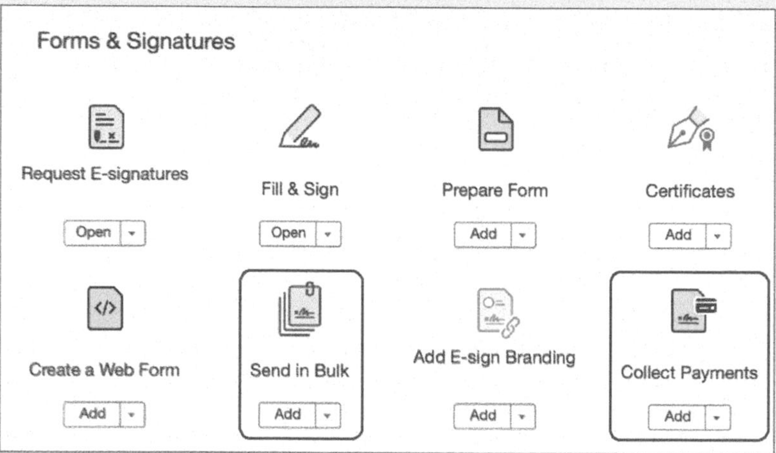

Sending forms in bulk

Upload a form to use as a template for unique agreements, each created for a single signer and kept separate and confidential. As the sender, you can access all the agreements, track their status, and export field-level data from completed agreements into CSV format.

To send forms in bulk:

1 Select the Send In Bulk tool in the Tools Center in Acrobat.

Acrobat opens the Request Signatures in Bulk tool in your web browser. (You can also access the tool by choosing Send In Bulk from the E-sign menu in Acrobat for the web.)

2 Click Select Files and choose a method to add the base file.

3 Add the list of signers' email addresses, separated by commas. Then click the key icon to confirm the authentication method (email or password) for each participant.

4 Follow the on-screen instructions to prepare the forms and send them.

Requesting payment

Make it easy for your customers to pay you when they sign the contract. Use Acrobat on the Web to request payment along with an e-signature using Braintree, a PayPal service. Once your Braintree account is set up, select the Collect Payments tool in the Tools Center in Acrobat, or choose Collect Payments from the E-sign menu in Acrobat for the web to integrate convenient, secure payment options into your PDF forms. To learn more, see Adobe Acrobat Help.

Signing the document

Acrobat Sign sends an email message to the first address you listed. You'll complete the form for the signer, and then complete it for the sender.

1 Log in to the email account whose address you entered first, the one that would be for the GlobalCorp representative. (If you used a colleague's email address, ask them to access their account.)

2 Open the message with the subject line "Signature requested on "Statement of Work."

3 Read the message, and then click Review And Sign.

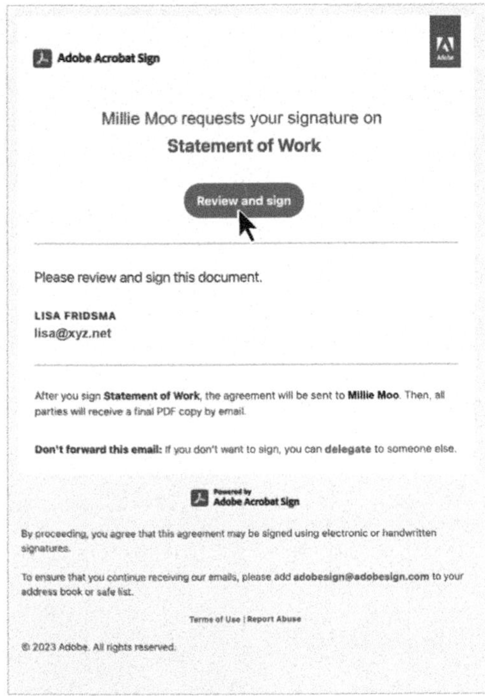

Acrobat Sign opens in your default browser.

4 If prompted, sign out of Acrobat Sign, and then click the link in the email message again to open the document as the signer.

5 Click the yellow arrow labeled Start to go to the first field that requires your input.

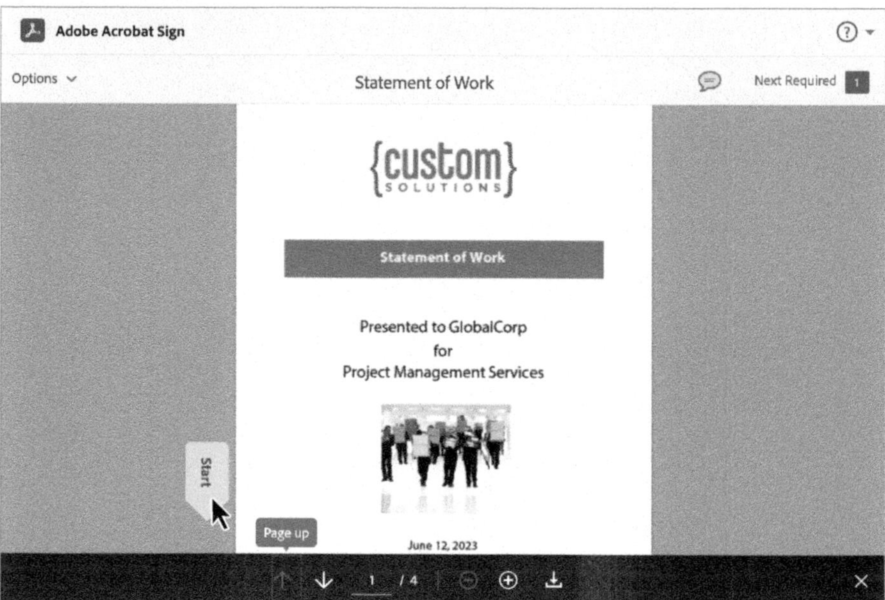

6 Click the GlobalCorp signature field.

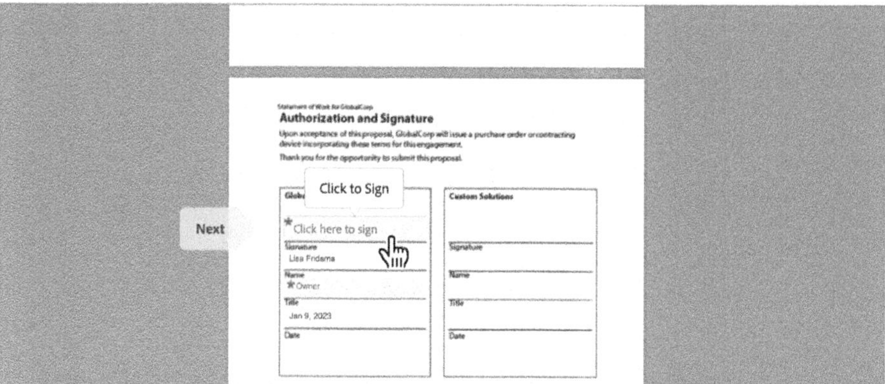

A signature dialog box opens.

7 Type your name. If you want it to look like your manual signature, click Draw, and then draw your signature using a stylus, tablet, or touch screen. You can also create a signature on a mobile device. Click Image if you want to use an image or logo for your signature. (You can use an image of your written signature.) When you're satisfied with your signature, click Apply.

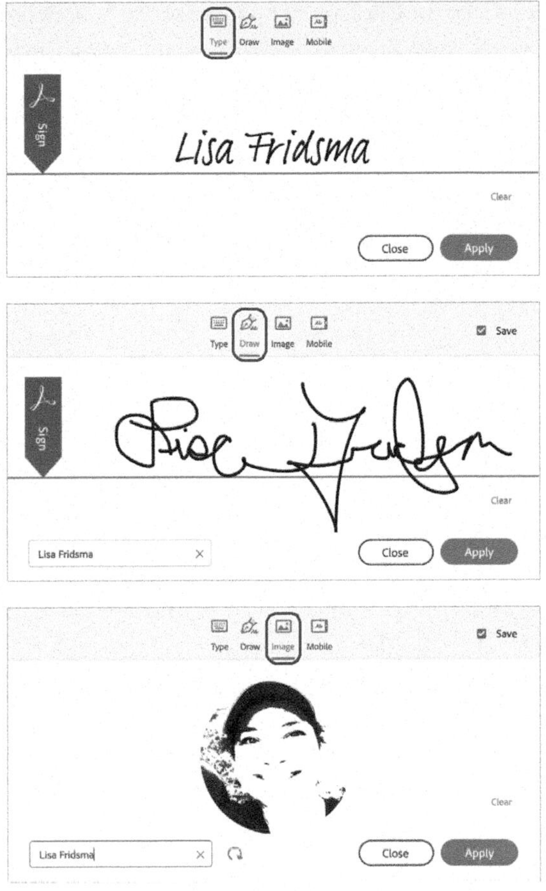

Whether you select Type, Draw, or Image in the signature dialog box, you must type your name so that it is officially recorded in the Acrobat Sign transaction. Acrobat Sign automatically fills in the Name field with that information.

8 Type a title in the Title field, if it hasn't been automatically filled. (If you've created a profile that includes a title, Acrobat Sign automatically uses that.)

9 Click the Click To Sign button at the bottom of the screen.

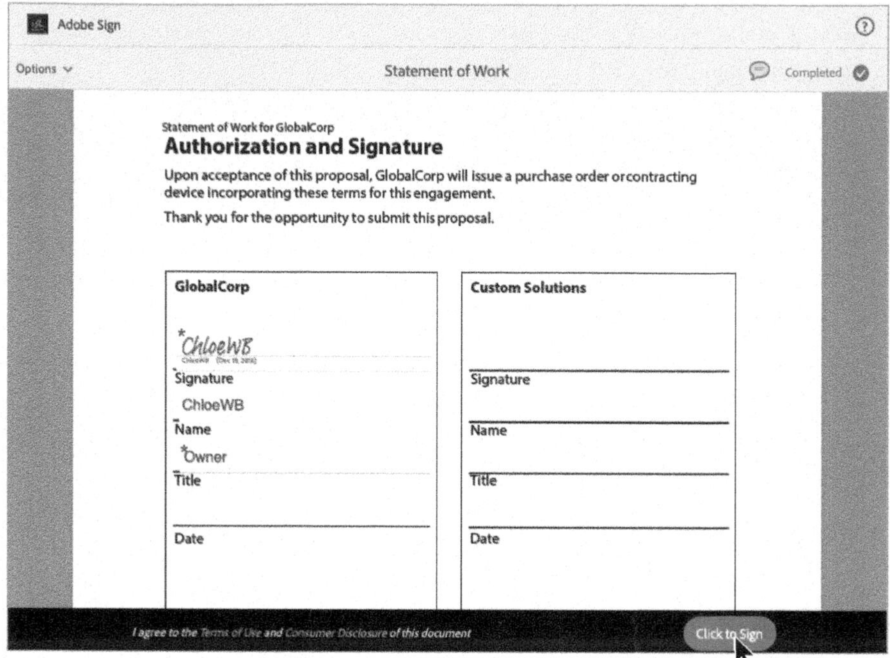

Now that the first person has signed, Acrobat Sign sends the document to the second email address, which is yours, as the sender.

10 Log in to the email address you used to send the document (the email address associated with your Adobe ID).

11 Open the message with the subject line that reads "Your signature is required on Statement of Work."

The subject line is different from the one in the email message you opened before, because this one is addressing the document's sender.

12 In the message, click Click Here To Review And Sign Statement of Work.

13 Acrobat Sign opens with the same document. Click the yellow arrow labeled Start.

The GlobalCorp fields are completed. The Custom Solutions fields are now active.

14 Repeat steps 6-9 to sign and complete the Custom Solutions fields and to submit the signed document.

Acrobat Sign sends messages to all parties informing them that the document has been signed and filed, and it attaches a PDF file of the final signed document to the message.

15 Close any open documents and Acrobat.

Using digital IDs

Acrobat Sign is usually the most convenient secure method of signing a document electronically. However, you can also sign PDF files electronically or certify their contents using certificates and digital IDs.

A digital ID is similar to a driver's license or passport. It proves your identity to people with whom you communicate electronically. A digital ID usually contains your name and email address, the name of the company that issued your digital ID, a serial number, and an expiration date. A digital ID lets you create a digital signature or decrypt a PDF document that has been encrypted. You can create more than one digital ID to reflect different roles in your life.

With a self-signed ID, you share your signature information with other users using a public certificate. (A certificate is a confirmation of your digital ID and contains information used to protect data.) While this method is adequate for most unofficial exchanges, a more secure approach is to obtain a digital ID from a third-party provider.

When you create a self-signed digital ID in Acrobat, you can set the appearance of your digital signature, select your preferred signing method, and determine how digital signatures are verified in the Security preferences. You should also set your preferences to optimize Acrobat for validating signatures before you open a signed document.

Creating a digital ID

To create a digital signature and a digital ID:

1 Choose Edit > Preferences (Windows) or Acrobat > Preferences (macOS), and select Signatures from the categories on the left.

2 In the Creation & Appearance area of the dialog box, click More. In the Appearances section of the dialog box, click New.

3 Personalize your digital signature by adding a graphic and specifying which information appears.

4 When you're satisfied, click OK, and then click OK again to return to the Signatures Preferences dialog box.

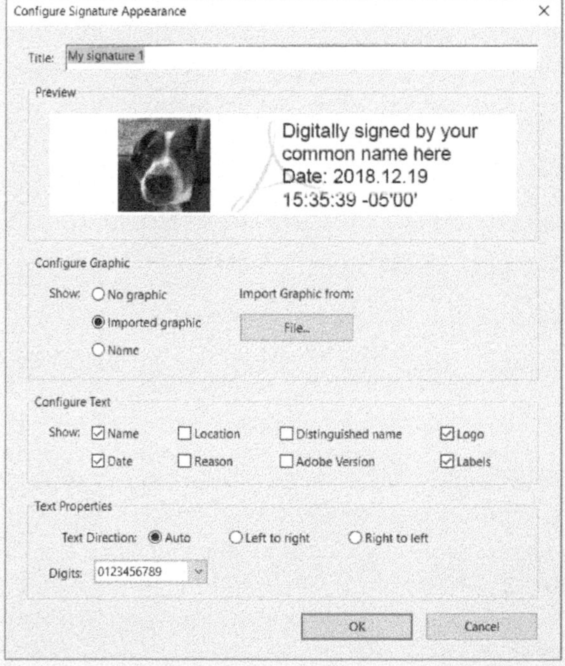

continues on next page

Using digital IDs (continued)

5 Click More in the Identities & Trusted Certificates area of the Digital Signatures Preferences dialog box. Then select Keychain Digital IDs in the left pane, and click the Add ID button.

6 Select A New Digital ID I Want To Create Now, click Next, choose where to store your digital ID (Windows only), and enter your personal information. Choose a level of security and how you want to use the digital ID (e.g., signatures and data encryption). Click Next, create a password, and click Finish to save the digital ID file. Close the Digital ID and Preferences dialog boxes.

Signing a document digitally with certificates and digital IDs

To use a digital ID to sign a document:

1 In the Forms & Signatures section of the Tools Center, click Certificates.

2 Click Digitally Sign in the Certificates toolbar, and then drag to create a signature field on the page.

3 Click Sign if prompted, select the digital ID you want to use, and click Continue. Enter the password, choose a signature appearance, and enter any required information (such as a reason for signing).

4 Click Sign to apply your signature, and click Save to save the signed file. Click Yes or Replace to replace the original file.

To see whether a signature is valid, open the Signatures panel in the navigation pane. Expand the signature line and the Signature Details entry.

Certifying PDF files

You can also certify the contents of a PDF document, which is useful if you want the user to be able to make approved changes to a document. When you certify a document and a user makes approved changes, the certification is still valid. You can certify forms, for example, to guarantee that the content is valid when the user receives the form. As the creator of the form, you can specify what tasks the user can perform. For example, you can specify that readers can fill in the form fields without invalidating the document. However, if a user tries to add or remove a form field or a page, the certification will be invalidated.

To certify a PDF file:

1 Click Tools, and then open the Certificates tool.

2 Click Certify (Visible Signature) in the Certificates toolbar. In the dialog box that appears, click Drag New Signature Rectangle, and then click OK in the Save As Certified Document dialog box.

3 Drag anywhere in the document to create a signature field, and then select the digital ID to use. Click Continue, enter the password, choose an appearance, and enter any additional information. Choose an option from the Permitted Actions After Certifying menu, click Review to see any warnings about content, click OK, and then click Sign.

When you open a certified document, you'll see a Certification icon at the left of the message bar. You can click this icon at any time to see certification information for the document.

For more information about creating and using digital IDs, sharing certificates, and certifying PDF files, see Adobe Acrobat Help.

Review questions

1 What is Acrobat Sign?

2 Why would you want to apply password protection to a PDF file?

3 Why would you apply permissions protection to a PDF file?

Review answers

1 Acrobat Sign is an electronic signature service that makes it easier for individuals and businesses to sign documents quickly and securely. If you have an Acrobat or Creative Cloud subscription, you can use Acrobat Sign to send documents for signatures and to track and manage those documents.

2 If you have a confidential document that you don't want others to read, you can apply password protection. Only users with whom you share your password will be able to open the document.

3 Permissions protection limits how someone can use or reuse the contents of your Adobe PDF file. For example, you can specify that users cannot print the contents of your file, or copy and paste the contents of your file. Permissions protection allows you to share the content of your file without losing control over how it is used.

10 USING ACROBAT IN A REVIEW CYCLE

Lesson overview

In this lesson, you'll do the following:

- Discover multiple ways to use Acrobat in a document review process.
- Annotate a PDF file with the Acrobat commenting and markup tools.
- View, reply to, search, and summarize document comments.
- Import comments.
- Initiate a shared review.
- Compare versions of a document (Acrobat Pro only).

This lesson will take approximately 60 minutes to complete. Download the project files for this lesson, following the instructions in the Getting Started section under "Accessing the lesson files and Web Edition," if you haven't already done so. As you work on this lesson, you'll preserve the start files. If you need to restore the start files, download them from your Account page.

Robust commenting tools and collaboration features in Acrobat keep review cycles efficient and make it easy for stakeholders to give feedback.

About the review process

There are several ways to use Acrobat in a document review process. No matter which method you use, the workflow contains some core elements: the review initiator invites participants and makes the document available to them, reviewers comment, and the initiator gathers and works with those comments.

You can share any PDF document by email, on a network server, or on a website, and ask individuals to comment on it using Acrobat Reader or Acrobat. If you post the document or email it manually, you'll need to keep track of returned comments and merge them as you receive them. If you're requesting feedback from only one or two other people, this might be the most efficient way for you to work. For most reviews, however, you can gather comments more efficiently using a shared review process. Additionally, in a shared review, reviewers can see and respond to each others' comments.

When you initiate an email-based review in Acrobat, you send the PDF file as an email attachment, track responses, and manage the comments you receive. Anyone with Acrobat or Acrobat Reader can add comments to the PDF file.

When you initiate a shared review in Acrobat, you post the PDF file to Adobe's cloud storage, a network folder, WebDAV folder, or SharePoint or Office 365 subsite. Then you email invitations to reviewers, who can access the shared document, add comments, and read others' comments using Acrobat or Acrobat Reader.

Getting started

In this lesson, you'll add comments to a PDF document, view and manage comments, and initiate a shared review. By definition, collaboration requires you to work with other people. Therefore, many of the exercises in this lesson will be more meaningful if you work through them with one or more colleagues or friends. However, if you are working independently, you can complete the exercises using alternative email addresses, available through web services such as Gmail or Yahoo Mail. (See the legal agreements on their websites for information about how you may use their email accounts.)

First, open the document you'll work with.

1 In Acrobat, choose File > Open.

2 Navigate to the Lesson10/Assets folder, and double-click the Profile.pdf file.

3 Click Comment in the Tools pane.

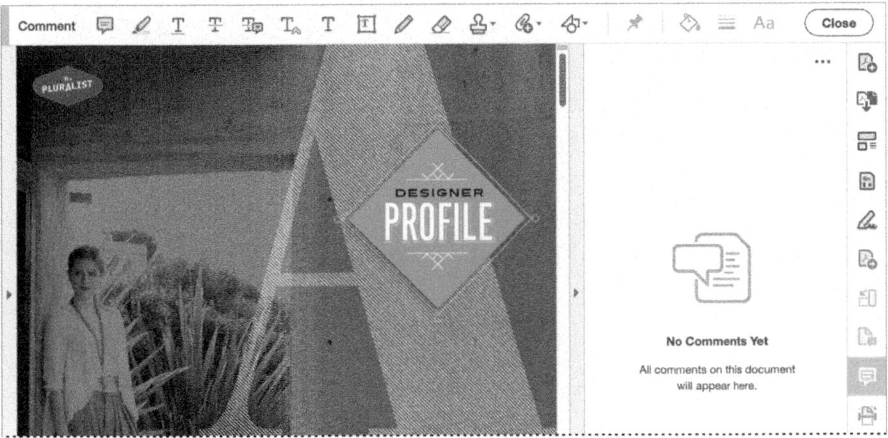

Adding comments to a PDF document

You can add comments to any PDF file, unless security has been applied to the document to prohibit commenting. In most cases, you'll use the commenting features to provide feedback to a document's author, but you may also find them useful to write notes to yourself as you're reading documents. Acrobat includes several commenting tools. You'll recognize some of them from the physical world. For example, the Sticky Note and Highlight Text tools are electronic versions of physical tools you may have on your desk.

In this exercise, you'll use some of the commenting tools to provide feedback on an article about a fashion designer.

About the commenting tools

Acrobat provides several commenting and markup tools, designed for different commenting tasks. Most comments include two parts: the markup or icon that appears on the page, and a text message that appears in a pop-up note when you select the comment. Markup and icon tools are available in the Comment toolbar when the Comment tool is open. For detailed information about using each tool, see Adobe Acrobat Help.

> **Tip:** You can add comments to a PDF file on a tablet or phone using the Acrobat Reader mobile app. To learn more, see Lesson 6, "Using Acrobat on Mobile Devices."

- **Sticky Note tool** ( ) – Create sticky notes, just as you would in the physical world. Click wherever you want the note to appear. Sticky notes are useful when you want to make overall comments about a document or a section of a document, rather than commenting on a particular phrase or sentence.
- **Highlight Text tool** ( ) – Highlight text. To add a comment, click the highlight on the page.
- **Underline Text tool** ( ) – Indicate which text should be underlined.
- **Strikethrough Text tool** ( ) – Indicate which text should be deleted.
- **Replace Text tool** ( ) – Indicate which text should be removed, and type the text that should replace it.
- **Insert Text tool** ( ) – Add text at the insertion point. As with all the text commenting tools, your comments don't affect the text in the PDF document, but they make your intention clear.
- **Add Text tool** ( ) – Type text that appears directly on the page; like other comments, it won't change the document itself. You can move it, but unlike a pop-up note, you can't hide it.
- **Add Text Box tool** ( ) – Create a box that contains text, positioned anywhere on the page, and at any size. It remains visible on the page.
- **Pencil tool** ( ) – Draw freeform lines and shapes on the page.
- **Eraser tool** ( ) – Erase lines, or portions of lines, that you've drawn.
- **Stamp tool** ( ) – Use a virtual rubber stamp to approve a document, mark it confidential, or perform several other common stamping tasks. You can also create custom stamps for your own purposes.
- **Attach File tool** ( ) – Attach a file, in any format, to the PDF document.
- **Record Audio tool** ( ) – Clarify your feedback with an audio recording. The Record Audio tool is hidden beneath the Attach File tool. To record audio, you must have a built-in or removable microphone on your system.

> **Tip:** To create a custom stamp, click the Stamp tool, and choose Custom Stamps > Create. Then select the image file you want to use.

- **Drawing tools** (icon) – Use the drawing tools to emphasize areas on the page or communicate your thoughts visually, especially when reviewing graphical documents. You can use the **Line** (icon), **Arrow** (icon), **Rectangle** (icon), **Oval** (icon), **Text callout** (icon), **Polygon** (icon), **Cloud** (icon), and **Connected Lines** (icon) tools. You can expand the drawing tools to include all of them on the Comment toolbar.

Note: Text callouts let you specify the area you're commenting on without obscuring it. Callout markups have three parts: a text box, a knee line, and an end-point line. Drag handles to resize each part and position it exactly where you want it.

Commenting in Acrobat Reader

Acrobat Reader for the desktop includes all the commenting and markup tools that are available in Acrobat. The Acrobat Reader mobile app provides several commenting and markup tools: the Sticky Note, Highlight Text, Strikethrough, Underline, and Pencil tools. When a PDF file has been shared for review, Acrobat on the web provides the same commenting tools as the Acrobat Reader mobile app.

Adding sticky notes

You can attach a sticky note anywhere in a document. Because notes can easily be moved, they are best suited to comments about the overall content or layout of a document, rather than to specific phrasing. You'll add a sticky note on the first page of this document.

1 Select the Sticky Note tool (icon) in the Comment toolbar.

2 Click anywhere on the page.

A sticky note appears where you clicked. In the right-hand pane, the name in the Identity panel of the Acrobat Preferences dialog box automatically appears on the note, as well as the time.

3 Type **Looks good so far. I'll look again when it's finished.**

4 Right-click or Control-click the Sticky Note dialog box, and choose Properties from the pop-up menu.

▶ **Tip:** You can also change the color, line thickness, or text properties of comments using tools in the Comment toolbar.

5 Click the Appearance tab, and then click the Color swatch.

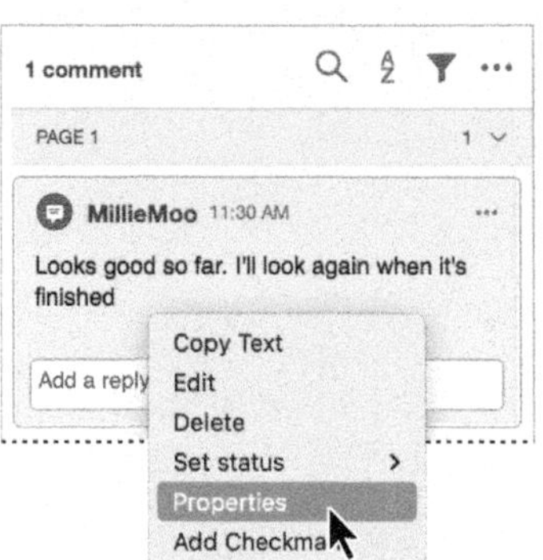

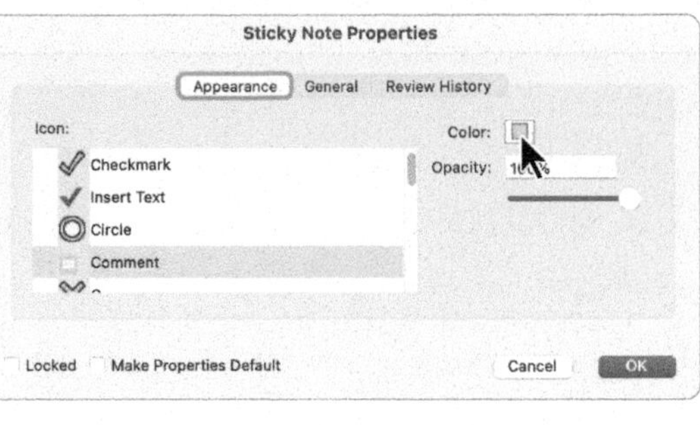

6 Select a blue swatch. If you're using macOS, close the Colors dialog box. The sticky note changes color automatically.

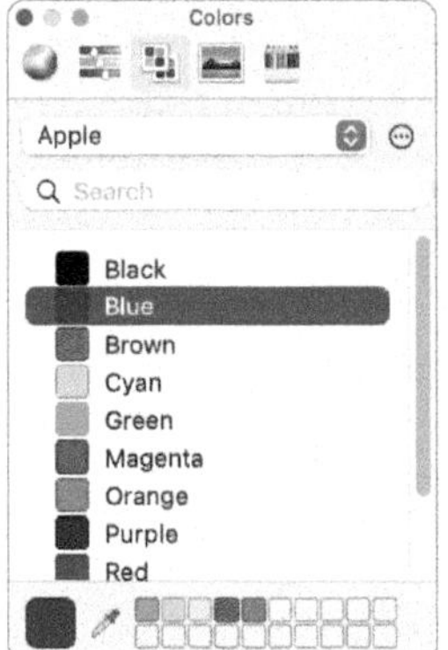

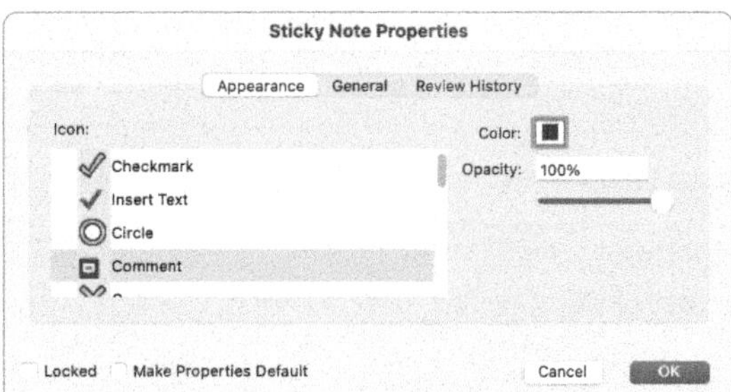

7 Click the General tab and then, in the Author box, type **Reviewer A**.

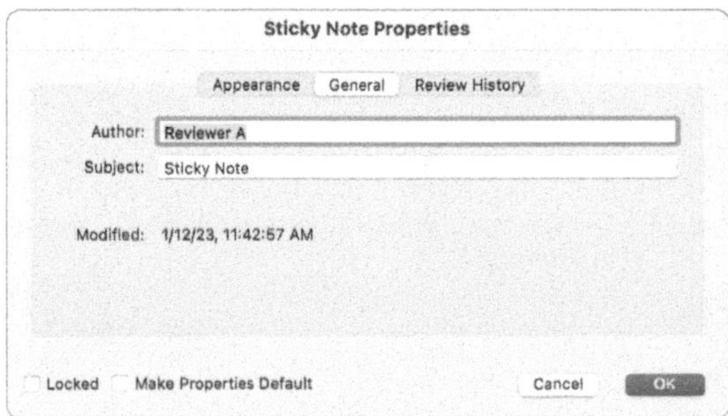

You can change the name attached to a comment. You may want to do that, for example, if you are using someone else's computer.

8 Click OK.

The contents of your note are displayed in the right-hand pane. The blue sticky note is closed on the page. To view it, just roll the cursor over the sticky note icon.

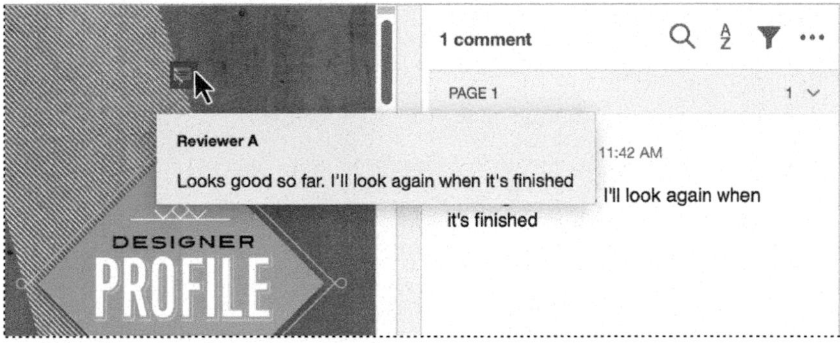

Emphasizing text

Use the Highlight Text tool to emphasize specific text in a document. After highlighting the text, you can also add a message. You'll make a comment using the Highlight Text tool in this document.

1 Scroll to page 3 in the document.

2 Select the Highlight Text tool (✎) in the Comment toolbar.

3 Drag the pointer over "ital" at the bottom of the second paragraph on the page. The text is highlighted in yellow.

4 A comment message box opens in the comments list.

5 Type **bad line break**.

6 Click Post to save your comment.

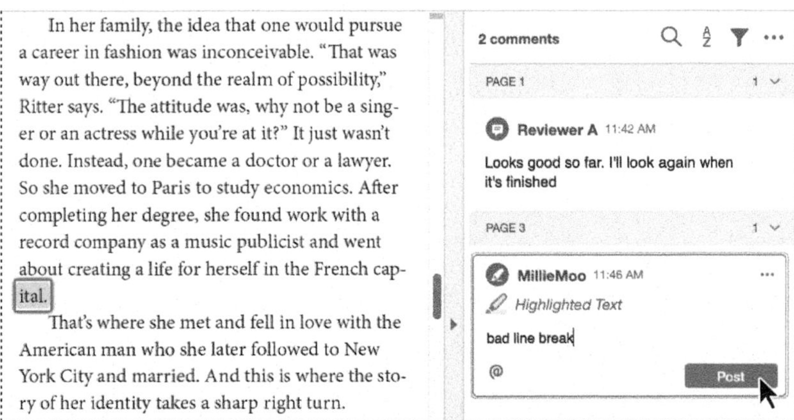

Marking text edits

You can clearly communicate which text should be deleted, inserted, or replaced using the text-editing tools. You'll suggest some text changes to the profile article.

1 Scroll to page 2 of the document.

2 Select the Replace Text tool (![icon]) in the Comment toolbar.

3 Select the words "Self reinvention" at the top of the page.

The original text is crossed out, and an insertion point appears. A comment field is created in the comments list.

4 Type **Self-reinvention** to replace the original text, and click Post.

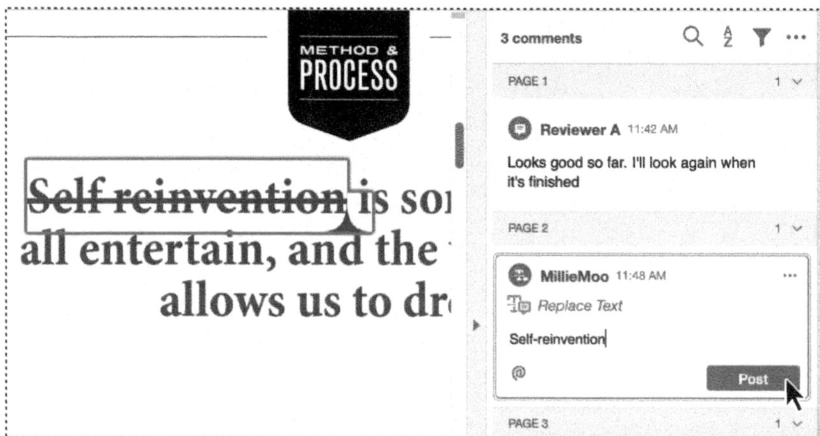

5 Select the Insert Text tool (![icon]) in the Comment toolbar. Then click an insertion point after "dress" in the last paragraph in the right column.

An insertion point icon appears in the original text, and a comment field appears in the comments list.

6 Type a dash (-) to indicate that a hyphen should be inserted in the text, and click Post.

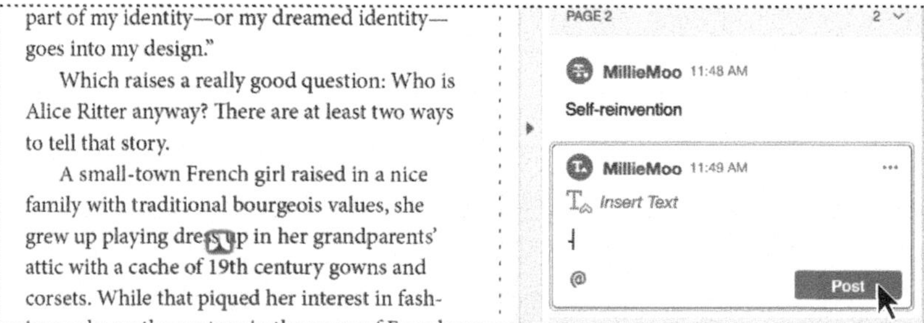

7 Select the Strikethrough tool (T̶) in the Comment toolbar.

8 Select the words "Which raises a really good question:" in the second paragraph in the right column.

A red line appears through the text, indicating deletion.

9 Go to page 5, and select the Underline tool (T̲).

10 Select the word "Emmanuelle" at the bottom of the left column. The word is underlined in the PDF file.

11 Double-click the area you underlined if the comment field isn't open in the comments list, and then type **Italicize movie title**, and click Post.

12 Choose File > Save As. Save the file in the Lesson10/Finished_Projects folder, and name the file **Profile_review.pdf**.

Working with comments

You can view comments on the page, in a list, or in a summary. You can import, export, search, and print comments. You can also reply to comments if you're participating in a shared review or will be returning the PDF file to a reviewer in an email-based review. In this exercise, you'll import comments from reviewers, sort comments, show and hide comments, search for comments, and change their status.

Importing comments

If you use a shared review process, comments are imported automatically. However, if you're using an email-based review process or collecting feedback informally, you can import comments manually. You'll import comments from three reviewers into the draft of the designer profile.

1 With the Profile_review.pdf file open, notice the comments in the right-hand pane. The only comments in the document are the ones you added.

2 From the options menu (•••) in the right-hand pane, choose Import Data File.

3 Navigate to the Lesson10/Assets/Comments folder.

4 Shift-click to select all three files in the folder: profile_Art_Director.pdf, profile_Linda.pdf, and profile_Stan.fdf.

5 Click Open (Windows) or Select (macOS).

6 Click OK or Yes if you see a message that comments were made on a different version of the document.

Two of the documents are PDF files with comments included; the FDF file is a data file that contains comments that a reviewer exported.

Tip: As a reviewer, you can export comments to a data file (named with an .fdf extension) to reduce file size, especially if you're submitting comments by email. To export comments, choose Export All To Data File or Export Selected To Data File from the options menu in the right-hand pane when the Comment tool is open.

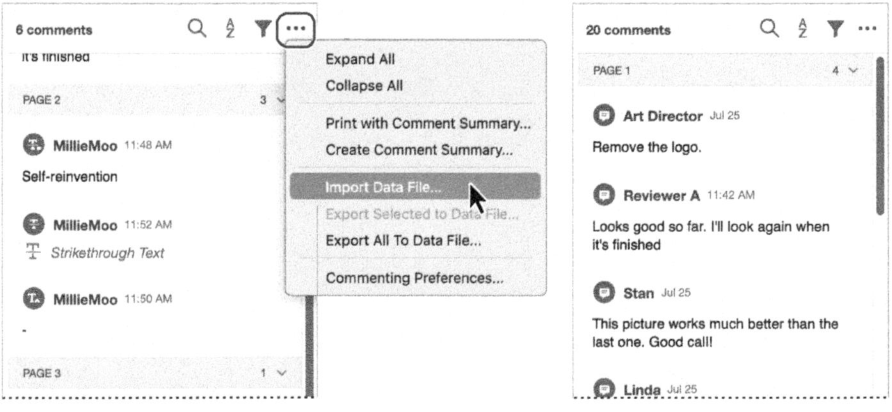

Acrobat imports the comments and displays them in the comments list.

Viewing comments

The comments list includes every comment in the document, with the comment author's name, the type of comment, and the comment itself.

1 Scroll through the comments list. By default, comments are listed in the order they appear in the document.

2 Above the comments list, click the Sort Comments button (A/Z), and then choose Author.

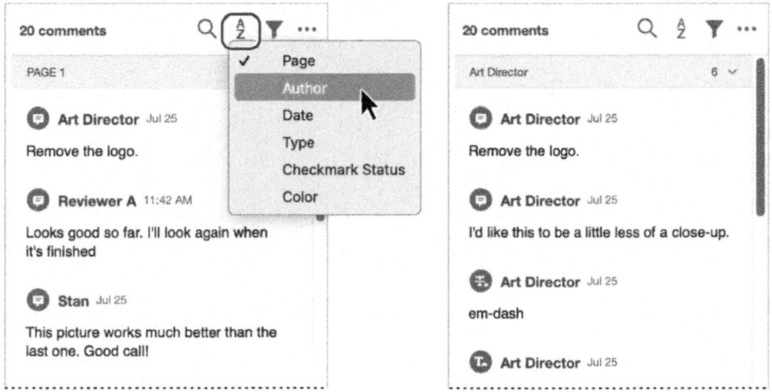

Acrobat rearranges the comments so that they are categorized by author name, with authors appearing in alphabetical order.

3 Click the Art Director's comment about a hyphen. When you click it, Acrobat moves the page to the comment location so that you can see it in context.

4 From the options menu in the comment field, choose Add Checkmark.

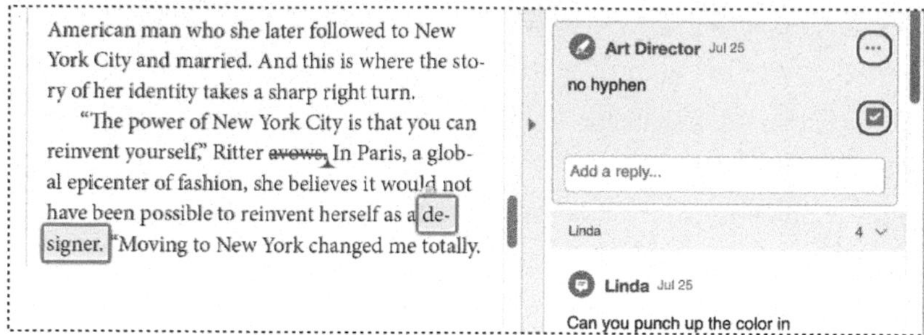

You can add check marks to indicate that you've read a comment, replied to it, discussed it with someone, or anything else that is meaningful to you.

5 Click the Filter Comments button (▽) above the comments list, select Unchecked, and click Apply.

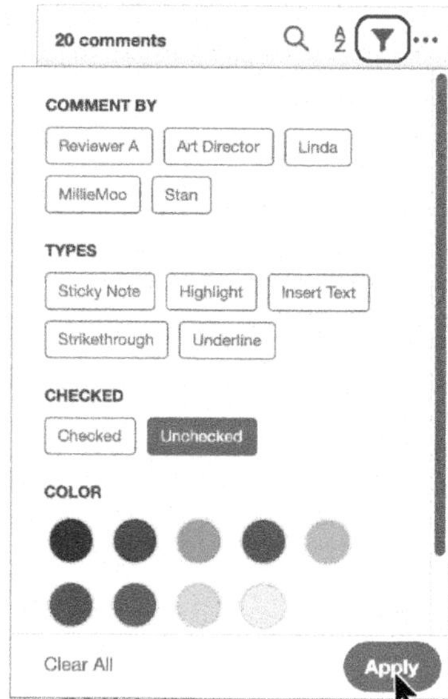

The comment you checked is no longer listed, but it remains in the document. You can use the filter options to declutter the comments list and focus on the comments you want to work with, whether you want to see only text edits, comments by a particular reviewer, or comments labeled with a particular color.

6 Click the Filter Comments button again, and click Clear All.

All the comments are listed again.

7 Above the comments list, click the Search button (🔍), and then type **logo** in the Search box.

Only one comment appears in the list, the only comment that includes the word "logo." You can use the Search box to search for any text in comments.

8 Select the comment. A reply field opens beneath the comment.

9 Type **Legal says the logo is required, per Janet**. Then click Post. Your name appears next to the reply, which is indented to show its position in the thread.

Note: The reviewer will see your reply only if you are using a shared review process or if you email a saved copy of the PDF file to the reviewer.

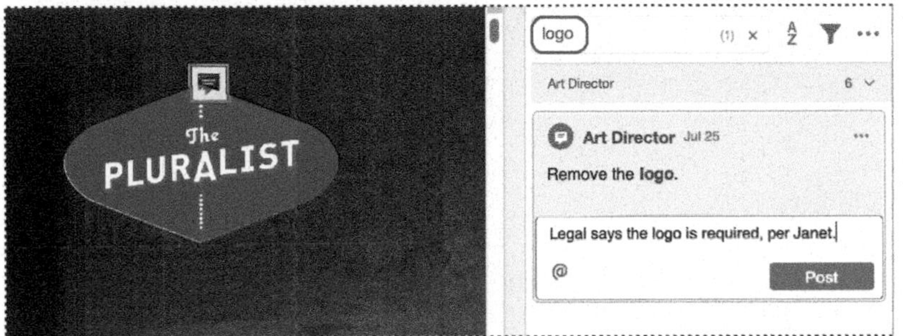

10 With the last comment still selected, right-click or Control-click the comment, and choose Set Status > Completed.

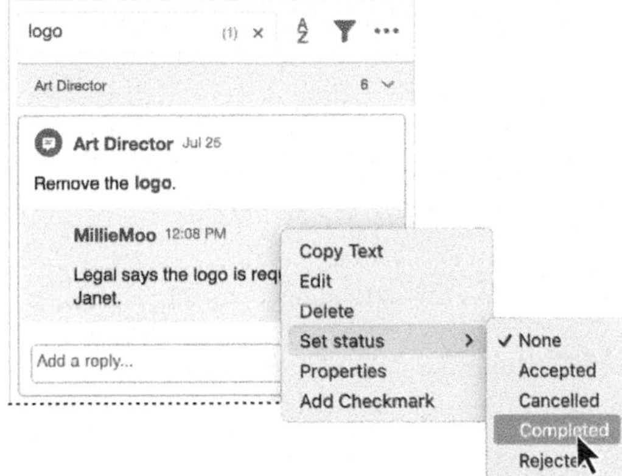

You can set the status of each comment for your own records and to show reviewers how their comments were handled.

11 Close the document, saving the changes if you like.

Summarizing comments

You can create a summary of comments, either as a list of only the comments, or as the document with comments referenced. From the options menu above the comments list, choose Create Comment Summary. In the Create Comment Summary dialog box, select the layout and other options for your summary. Then click Create Comment Summary. Acrobat creates and opens a separate PDF file with the comments summary layout you selected. You can view the summary onscreen or print it if you prefer to work with paper.

Initiating a shared review

In a shared review, you post the PDF file to a common server, such as Adobe's cloud storage, and invite reviewers to comment; all comments are automatically consolidated in the review version of the PDF file. All participants can view and respond to each others' comments. Using a shared review is an effective way to let reviewers resolve conflicting opinions, identify areas for research, and develop creative solutions during the review process.

For this exercise, you'll need to invite at least one other person to participate. If you are working on your own, you may want to create an alternative email address using a free web service such as Gmail or Yahoo Mail.

Inviting reviewers

You'll invite reviewers to comment on the document. Your file will be uploaded to Adobe's cloud storage, where the people you invite will have access to it.

1 Decide who you will invite to participate in the review, and make sure you have their email addresses. If you are working on this lesson alone, create an alternative email address that you can send an invitation to.

2 Choose File > Open.

3 Navigate to the Lesson10/Assets folder, and double-click the Registration.pdf file.

4 Click the Share With Others icon (icon) in the toolbar.

5 Type an email address in the Share With Others dialog box, and then press Enter or Return. You can enter more than one email address. To access your address book, click the Address Book button in the email field.

Instead of entering email addresses here, you could choose to email a link to reviewers. If you're asking for comments from numerous people subscribed to an email list, for example, it's more efficient to send a link once to the entire list. To do that, click the Share A Link icon in the toolbar, make sure Allow Comments is selected, and then click Create Link. When Acrobat has uploaded the PDF document to Adobe's cloud storage, click Copy Shared Link, and then paste that link into an email message. Once the link is created, you can access it again by clicking the Share A Link icon. You don't need a link when you're creating a shared review.

6 Make sure Allow Comments is enabled.

7 Customize the message for reviewers, if you want to.

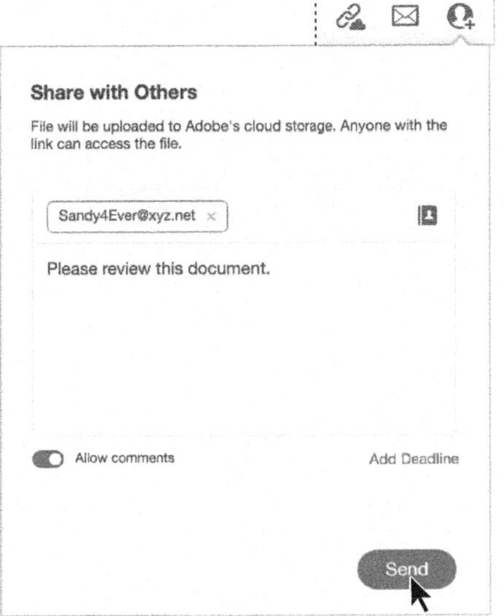

If you want to set a deadline for reviewers, click Add Deadline, select a date, and decide whether to send a reminder. For this exercise, no deadline is needed.

8 Click Send.

Acrobat copies the document to Adobe's cloud storage, and it sends email to reviewers using your default email application. The document is synced with the one in cloud storage. Acrobat shows a list of people you shared the document with and options to add more people, unshare the link, and download a copy to work with offline.

9 Close the PDF file in Acrobat.

Sending PDF files as email attachments

Instead of sharing the PDF file on Adobe's cloud storage, you can send it to reviewers as an email attachment. To do so, click the Send File By Email icon in the toolbar, select an email application, deselect Attach A Link, and click Next. Then, send the messages from your email account. In an email-based review, you'll need to gather and consolidate comments separately.

Participating in a shared review

You or your colleague will participate in the shared review, adding comments about the document.

Note: Though you're using a different email address, Acrobat may recognize your Creative Cloud account, so it may recognize that you're commenting on your own document.

1 If you're working alone, open the email invitation you sent to an alternative email address. If you're working with a colleague or friend, ask them to open the email invitation you sent and to follow the steps below.

2 Click Open in the email.

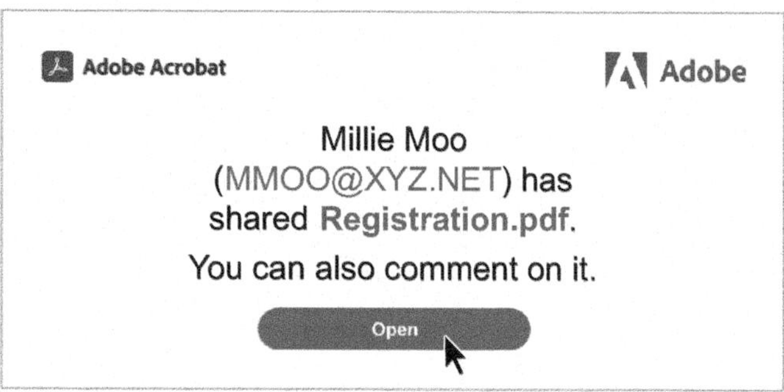

The document opens in Acrobat on the web in your default browser.

3 Add several comments to the PDF file using the commenting tools. If you aren't signed in to a Creative Cloud account, continue as a guest when prompted, and type in a name to appear on your comments. If you use the @ symbol to address someone in a comment, they'll receive a notification in Acrobat.

4 When you've finished reviewing the document, close the browser window.

Tracking review comments

You can keep track of reviewers' comments and reply to comments yourself from within Acrobat. You'll track the progress in your version of the document.

1 In Acrobat, click Home to see the Home view, if you're not there already.

2 In the Shared area on the left, click Shared By You. The Registration PDF file is listed. (You may need to close Acrobat and open it again to see the file.)

3 Select the Registration PDF file. Information about the review process appears on the right. You can see who you invited, and when the last activity in the document occurred.

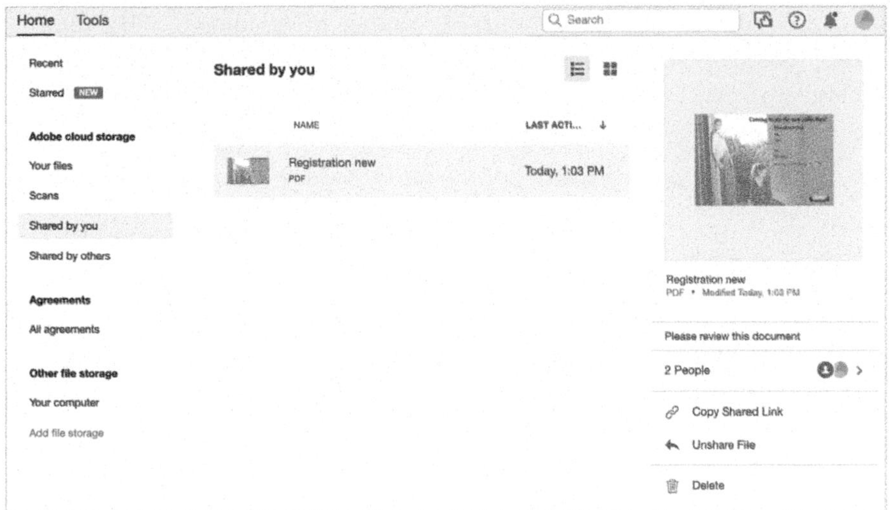

4 Double-click the Registration document to open it. Comments you made in the document in Acrobat and any comments made in Acrobat on the web appear in the comments list.

Note: Comments are synced as long as Acrobat can access Adobe's cloud storage.

5 Close the PDF file, but leave Acrobat open.

Using a network folder for a shared review

By default, Acrobat copies PDF files for review to Adobe's cloud storage. But you can also host a shared review on a network folder, WebDAV folder, SharePoint workspace or subsite, or Office 365 site.

To host a shared review on a network folder, first change your preferences: Choose Edit > Preferences (Windows) or Acrobat > Preferences (macOS), select Reviewing on the left, deselect Share For Review Using the Adobe's Cloud Storage, and click OK. Then, click the Send for Comments tool in the Tools pane, and click Send For Shared Commenting in the Send For Comments toolbar. Follow the steps in the wizard to share the file on your server and invite reviewers.

Comparing versions of documents (Acrobat Pro only)

In Acrobat Pro, you can see what's changed between two versions of a PDF document. This can be particularly helpful if you're working on a document that multiple people have edited. You'll compare the initial version of the Facilities.pdf file with the edited version.

1 Choose File > Open, navigate to the Lesson10/Assets folder, and double-click the Facilities.pdf file.

2 Click Tools to open the Tools Center, and then click Compare Files (in the Share & Review section) to open it.

Acrobat prompts you to choose the files you want to compare.

3 If the open document is selected in the New File column, click Swap Documents to move it to the Old File column.

4 Under New File, choose Browse For File from the Select File pop-up menu. Then double-click the Facilities_edited.pdf file in the Lesson10/Assets folder.

5 Click Settings.

You can compare specific pages, and you can tell Acrobat what sort of document you're working with. By default, Acrobat compares all the pages in the document, and it detects what kind of document it is.

6 Click OK to accept the default settings. Then click Compare.

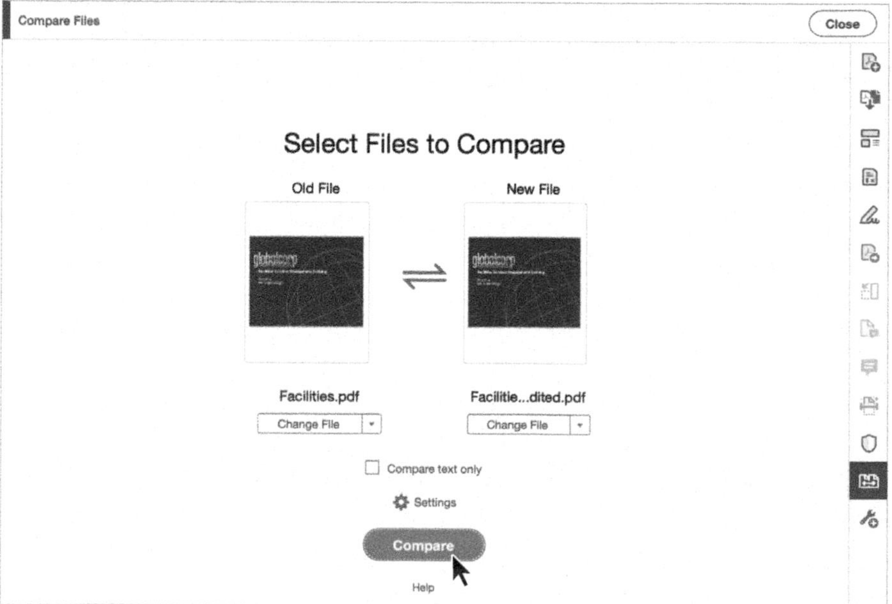

Acrobat displays a progress bar as it compares the documents. When it's made its analysis, it opens the Compare Report, which summarizes and identifies the differences between the files. The summary reports the number and kinds of changes in the document.

7 Click Go To First Change (Page 2).

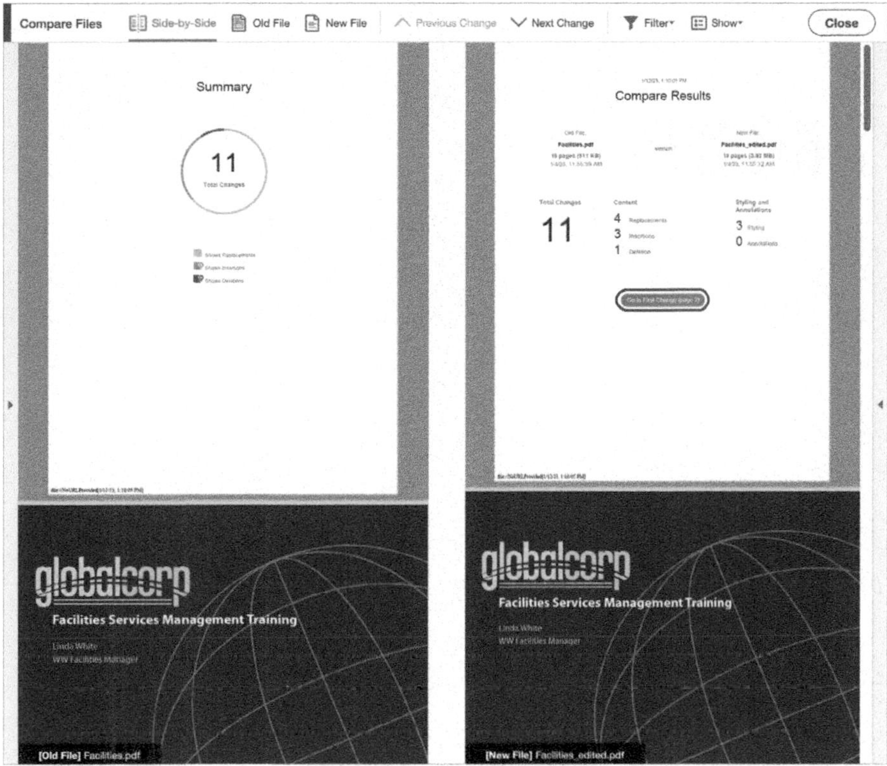

Acrobat displays page 2 in each of the files and identifies the change; in this case, text was deleted.

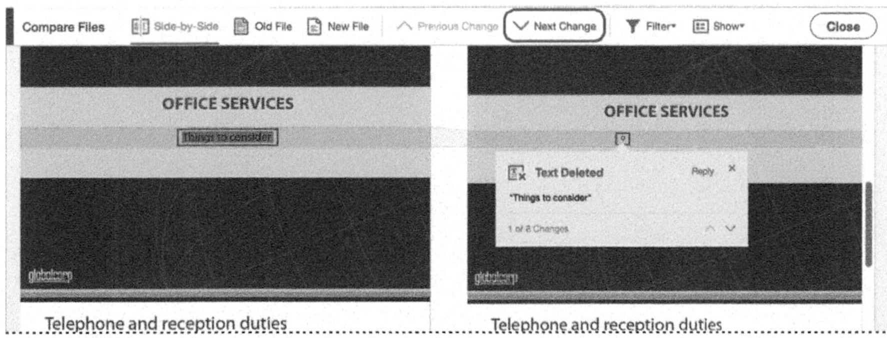

8 Click Next Change in the Compare Files toolbar. Acrobat displays the next change in the document. It's an image that was replaced.

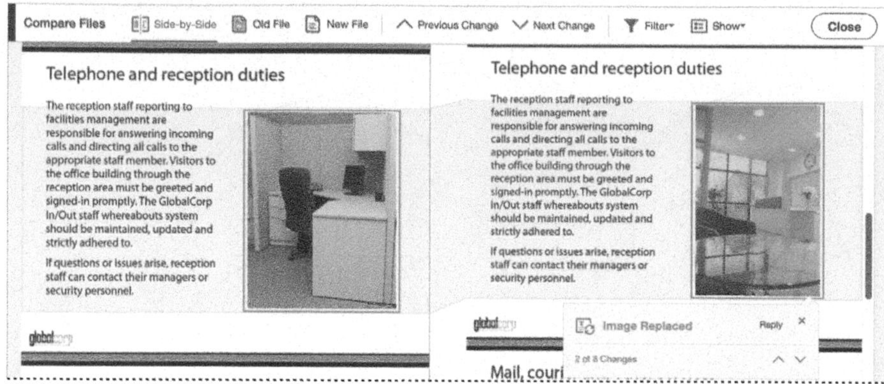

9 Continue clicking Next Change until you've seen all the changes in the document.

You can use options in the Compare Files toolbar to view one document at a time or to see both at once (the default), to filter the kinds of changes Acrobat identifies, and to see the summary again. You can also save the report to document the changes.

10 Close all open documents.

Review questions

1 How do you add comments to a PDF document?

2 How can you consolidate comments made by several reviewers?

3 What are some benefits of a shared review process?

Review answers

1 You can add comments to a PDF document using any of the commenting and markup tools in Acrobat. Open the Comment tool to see all the tools available in the Comment toolbar. To use a tool, select it, and then select the text you want to edit, draw your markup, or click to create a sticky note.

2 To consolidate review comments, open the original PDF file that you sent out for review, and then choose Import Data File from the Comments List panel menu. Select the PDF or FDF files that reviewers returned to you, and click Select. Acrobat imports all the comments into the original document.

3 In a shared review process, you post the PDF document to Adobe's cloud storage or another network folder, and then invite reviewers to make their comments. When reviewers post comments, they can be seen by all other reviewers, so everyone can respond to each other. Using a shared review is an effective way to let reviewers resolve conflicting opinions, identify areas for research, and develop creative solutions during the review process.

11 WORKING WITH FORMS IN ACROBAT

Lesson overview

In this lesson, you'll do the following:

- Create an interactive PDF form.
- Add form fields, including text boxes, radio buttons, and action buttons.
- Distribute a form.
- Track a form to determine its status.
- Learn how to collect and compile form data.
- Validate and calculate form data.

This lesson will take approximately 45 minutes to complete. Download the project files for this lesson, following the instructions in the Getting Started section under "Accessing the lesson files and Web Edition," if you haven't already done so. As you work on this lesson, you'll preserve the start files. If you need to restore the start files, download them from your Account page.

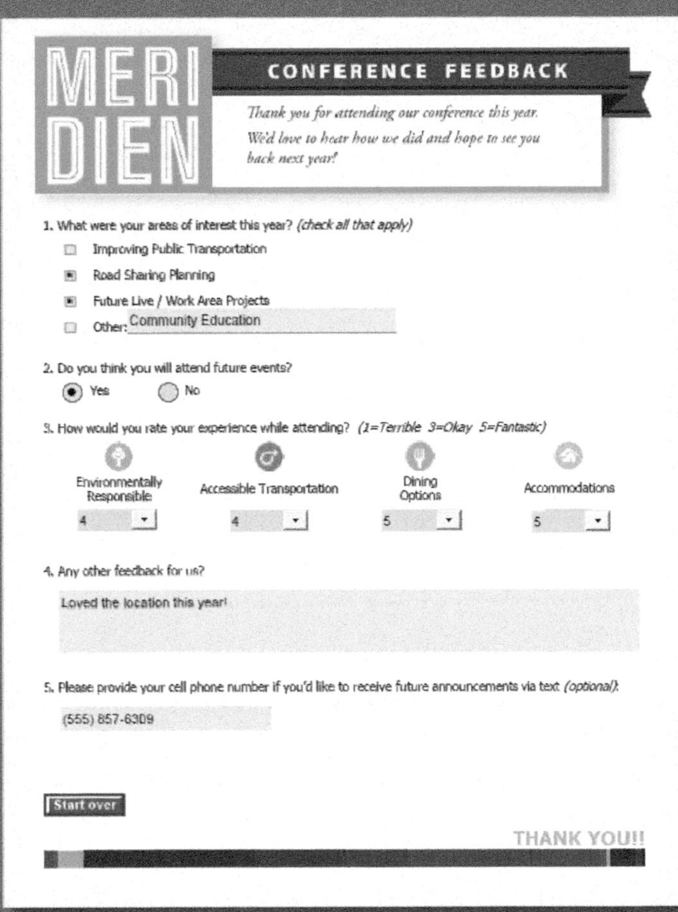

MERI DIEN

CONFERENCE FEEDBACK

Thank you for attending our conference this year. We'd love to hear how we did and hope to see you back next year!

1. What were your areas of interest this year? *(check all that apply)*
   - [ ] Improving Public Transportation
   - [x] Road Sharing Planning
   - [x] Future Live / Work Area Projects
   - [ ] Other: Community Education

2. Do you think you will attend future events?
   (•) Yes ( ) No

3. How would you rate your experience while attending? *(1=Terrible 3=Okay 5=Fantastic)*

Environmentally Responsible	Accessible Transportation	Dining Options	Accommodations
4	4	5	5

4. Any other feedback for us?
   Loved the location this year!

5. Please provide your cell phone number if you'd like to receive future announcements via text *(optional)*:
   (555) 857-6309

Start over

THANK YOU!!

You can convert any Acrobat document, including a scanned paper file, into an interactive form for online distribution, tracking, and collection.

Getting started

In this lesson, you'll prepare a feedback form for the fictitious Meridien conference. You'll convert an existing PDF document into an interactive form and use the form tools in Acrobat to add form fields that users can complete online. Then you'll distribute the form, track it, collect the responses, and analyze the data, all using tools within Acrobat.

Converting PDF files to interactive PDF forms

With Acrobat, you can create interactive PDF forms from documents you've created in other applications, such as Microsoft Word or Adobe InDesign, or scanned in from existing paper forms. You will start by opening a flat form that has already been converted to PDF. You will then use the form tools to make it an interactive form.

1 Start Acrobat. Then choose File > Open, and navigate to the Lesson11/Assets folder. Open the MeridienFeedback.pdf file.

The PDF document contains the text for the form, but Acrobat doesn't recognize any form fields in the document yet.

2 If the Prepare Form tool is not in the Tools pane, click Tools to open the Tools Center, and then click Add under Prepare Form. Click the Meridien Feedback tab to return to the form.

3 Click the Prepare Form tool in the Tools pane.

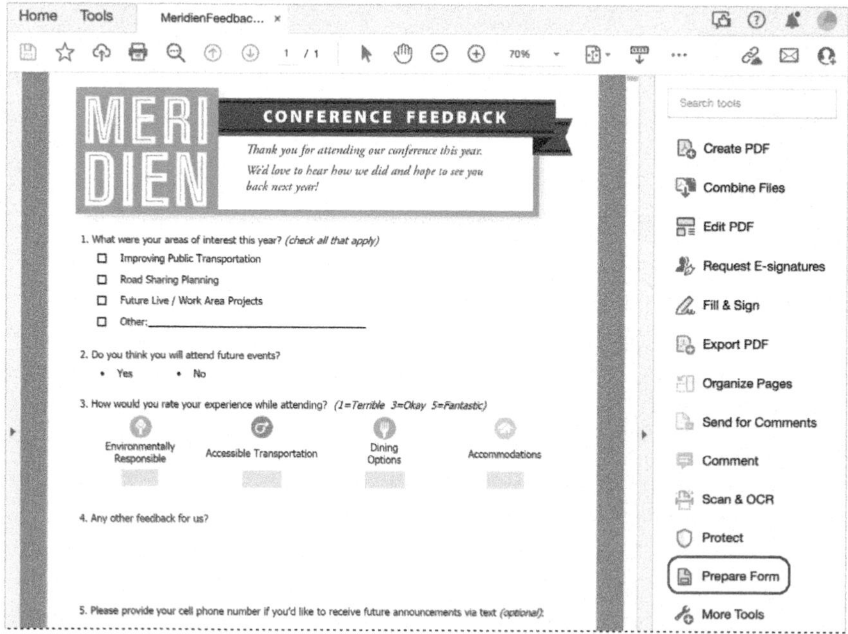

4 Make sure the MeridienFeedback.pdf file is selected, that This Document Requires Signatures is not selected, and that form field auto detection is on. Then click Start. (To enable form field detection, click Change, and then select Automatically Detect Form Fields in the Preferences dialog box, and click OK.)

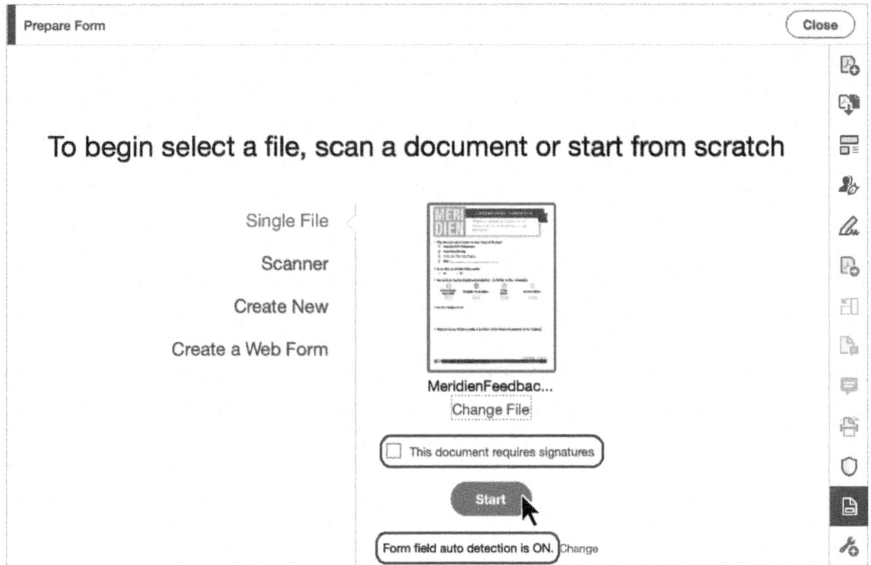

Acrobat analyzes the document and adds interactive form fields. You can inspect the document to ensure that Acrobat added form fields appropriately, and you can add fields manually where necessary.

Acrobat lists the form fields it added in the Fields panel on the right. The Prepare Form toolbar and the right-hand pane display the tools available for editing forms.

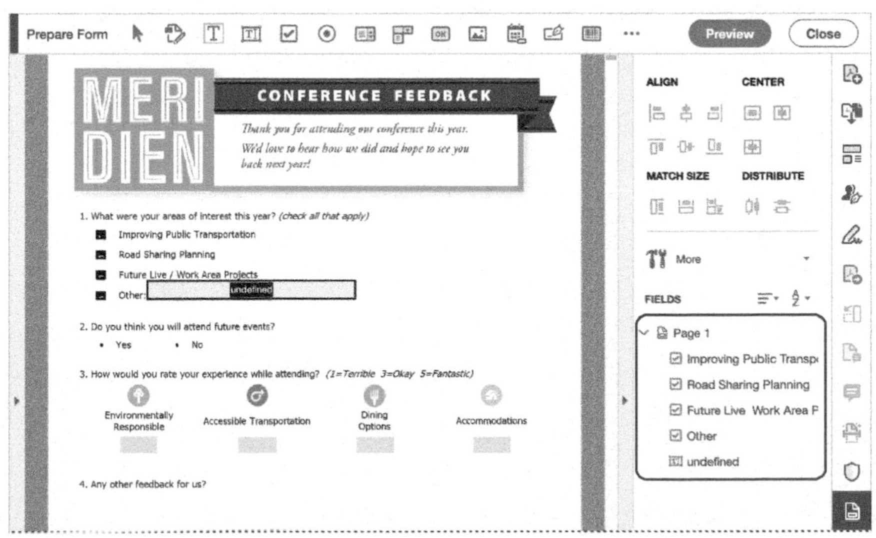

Note: If you see different tools, choose Revert To Acrobat Form from the More pop-up menu in the right-hand pane. Acrobat provides different tools to prepare a document for Acrobat Sign than for your own distribution.

Types of form fields

You can include the following types of fields in a PDF form you create in Acrobat:

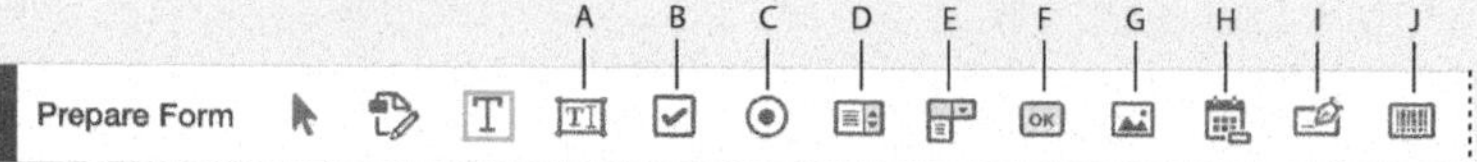

A. Text field B. Check box C. Radio button D. List box E. Dropdown list F. Button G. Image field H. Date field I. Digital signature J. Barcode

- **Barcodes** encode the input from selected fields and display it as a visual pattern that can be interpreted by decoding software or hardware (available separately).
- **Buttons** initiate an action on the user's computer, such as opening a file, playing a sound, or submitting data to a web server. You can customize buttons with images, text, and visual changes triggered by moving or clicking a mouse.
- **Check boxes** present yes-or-no choices for individual items. If the form contains multiple check boxes, users can typically select as many of these as they want.
- **Date fields** let the user type a date or select one from a pop-up calendar.
- **Dropdown lists** let the user either choose an item from a menu or type in a value.
- **Digital signature fields** let the user electronically sign a PDF document with a digital signature.
- **Image fields** let the user insert a photo or illustration.
- **List boxes** display a list of options the user can select. You can set a form field property that enables the user to Shift-click, Ctrl-click, or Command-click to select multiple items on the list.
- **Radio buttons** present a group of choices from which the user can select only one item. All radio buttons with the same name work together as a group.
- **Text fields** let the user type in text, such as name, address, email address, or phone number.

You can edit the form fields Acrobat creates. You'll edit the field marked "undefined" to give it a useful name and tooltip.

5 Double-click the field labeled "undefined" to edit it.

6 In the Text Field Properties dialog box, click the General tab. Then type **Other text** in both the Name and the Tooltip boxes, and click Close.

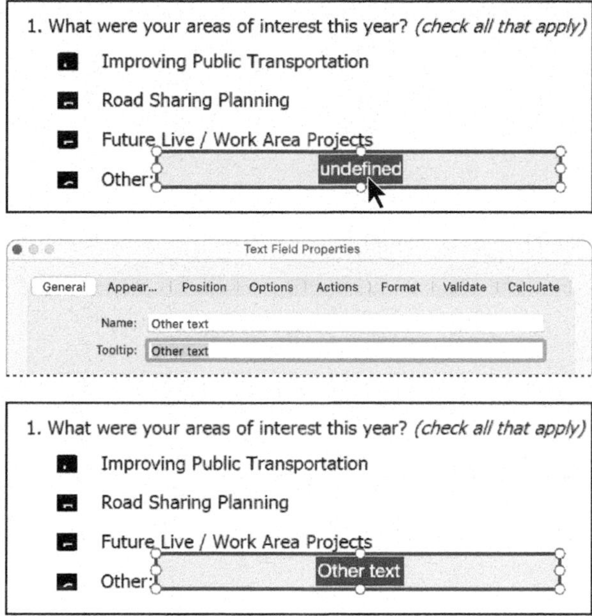

Adding form fields

You can use the form tools in Acrobat to add form fields to any document. Each form field has a name, which should be unique and descriptive; you'll use this name when you collect and analyze data, but it does not appear on the form the user sees. You can add tooltips and labels to help users understand how to complete form fields.

Note: If a document has been password-protected to prevent editing, you must know the password to add or edit fields.

Adding text fields

Acrobat identified some fields, but missed others. You'll add a text field for a cell phone number. Text fields enable users to enter information, such as their name or telephone number, on a form.

▶ **Tip:** To position fields exactly where you want them, use the Position tab in the field's Properties dialog box. To change the width, height, or position of multiple fields at once, select them, and make the change in the Properties dialog box for one of the fields. You can also lock the width and height of a field so you don't accidentally resize it as you move it.

1 Select the Text Field tool (▢) in the Prepare Form toolbar. Your pointer becomes a text box.

2 Click just below "5. Please provide your cell phone number" to place the text field.

3 Type **cell phone number** in the Field Name box. Do not select Required Field, because this is an optional field.

4 Click All Properties to change the properties for the field.

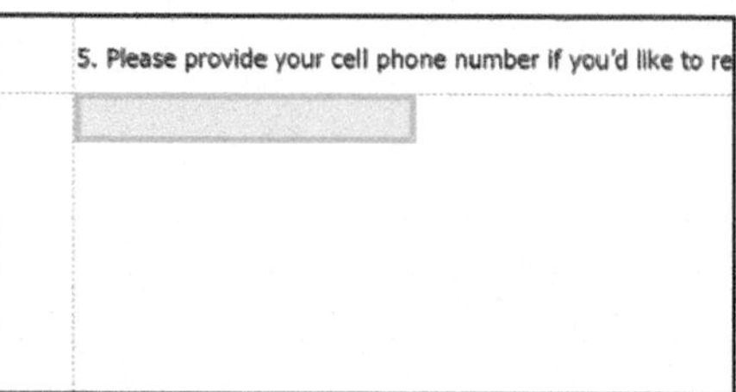

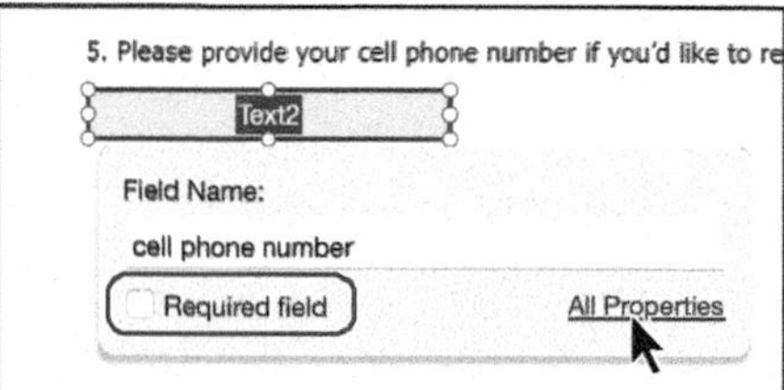

5 In the Text Field Properties dialog box, click the Format tab.

6 Choose Special from the Select Format Category pop-up menu. Then select Phone Number, and click Close.

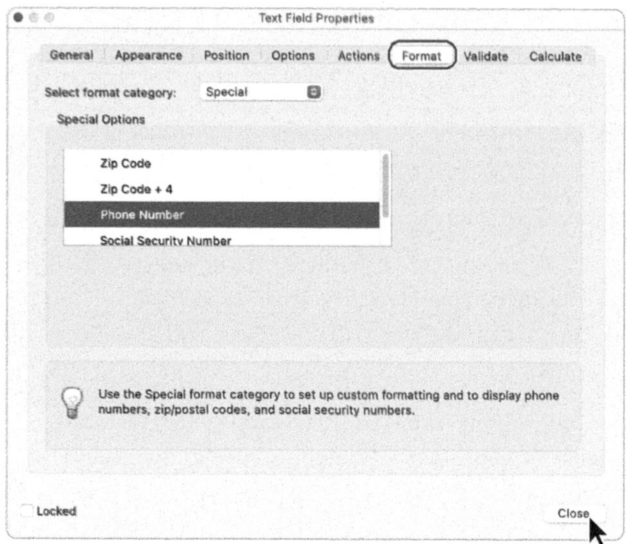

Now the field will accept phone numbers, but no other text.

7 Drag the right edge of the text field to make it longer.

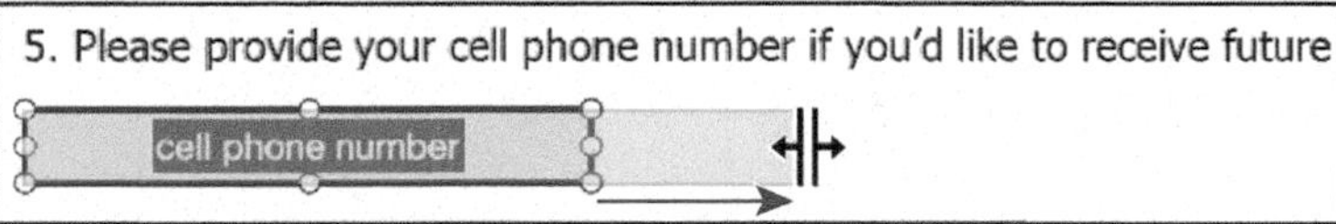

Specifying an answer format

You can use special formatting to restrict the type of data that is entered into a text field or to automatically convert data into a specific format. For example, you can set a zip code field to accept only numbers, or a date field to accept only a specific date format. And you can restrict numerical entries to numbers within a certain range.

To restrict the format for a text field, open its properties. Click the Format tab, select the format category, and then select the appropriate option for your field.

Adding a multiline text field

The next field you'll add is for additional feedback. Someone completing the form might type just a few words or a complete paragraph, so you'll create a text field that supports multiple lines.

1 Select the Text Field tool in the Prepare Form toolbar.

2 Click below "4. Any other feedback for us?" and drag a text box large enough to contain multiple lines of text.

3 Type **other feedback** in the Field Name box. This is another optional field, so do not select Required Field.

4 Double-click the text field to edit its properties.

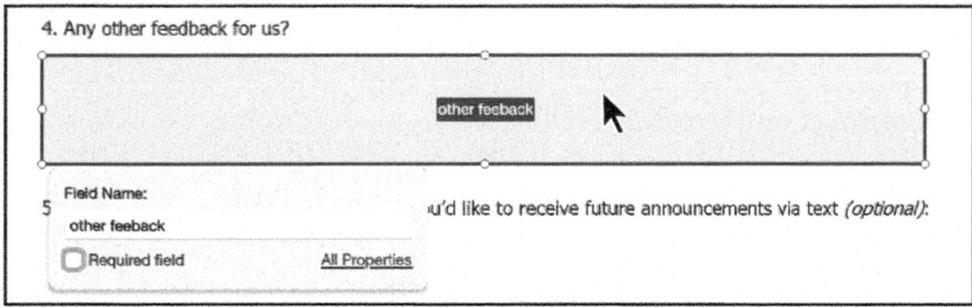

5 In the Text Field Properties dialog box, click the Options tab.

6 Select Multi-line and Scroll Long Text.

7 Select Limit Of _ Characters, and type **350** for the limit.

8 Click Close.

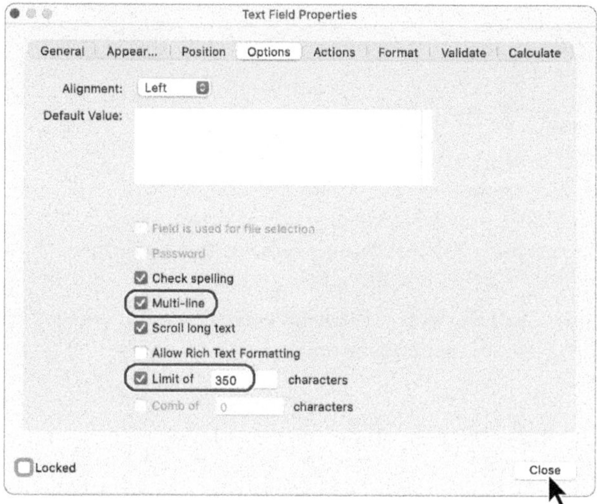

9 Click Preview in the Prepare Form toolbar.

In Preview mode, form fields appear as they will to the person completing the form.

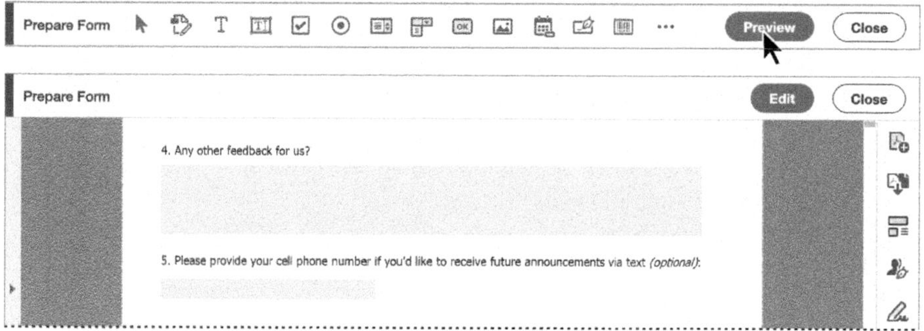

10 Type a few sentences into the other feedback field to see how the text wraps. You can also enter a phone number in the cell phone number field.

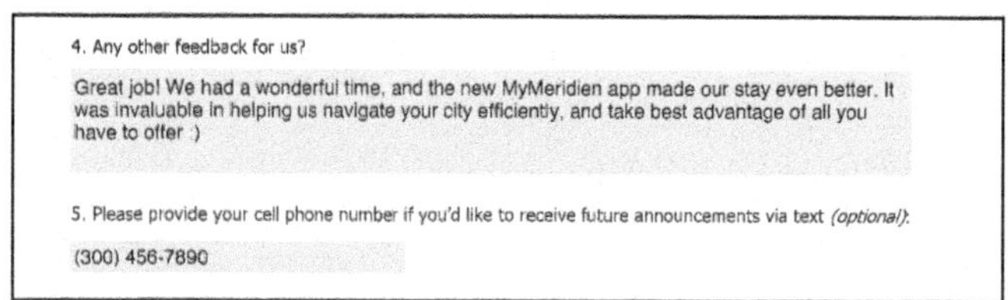

Adding radio buttons

The second question on the feedback form requires a yes-or-no answer. You'll create radio buttons for that question. Radio buttons let the user select one—and only one—option from a set of options.

1 If you're in Preview mode, click Edit in the Prepare Form toolbar to return to Form Editing mode.

2 Select the Radio Button tool (◉) in the Prepare Form toolbar.

3 Click over the circle next to the word "Yes" after question 2.

4 Select Required Field.

5 Type **Yes** in the Radio Button Choice box.

6 Type **attend again** in the Group Name box.

7 Click Add Another Button at the bottom of the dialog box. Your pointer becomes a box again.

Note: All radio buttons in a set need to have the same group name.

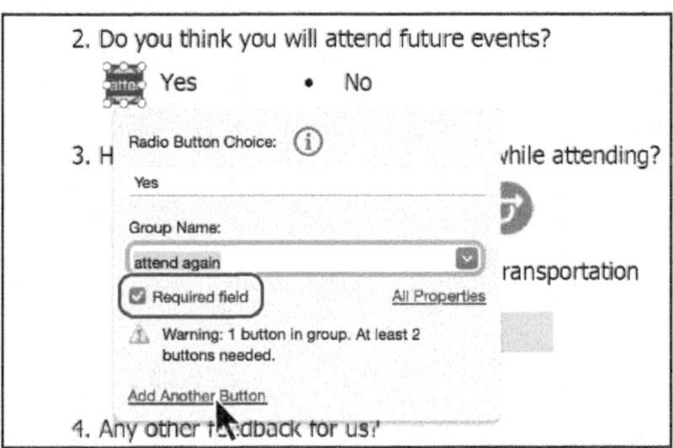

8 Click the circle next to "No."

9 Type **No** in the Radio Button Choice box, and confirm that the group name is "attend again" and that Required Field is selected. Then click outside the dialog box to close it.

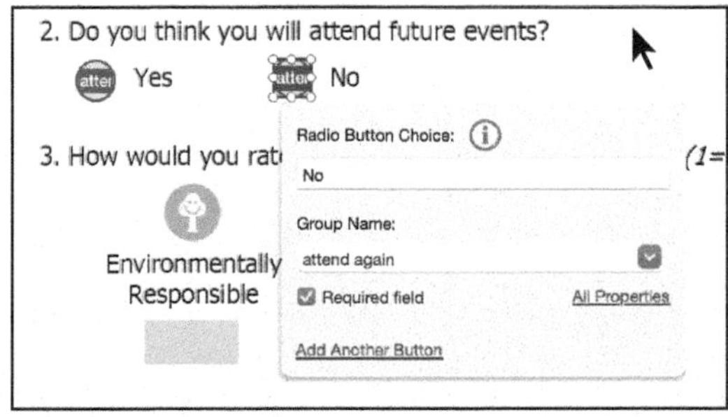

10 Click Preview in the Prepare Form toolbar. For the second question, click Yes, and then click No. Notice that you can select only one radio button at a time.

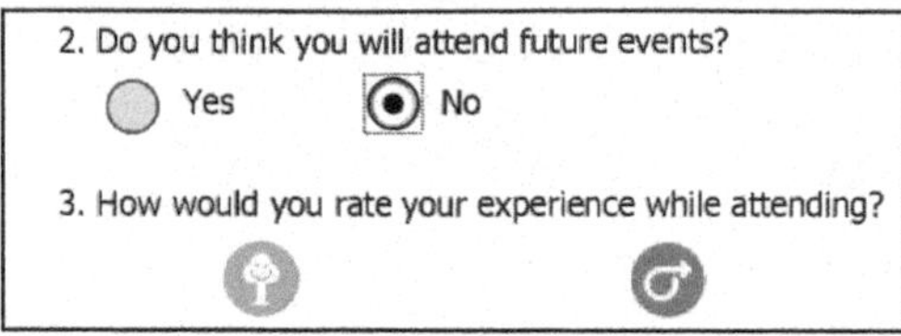

Adding a dropdown list

Dropdown lists let users choose an option from a pop-up menu or, if the form creator has allowed it, type in a value. You'll add dropdown lists for the third question, which asks participants to rate their experience.

1 Click Edit in the Prepare Form toolbar to return to Form Editing mode.

2 Select the Dropdown List tool (▤) in the Prepare Form toolbar.

3 Click beneath "Environmentally Responsible" to create the pop-up menu.

4 Name the field **environment**.

5 Click All Properties.

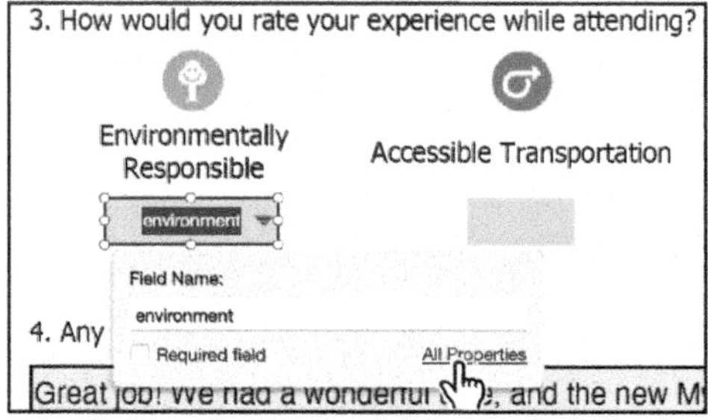

6 Click the Options tab, and then type -- in the Item field, and click Add.

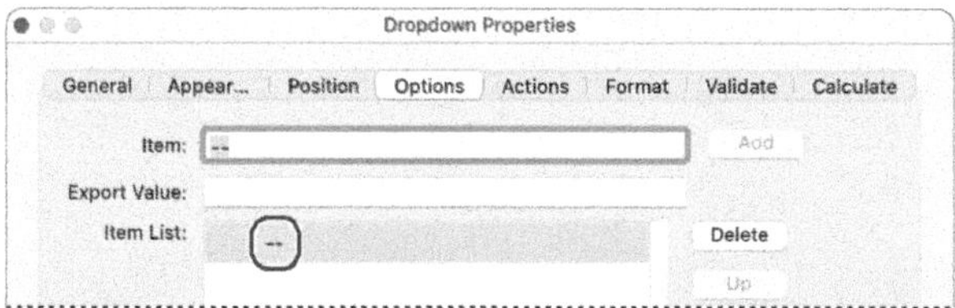

Acrobat adds -- to the menu.

7 Type **1** in the Item field, and click Add.

8 Repeat step 7 for the numbers 2–5, so that the menu includes the following options: --, 1, 2, 3, 4, 5.

9 Select the first option (--) to make it the default. This is the option that will appear on the form when it's first opened.

10 Click Close.

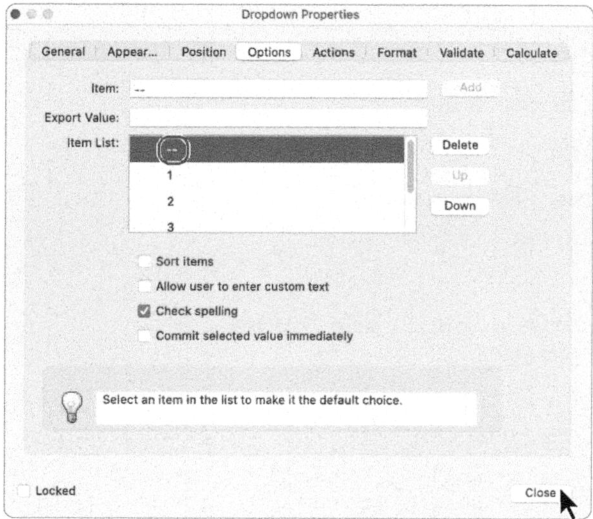

11 Resize the field to match the gray box on the form.

12 Repeat steps 2–11 to add dropdown lists for the other three ratings categories. Name them **transportation**, **dining**, and **accommodations**.

13 Click Preview in the Prepare Form toolbar.

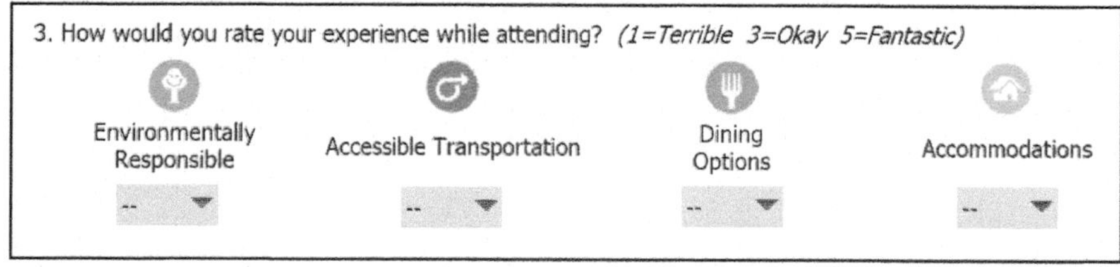

14 Select a rating from each menu to see how users will experience the form.

▶ **Tip:** After you've created one dropdown list, you can copy the field and paste it to create the others. Just remember to change the field name!

Using image buttons

Sometimes you want form users to provide a photo or illustration. For example, you may want to include an image field in a contest submission form, an application form, or a form that documents an issue or incident. In Acrobat, it's just as easy to create an image field as it is to create any other field. Select the Image Field tool () in the Prepare Form toolbar, click on the page to add the field, and then customize its appearance. When someone clicks the field in a form, they'll be prompted to browse for an image.

1. Where is the issue?

On 15th Ave, just north of Union.

2. Describe the issue.

No parking sign is obscured by pole.

3. If you have a photo, add it here.

Adding an action button

Buttons let users perform an action, such as going to a different page or submitting a form. You'll create a reset button that will clear the fields on this form so the user can start over.

1 Click Edit in the Prepare Form toolbar to return to Form Editing mode.

2 Select the Button tool () in the Prepare Form toolbar.

3 Click in the bottom left corner of the form to create the button.

4 Type **Reset** in the Field Name box, and then click All Properties.

5 Click the Options tab.

6 Type **Start over** in the Label box.

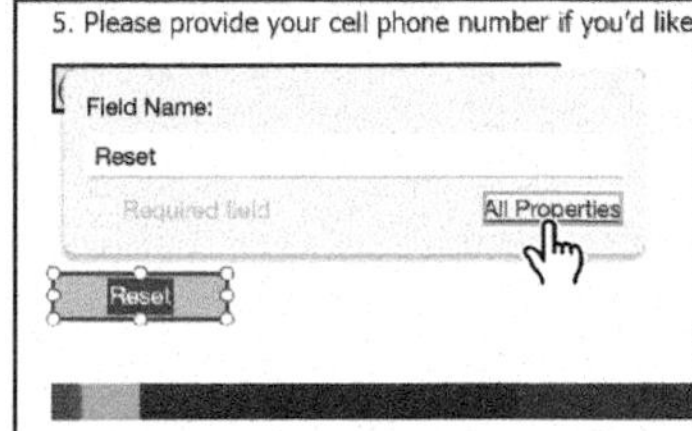

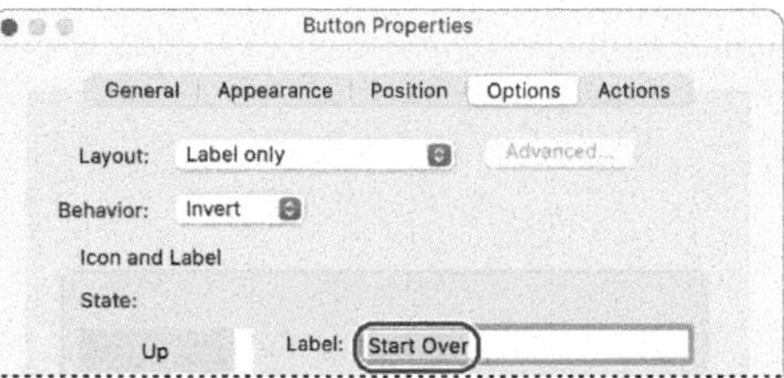

The field name is used to collect and analyze data, but does not appear on the form itself. The label, however, appears in the field when the user is completing the form.

7 Click the Actions tab.

8 Choose Mouse Up from the Select Trigger menu, and then choose Reset A Form from the Select Action menu. Click Add.

When the user clicks the button and releases the mouse (Mouse Up), the form will reset.

9 Click OK in the Reset A Form dialog box to reset the selected fields. By default, all form fields are selected.

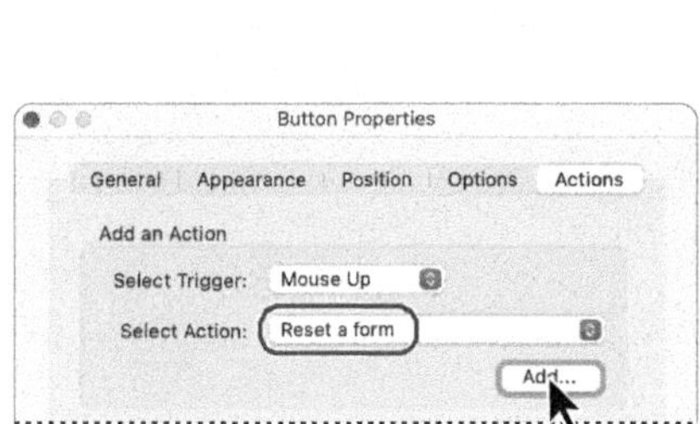

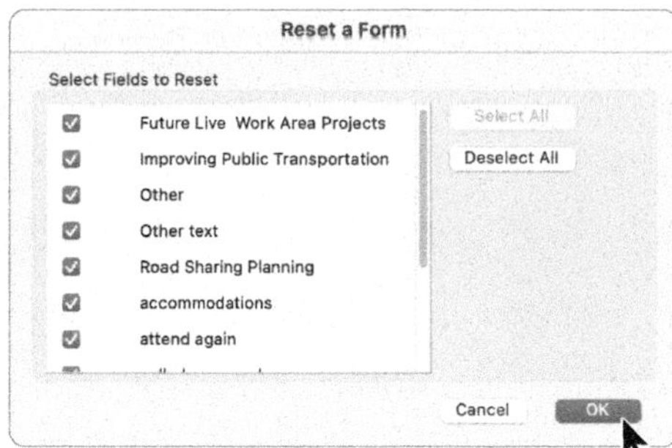

10 Click the Appearance tab.

11 Click the Border Color swatch, and select a dark shade of red. In macOS, deselect Transparent. Then close the Colors panel.

12 Click the Fill Color swatch, select a lighter shade of red, and then close the panel.

13 Choose Beveled from the Line Style menu, Medium from the Line Thickness menu, and white for the Text Color.

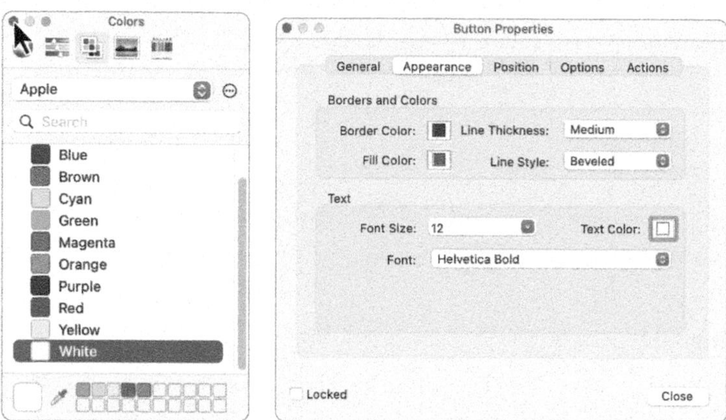

The button will appear with a red background, dark red outline, and white text. The beveled line will make it appear to be three-dimensional.

14 Click Close to close the Button Properties dialog box.

15 Click Preview. Select options for a few questions, and then click the Start Over button you created. The fields reset.

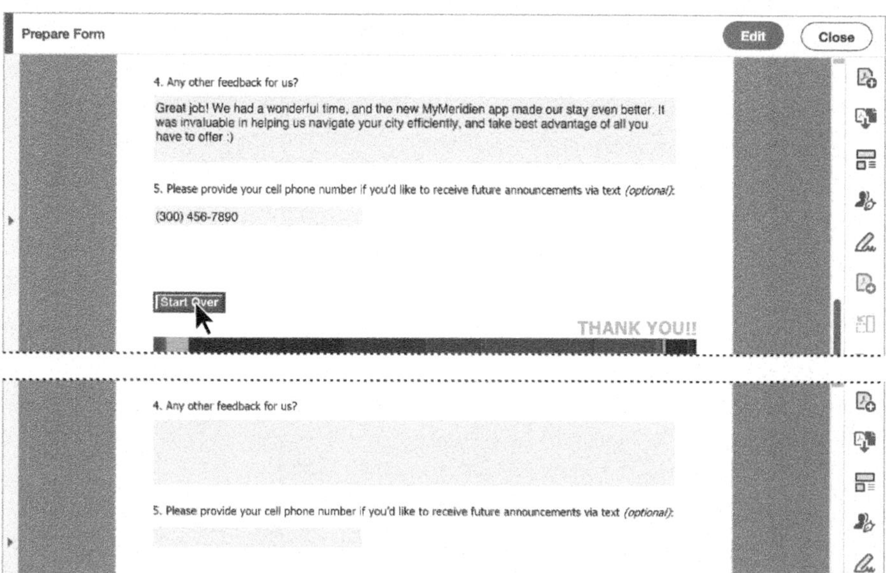

16 Click Edit to return to Form Editing mode.

17 Choose File > Save As. In the Save As PDF dialog box, name the file **MeridienFeedbackForm.pdf**, and save it to the Lesson11/Finished_Projects folder.

Distributing forms

After you have designed and created your form, you can distribute it in several different ways. If you have an email account, you'll send the feedback form to yourself, and then collect the response in email. You'll use the tools in Acrobat to distribute the form.

1 Click Distribute in the right-hand pane.

2 Click Save if you are prompted to save.

3 In the Distribute Form dialog box, select Email, and then click Continue. Click Yes if you are prompted to clear the form before distributing it.

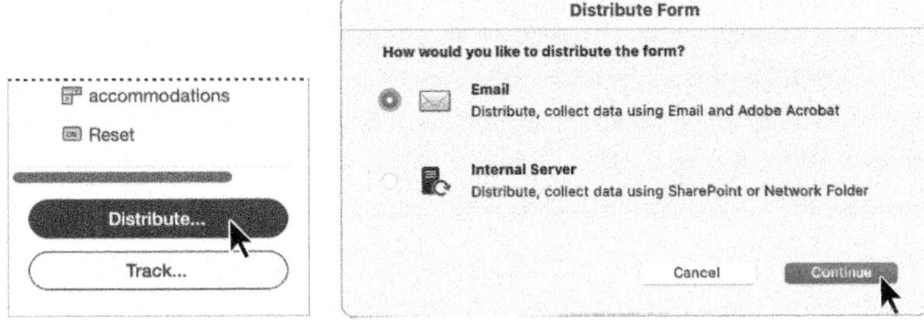

4 If prompted, in the Distribute Form dialog box, enter or verify your email address, name, title, and organization name, and then click Next. If you've entered that information previously, Acrobat uses the information it has stored.

5 Click Send Using Adobe Acrobat, and click Next.

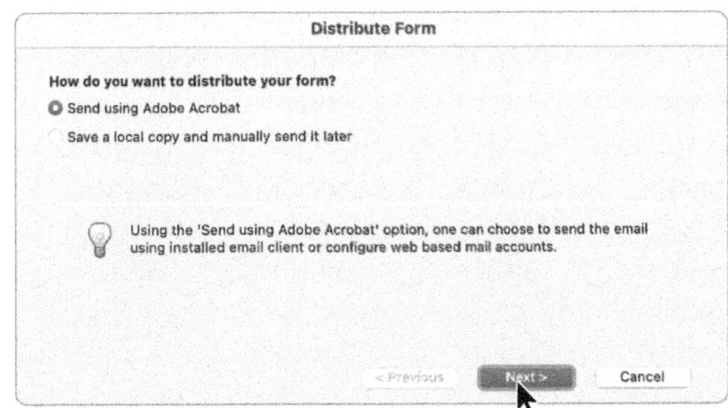

Note: You can customize the subject line and email message that accompanies your form, and you can send the form to multiple people at once. You may want to provide instructions for recipients completing the form on the mobile app, as they won't see a Submit button.

6 Type your email address in the To box. Make sure Collect Name & Email From Recipients To Provide Optimal Tracking is selected. Then click Send.

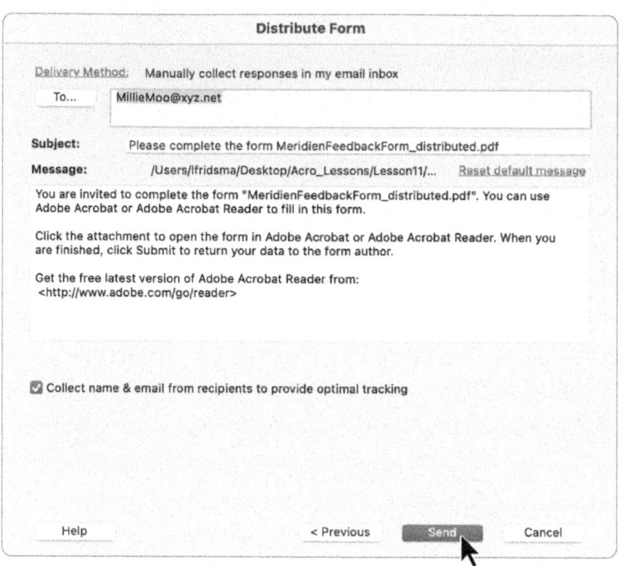

Note: If you receive a message that you don't have a default email application, click OK. Acrobat then opens the Send Email dialog box.

7 In the Send Email dialog box, select Default Email Application if you want to send the message from an email application installed on your computer. If you want to use an online service such as Gmail or Yahoo Mail, select Use Webmail, enter your email address when prompted, and then click OK.

8 Click Continue.

9 If you are sending email through a webmail account, sign in when prompted, read any security messages, and grant access as required. Enter email addresses for recipients, and send the message.

If you choose to send the message through your default email application, Acrobat opens it and sends the message with the attached form. Depending on your email application, you may have to grant access or click Send in the application.

10 Check your email, and open the attached PDF file to complete the form.

The form opens in Acrobat, and a document message bar appears above it.

Note: If form recipients are using earlier versions of Acrobat or Reader, the document message bar may not be visible or may contain different information.

The document message bar displays information about the form. If the form does not contain a Submit Form button, one is included in the document message bar. Additionally, the document message bar specifies whether a form is certified or contains signature fields.

Tracking forms

If you've used Acrobat to distribute your forms, you can manage the forms that you have distributed or received. Use Tracker to view and edit the location of the response file, track who has responded, add more recipients, email all recipients, and view the responses for a form.

To track forms in Tracker:

1 Open the form you want to track, open the Prepare Form tool, and click Track in the right-hand pane.

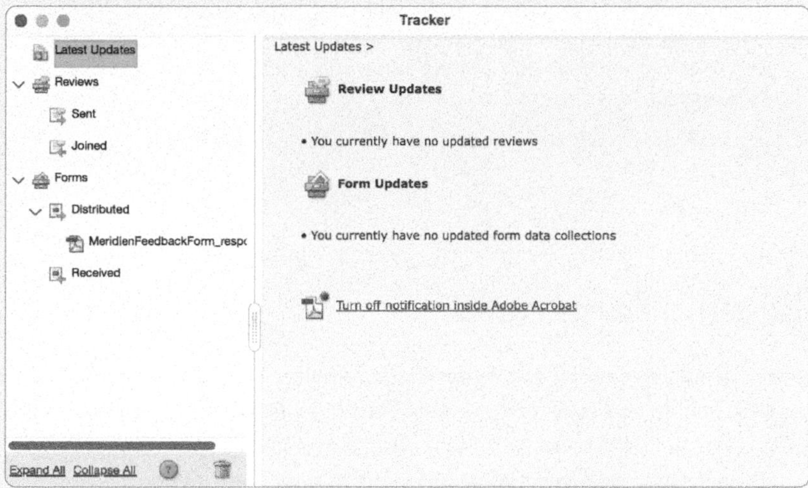

Tracker displays reviews you've initiated and forms you've distributed.

2 In the left navigation pane, expand Forms, and click Distributed.

3 Select the form you want to track.

In the main pane, Tracker displays the location of the response file, the method used to distribute the form, the date it was distributed, the list of recipients, and whether each recipient has responded.

4 Do one or more of the following:

- To view all responses for a form, click View Responses.
- To modify the location of the response file, in Response File Location, click Edit File Location.
- To view the original form, click Open Original Form.
- To send the form to more recipients, click Add Recipients.
- To send email to everyone who received the form, click Email All Recipients.
- To remind recipients to complete the form, click Email Recipients Who Haven't Responded.

Options for distributing forms

There are several ways to get your forms to the people who need to fill them out. You can simply post a form on a website, for example, or send it directly from your email application. To take advantage of Acrobat form-management tools to track, collect, and analyze data, use one of these options:

- Send the form as an email attachment, and manually collect responses in your email inbox.
- Send the form using a network folder or a Windows server running Microsoft SharePoint services. You can automatically collect responses on the internal server.
- Create a web form. In Acrobat for the web (acrobat.adobe.com), click the Create A Web Form tool, and follow the onscreen instructions to load your PDF, prepare the form, and publish a link.

To learn more about distributing forms, see Adobe Acrobat Help.

Collecting form data

Electronic forms aren't simply more convenient for users; they also make it easier for you to track, collect, and review form data. When you distribute a form, Acrobat automatically creates a PDF document for collecting the form data. By default, this file is saved in the same folder as the original form, and is named [filename]_responses.

You'll complete the form and submit it, and then collect the form data.

1 Complete the form you opened, and select options for each question, as if you were the recipient. Type a few words in the multiline field for number 4. Then click Submit Form.

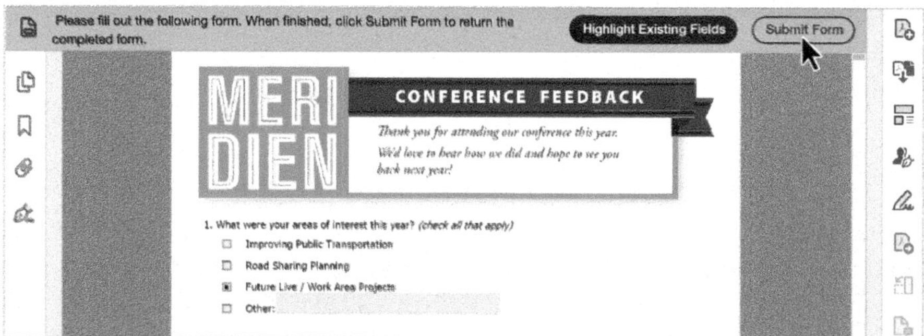

2 In the Send Form dialog box, verify the email address and name you're using to send the data, and then click Send.

3 In the Send Email dialog box, select your default email application or Webmail, click Continue, and follow any prompts necessary to sign in. Click Continue or Allow if a warning dialog box appears.

Note: Depending on the security settings in your email application, you may need to approve the message before it is sent.

If you receive a message about sending the email, click OK. Depending on settings in your email application, you may need to send the message manually.

4 Check your email. The completed form arrives in a message with the subject line "Submitting Completed Form," or the subject line you used if you mailed it manually. Open the attachment in that message.

5 Select Add to An Existing Response File, and accept the default filename. Then click OK.

Acrobat compiles the data in the response file that was created when you distributed the form.

Form data you've collected is listed in the table in the PDF responses document. Responses are listed in the columns for the corresponding questions. If there are too many columns to fit on the page, scroll to see additional data.

Note: You can add multiple form responses to the responses file at once. Click Add, and then navigate to the responses you want to include. With some email applications, you may need to use this method to add files, rather than double-clicking an attachment.

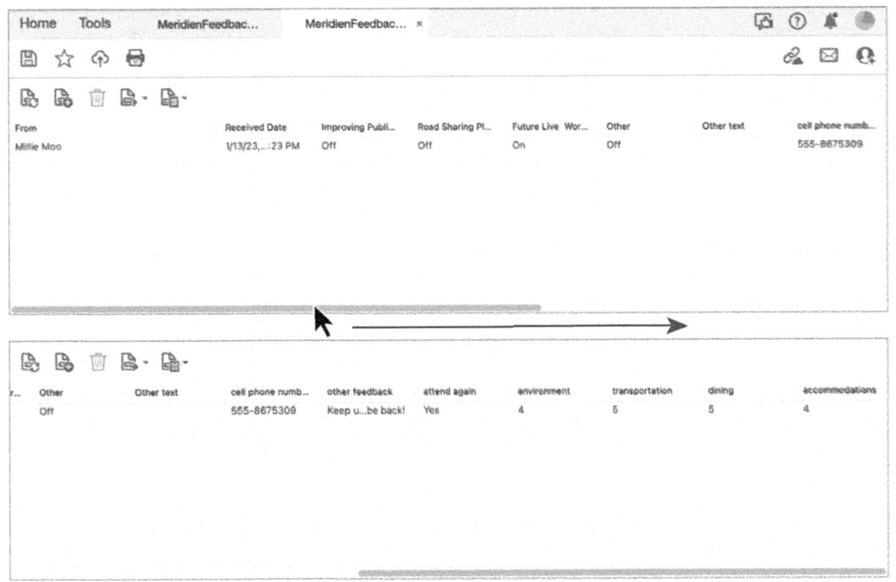

Working with form data

Once your data has been compiled, you can view each response, sort responses, export the data to a CSV or XML file for use in a spreadsheet or database, or archive the data for access later. You'll sort the data from the feedback form and then export it to a CSV file. If you have only one set of responses in the document, consider submitting the form a few times, with varying answers to questions, so that the sorting operation is more obvious.

1 Right-click (Windows) or control-click (macOS) the table.

2 Choose Sort By > Attend Again.

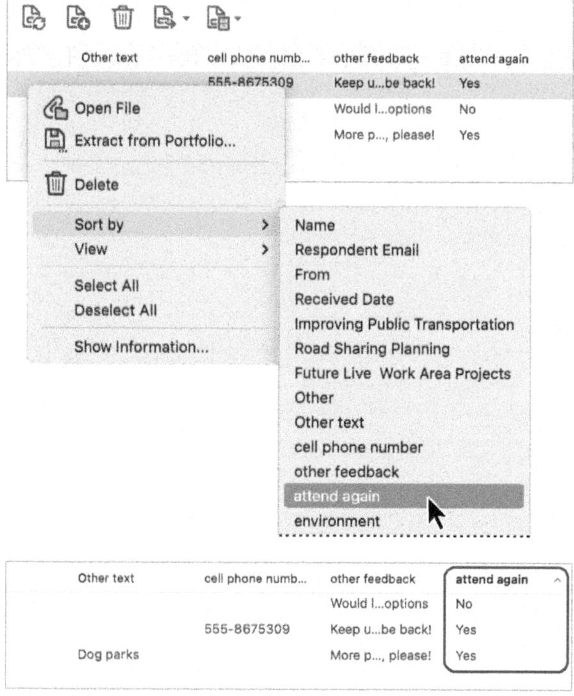

Acrobat sorts the entries by the answer to the attend again field.

3 Right-click or control-click the table again, and choose View > Respondent Email.

A new column appears, displaying the respondents' email addresses.

4 Right-click or control-click the first set of responses in the table, and choose Open File.

Acrobat opens the completed form whose responses are listed in that row.

5 Close the form you just opened, and return to the responses document.

6 Click the Export button (icon) in the toolbar, and choose Export All.

7 Choose CSV as the format, and click Save.

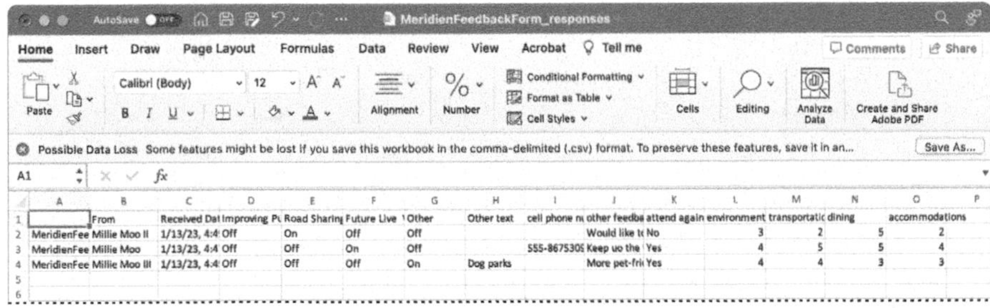

Acrobat creates a comma-separated data file that contains the data from the selected responses. You can open a CSV file in Microsoft Excel or another spreadsheet or database application.

8 Close any open PDF files and Tracker.

Calculating and validating numeric fields

Acrobat offers many ways to ensure that users fill out your forms correctly. As you learned earlier, you can create fields that will allow the user to enter only information of a specific type. You can also create fields that automatically calculate values based on entries in other fields.

Validating numeric fields

To ensure that correct information is entered into form fields, use the Acrobat field validation feature. For example, if a response must be a number with a value between 10 and 20, restrict entries to numbers within this range. Here, you'll limit the price of merchandise on an order form to no more than $1,000.

1 Choose File > Open, navigate to the Lesson11/Assets folder, and open the Merch_order.pdf file. This PDF file already has form fields in place.

2 Click Prepare Form in the Tools pane to edit the form.

3 Double-click the Price.0 field (the first cell in the Price Each column).

4 In the Text Field Properties dialog box, click the Format tab, and set the following values:

- For Select Format Category, choose Number.
- For Decimal Places, choose 2 (to allow cents to be entered).
- For Separator Style, choose 1,234.56 (the default).
- For Currency Symbol, choose $ (the dollar sign).

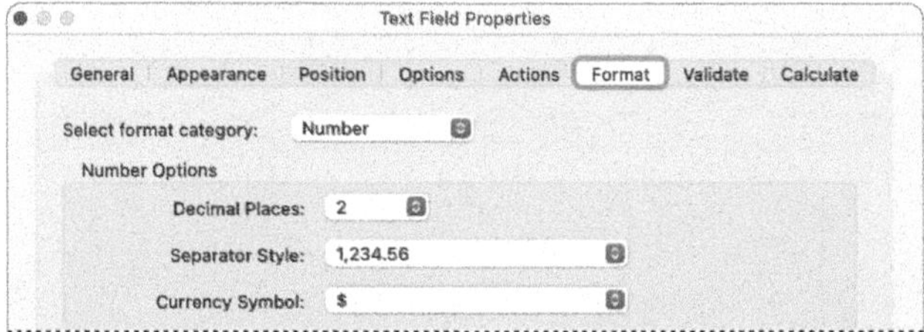

Now you'll specify a validation check on the data entered in this field.

5 Click the Validate tab, and then select Field Value Is In Range. In the range fields, type **0** in the From box and **1000** in the To box. Click Close.

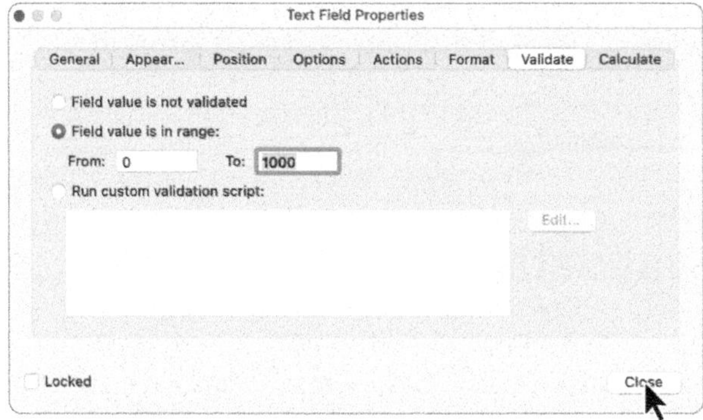

6 Click Preview in the Prepare Form toolbar. Then type **2000** in the field you just edited (the first cell in the Price Each column), and press Enter or Return. A message warns you that the entry you have tried to make is unacceptable.

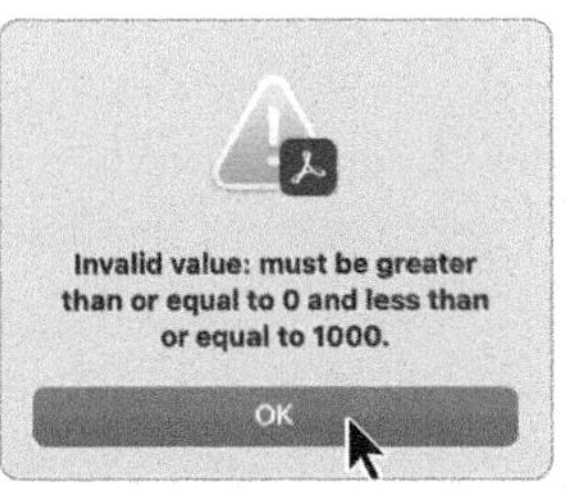

7 Click OK to close the warning dialog box.

Calculating numeric fields

In addition to verifying and formatting form data, you can use Acrobat to calculate values used in form fields. For your PDF order form, you will calculate the cost for each line item, based on the quantity that has been ordered. You will then have Acrobat calculate the total cost of all items that have been ordered.

1 If you're in Preview mode, click Edit.

2 Double-click the Total.0 field (the first cell in the Item Total column).

3 In the Text Field Properties dialog box, click the Calculate tab, and do the following:

- Select the Value Is The option.
- For the value, choose Product (x). You'll be multiplying two fields.
- Click Pick to select the fields to multiply.

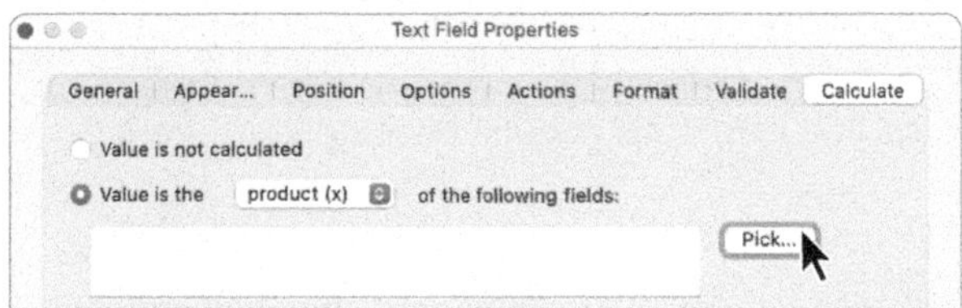

- In the Field Selection dialog box, select the boxes next to Price.0 and Quantity.0. (To scroll through the list of fields, select one, and then press the Down Arrow key.)

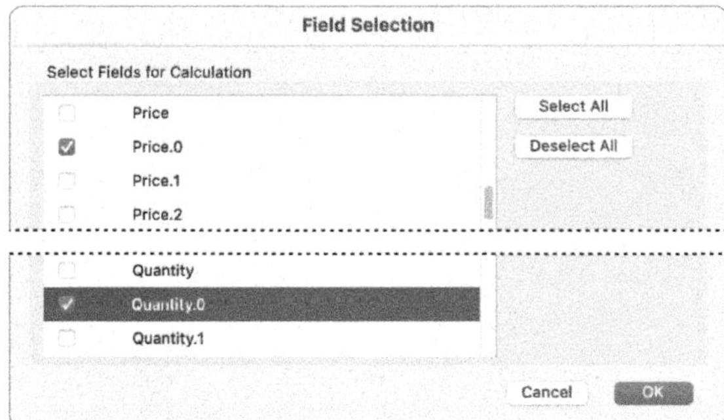

4 Click OK to close the Field Selection dialog box.

5 Click Close to exit the Text Field Properties dialog box.

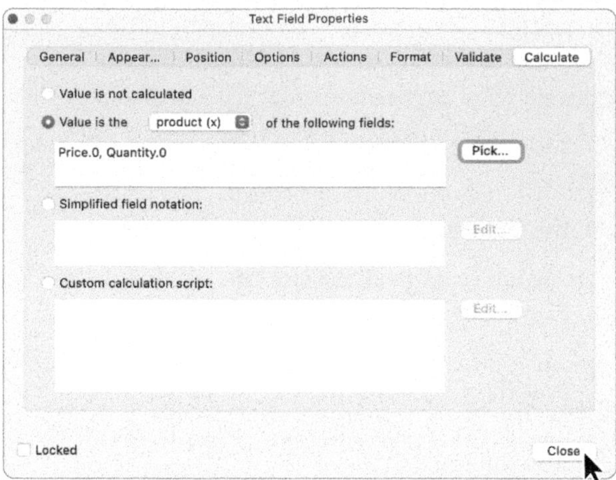

6 Click Preview. Then enter **1.50** for the price and **2** for the quantity in the first row, and press Enter or Return. The Item Total column displays $3.00.

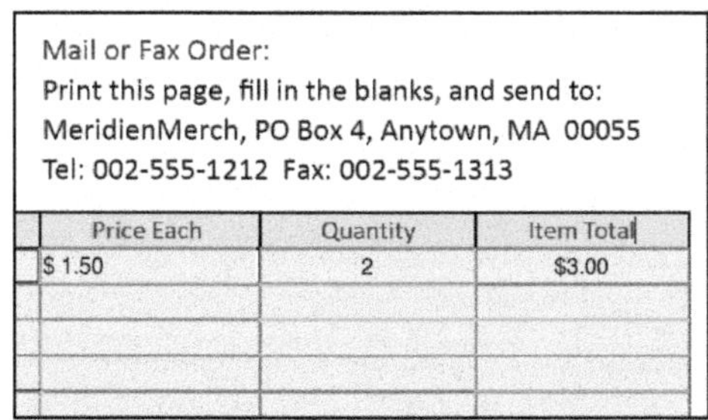

Mail or Fax Order:
Print this page, fill in the blanks, and send to:
MeridienMerch, PO Box 4, Anytown, MA 00055
Tel: 002-555-1212 Fax: 002-555-1313

Price Each	Quantity	Item Total
$ 1.50	2	$3.00

7 Close any open files, and quit Acrobat when you are finished.

Review questions

1 How can you convert an existing document into an interactive PDF form in Acrobat?

2 What is the difference between a radio button and a button in an interactive PDF form?

3 How can you distribute a form to multiple recipients and track the responses you receive?

4 Where does Acrobat compile form responses?

Review answers

1 To convert an existing document into an interactive PDF form, open the document in Acrobat. Then open the Prepare Form tool, select the current document, and click Start.

2 Radio buttons permit the user to select just one of a set of two or more options. Buttons trigger actions, such as playing a movie file, going to another page, or clearing form data.

3 You can email the form to recipients or post the form on an internal server. Click Distribute in the right-hand pane when the Prepare Form tool is open to select a distribution option.

4 When you use Acrobat to distribute a form, Acrobat automatically creates a PDF document for your responses. By default, the file is in the same folder as the original form, and the word "_responses" is appended to the name of the original form.

12 USING ACTIONS (ACROBAT PRO)

Lesson overview

This lesson requires Acrobat Pro. In this lesson, you'll do the following:

- Run an action.
- Create an action.
- Create an instruction step for an action.
- Set options in steps so the user doesn't need to provide input.
- Prompt the user for input on specific steps.
- Share an action.

This lesson will take approximately 45 minutes to complete. Download the project files for this lesson, following the instructions in the Getting Started section under "Accessing the lesson files and Web Edition," if you haven't already done so. As you work on this lesson, you'll preserve the start files. If you need to restore the start files, download them from your Account page.

THOMAS BOOKER

Founder, President and CEO of Aquo

Biography

Thomas Booker founded Aquo Energy Drinks Ltd. in August 2006, and currently acts as the company's President and Chief Executive Officer. Mr. Booker is responsible for overseeing all Aquo business units, including Aquo energy drink and water brands, and also remains a driving force behind Aquo's product development. He has served on the boards of many large public companies, consulting them on environmentally sustainable business practices throughout his career. He currently serves as chairman of the California Corporate Green Building Council. Prior to founding Aquo, Mr. Booker was Director of Research and Development at Purely Natural Energy Company, the ground breaking Northwestern energy bar company that was the first to introduce a 100% organic bar to the national market in 1996. He earned a B.S. from the University of Virginia in 1987, and a MBA from the College of William & Mary in 1990. He was named *Better* magazine's 2006 "Most Environmentally Responsible CEO of the Year."

Actions in Adobe Acrobat Pro automate tasks and make processes more consistent. You can use the actions that come with Acrobat or create your own to use and share.

About actions

In Adobe Acrobat Pro, you can use actions to automate multistep tasks and share processes with others. An action is a collection of steps. Some steps, such as adding tags to a document, can be performed automatically by Acrobat. Some steps, such as removing hidden information, require input as to which information to remove or add, or which settings to use. Other steps, such as adding bookmarks, cannot be done automatically because you need to use human discretion to create and name the bookmarks; in those cases, an action includes instructions for the user to perform the necessary step before the action continues.

Acrobat Pro includes several actions in the Action Wizard tool. You can use these actions to perform common tasks, such as preparing documents for distribution or creating accessible PDF documents. You can also create your own actions, assembling steps in the order that works for your process, and including informational steps where appropriate for the people who will be using each action.

Actions that contain automated steps are particularly useful for tasks you perform frequently. In general, actions are handy for tasks you perform less frequently, but which require the same steps each time. Using actions, you can ensure that critical steps are included in the process.

Using predefined actions

To use an action, open the Action Wizard tool, and select the action in the Actions List in the right-hand pane. In this exercise, you'll use the Prepare For Distribution action to prepare a document before posting it on an external website.

1 Start Acrobat Pro, and choose File > Open. Navigate to the Lesson12/Assets folder, select Aquo_CEO.pdf, and click Open.

The Aquo_CEO.pdf document is a biography of the chief executive of a fictitious beverage company.

2 Click Tools in the main toolbar, scroll to the Customize category, and then click Action Wizard to open it.

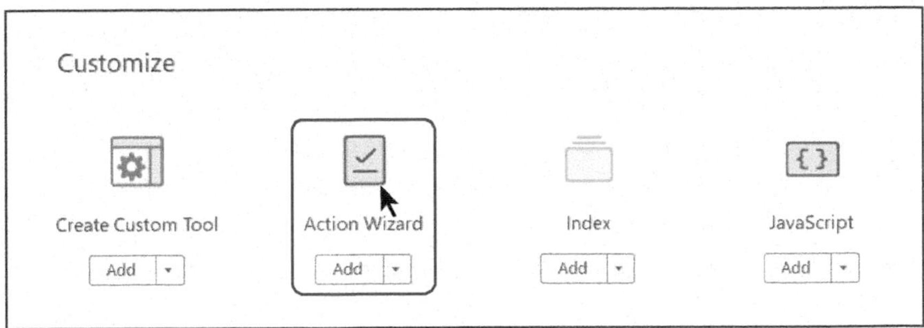

3 Select Prepare For Distribution in the Actions List in the right-hand pane.

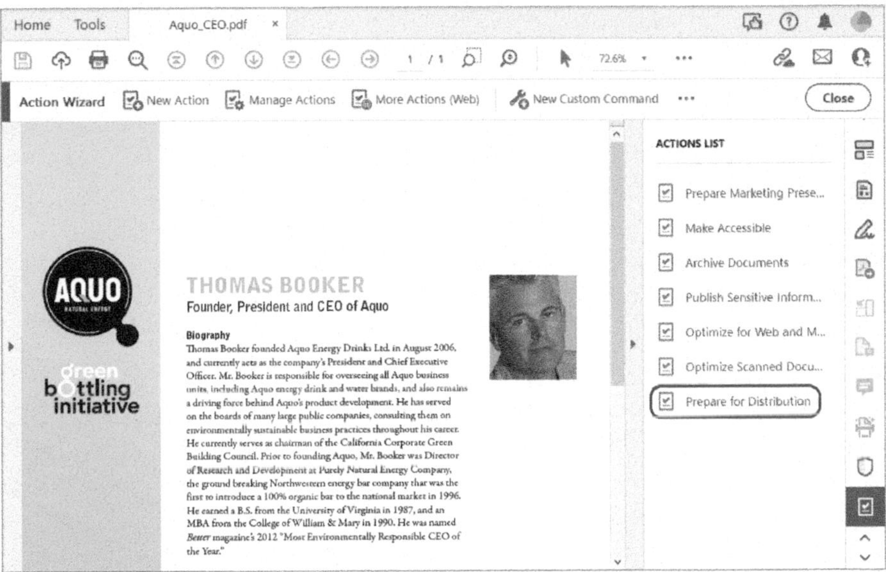

The action steps and information appear where the Actions List was. The action pane names the files to be processed, lets you add files if you want to, and then lists the steps and information for the action itself.

4 Review the steps for this action. When you've read the information, click Start to proceed to the first step.

The Start button changes to a Stop button, which you can click at any time to stop the action. The Remove Hidden Information dialog box appears, and that step is highlighted in the action pane.

5 Click OK in the Remove Hidden Information dialog box to accept the default selections.

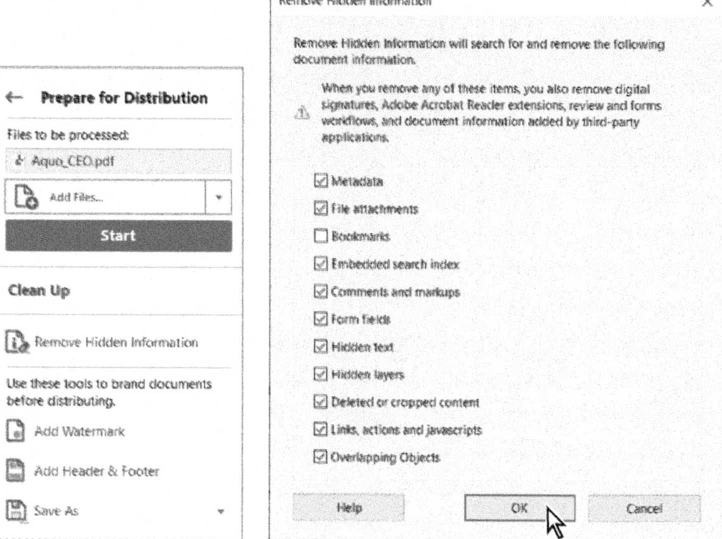

6 In the Add Watermark dialog box, do the following:

- Click an insertion point in the Text box, and type **Copyright Aquo 2023**.
- Select 20 for the font size
- Set the Opacity to 20%.
- In the Position area of the dialog box, choose Points, and enter **1** for the Vertical Distance. Then choose Bottom from the From menu.
- Choose Right from the From menu for Horizontal Distance.

The watermark should appear in the lower right corner of the document in the Preview pane.

7 Click OK to accept the watermark.

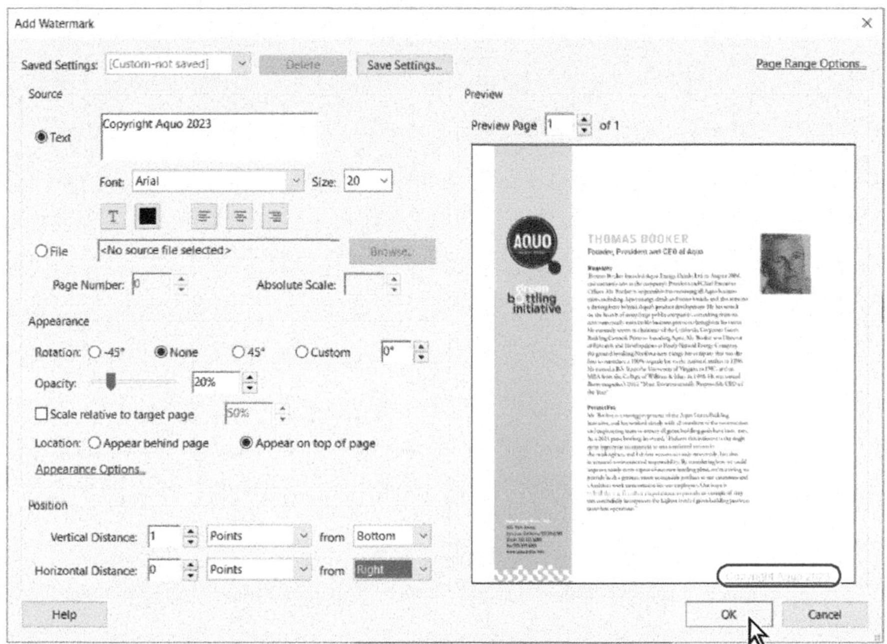

▶ **Tip:** To add a header or footer when you're not using an action, open the Edit PDF tool, and choose Header & Footer > Add.

8 In the Add Header And Footer dialog box, click an insertion point in the Center Header Text box, and then type **Aquo Corporate Information**. Change the font size to 9. The header appears in the preview area. Click OK to add the header and close the dialog box.

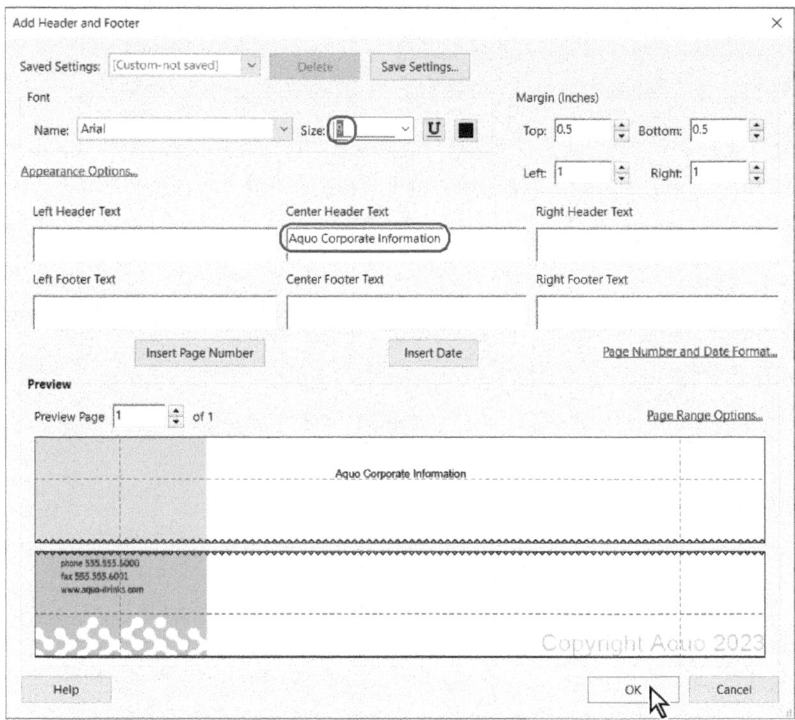

● **Note:** By default, Acrobat saves the new file to the folder that contains the original file. You can specify a different location.

9 In the Save As PDF dialog box, name the document **Aquo_CEO_dist.pdf**, save it to the Lesson12/Finished_Projects folder, and click Save.

The action pane now shows the word Completed where the Stop button was.

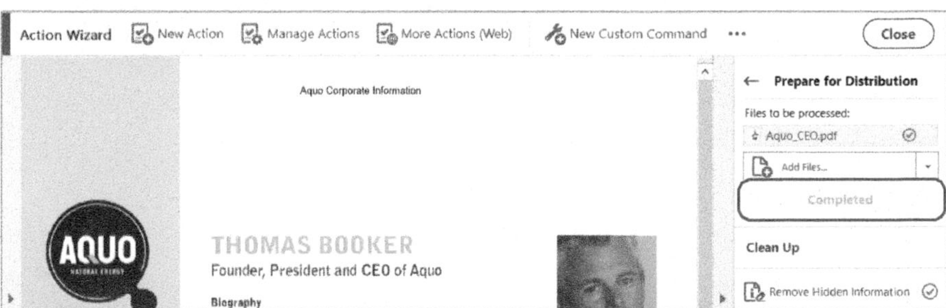

10 Click Full Report at the bottom of the action pane to see an itemized list of the tasks performed by the action. The report opens in a browser window. When you're done reviewing it, close the browser.

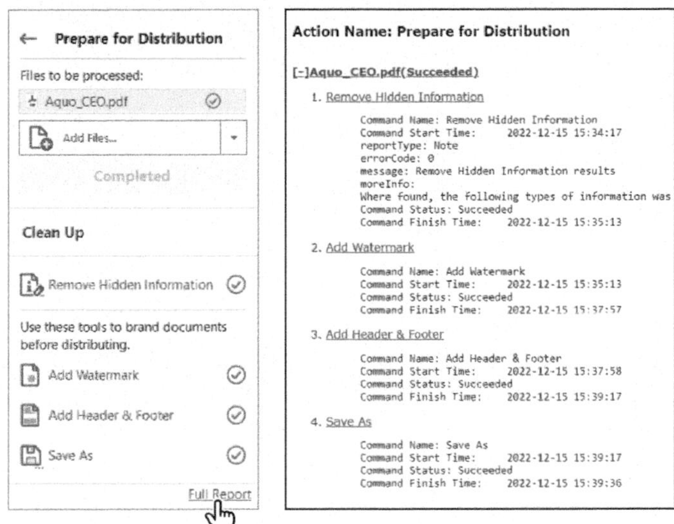

11 In Acrobat Pro, leave the Action Wizard tool and the document open.

Creating an action

You can create your own actions, assembling Acrobat steps and instructional steps to automate a process or to make it more consistent. Before you create an action, consider the steps involved and the logical order for those steps. For example, encrypting a document with password protection should be among the last steps in an action.

You'll create an action for preparing a multimedia presentation in Acrobat Pro. The steps you'll include are adding a header or footer to visually link the pages to each other, creating page transitions, setting the file to open in Full Screen mode, and then adding a password to the document to prevent others from making changes.

1 In the Action Wizard toolbar, click New Action.

The Create New Action dialog box is divided into two panes. The left pane displays tools that you can include in the action (arranged by category). In the right pane of the dialog box are options for files to be processed and the steps you've added to the action. Use the buttons on the far right to design the action's appearance; you can add dividers, panels, and instructions.

2 In the Create New Action dialog box, make sure Add Files is chosen from the Default Option menu.

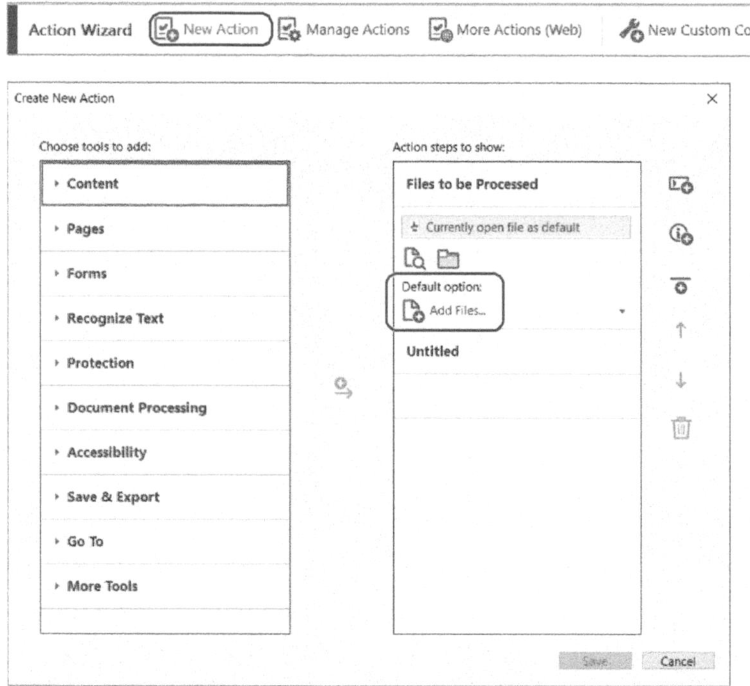

You can apply an action to an open file, or the action can prompt the user to select a file or folder, require the user to scan a document, or open a file from cloud storage.

Adding steps to an action

Now you're ready to add the steps.

1 Expand the Pages category in the left pane of the dialog box, and select Add Header & Footer.

2 Click the Add To Right-Hand Pane button ( ) in the middle of the dialog box. The Add Header & Footer step appears in the panel in the list on the right.

3 Make sure Prompt User is selected for the step. When the action runs, the user can customize the header or footer for the presentation.

Tip: If you change your mind about a step, you can delete it: Select the step, and then click the Remove button ( ) on the right side of the dialog box. To change the order of steps, use the Move Up and Move Down buttons.

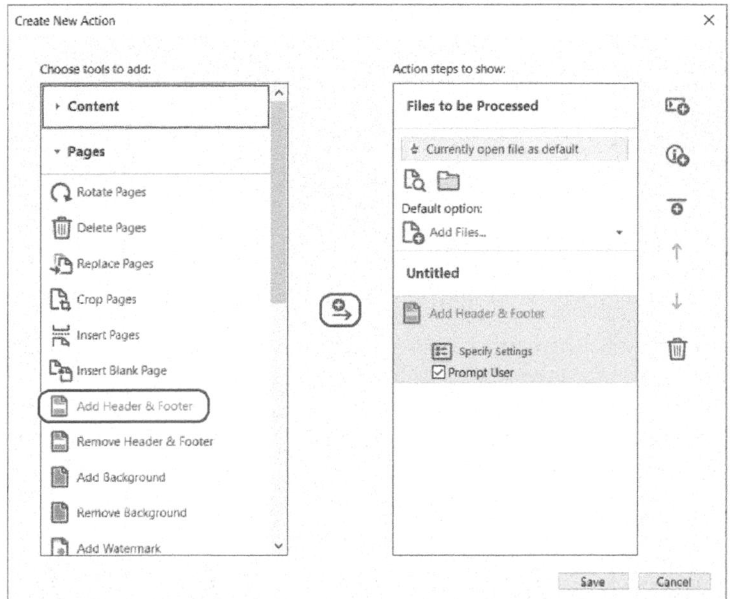

The company's legal department has asked that headers follow a particular convention. You'll add an instruction step for the user.

4 Click the Add Instruction button () on the right side of the dialog box.

5 In the Add Or Edit Label dialog box, type **Aquo Legal requests that all marketing presentations use the full company name, Aquo Natural Energy, in the header.** Then click Save.

▶ **Tip:** While an action is running, you can't access the Tools pane or the Tools Center. So if you need users to access a tool, add a Go To step.

You can add as much or as little information as you want in an instruction step. If you're sharing your action with people who are less familiar with Acrobat, consider providing detailed steps. If you're creating an action for yourself, a reminder to perform the step, such as "Use full company name," may be enough.

6 Click Pause for the step you created to give the user time to read your instructions.

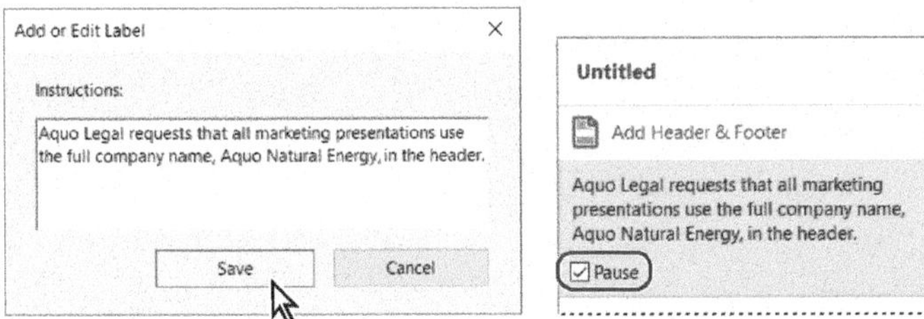

You want the user to read the instructions before the action opens the Add Header & Footer dialog box. You'll move the instructions up in the action.

7 Select the Add Header & Footer action, and click the down arrow (↓) on the right side of the Create New Action dialog box.

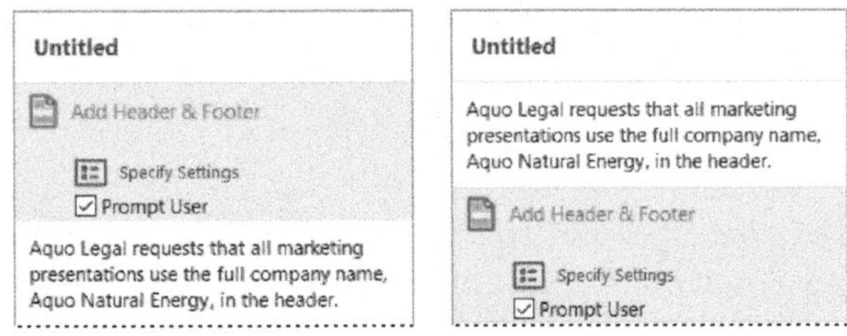

The Add Header & Footer action will now open after the user has read the instruction.

8 Expand the Document Processing category in the left pane, and double-click Page Transitions.

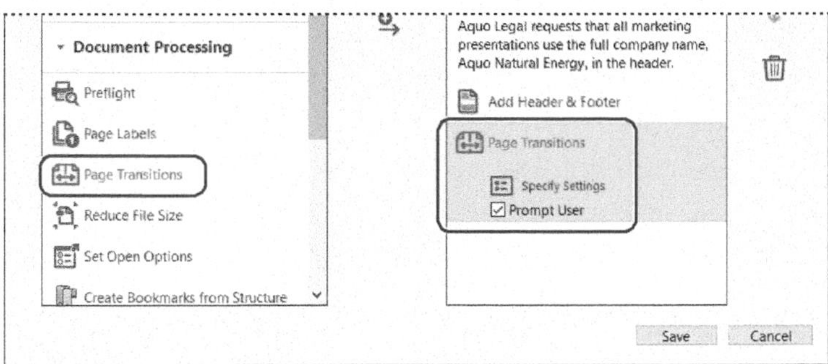

When you double-click an option on the left side, it's automatically added as a step on the right.

9 Click the Specify Settings button in the Page Transitions step.

10 Choose Dissolve from the Transition menu, and then choose Medium from the Speed menu. Then click OK.

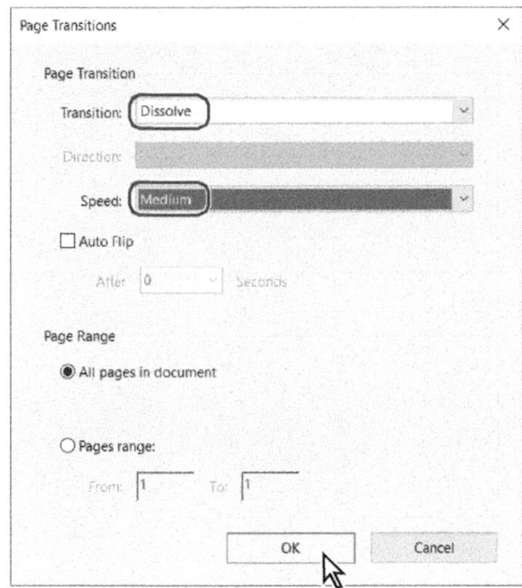

11 Deselect Prompt User in the Page Transitions step.

Acrobat will automatically apply the options you select for the Page Transitions step, without prompting the user.

12 In the left pane, double-click Set Open Options in the Document Processing category.

13 Deselect Prompt User, and then click the Specify Settings button for the new step.

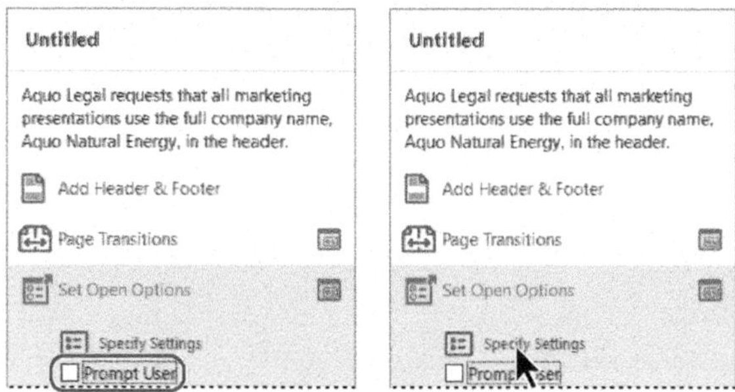

14 In the Set Open Options dialog box, choose Yes from the Open In Full Screen Mode menu, and then click OK.

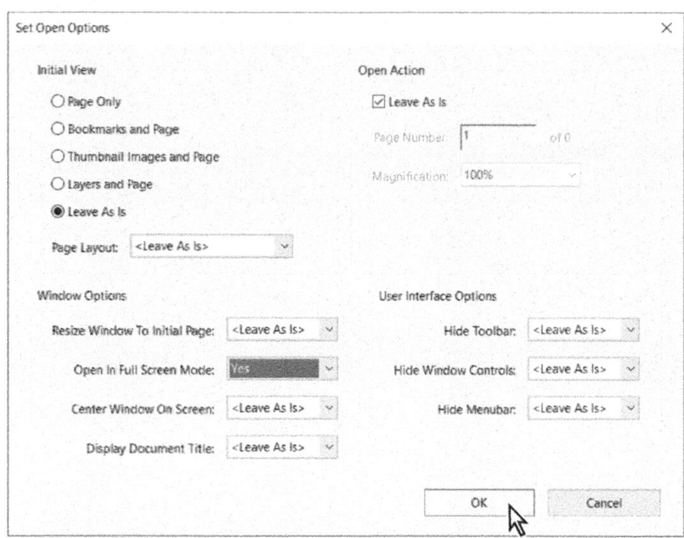

15 Expand the Protection category, and then double-click Encrypt. Make sure that Prompt User is selected in the Encrypt step so that each user can set an individual password.

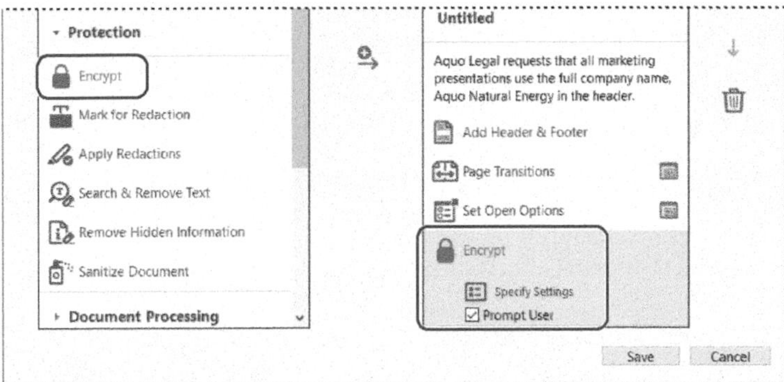

Saving an action

When you've added all the steps, confirmed that they're in the appropriate order, and specified the options you want, save and name the action.

1 Click Save.

2 Name the action **Prepare Marketing Presentation**.

3 For the action description, type **Add headers, transitions, and a password to a presentation**. Then click Save.

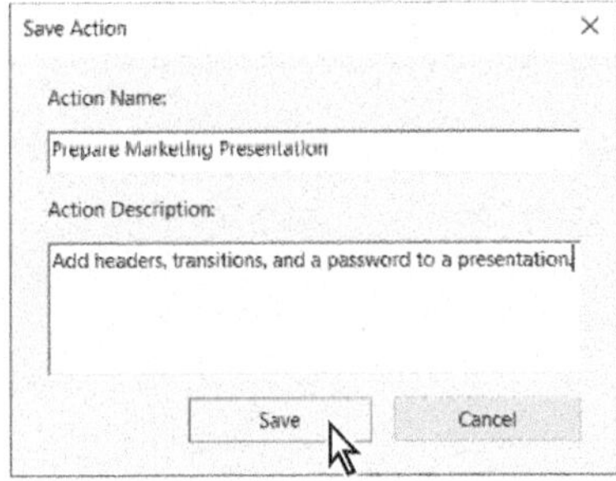

Give actions names that help you remember what the actions do. It's usually a good idea, especially if you'll be sharing the action, to describe the product of the action or when you should use it, such as when you're preparing documents for a particular client or purpose.

Testing an action

Now you'll test-drive your action to ensure it works the way you expect. You'll prepare a presentation for a fictitious beverage company.

1 Choose File > Open, and open the Aquo_presentation.pdf file in the Lesson12/ Assets folder.

2 Click Tools, and then open the Action Wizard tool.

3 In the Actions List, select Prepare Marketing Presentation. The action steps replace the Actions List, and the open document is the default file to be processed.

4 Click Start to proceed to the first step in the action.

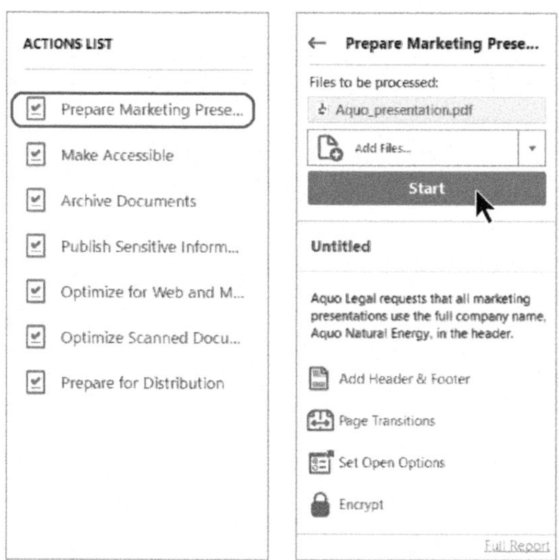

The instruction step you created appears on the screen. Because you selected the Pause option for the step, the user must click Click To Proceed in order to continue working through the action.

5 Click Click To Proceed.

6 In the Add Header And Footer dialog box, click an insertion point in the Left Header Text box, and then type **Aquo Natural Energy Shareholders Meeting 2023**. Change the font size to 10, and then click OK.

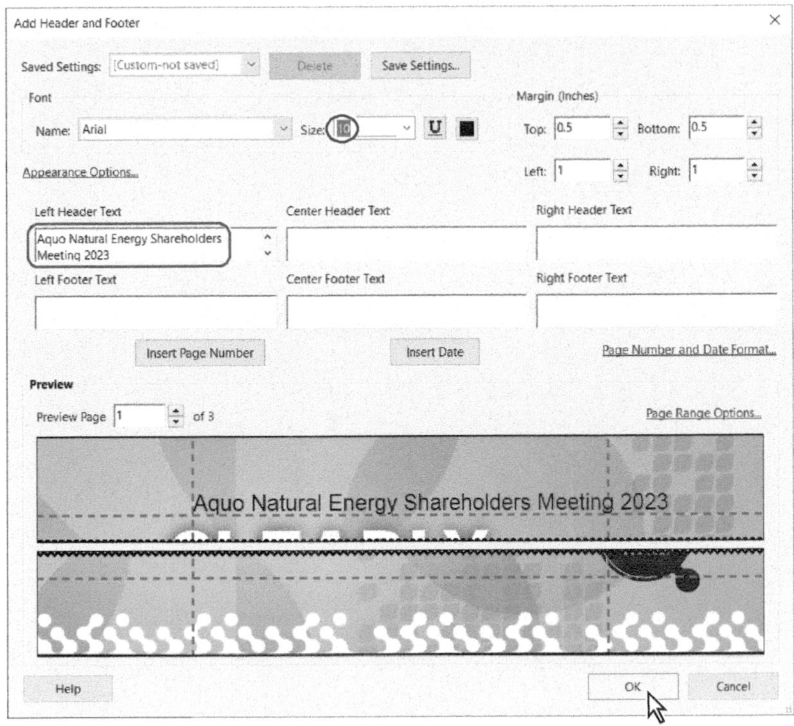

Acrobat automatically performs the next two steps—adding page transitions and setting the presentation to open in Full Screen mode—because no input is required. The final step is adding a password, which does require input.

7 In the Document Security dialog box, choose Password Security from the Security Method menu.

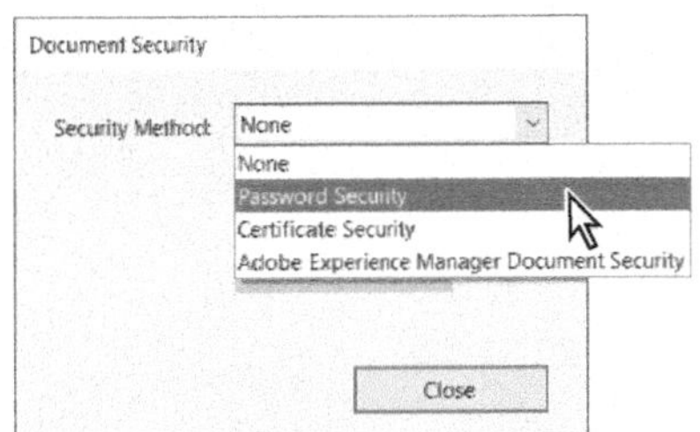

Note: Acrobat reports how secure your password is when you create it. To help you work through the action quickly, we're using a very simple password with only a Medium rating. When you create passwords, strive for a Strong rating.

8 In the Permissions area of the Password Security – Settings dialog box, select Restrict Editing And Printing Of the Document. In the Change Permissions Password box, enter **Aquo1234** as the password. Then click OK.

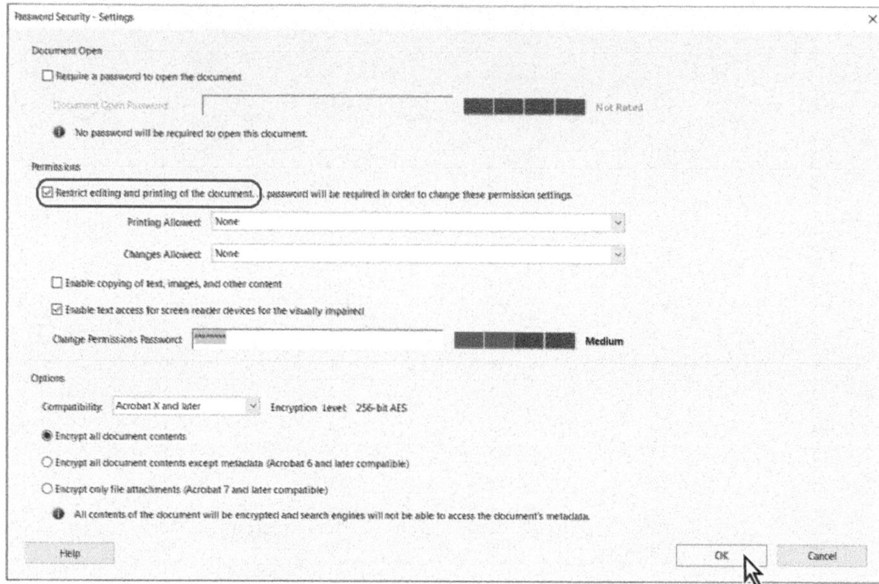

9 Click OK in the informational dialog box, enter the password again when prompted, and then click OK. Click Close to close the Document Security dialog box.

The Action Wizard pane shows that the Prepare Marketing Presentation action has been completed.

10 Choose File > Save As, name the presentation file **Aquo_meeting.pdf**, save it to the Lesson12/Finished_Projects folder, and then click Save.

11 Close the document. If you want to see the presentation open in Full Screen mode with its header and page transitions, open the Aquo_meeting.pdf file in Acrobat. When you're done, press the Esc key to exit Full Screen mode, and then close the file.

Sharing actions

You can share actions you create or edit with other users.

> ▶ **Tip:** You can edit actions after you create them: Click Manage Actions. In the Manage Actions dialog box, select the action name, and click Edit.

1 If you're using macOS, open a PDF file so that you can access tools.

2 Open the Action Wizard tool.

3 Click Manage Actions in the Action Wizard toolbar.

4 Select the Prepare Marketing Presentation action, and click Export.

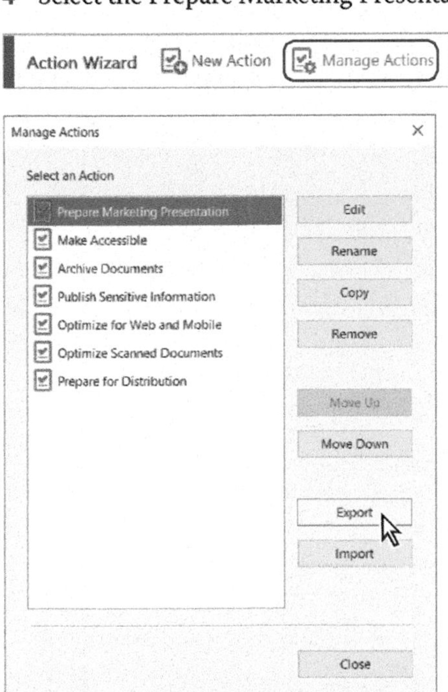

5 Name the action **Prepare Marketing Presentation** (the default name), save it in the Lesson12/Finished_Projects folder, and click Save.

The action file is saved with the .sequ extension. You can copy .sequ files or email them to other users. To open an .sequ file that someone has sent you, click Import in the Manage Actions dialog box, and select the action file.

6 Click Close to close the Manage Actions dialog box. Then close any open documents, and quit Acrobat.

Avoiding the Full Screen mode warning

By default, Acrobat warns you when a PDF file is set to be opened in Full Screen mode, because it is possible for malicious programmers to create PDF files that appear to be other applications. If you click Remember My Choice For This Document, Acrobat will not show the warning again when you open the presentation on this computer. If you are presenting material on your own computer, you can change the preference so that Acrobat will not display the warning at the beginning of your presentation. To change the preference, choose Edit > Preferences (Windows) or Acrobat > Preferences (macOS), and then click Full Screen on the left. Deselect the Alert When Document Requests Full Screen option.

Review questions

1 What is an action in Acrobat Pro?

2 How can you provide additional information to the user?

3 How can you share an action with others?

Review answers

1 An action is a collection of steps. Some steps, such as adding tags to a document, can be performed automatically by Acrobat. Some steps, such as removing hidden information, require input as to what to remove or add, or which settings to use. Other steps, such as adding bookmarks, cannot be done automatically, because you need to use human discretion to create and name the bookmarks.

2 To add a message for the user, click the Add Instruction button, and then type the information you want to provide.

3 To share an action, click Manage Actions in the Action Wizard toolbar, select the action you want to share, and click Export. Then send the resulting .sequ file to the person you want to share the action with.

13 USING ACROBAT IN PROFESSIONAL PRINTING

Lesson overview

In this lesson, you'll do the following:

- Learn how to create Adobe PDF files suitable for high-resolution printing.
- Preflight an Adobe PDF file to check for quality and consistency (Acrobat Pro).
- View how transparent objects affect a page (Acrobat Pro).
- Configure color management.
- Use Acrobat to generate color separations.

This lesson will take approximately 60 minutes to complete. Download the project files for this lesson, following the instructions in the Getting Started section under "Accessing the lesson files and Web Edition," if you haven't already done so. As you work on this lesson, you'll preserve the start files. If you need to restore the start files, download them from your Account page.

Self reinvention is something we all entertain, and the way fashion allows us to dream.

Alice Ritter is kneeling at the feet of a long-limbed model, one of a dozen milling around a photography set in clothes from her Fall-Winter 2011 collection. It is crucial that she get the girl's pant legs scrunched just so for the shoot. Precise, but with an unstudied symmetry that somehow comes off as casual. She readily admits to being obsessed with this level of detail, because it's where story springs from. "Design is storytelling," Ritter explains. "You start to draw, then you go into the details and the story takes over."

As much as detail is the motor that drives the story inherent in an Alice Ritter piece, it's also what provokes an emotional response to the item. "The piece has to trigger an emotion," Ritter believes, and the seat of emotion is detail. Detail grabs you by the scruff of the neck. It slips its hand in yours. It follows you home. Detail is what makes an item "really special," she says, "the one dress you'll wear for ten years."

So she sweats the small stuff, crafting and editing a fresh batch of stories with each new collection. The unifying design element--the signature plotline threading one season to the next--is the vision of a better Alice. One who regularly tumbles down the rabbit hole to see where the

path might lead her. The story she's telling and the design process that leads her there is "a reflection of my journey, my self-discovery. A big part of my identity—or my dreamed identity—goes into my design."

Which raises a really good question: Who is Alice Ritter anyway? There are at least two ways to tell that story.

A small-town French girl raised in a nice family with traditional bourgeois values, she grew up playing dress up in her grandparents' attic with a cache of 19th century gowns and corsets. While that piqued her interest in fashion early on, the couture in the pages of French Vogue—Chanel, Yves Saint Laurent and Balmain and the rest—hooked her for life on design. "I

Acrobat Pro provides professional printing tools, including preflighting and transparency previews, to help you achieve high-quality output.

Creating PDF files for print and prepress

As you learned in Lesson 2, there are many ways to create a PDF file from your original document. No matter which method you choose, however, you need to use the appropriate PDF preset for your intended output. For high-resolution, professional printing, specify the Press Quality PDF preset or a custom PDF preset provided by your printer.

About Adobe PDF presets

A PDF preset is a group of settings that affect the process of creating a PDF file. These settings are designed to balance file size with quality, depending on how the PDF file will be used. Most predefined presets are shared across Adobe Creative Cloud applications, including Adobe InDesign, Adobe Illustrator, Adobe Photoshop, and Acrobat. You can also create and share custom presets to meet your own needs.

Presets that include "(Japan)" in their names are specifically designed for Japanese print workflows. For more detailed descriptions of each preset, see Adobe Acrobat Help.

- **High Quality Print** creates PDF documents for quality printing on desktop printers and proofing devices.
- **Oversized Pages** creates PDF files suitable for viewing and printing engineering drawings larger than 200 by 200 inches.
- **PDF/A-1b (CMYK and RGB)** standards are used for the long-term preservation (archival) of electronic documents.
- **PDF/X-1a** standards minimize the number of variables in a PDF document to improve reliability. PDF/X-1a files are commonly used for digital ads that will be reproduced on a press.
- **PDF/X-3** files are similar to PDF/X-1a files, but they support color-managed workflows and allow some RGB images.
- **PDF/X-4** has the same color-management ICC color specifications as PDF/X-3, but includes support for live transparency.
- **Press Quality** creates PDF files for high-quality print production (for example, for digital printing or for separations to an imagesetter or platesetter).
- **Smallest File Size** creates PDF files for displaying on the web or a local network, or for distribution through an email system.
- **Standard** creates PDF files to be printed to desktop printers or digital copiers, published on a disc, or sent to a client as a publishing proof.

Guidelines for creating print-ready PDF files

By the time you submit a PDF file to a printer, the die has been cast. A printer can coax a quality print-out from some less-than-optimal PDF files, but for the most part, the printer is restricted by decisions made during the creative process. Following these guidelines, you can deliver the strongest, highest-quality PDF files to a printer:

- **Remember that the end product is only as good as its components.** For high-quality printing, a PDF file must contain the appropriate images, fonts, and other components.
- **Convert only when absolutely necessary.** Every time you convert text, objects, or color, you compromise the integrity of the file. The printed product will most closely resemble your original intent if you minimize conversions. Keep text in its original form, as fonts, rather than outlining or rasterizing it. Keep gradients live. Maintain live transparency as long as possible. And don't convert colors from device-independent or high-gamut color spaces, such as RGB, to device-specific or low-gamut color spaces, such as CMYK, unless advised to do so.
- **Use transparency efficiently.** Transparency comes into play any time you apply a blending mode or change the opacity of an object. For the best results, keep transparency live as long as possible; place objects you don't want the flattener to affect (such as text and line objects) above all nearby sources of transparency, preferably on a separate layer; and use the highest quality flattener settings if and when you flatten transparency.
- **Proof and preflight before creating the PDF file.** Early in the workflow, you have more context for problems, and more options for fixing them. Carefully proof the content and formatting before creating a PDF file. Additionally, if the authoring application provides a preflight feature, use it to identify missing fonts, unlinked images, or other issues that could result in problems down the road. The earlier you can identify and fix a problem, the easier and less expensive it is to fix. Certainly, technical problems found while you're still working in the authoring program are easier to fix than problems found in Acrobat or on a printing press.
- **Embed fonts.** To minimize the chance of complications, embed fonts in the PDF file. Read the end user license agreement (EULA) before purchasing a font to ensure it permits embedding.
- **Use the appropriate PDF settings file.** When you create the PDF file, make sure you're using the appropriate settings. The PDF settings file determines how image data is saved, whether fonts are embedded, and whether colors are converted. By default, Acrobat PDFMaker in Microsoft Office creates PDF files using the Standard settings file, which does not meet the requirements for most high-end printing. No matter what application you're using to create a PDF file for professional printing, ensure that you're using the PDF/X-1a or Press Quality PDF settings file, or the settings file recommended by your printer.
- **Create a PDF/X file if appropriate.** PDF/X is a subset of the Adobe PDF specification, requiring that PDF files meet specific criteria for the printing industry, resulting in more reliable PDF files. Using PDF/X-compliant files eliminates the most common errors in file preparation: fonts that aren't embedded, incorrect color spaces, and overprinting issues. PDF/X-1a, PDF/X-3, and PDF/X-4 are the most popular formats; each is designed for a different purpose. Ask your printer whether you should save your file in a PDF/X format.

Creating the PDF file

You can create a PDF file from any application using the Print command. Because we do not know which applications you use, we have not included a file for this exercise. You can use any existing document or create a new document. The following steps are appropriate for most applications.

1 Open any document in its original application.

> **Note:** Some applications don't use the standard Print dialog boxes to create PDF files. For example, to save a PDF file from Adobe InDesign, use the Export command.

2 Choose File > Print.

3 Do one of the following:

In Windows: Choose Adobe PDF from the list of available printers. Then click Properties, Preferences, Printer Properties, or Setup, depending on the application. Choose Press Quality or a custom PDF settings file.

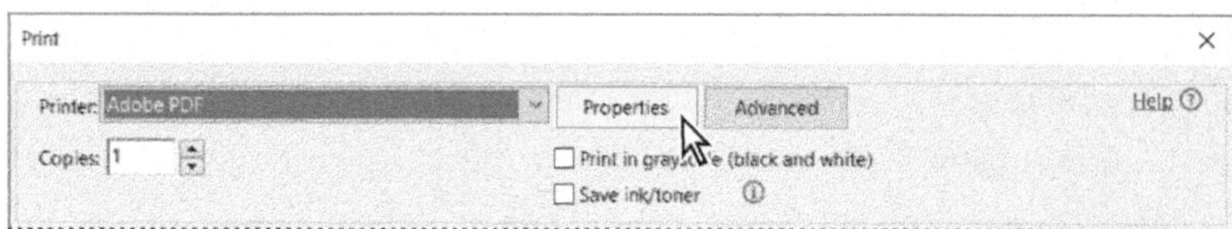

In macOS: Click PDF, and choose Save As Adobe PDF from the menu. Then, in the Save As Adobe PDF dialog box, select the Press Quality settings file or a custom settings file from the Adobe PDF Settings menu, and click Continue.

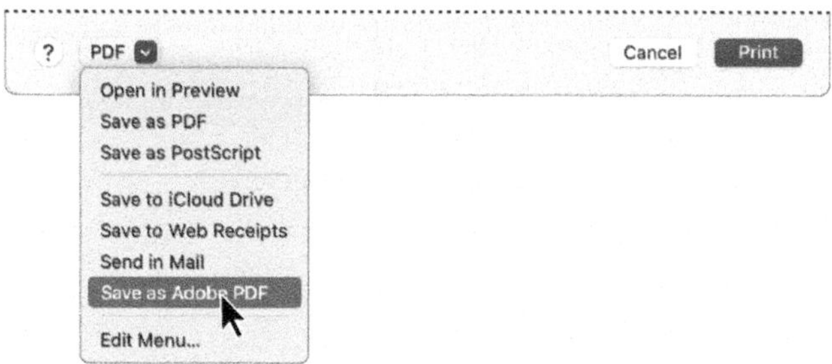

4 In Windows, choose Prompt For Adobe PDF Filename from the Adobe PDF Output Folder menu, and then click OK. If you do not select this option, the Adobe PDF printer saves the file in the My Documents folder. (In macOS, you will be prompted for a filename and location automatically.)

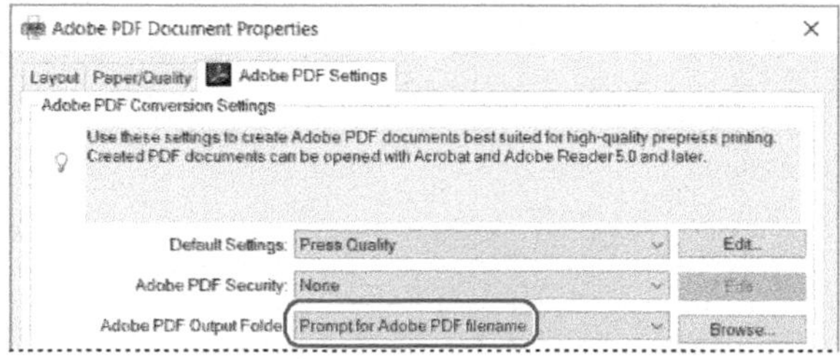

5 In Windows, click Print or OK.

6 Specify a filename and folder for the PDF file when prompted, and click Save.

7 Close the PDF file and the original document.

For more information about selecting presets, see Adobe Acrobat Help.

Preflighting files (Acrobat Pro)

Before you hand off a PDF file to a print service provider, preflight it to verify that the document meets the criteria for print publishing. Preflighting analyzes a document against the criteria listed in the preflight profile you specify; in addition to identifying potential issues, many preflight profiles contain fixups that can correct problems for you.

Ask your print service provider which preflight profile to use to accurately preflight your document. Many print service providers provide custom preflight profiles to their customers.

You'll preflight a file to determine whether it's ready for digital printing.

1 In Acrobat Pro, choose File > Open, and navigate to the Lesson13/Assets folder. Select the Profile.pdf file, and click Open.

2 Click Tools to open the Tools Center. Then, choose Add Shortcut in the menu beneath the Print Production tool (in the Protect & Standardize category) to add the tool to the Tools pane if it's not already there. You'll use the tool multiple times in this lesson.

3 In the Tools pane, click Print Production.

4 Click Preflight in the right-hand pane.

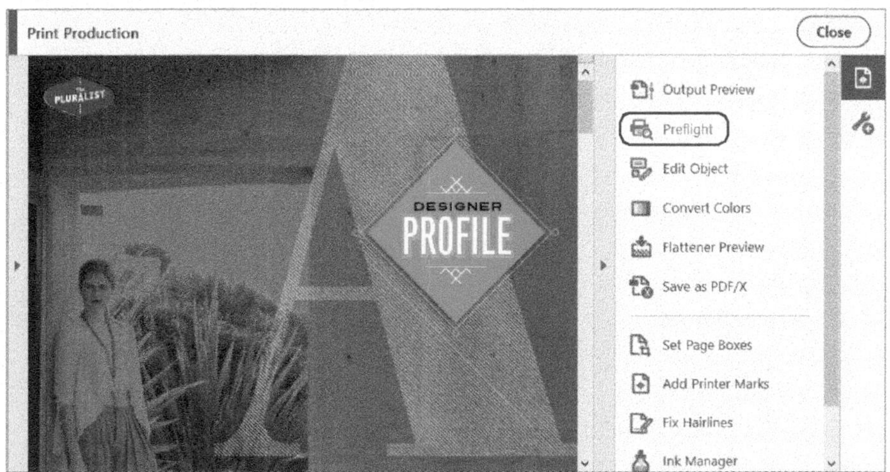

The Preflight dialog box lists the available preflight profiles, grouped into categories that describe the tests they perform.

5 Click the triangle next to Digital Printing And Online Publishing to expand the category.

6 Select the Digital Printing (Color) profile.

When you select the profile, Acrobat displays its description.

7 Click Analyze And Fix.

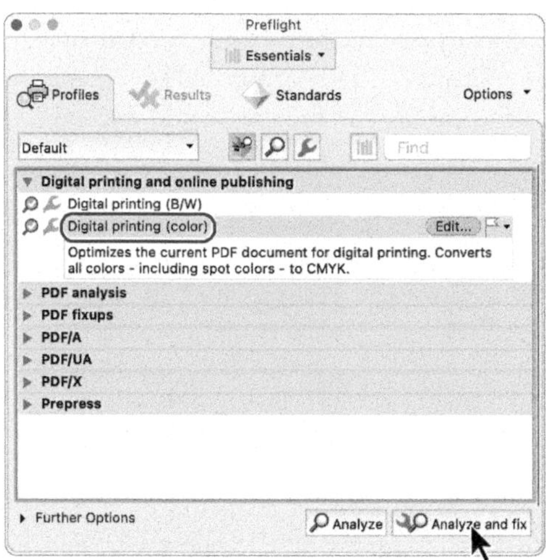

8 In the Save As PDF dialog box, name the fixed file **Profile_fixed.pdf,** save it to the Lesson13/Finished_Projects folder, and click Save.

Because the profile applies fixups, it makes changes to the file. Saving the file to a different name ensures that you can return to the original if you need to.

9 Review the results of the preflight.

Acrobat displays the results of the preflight in the Results pane. In this file, Acrobat performed several fixups, applying compression, color conversion, and transparency flattening, as well as other changes.

The Results pane also notes that a white object is not set to knock out. If you were professionally printing this document, you might want to contact your print service provider to ensure that any factors reported in the Results pane won't cause problems when your document is printed.

10 Click Create Report.

11 Navigate to the Lesson13/Finished_Projects folder, and then click Save to save the report with the default name **Profile_fixed_report.pdf**.

Acrobat creates the preflight summary report as a PDF and opens it in Acrobat.

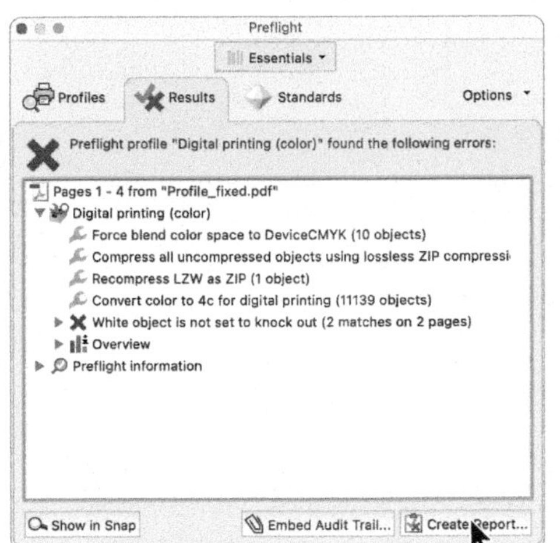

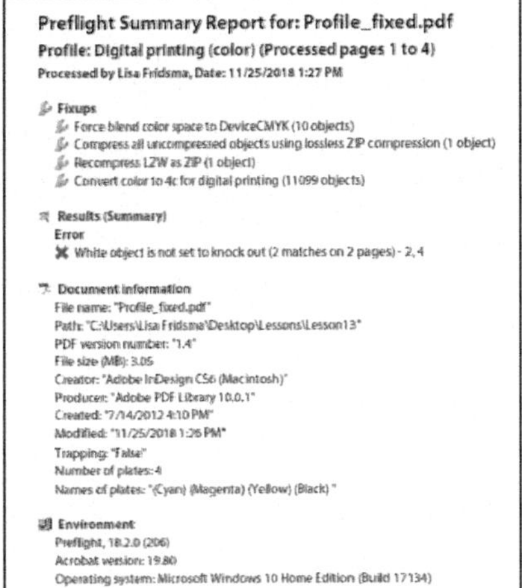

Preflight Summary Report for: Profile_fixed.pdf
Profile: Digital printing (color) (Processed pages 1 to 4)
Processed by Lisa Fridsma, Date: 11/25/2018 1:27 PM

Fixups
Force blend color space to DeviceCMYK (10 objects)
Compress all uncompressed objects using lossless ZIP compression (1 object)
Recompress LZW as ZIP (1 object)
Convert color to 4c for digital printing (11099 objects)

Results (Summary)
Error
White object is not set to knock out (2 matches on 2 pages) - 2, 4

Document information
File name: "Profile_fixed.pdf"
Path: "C:\Users\Lisa Fridsma\Desktop\Lessons\Lesson13"
PDF version number: "1.4"
File size (MB): 3.05
Creator: "Adobe InDesign CS6 (Macintosh)"
Producer: "Adobe PDF Library 10.0.1"
Created: "7/14/2012 4:10 PM"
Modified: "11/25/2018 1:26 PM"
Trapping: "False"
Number of plates: 4
Names of plates: "(Cyan) (Magenta) (Yellow) (Black) "

Environment
Preflight, 18.2.0 (206)
Acrobat version: 19.80
Operating system: Microsoft Windows 10 Home Edition (Build 17134)

12 Close the Preflight dialog box, and review the preflight summary report.

You can send the preflight summary report to your print service provider if you have any questions about preparing the file. Note that there are five pages to the report: The first page provides a summary of fixups and errors. The summary page is followed by the document itself, with comments identifying where errors occur.

13 Choose File > Close File to close the preflight summary report, and then choose File > Close File again to close the Profile_fixed.pdf file.

Tip: You can hide or show individual layers that were created in the authoring application, and determine which ones will print. To learn about showing, hiding, and printing layers, see Adobe Acrobat Help.

Custom preflight profiles

You can customize the preflight profiles included with Acrobat, import profiles provided by your print service provider, or create your own custom profiles.
To create a new profile, open the Preflight dialog box, and choose Options > Create Profile. To modify an existing profile, select it, click Edit next to its name, and then, if it's locked, choose Unlocked, and give the custom version a new name. Next, choose a group for the profile. Then expand the profile, click a category of criteria, and add or remove specific checks or fixups. Save the profile when you're done.

To import a preflight profile, open the Preflight dialog box, and choose Options > Import Profile. Navigate to the custom profile, which has a .kfp extension, and click Open.

To export a profile, select the profile you want to share, and then choose Options > Export Profile. Define the display name of the profile, and then specify the location where you want to save it.

Working with transparency (Acrobat Pro)

Adobe applications let you modify objects in ways that can affect the underlying artwork, creating the appearance of transparency. You may create transparency by using an opacity slider in InDesign, Illustrator, or Photoshop, or by changing the blending mode for a layer or selected object. Transparency also comes into play whenever you create a drop shadow or apply feathering. Adobe applications can keep transparency "live," or editable, as you move documents from one application to another, but transparency must typically be flattened before printing. In Acrobat Pro, you can see which areas of your document are affected by transparency and how those areas will print.

Previewing transparency

Note: If your print service provider is using a RIP (raster image processor) that includes the Adobe PDF Print Engine, you may not need to flatten transparency.

When you print to most printers, transparency is flattened. The flattening process separates overlapping areas of artwork into discrete sections that are converted either into separate vector shapes or rasterized pixels to retain the look of the transparency.

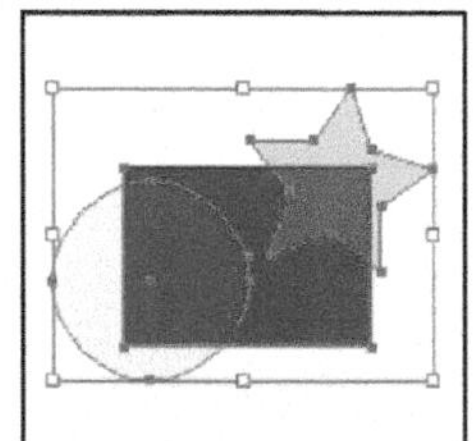

Objects before flattening

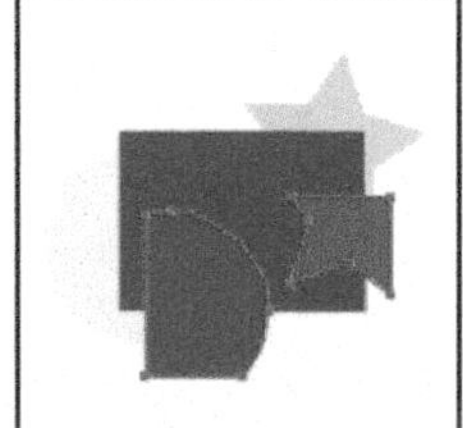

Objects after flattening

(Overlapping art is divided when flattened.)

Before flattening occurs, you can determine how much of the transparent area remains vector, and how much becomes rasterized. Some effects, such as drop shadows, must be rasterized in order to print correctly.

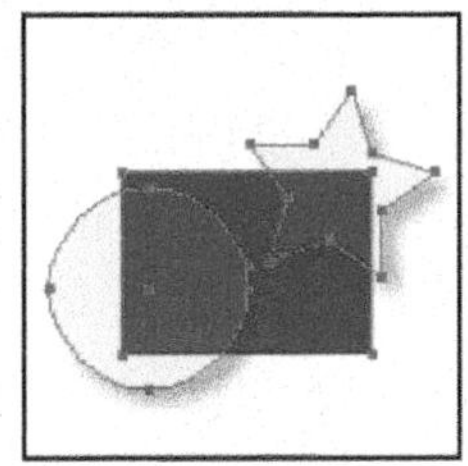

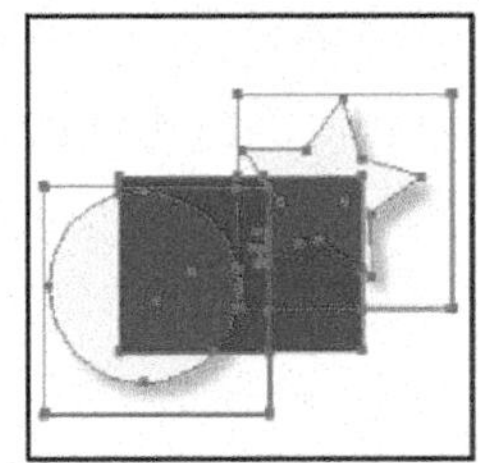

If you receive a PDF file created by someone else, you may not know if or where transparency has been applied. The Acrobat transparency preview shows you where transparency is used in a document. This feature can also help you determine the best flattener settings to use when printing the document.

▶ **Tip:** In Acrobat Pro, you can quickly see whether a PDF file includes transparency: Select Output Preview in the right-hand pane of the Print Production panel. At the bottom of the Output Preview dialog box, Acrobat reports whether the page has transparency. If it doesn't, there's no need to flatten it.

PDF standards

PDF standards are internationally defined standards designed to simplify the exchange of graphic content (PDF/X), archived documents (PDF/A), or engineering workflows (PDF/E). The most widely used standards for a print publishing workflow are PDF/X-1a, PDF/X-3, and PDF/X-4.

You can validate PDF content against PDF/X, PDF/A, or PDF/E criteria in Acrobat Pro and save a copy of the document as PDF/X, PDF/A, or PDF/E, provided it complies with the specified requirements. You can also save a PDF file as a PDF/X or PDF/A file when you create the file using the Print command or the Export or Save command in an Adobe application.

In Acrobat or Acrobat Reader, you can use the Standards pane to see information about the file's conformance. The Standards pane is available only if an open document conforms to a standard; choose View > Show/Hide > Navigation Panes > Standards to open it. If you are using Acrobat Pro, you can also click Verify Conformance in the Standards pane to use the preflight feature to verify that the PDF file is a valid PDF/X or PDF/A file.

To save a copy of an existing PDF file as a PDF/X, PDF/A, or PDF/E file in Acrobat Pro:

1 Choose File > Save As.

2 Select a destination folder for the file.

3 In the Save As dialog box, choose PDF/A, PDF/E, or PDF/X from the Save As Type or Format menu, and click Settings.

4 Select the version of the standard and any other options, and click OK.

5 In the Save As dialog box, name the converted file, and click Save.

Acrobat converts the file, displaying messages about its progress.

You'll preview transparency in the Profile.pdf file.

1 Open the Profile.pdf file from the Lesson13/Assets folder.

2 Navigate to page 1 of the document. If the entire page is not visible, choose View > Zoom > Zoom To Page Level.

3 Open the Print Production tool, and then click Flattener Preview in the right-hand pane.

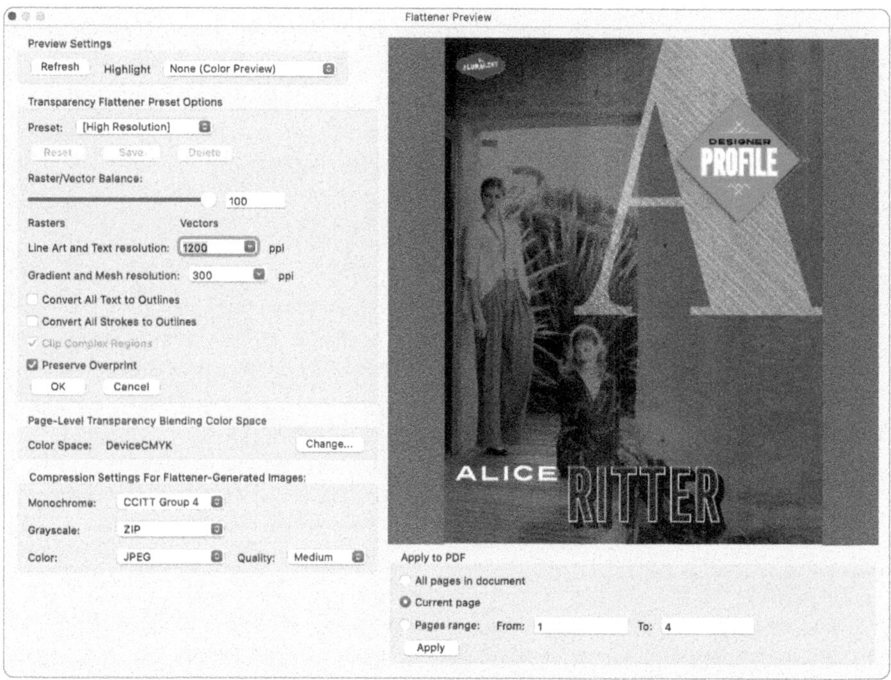

The Flattener Preview shows a preview of page 1 of the document on the right side of the dialog box.

Specifying flattener preview settings

You can select different settings to preview different aspects of the way transparency interacts with objects in the document.

1 In the Flattener Preview dialog box, choose All Affected Objects from the Highlight menu. Nearly the entire page is highlighted in red, indicating that the objects themselves have transparent properties or interact with objects that have transparent properties. Only a few items, including the text at the bottom of the page, are not affected by transparency.

2 Choose High Resolution from the Preset menu in the Transparency Flattener Preset Options area. The preset determines how much of the artwork remains vector and how much is rasterized. For professional printing, use the High Resolution preset unless your print service provider advises you differently.

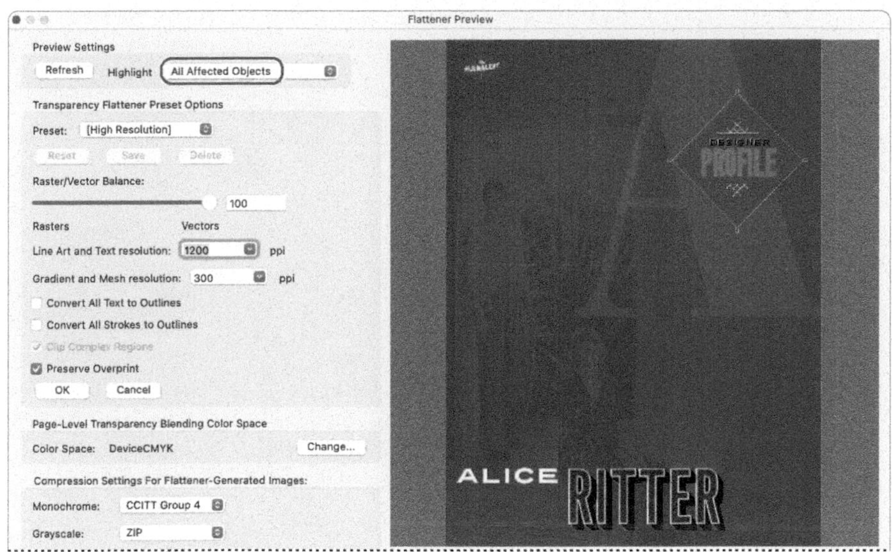

What is rasterization?

Rasterization is the process of changing vector objects, including fonts, into bitmap images to display or print them. The number of pixels per inch (ppi) is referred to as the *resolution*. The higher the resolution in a raster image, the better the quality. When flattening occurs, some objects may need to be rasterized, depending upon flattening settings.

Vector Object Rasterized at 72 ppi Rasterized at 300 ppi

3 Click the left end of the Raster/Vector Balance slider, or type **0** in the box. Then click Refresh in the Preview Settings area, and choose All Affected Objects from the Highlight menu. Everything on the page is highlighted in red, indicating that everything would be rasterized at this setting.

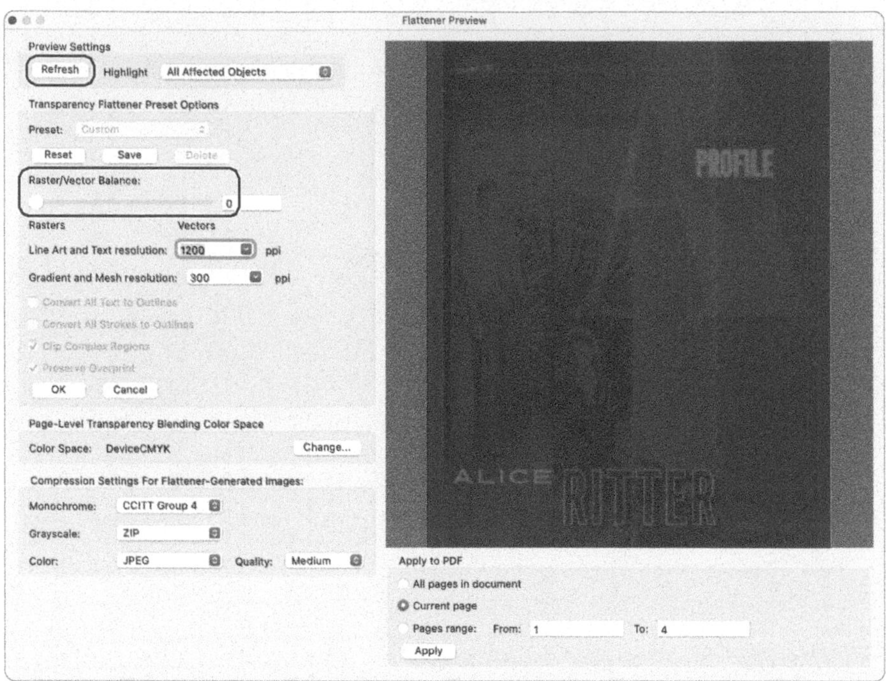

▶ **Tip:** You can find more information about printing transparency on the Adobe website at www.adobe.com.

4 Make other selections to see how the settings affect the document. When you are finished, click the close button in the upper right (Windows) or upper left (macOS) corner of the window to close the Flattener Preview window without applying your settings.

If you want to use the selected transparency flattener settings when printing, click Apply in the Flattener Preview dialog box.

About flattening options in the Flattener Preview dialog box

- **Line Art And Text Resolution** determines the resolution at which line art and text are rasterized. Because line art and text involve a sharper contrast around the edges, they need to be rasterized at a higher resolution to maintain a high-quality appearance. A resolution of 300 ppi is sufficient when proofing, but this should be increased to a higher resolution for final high-quality output. A resolution of 1200 ppi is typically sufficient for high-quality output.
- **Gradient And Mesh Resolution** determines the resolution at which gradients and meshes, which are sometimes called *blends*, will be rasterized. The resolution should be set appropriately for your specific printer. For proofing to a general-purpose laser printer or inkjet printer, the default setting of 150 ppi is appropriate. For printing to most high-quality output devices, such as a film or plate output device, a resolution of 300 ppi is usually sufficient.
- **Convert All Text To Outlines** ensures that the weight of all text in the artwork stays consistent. However, converting small fonts to outlines can make them appear noticeably thicker and less readable (especially when printing on lower-end printing systems).
- **Convert All Strokes To Outlines** ensures that the weight of all strokes in the artwork stays consistent. Selecting this option, however, causes thin strokes to appear slightly thicker (especially when printing on lower-end printing systems).
- **Clip Complex Regions** ensures that the boundaries between vector artwork and rasterized artwork fall along object paths. This option reduces stitching artifacts that result when part of an object is rasterized while another part remains in vector form (as determined by the Raster/Vector slider). Selecting this option may result in extremely complex clipping paths, which take significant time to compute, and can cause errors when printing.
- **Preserve Overprint** blends the color of transparent artwork with the background color to create an overprint effect. Overprinted colors are two or more inks printed on top of each other. For example, when a cyan ink prints over a yellow ink, the resulting overprint is a green color. Without overprinting, the underlying yellow would not be printed, resulting in a cyan color.

Setting up color management

Using color management can help you achieve consistent color throughout your workflow. Color profiles describe the characteristics of each device. Color management uses those profiles to map the colors possible for one device, such as a computer monitor, with the colors possible on another device, such as a printer.

1 Choose Edit > Preferences (Windows) or Acrobat > Preferences (macOS), and select Color Management from the list on the left.

2 From the Settings menu, choose North America Prepress 2. With this setting, Acrobat displays colors as they generally appear when printed using North American printing standards.

Note: You can synchronize color management settings for all the Adobe Creative Cloud applications in Adobe Bridge, which is available as part of a Creative Cloud membership. See Bridge Help for more information.

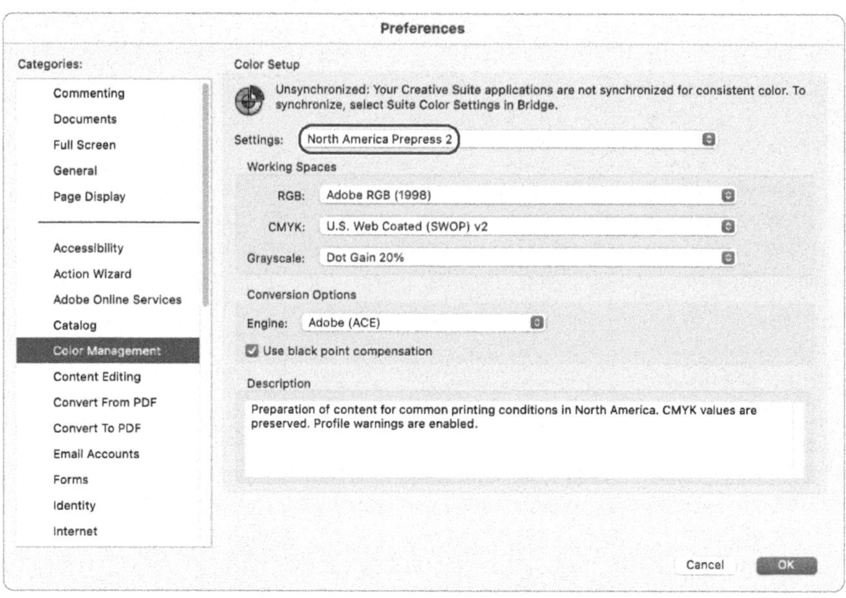

The setting you select determines which color working spaces are used by the application and how the color management system converts colors. To view a description of a setting, select the setting. The description appears at the bottom of the dialog box.

ACE (Adobe Color Engine) is the same color management engine used by other Adobe graphics software, so you can be confident that color management settings applied in Acrobat will mirror those applied in your other Adobe applications.

3 Click OK to close the Preferences dialog box.

Previewing your print job (Acrobat Pro)

You've already previewed how transparency will print. Now you'll preview color separations and verify the resolution of individual objects. You'll also perform a *soft proof*—that is, you'll proof the document on the screen without having to print it.

Previewing color separations

To reproduce color and continuous-tone images, printers usually separate artwork into four plates, called *process colors*—one plate for each of the cyan, magenta, yellow, and black portions of the image. You can also include custom pre-mixed inks, called *spot colors*, which require their own plates. When inked with the appropriate color and printed in register with one another, these plates combine to reproduce the original artwork. The plates are called *color separations*.

You will preview color separations from this document using the Output Preview dialog box.

1 Make sure you're viewing page 1 of the document, and that the Print Production tool is open.

2 Click Output Preview in the right-hand pane.

3 Choose Separations from the Preview menu.

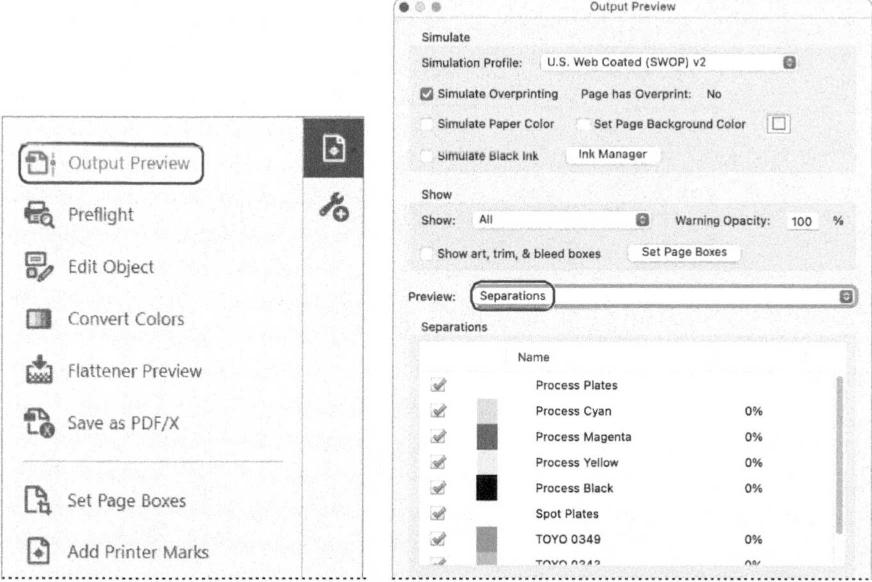

The Separations area of the dialog box lists all the inks that are included in this document for printing. There are four process inks (cyan, magenta, yellow, and black) and two spot colors (TOYO 0349 and TOYO 0343).

4 Drag the Output Preview dialog box to the side so that you can see the document. Then, in the Output Preview dialog box, deselect every ink except TOYO 0349. The items that remain on the page use the selected ink.

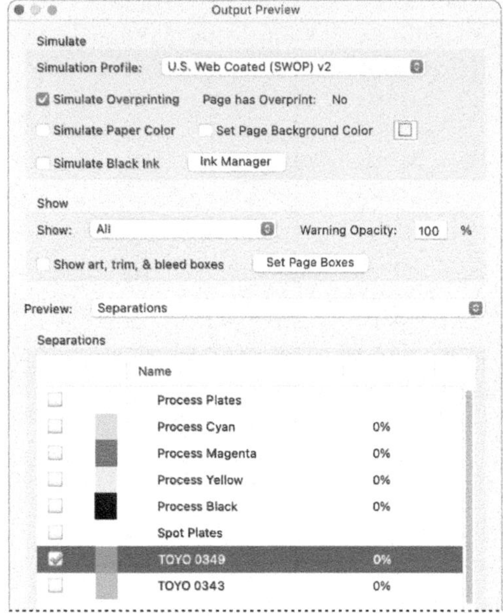

5 Deselect TOYO 0349, and select Process Magenta. Only those items that would print on the magenta plate appear.

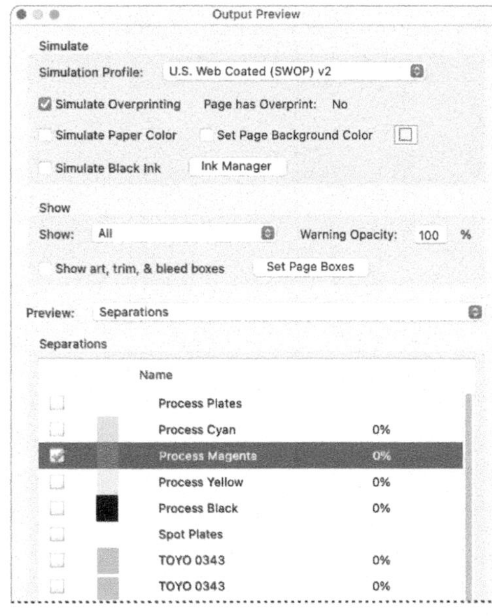

▶ **Tip:** If you wanted to remap a spot color to a process color in order to limit the number of plates, and thus the expense, of a print job, you could use the Ink Manager, also available in the Output Preview dialog box.

6 Select all the inks again.

Soft-proofing your document

You can use the Output Preview dialog box to soft-proof a document, so that you can see onscreen how your document will look when printed. Use the simulation settings to approximate the color.

As you change the profile chosen in the Simulation Profile menu, color shifts on the monitor. When you soft-proof a document, select the simulation profile that matches your output device. If you use accurately calibrated ICC profiles and have calibrated your monitor, the onscreen preview should match the final output. If you haven't calibrated your monitor or your profiles, the preview may not provide an exact match. For information about calibrating your monitor and profiles, see Adobe Acrobat Help.

Note: If you're working with a PDF/X or PDF/A file, the color profile that is embedded in the file as its output intent is automatically selected.

Inspecting objects in a PDF file

You can take a closer look at individual graphics and text in a PDF file using the Object Inspector. The Object Inspector displays the image resolution, color mode, transparency, and other information about the selected object.

You'll check the resolution of the image on page 2.

1 Choose Object Inspector from the Preview menu in the Output Preview dialog box.

2 Scroll to page 2, and click the image of the woman.

PROCESS

Self reinvention is something we all entertain, and the way fashion allows us to dream.

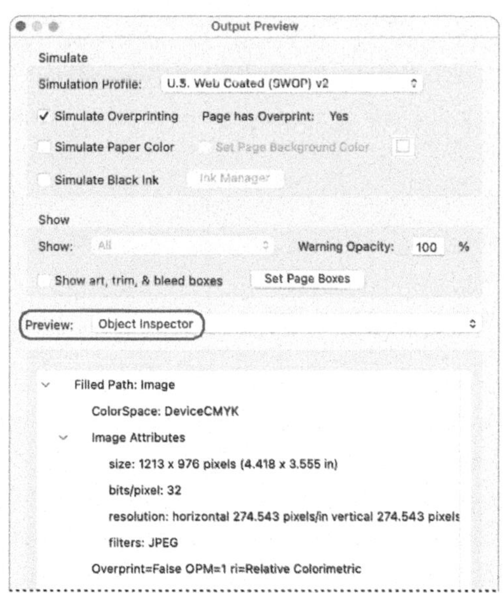

Tip: You can document the information the Object Inspector reports for easy access later. Shift-click an area, create a sticky note, and record the information.

The Object Inspector lists attributes of the image you clicked, including the image resolution: 274.543 by 274.543 pixels.

3 Click the body text on the page. The Object Inspector displays information about the text, including the font and type size.

4 Close the Output Preview dialog box, and then close the Print Production tool.

Advanced printing controls

Tip: Overprinting is automatically displayed accurately in PDF/X files in all versions of Acrobat and Acrobat Reader. You can change the settings to display overprinting accurately for all files in the Page Display pane of the Acrobat Preferences dialog box.

You'll use the advanced printing features of Acrobat Pro to produce color separations, add printing marks, and control how transparent and complex items are imaged.

1 Choose File > Print.

2 In the Print dialog box, choose a PostScript printer. In Windows, if you do not have a PostScript printer available, you can choose Adobe PDF.

Some advanced printing options, including color separations, are available only for PostScript printers. The Adobe PDF printer uses a PostScript printer driver, so it provides access to the options covered in this exercise.

3 In the Pages To Print area, select All.

4 In the Page Sizing & Handling area, select the Size tab, and then select Fit.

The Fit option reduces or enlarges each page to fit the paper size.

5 Click Advanced near the top of the Print dialog box.

There are four options on the left side of the dialog box: Output, Marks And Bleeds, PostScript Options, and Color Management.

6 Select Output, and then choose Separations from the Color menu.

7 Click the Ink Manager button in the Ink Manager area.

8 In the Ink Manager dialog box, select the icon to the left of TOYO 0349. The icon changes into a CMYK color swatch, indicating that this color will be printed as a process color, using the cyan, magenta, yellow, and black plates.

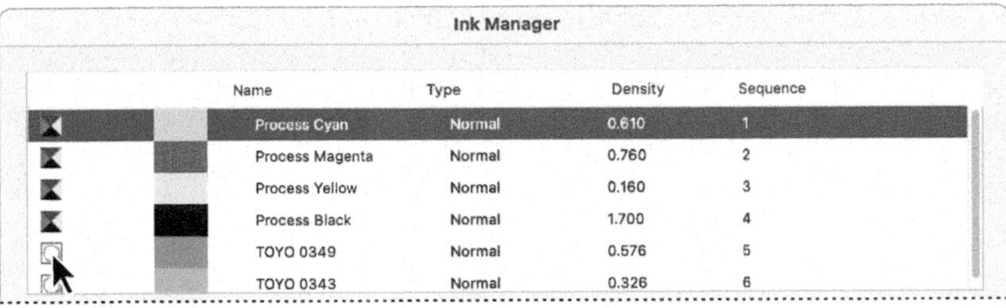

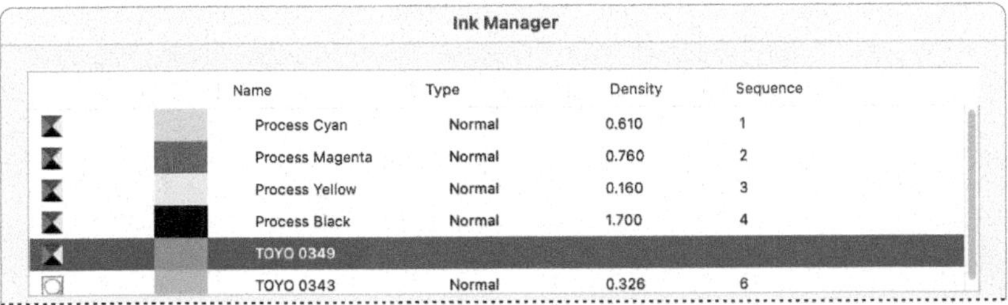

Acrobat will mix cyan and black to simulate the dedicated ink that is used to produce the TOYO 0349 spot color. In many cases, it is more cost-effective to use a mixture of CMYK inks than to add an entirely new spot color ink.

To globally convert all spot colors to their CMYK equivalents, select Convert All Spots To Process.

9 Click OK to close the Ink Manager dialog box.

10 In the Advanced Print Setup dialog box, select Marks And Bleeds from the list on the left. Select All Marks to enable trim marks, bleed marks, registration marks, color bars, and page information to print on each plate, outside the edges of the document.

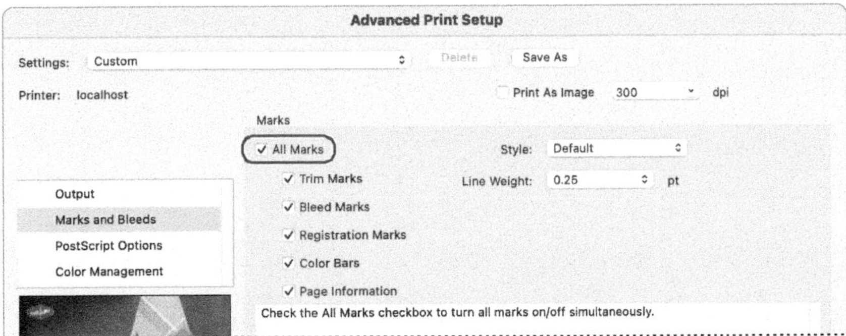

11 Select Color Management from the list on the left.

12 Choose Acrobat Color Management from the Color Handling menu.

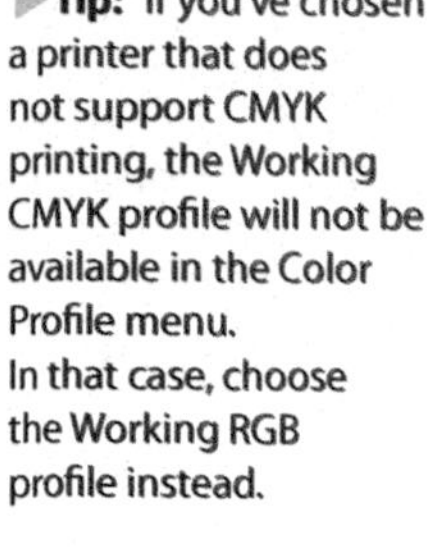

▶ **Tip:** If you've chosen a printer that does not support CMYK printing, the Working CMYK profile will not be available in the Color Profile menu. In that case, choose the Working RGB profile instead.

13 Choose Working CMYK: U.S. Web Coated (SWOP) v2 from the Color Profile menu.

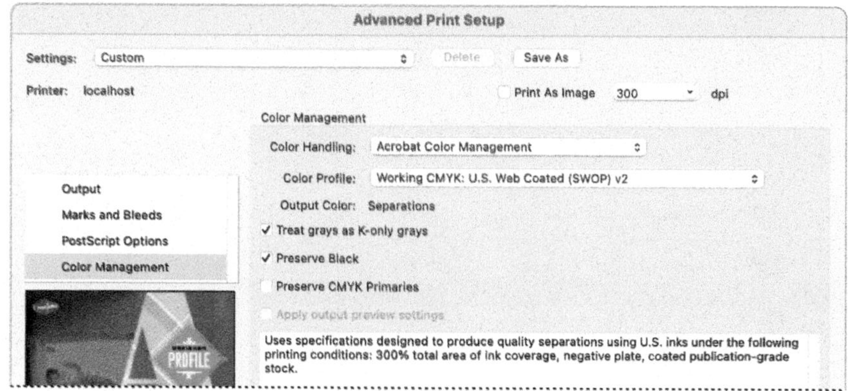

The color profile you select should match the device you will be printing to.

14 Click Save As at the top of the Advanced Print Setup dialog box, and save your settings using the name **Profile**. Then click OK.

Saved settings are added to the settings menu, so you can reuse them for future print jobs without having to re-enter the settings for recurring publications or specific output devices.

15 Click OK to exit the Advanced Print Setup dialog box. Then either click Print to print this document, or click Cancel if you prefer not to print at this time.

16 Close the document, and quit Acrobat.

Review questions

1 What is a PDF preset?

2 How can you select a settings file when you create a PDF document using the Print command in macOS?

3 What problems can Preflight detect within a PDF file?

4 What is a spot color, and how can you remap it to a process color when you print color separations?

Review answers

1 A PDF preset is a group of settings that affects the process of creating a PDF file. These settings are designed to balance file size with quality, depending on how the PDF file will be used.

2 To change the settings file in macOS, first choose Save As Adobe PDF from the PDF menu in the Print dialog box. Then choose a preset from the Adobe PDF Settings menu.

3 Use the Preflight command to check for all areas of concern within a PDF document. For example, if you are sending a PDF file to a professional printer, preflight the document to verify that fonts are embedded, graphics have the appropriate resolution, and colors are correct.

4 A spot color is a special premixed ink that is used instead of, or in addition to, CMYK process inks, and that requires its own printing plate on a printing press. If absolute color accuracy is not critical, and it is not practical to print a spot color plate as well as CMYK plates, you can remap the spot color to a process color for printing using the Ink Manager. In the Advanced Print Setup dialog box, select Separations, and then click Ink Manager. In the Ink Manager, click the icon to the left of the spot color to remap it to a process color for the print job.

INDEX

A

Accessibility Checker panel 84–86

accessibility features 82–95

Accessibility Setup Assistant 92

Accessibility tool 84

accessible text, copying text as 132

ACE (Adobe Color Engine) 304

Acrobat. *See* Adobe Acrobat

Acrobat PDFMaker

- about 51, 162
- dialog box 163, 171

Acrobat Reader. *See* Adobe Acrobat Reader

Acrobat ribbon in Microsoft Office 162

actions

- about 272
- adding steps to 279
- adding to form fields 257
- creating 277–286
- editing 287
- exporting 287
- instruction steps in 280
- naming 283
- reviewing tasks performed by 277
- saving 283
- sharing 287
- using 272–277, 284

Action Wizard tool 272

Actual Size view 69

Add Header And Footer dialog box 276

Add Image tool 130

adding

- barcodes 248
- blank pages 50
- bookmarks 113
- bullet points 126–127
- comments 225–231
- files to combined files 183
- form fields 247, 249–255
- headers and footers 276, 285
- images 130
- keywords 118
- navigational tools to the toolbar 73
- page numbers 107
- passwords 201–204
- security 201–221
- steps to actions 279
- sticky notes 227
- tags 90–91
- text 126
- text fields 249
- tools to the Quick Tools toolbar 32
- tools to the Tools pane 20
- watermarks 275

Add Text Box tool 226

Add Text tool 82, 127, 213, 226

Add Watermark dialog box 275

Adobe Acrobat
about 10–12
installing 2
options for purchasing 3
starting 3

Adobe Acrobat Classroom in a Book, Fourth Edition
about 1
prerequisites 2

Adobe Acrobat Help 36

Adobe Acrobat online 144

Adobe Acrobat Pro
compared with Acrobat Standard 2
lessons requiring 2

Adobe Acrobat Reader
about 11
commenting in 227
distributing 12
installing 12
security in 11
using Protected Mode in 198

Adobe Acrobat Reader app 145–151

Adobe Acrobat Sign
preparing a form for 207–210
sending for signatures 210–212
signing a document in 215–219
using 206–216

Adobe Acrobat Sign app 144

Adobe Acrobat Standard 2

Adobe Color Engine (ACE) 304

Adobe Fill & Sign app
about 12, 144
creating a profile in 155
using 154–158

Adobe LiveCycle Rights Management 199

Adobe online services 13

Adobe PDF files
about 10
accessible 82–91
adding security to 199–221
advantages of 10
combining 182–195
consolidating and converting source files 45, 182–195
converting to Microsoft Word documents 137
creating 38–65
creating by dragging and dropping 44
designing for online viewing 31
from Microsoft Excel files 170–175
from Microsoft Word documents in Windows 163–168
from Microsoft Word documents on macOS 169–170
from web pages 60–64
navigating 22–26, 68–76
on the web 13
opening 15
optimizing 55–56
reading 68–74
reflowing 91
searching 74–76
structured 83
tagged 83, 84

Adobe PDF Print Engine 298

Adobe PDF Printer 51–52

Adobe Scan app
about 12, 144
using 156–157

Adobe's cloud storage 145

alignment, changing 126

Allow Fast Web View option 32

Allow Speculative Downloading In The Background option 32

alt text 89–90

analyzing
form data 264
PDF files for printing 295

Append To Document, web pages 62

apps for Acrobat 12

Arrow tool 227

Attach File tool 226

attaching the original Word file to a PDF 166

automatic scrolling 93

automating tasks using actions 272

Autotag Document option 90

B

barcodes, adding 248

Bates numbering 108

blank pages, inserting 50

bolding text 126

booklets, printing 80

bookmarks
- changing destinations for 114–115
- creating 26, 113–114, 116
- for converted web pages 61
- from Word headings and styles 163
- generating automatically 25
- in combined files 192
- increasing text size in 94
- moving 115
- naming automatically 116
- navigating with 25
- nesting 26, 115

Bookmarks button in navigation pane 25, 100

Bookmarks panel 100, 113

Bookmarks tab, PDFMaker 164

bounding boxes, moving 127

Box, saving PDF files to 44

brightness setting 35

bullets, in text 124, 126–127

buttons, adding to forms 256, 257

C

cascading multiple documents 27–28

changing text in a PDF 123–127

check boxes, adding to forms 248

checking accessibility 84

check marks in the Comments list 234

checks in preflighting 295

clipboard, creating PDF files from 43

Clip Complex Regions, when flattening transparency 303

Cloud tool 227

collecting form data 262–263

Collect Payments tool 214

color management
- setting up 304
- when printing 310

color of text, changing 126

color separations
- previewing 305
- printing 308

Combine Files tool 45–49
- arranging pages in 188–190
- browsing thumbnails in 185
- displaying contents as list in 190
- opening 183
- page size options in 191
- setting options in 191–192
- zooming in on thumbnails in 185

combining files 180–195
- in PDF Portfolios 182, 193–194

commenting tools 226–227

comments
- about 226
- adding in Acrobat Reader 227
- adding to a PDF 225–231
- changing the status of 235
- exporting 232
- filtering 234
- importing 232–233
- including in a PDF from a Word document 165–166
- inserting text with 230
- marking text edits in 230–232
- replying to 235
- sorting 233
- summarizing 236
- viewing 232, 233

Comments List 234

Comment tool 19, 225

Compare Files tool 240–242

completing forms 81–83

compression 55

Connected Lines tool 227

conversion settings in PDFMaker 166

Convert All Strokes To Outlines option 303

Convert All Text To Outlines option 303

Convert Displayed Comments To Notes In Adobe PDF option 165

converting
- and combining files 45
- a page range 47
- comments to PDF notes 165
- spot colors to process colors 308
- web pages 60

Convert Multimedia and Preserve Slide Transitions option 177

Convert To PDF preferences 42

copying text and images 132–134

Copy With Formatting command 133

Create Link dialog box 112

Create New Action dialog box 278

Create PDF tool 19, 40

creating
- actions 277
- bookmarks 26, 116
- custom preflight profiles 298
- forms 246
- links in PDF files 111

creating Adobe PDFs
- about 40
- by dragging and dropping 44
- by scanning 56–58
- comparing methods for 40
- for print and prepress 292
- from Office applications 162–179
- from the clipboard 43
- from web pages 60–63
- using the Adobe PDF Printer (Windows) 51–52
- using the Create PDF tool 40
- using the Print command 51–52
- using the Save As Adobe PDF option (macOS) 53

cropping images 130

customizing
- interface brightness 35
- preflight profiles 298
- stamps 226
- the toolbar 32–34

D

date fields, creating 251

default
- tools 18
- work area 15

deleting
- blocks of text 122–123
- pages 48, 105
- pages when combining files into a single PDF 187–188

description, adding 117

digital IDs
- about 207
- creating 219–220
- using 219–220

digital signatures
- about 206
- adding to forms 248
- creating 219–220
- creating fields for 208
- sending documents for 207–217

Display In Read Mode By Default option 32

display, onscreen 68

distributing
- Acrobat Reader 12
- PDF forms 259, 262

dividing a spreadsheet into sections for viewing 175

Document Cloud. *See* Adobe online services

document message bar 260

Document Open password 201

document properties, setting 117, 199, 200

document review processes 224

document title 117

document window 16

downsampling 56

dragging and dropping to create PDFs 44

Dropbox, saving files to 44

dropdown menus, adding to forms 248

duplex printing 80

Dynamic Zoom tool 73

E

editing
- actions 287
- images in Acrobat 129–132
- images in another application 131
- PDF files in Acrobat Reader app 150
- text 122–127

Edit PDF tool 19, 21, 122, 129

email-based reviews
- about 224
- importing comments from 232

email, distributing forms through 262

Enable Accessibility And Reflow With Tagged PDF option 171

encrypting PDF files 199

Enter key, navigating with 69

Eraser tool 226

Excel spreadsheets
- converting to PDF 170–175
- saving PDF tables as 139

expanding documents in the Combine Files dialog box 186–187

exporting
- actions 287
- comments 232
- images 132–133
- PDF files as Word documents 137
- preflight profiles 298
- presentations to PowerPoint 134–135
- tables from PDF as Excel spreadsheets 139

Export PDF tool 19, 137

F

Fields panel 247

file size, reducing 54–55

filling out PDF forms 81

Fill & Sign app. *See* Adobe Fill & Sign app

Fill & Sign tool 19, 213

filtering comments 234

Find command 74

finding and replacing text 125

Find panel 125

First Page button 74

First Page command 70

Fit Height command 22

Fit One Full Page button 43

Fit To Paper Width option 172

Fit Visible command 69

Fit Width command 68, 71

Fit Worksheet To A Single Page option in Excel 172

fixing PDF files for printing 295

flat forms, converting into interactive forms 81, 246

Flattener Preview 300

flattening transparency 299–304

floating toolbar 31

font, changing 126

formatting
- text field responses 251
- text in Acrobat 126, 127

Form Editing mode 247

form fields
- adding actions to 257
- adding automatically 247
- barcodes 248
- buttons 256, 257
- check boxes 248
- date fields 251
- digital signatures 248
- dropdown menus 248
- editing properties for 251
- labels for 257
- list boxes 248
- naming 249
- phone number fields 251
- positioning 250
- previewing 252
- radio buttons 248, 253
- restricting answer formats for 251
- reviewing in Fields panel 247
- scrolling text fields 252
- text fields 248–249
- types 248
- zip code fields 251

form responses
- analyzing 265
- tracking 261

forms
- adding a reset button to 256
- adding text fields to 249
- collecting data from 262
- compiling responses from 263
- creating from scanned documents 246
- creating from Word documents 246
- distributing 259, 262
- document message bar in 260
- filling out 81
- flat 81
- laying out precisely 250
- making interactive 246
- tracking 261
- working with 244–269

Full Screen mode
- about 29
- avoiding the warning message 288
- displaying navigation tools in 30
- exiting 29
- setting a file to open in 30
- setting preferences for 30
- viewing PDFs in 29–31, 118

G

Go To Page dialog box 23

Gradient And Mesh Resolution option 303

H

Hand tool 18, 25, 68

headers and footers 276, 285

headers, viewing in a spreadsheet while scrolling 175

headings and styles in Word, converting to bookmarks 163

hiding
- layers when printing 297
- text (redacting) 128

highlighting areas affected by transparency 300–301

Highlight Text tool
- in Acrobat 226, 229
- in Acrobat Reader app 149

Home view
- in Acrobat 14
- in Acrobat Reader app 146

I

image fields, adding to forms 248, 256

images
- adding 130
- converting to PDF 40
- copying 132–134
- cropping 130
- editing in Acrobat 129–132
- editing in another application 131
- exporting from Acrobat 132–133
- replacing 129
- saving 134

importing
- actions 287
- comments 232
- preflight profiles 298

initial view, setting to Full Screen mode 30

Initial View tab in the Document Properties dialog box 117

Ink Manager 306, 308

inserting
- blank pages 50
- images 130
- pages from one PDF file into another 104

Insert Pages dialog box 50, 104

Insert Text tool 226, 230

inspecting objects in a PDF file 307

installers, Acrobat Reader 12

installing Acrobat 2

instruction steps, adding to actions 280

interactive forms, creating 246

Internet settings, for converting web pages 60

inviting reviewers 236

K

keyboard shortcuts 94

keywords, adding to a PDF 118

L

labels, adding to form fields 257

layers, printing 297

layout of forms 250

learning resources 5

Line Art And Text Resolution option 303

links
- about 73
- adding actions to 109
- changing the destination of 109
- creating 111
- editing 109

list boxes, adding to forms 248

LiveCycle Rights Management 199

M

magnification
- about 68
- changing 18, 22

mail merge, converting Word files to PDF 168

Make Accessible action 87–89

Make Searchable option 58

Manage Actions dialog box 287

markup tools 226–227

Marquee Zoom tool 72

menu bar, reopening 16

merging files into a single PDF 180–195

metadata, adding to PDF files 117

Microsoft Excel
- exporting tables to 139
- using PDFMaker with, in Windows 170–175

Microsoft Office files
- including in combined files 182
- using Acrobat with 160–179

Microsoft PowerPoint
- exporting presentations to 134
- using PDFMaker with 176–178

Microsoft SharePoint
- saving PDF files to 44
- using in a review 224
- using to distribute forms 262

Microsoft Word
- exporting PDF files to 137
- including documents in combined files 182

Microsoft Word documents
- attaching source files to PDF files 166
- converting mail-merge to PDF files 168
- converting to Adobe PDF in Windows 163–168
- converting to Adobe PDF on Mac OS 169–170

Microsoft WordPad, creating PDF files from 52

mobile apps for Acrobat 12, 142–159

monitor resolution 68

moving
- pages 102
- text bounding boxes 127

multiline text fields, adding 251

multiple documents
- combining into a single PDF 45
- viewing 27

N

navigating
- in Full Screen mode 30
- PDF documents 22, 68–76
- with Enter and Return keys 69
- with scroll bar 70

Navigation Bar in Full Screen mode 30

navigation pane
- Bookmarks panel 100
- displaying 100
- Page Thumbnails panel 23
- Security Settings button in 200
- Tags panel 87

navigation tools, adding to the toolbar 73

New Acrobat Experience 6

New Bookmark button 26, 113, 116

Next Page button 26

Next Page command 23

Next View button 74

Number Pages command 106

O

Object Inspector 307

OCR, applying 58–59

omitting pages from combined files 187–188

onscreen display 68

opacity. *See* transparency

opening
- password-protected PDF files 204
- PDF files in Acrobat 15
- PDF files in Acrobat Reader app 146
- PDF files in Full Screen mode 30

optimizing PDF files 55–56

Organize Pages tool 19, 20, 104

organizing pages in the Combine Files dialog box 188–190

Output Preview dialog box 307

Oval tool 227

P

Page Controls toolbar 17

Page Display preferences 94

page numbers, adding to a PDF 107

page preview box 71

page range, converting 47

pages
- arranging in the Combine Files dialog box 188–190
- deleting 105
- inserting 104
- moving with page thumbnails 102
- omitting from combined files 187–188
- printing 76
- renumbering 106–107
- rotating 105

page size
- displaying 16
- options in the Combine Files dialog box 191

Pages panel 19

page thumbnails 23–24

page view magnification 71

panning across a page 68

password-protected PDF files
- creating 201–202
- opening 204

password strength 203

PDF/A 299

PDF/E 299

PDF files. *See* Adobe PDF files

PDFMaker 51

PDF Optimizer 55

PDF Portfolios
- collecting form responses in 262
- creating 193–194

PDF settings files (presets)
- about 54, 292
- selecting 294

PDF standards 299

PDF tables, saving as Excel spreadsheets 139

PDF/X files 293, 299

Pencil tool 226

Permission Details in the Security Settings panel 200

Permissions password 201

phone number field, creating 251

pop-up menus, adding to forms 248

positioning form fields 250

PostScript printer driver 308

PowerPoint. *See* Microsoft PowerPoint

preferences
- Convert To PDF 42
- for web browsing 32
- Full Screen mode 30, 288
- Internet 32
- Page Display 94
- Reading 95

preflighting PDF files 295–297

preflight profiles 298

Prepare Form tool 207–218, 246

prepress, creating PDF files for 292

prerequisites for Classroom in a Book 2

presentations
- exporting to PowerPoint 134
- setting up 118
- viewing in Full Screen mode 29

Preserve Overprint option 303

presets for creating PDF files 54

previewing
- color separations 305
- documents in the Combine Files dialog box 185
- form fields 252
- printing 305
- transparency 298

Previous Page command 23

Previous View command 74, 101

Print command, using to create PDF files 51–52

printers' marks 309

printing
- booklets 80
- color separations 308
- comments 236
- PDF files 76
- printers' marks 309
- using color management 310

printing options 308

print preview 305

Print Production tool 295

professional printing, creating PDFs for 293

profiles in Fill & Sign app 155

Prompt For Conversion Settings option, in Excel 172

Prompt User option when creating actions 279

proofing onscreen 307

properties
- document 117
- editing for form fields 251

Protected Mode 11, 198

protecting PDF files 199–221

Protect tool 19, 202

Q

Quick Tools on toolbar 32

R

radio buttons 248, 253

rasterization 301

Raster/Vector Balance slider 302

reading
- comments 232
- PDF documents 68–74
- PDFs out loud 94

Reading preferences 94–95

Read mode 31–32

rearranging pages in a PDF 102

Recognition Report 88

Record Audio tool 226

Rectangle tool 227

redacting text 128

reducing file size 54–56

reflowing
- PDF files 91–93
- text 123

remapping spot colors to process colors 306, 308

Remove button in the Combine Files dialog box 187

Remove Selected Items button in the Combine Files dialog box 48

Remove Split command 29

removing pages from combined files 187

renumbering pages 106–108

Replace Text tool 226, 230

replacing
- images 129
- text 123–125

replying to comments 235

resampling images 56

reset buttons, adding to forms 256

resetting toolbars 74

resizing text boxes 127

resolution, checking 307

resources for learning Acrobat 5

response file, adding form data to 263

Results pane in the Preflight dialog box 296–297

Return key, navigating with 69

reviewers, inviting 236

Review mode in Acrobat online 153

reviews
- about 224
- commenting and markup tools for 226
- shared 224, 236–239
- sharing PDFs from Acrobat online 152
- types of 224
- using Acrobat in 222–243

rich text format, copying text as 132

roman numerals as page numbers 106

rotating pages 105

S

sandboxing 11, 198

Save As Adobe PDF option 53

saving
- actions 283
- as image files 134
- as RTF 132
- as Word documents 137
- to cloud accounts 44

scanning documents
- creating interactive forms from 246
- in Acrobat 56–58
- making text editable 58
- using Adobe Scan app 156
- using OCR 58

scrolling, automatic 93

searching PDF documents 74–76

security in PDF files
- about 199
- adding 196–221
- and accessibility 87
- settings 200

Security preferences 219

Security Settings button in the navigation pane 200

Selection tool 26

Send In Bulk tool 214

Set Bookmark Destination command 115

shared reviews
- about 224
- initiating 236–239
- using network folders for 239

SharePoint. *See* Microsoft SharePoint

sharing
- actions 287
- PDF files 95

showing and hiding layers when printing 297

signatures
- adding in Fill & Sign app 156
- adding to forms 248
- digital 206–221
- using Fill & Sign tool 213

smoothing text 94

Snapshot feature 133

soft-proofing a PDF file 307

sorting
- comments 233
- form data 264

source files, attaching to PDFs 166

splitting a document's view 28

spot colors, remapping to process 306

Spreadsheet Split command 175

Stamp tool 226

Start button in actions 274

sticky notes
- adding 227
- converting Word comments to 165–168

Sticky Note tool
- in Acrobat 226
- in Acrobat Reader app 149

Strikethrough tool 226, 231

structure in PDF files 83

styles in Word, converting to bookmarks 163–164

Submit Form button 260

summarizing comments 236

T

tables, exporting as spreadsheets 139

tagged PDF files 51, 83, 87, 90

Tags panel 87

Take A Snapshot command 133

task panes 20

text
- adding 126
- bolding 126
- changing properties of 123, 126
- color of 126
- copying 132–133
- deleting 122–123
- editing 122–127
- finding 125
- formatting 126
- inserting in comments 226, 230
- making editable 58
- marking for deletion 231
- marking up 230–232
- redacting 128
- reflowing 91–93, 123
- replacing 123–124
- repositioning on the page 127
- searching 74–76
- smoothing 94

text fields
- adding to forms 248, 249
- formatting for multiple lines 251

thumbnails
- browsing in the Combine Files dialog box 185
- highlighted area in 25
- moving pages with 102
- rearranging in the Combine Files dialog box 188–190
- viewing 23

TIFF files, converting to PDF 40

tiling documents 27

title, document 117

toolbar
- about 17
- adding tools to 73
- customizing 32
- resetting to default 74

tools
- Accessibility 84
- Action Wizard 273
- Add Text 213, 226
- Cloud 227
- Collect Payments 214
- Combine Files 183
- Comment 19, 225
- commenting and markup 226
- Create PDF 19, 40–43
- custom stamp 226
- Edit PDF 19, 21, 122, 129
- Export PDF 19
- Fill & Sign 19, 213
- Highlight Text 226, 229
- Organize Pages 19, 20, 104
- Oval 227
- Prepare Form 207–218, 246
- Print Production 295
- Protect 19, 202
- Redact 128
- selecting in the Tools pane 20
- Send In Bulk 214
- showing and hiding 72
- Stamp 226
- Sticky Note 226

Tools Center 20

Tools pane
- adding tools to 20, 84
- tools in 19

TouchUp Reading Order tool 87

Tracker 261

transitions, retaining in a PDF from a PowerPoint presentation 176

transparency
- about 298
- flattening 299–303
- previewing 298
- using efficiently for printing 293

type style, changing 126

U

Underline tool 226

Undo button in Acrobat Reader app 150

uploading files to Adobe's cloud storage 145

user interface, changes 6

V

validating form field data 265

versions of documents, comparing 240–242

View Adobe PDF Result option 166–168

viewing
- comments 232, 233
- documents in Protected Mode 198
- form responses 261
- multiple documents 26
- multiple views of a document 28
- PDFs in Full Screen mode 29–31
- PDFs in Read mode 31–32
- security settings 200
- spreadsheet headers while scrolling 175

View menu 23

views
  Actual Size 69
  changing 71
  Fit Visible 69
  Fit Width 69
  split 28
  Spreadsheet Split 175
  Zoom To Page Level 69

View settings in Acrobat Reader app 146

viruses, preventing 198

W

watermarks, adding 275

web browsing preferences for PDF files 32

web links, downloading and converting 62

web pages
  converting to PDF 60–63
  including PDFs in 13

Word. *See* Microsoft Word

Z

zip code fields, creating 251

Zoom In button 17

Zoom Out button 18

Zoom To command 23

zoom tools 18, 72
  Dynamic Zoom tool 73
  Marquee Zoom tool 72

Production Notes

Adobe Acrobat Classroom in a Book, Fourth Edition was created electronically using Adobe InDesign. Art was produced using Adobe InDesign, Adobe Illustrator, and Adobe Photoshop.

References to company names in the lessons are for demonstration purposes only and are not intended to refer to any actual organization or person.

Lesson files

Photographic images, illustrations, and other lesson files are intended for use only with the tutorials.

Typefaces used

Adobe Myriad Pro and Adobe Minion Pro are used throughout the lessons. For more information about OpenType and Adobe fonts, visit www.adobe.com/type/opentype/.

Team credits

The following individuals contributed to the development of *Adobe Acrobat Classroom in a Book, Fourth Edition*:

Writer: Brie Gyncild

Project Manager: Lisa Fridsma

Lesson Development: Brie Gyncild and Lisa Fridsma

Illustrator and Compositor: Lisa Fridsma

Technical Reviewer: Megan Ahearn

Indexer: Brie Gyncild

Interior design: Mimi Heft

Adobe Press Executive Editor: Laura Norman

Adobe Press Project Editor: Tracey Croom

Associate Sponsoring Editor: Anshul Sharma